THE NABATAEAN TEMPLE
AT KHIRBET ET-TANNUR, JORDAN

VOLUME 2

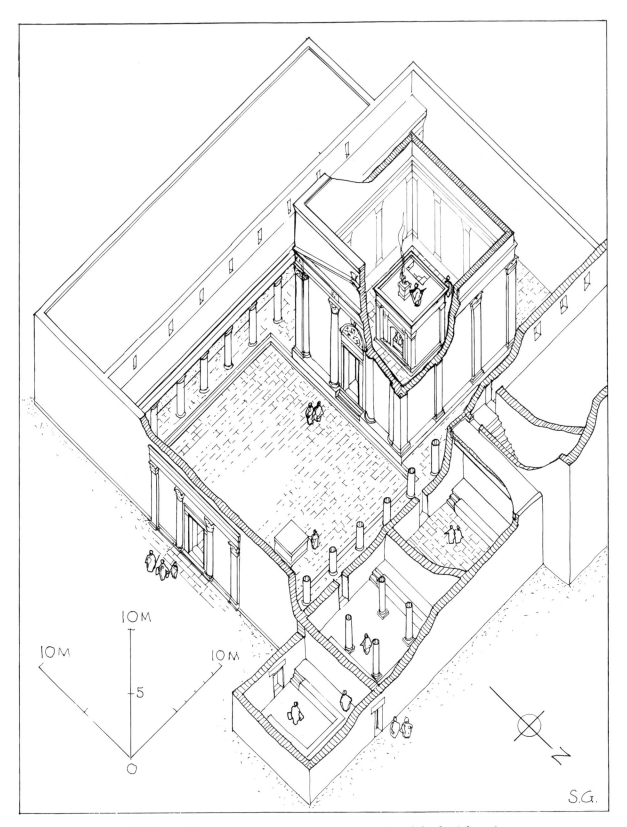

10M

10M

10M

5

0

S.G.

Khirbet et-Tannur, axonometric reconstruction (Sheila Gibson).

THE NABATAEAN TEMPLE
AT KHIRBET ET-TANNUR, JORDAN

VOLUME 2 — CULTIC OFFERINGS, VESSELS, AND OTHER SPECIALIST REPORTS

Final Report on Nelson Glueck's 1937 Excavation

by

Judith S. McKenzie, Joseph A. Greene, Andres T. Reyes,

Catherine S. Alexander, Deirdre G. Barrett, Brian Gilmour,

John F. Healey, Margaret O'Hea, Nadine Schibille, Stephan G. Schmid,

Wilma Wetterstrom, and Sarah Whitcher Kansa

with contributions by

Kate da Costa, Patrick Degryse, Katherine Eremin, Sheila Gibson,

Owen Gingerich, and Elias Khamis

American Schools of Oriental Research • Boston, MA
in collaboration with Manar al-Athar • University of Oxford

THE ANNUAL OF THE AMERICAN SCHOOLS
OF ORIENTAL RESEARCH
VOLUME 68

Series Editor
Joseph A. Greene

MANAR AL-ATHAR MONOGRAPH 2

The American Schools of Oriental Research

in collaboration with Manar al-Athar, University of Oxford

© American Schools of Oriental Research, Manar al-Athar, and individual authors, 2013

ISBN: 978-0-89757-036-7

Library of Congress Cataloging-in-Publication Data

McKenzie, Judith.
    The Nabataean temple at Khirbet et-Tannur, Jordan : final report on Nelson
        Glueck's 1937 excavation / by Judith S. McKenzie, Joseph A. Greene,
        Andres T. Reyes, Catherine S. Alexander, Deirdre G. Barrett, Brian
        Gilmour, John F. Healey, Margaret O'Hea, Nadine Schibille, Stephan
        G. Schmid, Wilma Wetterstrom, and Sarah Whitcher Kansa ; with
        contributions by Kate da Costa, Patrick Degryse, Katherine Eremin,
        Sheila Gibson, Owen Gingerich, and Elias Khamis.
    volumes cm. -- (Annual of the American Schools of Oriental Research ; v.
        67-68)
Includes bibliographical references and index.
ISBN 978-0-89757-035-0 (v. 1 : alk. paper) -- ISBN 978-0-89757-036-7 (v. 2 : alk.
        paper)
    1. Khirbet et-Tannur Site (Jordan) 2. Excavations (Archaeology)--Jordan--
        Khirbet et-Tannur Site. 3. Jordan--Antiquities. 4. Temples--Jordan. 5.
        Nabataeans. 6. Glueck, Nelson, 1900-1972. I. Title.
DS154.9.K49M35 2013
939.4'64--dc23
                                    2013034313

Printed in the United States of America on acid-free paper

Contents

VOLUME 1 – ARCHITECTURE AND RELIGION

Contents

ILLUSTRATIONS

TABLES

Preface and Acknowledgments

Nelson Glueck excavated Khirbet et-Tannur in 1937, but, delayed by World War II and a busy career, he only published its architectural sculpture in *Deities and Dolphins* in 1965, without any indication that he had the exceptional foresight to collect scientific samples of the non-architectural finds.

In 1982–86, when I was working in Petra on *The Architecture of Petra*, trying to solve the problem of the chronology of the classical facades, I examined the sculpture there in the hope that it might provide a solution. Consequently, I also studied the published record of the sculpture from Khirbet et-Tannur and, like the Abbé Jean Starcky in 1968, noticed that there were problems with the phases of the reconstructions (*Palestine Exploration Quarterly* 1988).

The visit by Queen Noor of Jordan in 1994 to Cincinnati Art Museum, where half of the Khirbet et-Tannur sculptures are stored, led to an exhibition organised by the late Glenn Markoe, *Petra: Lost City of Stone*, in the American Museum of Natural History in New York in 2003, before it toured North America. This exhibition re-united some of the fragments from Cincinnati and Amman, and also included sculptures from Petra, the Nabataean capital, and Khirbet edh-Dharih, the "mother" village of Khirbet et-Tannur. The request to write the chapter on Khirbet et-Tannur for the accompanying volume, *Petra Rediscovered*, led me to re-examine the evidence with Andres Reyes and the late Sheila Gibson. We presented the results of this, including my new elevations and her axonometric drawings, in *Palestine Exploration Quarterly* 2002.

After that article had been submitted, the material in the ASOR Nelson Glueck Archive in the Semitic Museum of Harvard University came to light. In addition to excavation records, architectural drawings, and photographs, there are scientific samples. These include remains of burnt cult offerings of bones, grains, and incense, as well as fragments of metal, glassware, lamps, and pottery vessels. It is only in recent years, as a result of further work at other sites, that useful information can be gleaned from this evidence. Rudolph Dornemann, on behalf of the American Schools of Oriental Research, granted me permission to work on this material and to publish it. What these finds reveal is summarized at the end of Chapter 1. I have worked very closely with Joseph A. Greene of the Semitic Museum throughout, without whom so many details could not have been followed up at a distance from Harvard. Just as Clarence Fisher's role in helping Glueck with reconstructing the temple at Khirbet et-Tannur cannot be stressed strongly enough, so too Joe Greene's role in the present volume was critical.

As the value of the material gradually became apparent, the work increased in scope. We initially asked Sarah Whitcher Kansa to examine the bones, Wilma Wetterstrom the seeds, and Deirdre Barrett the lamps. They quickly made significant discoveries, such as the fact that the bones had been deliberately burnt as offerings, that there are apparently remains of offering cakes in the samples of charred grains, and that the lamps include types chosen for sanctuary use. These results revealed the importance of the samples Glueck had collected over seventy years ago, and which only survived because, following his death, they had been stored in the Semitic Museum. (Their history prior to that is described in Chapter 1.) Even if not excavated with modern stratigraphic methods, they are valuable because, since the temple had no adjoining village and was not re-used as a church, these remains came from a site with a single function — for pagan worship.

Consequently, this study was expanded to include other categories of material. The sherds of the coarse ware and painted vessels were studied and many drawn by Stephan Schmid, with additional drawings by Catherine Alexander. The glassware was subjected to similarly detailed examination, with typological analysis by Margaret O'Hea, chemical analysis by Nadine Schibille, and isotope analysis by Patrick Degryse. I prepared a brief catalogue of the metal objects with help from Andres Reyes and Elias Khamis, while microstructural analysis of the iron hinge was done by Brian Gilmour. The evidence which had previously been published also needed to be re-examined in the light of discoveries since 1965. Thus, the Nabataean inscriptions were re-examined by John F. Healey. When I was trying to ascertain if it was possible to date the zodiac (and, thus, Period 2 of the temple) from the dots in the fields of some of the signs, Sara Schechner introduced us to Owen Gingerich, Professor Emeritus of Astronomy and History of Science at Harvard, who had been involved with attempts to date the zodiac at the time of its discovery, as he describes in Appendix 3.1.

I managed to establish the contexts for many of the finds from Glueck's excavation records (Vol. 2, Chapters 6–8). This re-examination made possible a new, more nuanced, interpretation of the chronology and phases, and thus the development and decline of the complex. I have presented this, along with the basis for the architectural reconstructions, in Chapter 2. With the help of Andres Reyes, I have attempted to place the results in a broader context, showing how the sculptures form a cohesive decorative programme, taking into account recent work, as well as considering what else the finds tell us about Nabataean religious practice (Chapters 4–5). It needs to be kept in mind that some of these conclusions might change as further evidence comes to light elsewhere. We are grateful to John Healey for reading those chapters.

The sculpture is in Cincinnati Art Museum, in Amman, or at the site. Photographs have been included of all architectural and sculptural fragments known from photographs in the Glueck Archive (assembled by Glueck and Eleanor Vogel, his assistant in Cincinnati), as well as of all fragments in Cincinnati. The staff at the Cincinnati Art Museum were most supportive and helpful. James Crump and Matthew Leininger facilitated Joe Greene's visit there in 2011. Jay Pattison sent us further details and photographs so that we could complete the list of fragments held there, and Jonathan Nolting provided further photographs. The records of the pieces in Jordan are complicated by the fact that the other half of the sculptures, not left at the site, was initially stored in the Palestine Archaeological Museum (the Rockefeller Museum) in Jerusalem and moved to Amman when the Jordan Archaeological Museum opened in 1951. Some were moved from it in 2011 to the new Jordan Museum, while others are probably in Department of Antiquities storage. Preparation of a full inventory of the fragments in Jordan remains a task for a future scholar.

We reached a point when it was best to publish what we had done and leave other work for the future, probably by others. Thus, we decided simply to publish our results from what Glueck had excavated in 1937 without further excavation, such as soundings. There are still possibly some places in the Inner Temenos Enclosure where new soundings could be made, which might provide stratified levels and pottery from below the paving. We did not initially do ^{14}C analysis on the bones or grains from the Altar Platform, because we thought they would not provide the required precision in the 1st century AD. However, as we now know the surviving evidence for worship on the Altar Platform spans a wider period than originally thought — the late 2nd century BC to mid-4th century AD — this might be expected to yield interesting results. But, I am also hesitant to do this because it is destructive of the samples. This caution is also suggested by the difficulties encountered when a range of samples in Petra was tested (as outlined in Saliège, J.-F.; Zazzo, A.; Hatt, C.; and Gauthier, C., "Radiocarbon Dating in Petra: Limitations and Potential in Semi-Arid Environments." Pp. 79–91 in *Men on the Rocks, The Formation of Nabataean Petra,* eds. M. Mouton and S. G. Schmid. Berlin, 2013.). Sometimes it is better to keep the samples for the future, as Glueck did. This especially applies to the vial containing a very small quantity of burnt incense scraped from the Alexander Amrou altar in 1937. Most of the remaining traces on it were cleaned off in 2003 in preparation for its inclusion in the New York exhibition. Fortunately, as the zodiac Tyche in the Cincinnati Art Museum has not been subjected to aggressive cleaning, traces of paint still survive on it. Chemical analysis of these should reveal the colours with which she was decorated. We had initially planned to do fabric analysis on the pottery to determine its origin — how much was brought from Petra or produced locally. However, as this field has developed so much in recent years and is so complex, this is best left for a future PhD or post-doctoral project, which also needs to include samples from Khirbet edh-Dharih and Petra for comparison.

Although this project was begun in 2001 and the main reports initially were completed in 2004, there was a pause until 2009, because I had other commitments. In hindsight, this was fortunate, because work done at other sites during this period has greatly improved our interpretation of the development of the site, the sub-phases, and chronology. As such work was very recent or still in progress, we were only able to benefit from it because colleagues kindly gave us pre-publication access to their results and discussed them in detail. We are most grateful to them, and they should take some of the credit for the results we have achieved. These include, in particular, our French colleague François Villeneuve and his team at Khirbet edh-Dharih, especially Jacqueline Dentzer-Feydy, Pascale Linant de Bellefonds, Charlène Bouchaud, Caroline Durand, Sébastien Lepetz, and Delphine Seigneuret, along with those excavating in Petra: Michel Mouton and François Renel. Other colleagues working in Petra have also been helpful: Khairieh ʿAmr, Joe Basile, Piotr Bienkowski, Zeyad al-Salameen, and Chris Tuttle; and at Jabal Haroun, Zbigniew Fiema and Tanja Tenhunen. I am especially grateful to Tali Erickson-Gini for all she taught me about pottery typology, and other timely assistance.

Martha Joukowsky made it possible for the same specialists who examined material from Khirbet et-Tannur to study finds from the Petra "Great Temple." This was particularly helpful for increasing the comparanda between Khirbet et-Tannur and Petra for the lamps, bones, and glassware. Allowing Nadine Schibille and Patrick Degryse to do chemical analysis on glass from the "Great Temple" excavations meant that meaningful results could be gained by comparing samples from the rural sanctuary with the metropolis. A comparison of the small corpus of Khirbet et-Tannur lamps with the large corpus from the "Great Temple" excavations was possible due to the study of both for Deirdre Barrett's PhD thesis. Kate da Costa was also exceptionally generous with access to her thesis, providing essential comparanda and comments. Her short note on the zodiac lamp from Petra does not reflect the full extent of her help. Laurent Tholbecq, who excavated the temple at Wādī Ramm, was independently making elevations of the complex at Khirbet et-Tannur when we first began our study and generously discussed this with us. Other colleagues working in the region also answered our questions or provided helpful discussion: John Bartlett, Ross Burns, Yael Gorin-Rosen, Tom Levy, Shaher er-Rababeh, and Don Whitcomb. We are also grateful to John Baines, Thomas Birch, J. J. Coulton, Cynthia Drakeman, Milet Gaifman, Galit Goldschmid, Monica Jackson, Ted Kaizer, Konstantin Klein, Andreas Kropp, Sean Leatherbury, Emma Libonati, Lidia Lozano, Zvi Maʿoz, David Milson, Martina Minas, the late Ehud Netzer, Sarah Norodom, Eleazer Oren, Orit Peleg-Barkat, Barbara Porter, and Thomas Weber. Tiffany Chezum provided sharp-eyed help with the editing. Ian Cartwright, Jane Inskipp, and Alison Wilkins provided help with the illustrations in Oxford, and Shannon Vanderhooft and Julie McIntosh Shapiro took additional photographs in Harvard.

Joe Greene's colleagues at the Semitic Museum were equally helpful, including Director Lawrence E. Stager, past and present Museum Curators James Armstrong and Adam Aja, and Museum Coordinator Tim Letteney. A number of interns there also provided logistic support, including Dana DePietro who sorted the photos in 2001, Carrie Duncan who sorted the pottery in 2002, Meseret Oldjira who munselled the pottery in 2011, and Hannah Wellman who examined the altars from Tell el-Kheleifeh. Other interns included Rose Eddy and Mary Grace Joseph, while Kristin Vagliardo did some scanning.

Many of Joe Greene's colleagues elsewhere in Harvard University also answered our questions: Carl Francis (Mineralogical Museum), Peter Burns (Zooarchaeological Laboratory, Peabody Museum), Sara Schechner (Collection of Historical Scientific Instruments), Jeff Howry (Research Associate, Semitic Museum), and Katherine Eremin (Straus Center for Conservation, Harvard Art Museums) who also sampled the glass. Carmen Arnold-Biucchi (Damarete Curator of Ancient Coins, Harvard Art Museums) re-examined the coin of Antiochus III.

Colleagues at other institutions where material is also held have been most generous. These include Gisela Walberg at the University of Cincinnati. Staff of the Hebrew Union College (of which Nelson Glueck had been President from 1947 to 1971) were very helpful in attempting to track down material: in Cincinnati, Nili Fox and Rabbi Jean Eglinton; and in Los Angeles, Catherine Aurora. As the sculpture from Khirbet et-Tannur was originally displayed in the Palestine Archaeological Museum in Jerusalem, there are still some records, largely photographs, in the archive of the Rockefeller Museum. For access to this material we are grateful to Silvia Krapiwko, and for answering other questions from their records to Alegre Savariego.

We would also like to thank the late Fawwaz al-Khraysheh and Ziad al-Saad, past Directors General of the Department of Antiquities of the Hashemite Kingdom of Jordan for their assistance. For other logistical help in Jordan we would like to thank: at the Amman Institute of the Council for British Research in the Levant (CBRL), Bill Findlayson and Nadja Qaisi; at the Department of Antiquities, Catreena Yousef, Tammam Khasawneh, Jihad Haroun, and Adnan Rafayah; at the Jordan Archaeological Museum, Ayda Naghawy; at the Jordan Museum, Fatma Marii; and at the Petra Archaeological Park, Mohammad Showbaki, as well as our driver Aiman el-Qadi. At the Kenyon Institute (CBRL) in Jerusalem we would like to thank Jaimie Lovell, Chloe Massey, and Maida Smeir.

For permission to see and publish material from the Nelson Glueck Archive in the Semitic Museum we are grateful to the American Schools of Oriental Research (ASOR). For assistance with organising this we would like to thank Joe D. Seger, former President of ASOR, and Rudolph Dornemann, former Executive Director of ASOR. We would also like to thank Timothy P. Harrison (ASOR President), Andrew Vaughn (ASOR Executive Director), Lawrence Geraty (former ASOR President), Douglas Clark (former ASOR Executive Director), and Cynthia Rufo (ASOR Archivist).

Essential support for the project was provided by the Semitic Museum which funded some of the specialist analyses, drawings, and photography, and contributed considerable staff and volunteer time for inventorying and scanning — all co-ordinated by Joe Greene and without which the research would not have been possible. An extensive project such as this also cannot succeed without research grants from a variety of organisations. We are most grateful to the British Academy, the Leverhulme Trust, the Wainwright Fund, the Palestine Exploration Fund, the Seven Pillars of Wisdom Trust, the Dillon Fund of Groton School, and, at the University of Oxford, the T. W. Greene and Meyers Funds of the Craven Committee, the Faculty of Oriental Studies, and the Oxford University Press John Fell Research Fund. Assistance and support from Andrew Fairweather-Tall, Neil McLynn, Nicholas Purcell, and Sam Sneddon ensured the success of the John Fell grants, making possible my final analysis of the material and completion of the text, which Andres Reyes helped edit.

Finally, we would like to thank those who made publication of both volumes possible with the Manar al-Athar Publication Fund, through Americans for Oxford and the University of Oxford. We are especially grateful to Elizabeth Macaulay-Lewis for her support, as well as Vernon Cassin, Adrien Duroc-Danner, Luke Duroc-Danner, Swift Edgar, Byron Fuller, and Morgane Richer la Flèche. We would also like to express our gratitude to Joseph A. Greene, as editor of the *ASOR Annual*, for his unfailing support, and to Susanne Wilhelm for her work on the design and production.

Judith S. McKenzie
Oxford, 26 December 2011

Abbreviations

ASOR	American Schools of Oriental Research
CAM	Cincinnati Art Museum
Ch.	Chapter
cm	centimetre(s)
DD	N. Glueck, *Deities and Dolphins*. London, 1965
diam.	diameter
E	east
FAN	Clarence Fisher's architecture notes, in GA
FFN	Clarence Fisher's field notes, in GA
FRN	Clarence Fisher's reconstruction notes, in GA
GA	ASOR Nelson Glueck Archive in the Semitic Museum, Harvard University
GA glass	numbers on the glass fragments in GA (assigned June 2010, same as their numbers in Chs. 15–16)
GA lamp	numbers on the lamps and lamp fragments in GA (assigned January 2010, same as their numbers in Ch. 17)
GA metal	number of metal object or sample in GA (same as their numbers in Ch. 13)
GA Unit	based on box and bag numbers in GA in 2002 (explained below on pp. 7–9)
GJ	Nelson Glueck's excavation journal, in GA (reproduced here in Ch. 7)
gm	gram(s)
GNAN	Nelson Glueck's notes on FAN, in GA
GP	Glueck's List of Pottery, in GA
GR	Glueck's Registration Book, in GA (reproduced here in Ch. 8)
h.	height
HUC	Hebrew Union College, Cincinnati
incl.	including
JAM	Jordan Archaeological Museum
l.	length
Locus	location marked in fig. 6.2 (explained below on p. 11)
m	metre(s)
ml	millilitre(s)
MNE	Minimum Number Estimate (i.e., of examples)
MNI	Minimum Number of Individuals (of animals)
no(s).	number(s)
N	north
NISP	Number of Identified Specimens (of animals)
PAM	Palestine Archaeological Museum
PFN	Carl Pape's field notes in GA
S	south

th.	thickness
TS	Type Series
Unit	GA Unit, in Ch. 18
w.	width
W	west

The Glueck Archive (GA) photograph numbering system is explained below on pp. 5–7. For abbreviations for pottery types and forms in the pottery catalogue, see Ch. 18, p. 213.

A Note on the Format: The figures in Vol. 1 have been numbered sequentially (figs. 1, 312, etc.), and a combined bibliography for the chapters given at the end of it. In this volume (Vol. 2), as some scholars may wish to copy individual specialist reports, the figures there have been numbered in the form, figs. 1.1, 13.1, etc., and the relevant bibliographies placed at the end of each chapter.

We have retained the older transliteration of the spelling of Khirbet et-Tannur, and also used the spellings for other sites as they generally appear in their excavators' reports for ease of recognition, although at the expense of a consistent system.

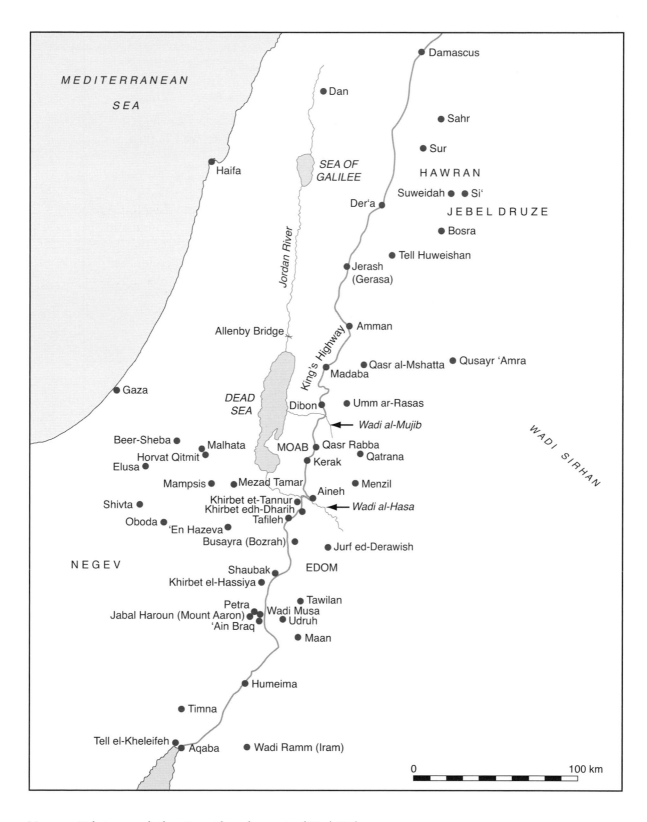

MAP 1   *Nabataean and other sites, with modern route of King's Highway.*

xix

MAP 2   *West of the Jordan River.*

xx

Chapter 6

Re-Establishment of Loci from Glueck's Excavation Records

by Judith S. McKenzie

The finds from the 1937 excavations of Khirbet et-Tannur in the ASOR Nelson Glueck Archive in the Semitic Museum, Harvard University, are basically scientific samples, which Glueck had kept with his other records of the site's excavations and its architecture: c. 5,700 pottery sherds, metal objects and metal specimens, some lamps and lamp fragments, glass fragments, and carbonized grains, wood, and animal bones. The present locations (in 2010) of these finds are summarized below, followed by detailed lists of the excavation records and photographs in the Glueck Archive. Finally, the methods used for re-establishing and naming the find places of the non-architectural finds (Loci and Units) are described, and these are presented in Table 6.1 at the end of this chapter.

LOCATIONS OF STONE ARCHITECTURAL FRAGMENTS, SCULPTURE, CULT STATUES, ALTARS, AND INSCRIPTIONS

The finds in the Glueck Archive do not include any carved architectural decoration, sculpture, cult statues, betyls, stone altars (Ch. 10), or inscriptions (Ch. 9). These carved pieces, nearly all of lime-stone, are in Amman in the Jordan Archaeological Museum, the Jordan Museum, or the Department of Antiquities Store, and in the Cincinnati Art Museum in Cincinnati, Ohio, with some architectural blocks left at the site itself.

The stone objects and blocks which had been in the Palestine Archaeological Museum in Jerusalem (Rockefeller Museum) were transferred to Amman in 1951 when the Jordan Archaeological Museum was opened, but it has not been possible to determine the present location of all of these.

LOCATIONS OF OTHER FINDS (POTTERY, LAMPS, GLASS, METALS, ANIMAL BONES, PLANTS, AND GYPSUM)

The finds from the Khirbet et-Tannur excavation which are not carved stone are nearly all in the Glueck Archive, except for some complete or nearly complete pots and lamps, as indicated in Table 6.1. Details are given in the relevant chapters.

The remains of pottery vessels consist of c. 5,700 sherds and some complete or partially complete pots. All currently known sherds are in the Glueck Archive (see Table 6.1). The pots which had been in the Palestine Archaeological Museum (Rockefeller

1

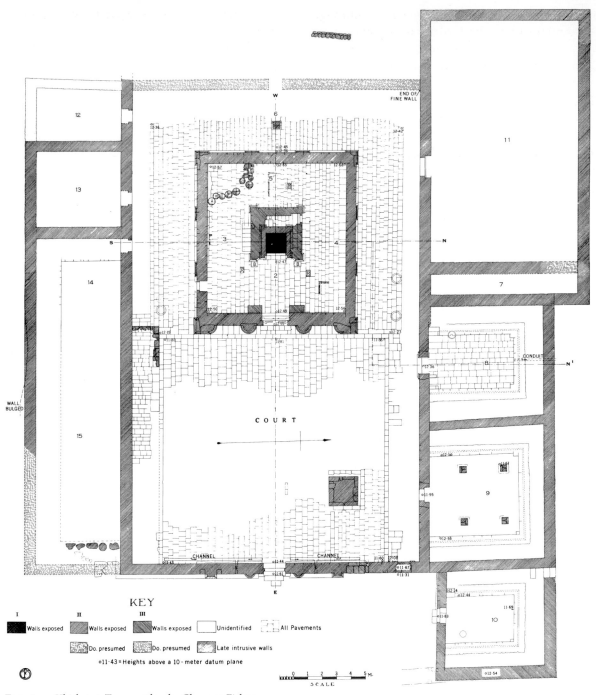

KEY

I		II		III					
■ Walls exposed		▨ Walls exposed		▧ Walls exposed		□ Unidentified		⬚ All Pavements	

	Do. presumed		Do. presumed		Late intrusive walls

o11·43 = Heights above a 10-meter datum plane

0 1 2 3 4 5 M.
SCALE

FIG. 6.1 *Khirbet et-Tannur, plan by Clarence Fisher.*

Museum) were transferred to Amman in 1951 when the Jordan Archaeological Museum was opened, but it has not been possible to determine the current whereabouts of all of these. The few complete or partially complete vessels which were tracked down are in the Cincinnati Art Museum, the

Jordan Archaeological Museum, and the Jordanian Department of Antiquities store (see Ch. 18).

All of the lamp fragments, except one polycandelon spout, are in the Glueck Archive, along with some partially complete examples. One complete lamp is in the Cincinnati Art Museum. We failed to locate the rest of the complete lamps, although some might be in the Jordanian Department of Antiquities store. There are none at Hebrew Union College in Cincinnati or Los Angeles.

The fragments of glass vessels are all in the Glueck Archive.

The iron samples (some from the temple doors) are in the Glueck Archive, along with the sealing ring, the *spatula*, and one Seleucid coin. The locations of the other coins are unknown, although the Nabataean one of Aretas IV is probably in the Jordanian Department of Antiquities store.

The carbonized grains, offering cakes, and wood, as well as the burnt and unburnt animal bones, are all in the Glueck Archive, along with one piece of worked bone.

The worked gypsum fragments, from wall-veneer or vessels,[1] are in the Glueck Archive, as well as some lumps of stucco.

RECORDS IN THE GLUECK ARCHIVE

A. Glueck's Excavation Records

These include:

1. Labels on the bags the finds were in or, sometimes, as in the case of pottery or lamps, written on the sherds themselves.
2. GJ = Glueck's excavation journal. There are three copies of this: the original one handwritten in the field, a typed copy, and its carbon. All three copies have later annotations of Glueck's further thoughts or clarifications, in particular concerning the stratigraphy. As these are not absolutely identical on all three copies, they have been checked against each other for the version reproduced here in Ch. 7.
3. GR = Glueck's Registration book. This is at the beginning of the first, 1938, Tell el-Kheleifeh registration book, and is reproduced here in Ch. 8.
4. GP = Glueck's list of pottery. Headed "Khirbet et-Tannur Pottery," this includes GR numbers, when relevant, and lists some, but not all, complete or nearly complete lamps and pots, and the metal objects, as well as their Palestine Archaeological Museum negative numbers.

An earlier copy of this lacks the first column of numbers.
5. Division Lists, largely of sculpture. These are the lists of which pieces were kept by the Transjordanian Department of Antiquities, although at the time stored in the Palestine Archaeological Museum in Jerusalem because there was no museum in Amman. Those allocated to the American School were sent to the Cincinnati Art Museum. The copy in the Rockefeller Museum has the Palestine Archaeological Museum numbers on it.
6. Typed record cards, made in February 1939, of the objects, largely sculpture, originally sent to the Palestine Archaeological Museum in Jerusalem.

B. Architectural Field Records

1. FFN = Clarence S. Fisher's field notes. These consist of measured drawings of mouldings on 3 ¼ × 4 ½ inch paper in two piles, one labelled "Temple facade II," and one labelled "Temple facade III," and also a pile of 5 × 8 inch cards beginning "Masonry Shrine Original I Casing."
2. PFN = Carl Pape's field notes, generally of architectural blocks. These are on 5 × 8 inch cards, beginning with "Kh. Tannur Base of large columns." They include cards by Clarence S. Fisher and S. Vernon McCasland. The numbers for the blocks on them are the same as those on Pape's inked drawings (reproduced in Vol. 1, Ch. 2) and Fisher's elevations and sections (*DD* plans B–C). When Pape's field notes provide additional details, they are reproduced in Vol. 1, Ch. 2.
3. Clarence Fisher's Level Book.
4. Notebook, 5 × 8 inches, of December 1937, with extra measurements taken by C. S. Steinbeck (includes pay records for workmen for December).

C. Architectural Analysis and Final Drawings

1. FAN = Clarence Fisher's 15-page architectural report, describing the building and its phases. Labelled "ARCHITECTURAL NOTES," there are two copies with different annotations by Glueck.

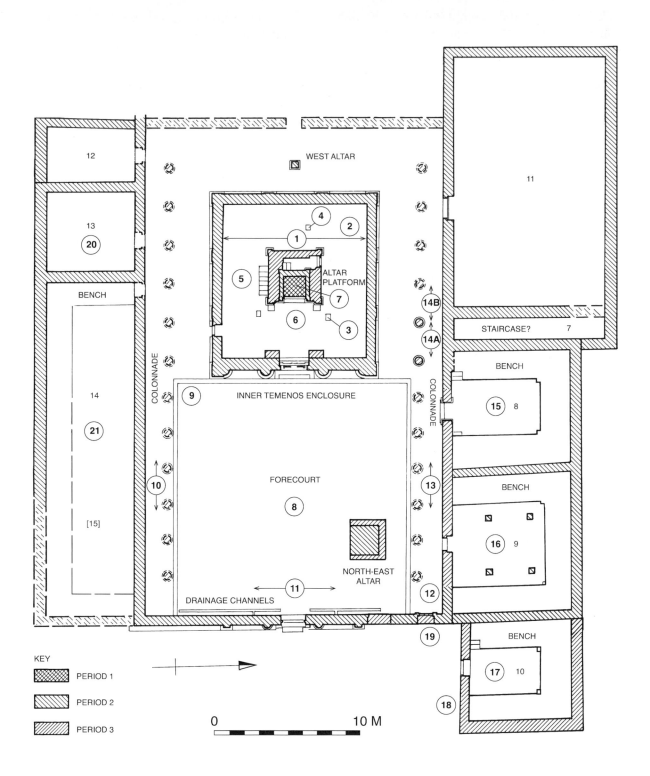

FIG. 6.2   *Khirbet et-Tannur, plan with loci numbers.*

2. GNAN = Glueck's handwritten notes on FAN. Labelled "Notes on Architectural Notes."

3. FRN = Clarence Fisher's 7 pages of typed notes on the reconstruction. Labeled "C. S. Fisher KHIRBET TANNUR," these apparently were written later than FAN, and include the first version of the List of Mouldings.

4. List of Mouldings. The numbers on this are the same as those on Carl Pape's inked profile drawings of the mouldings (below). There are four different typed drafts, as Glueck had trouble identifying them after Fisher's death.

5. Clarence Fisher's inked site plan (*DD* plan A) (Vol. 1, fig. 29; Vol. 2, fig. 6.1)

6. Clarence Fisher's inked elevations and sections (*DD* plans B–C).

7. Contour plan of Jabal et-Tannur (*DD* plan H) (Vol. 1, fig. 28b).

8. Carl Pape's inked drawings of profiles of mouldings, not published. All of these are reproduced in Vol. 1, Ch. 2, with his original numbers on them.

9. Carl Pape's inked drawings of some architectural details (such as the pilasters, friezes, and pediment of the Period 3 niches), not published. Used here for Vol. 1, figs. 171, 260a–b.

D. Other Records

Besides Glueck's description of his reconnaissance trip to the site in 1936, in his regular Newsletter to ASOR members, some passing references are found in other newsletters, his diary, and his letters in the Glueck Archive. Any of interest are mentioned in Vol. 1, Ch. 1.

Photographs in the Glueck Archive

A. Negatives and Prints

1. Photographs of the excavations at Khirbet-Tannur, with numbers in 100s.
Negatives on 2 ½ × 4 ¼ inch film, usually with contact prints. Glueck occasionally did not number these negatives in the exact order in which he took them. The prints are often labeled in detail on the back by Glueck.

Nos. 195 to 214 were taken by Peake Pasha on 10 September 1936.

The rest were taken by Glueck:

Nos. 321 to 349 at Khirbet et-Tannur on Glueck's reconnaissance visit on 17 November 1936.
Nos. 356 to 381 of blocks from Khirbet et-Tannur at ʿAbdullah Rīhānī Bey's house in Tafileh, 17 November 1936 (often out of focus).
Nos. 382 to 393 at Khirbet et-Tannur.
Nos. 394 to 397 of Peake Pasha with his Gipsy Moth at Kerak, 17 November 1936.

The folder with Nos. 400 to 500 (containing both negatives and contact prints) was not found in February 2011 although shipped to the Semitic Museum, Harvard University, in 1976. These probably included the Khirbet et-Tannur excavation photographs of February 1937.

Nos. 500 to 760, 796 taken during the excavation from March to April or May 1937. These have negatives and contact prints.

The folders with Nos. 800 to 1200, which included the Khirbet et-Tannur excavations May, November, and December 1937, were not found in February 2011 (although sent to the Semitic Museum in 1976). However, contact prints, the negatives, and enlarged prints of the most important of these are to be found in the large photograph file compiled by Eleanor Vogel (see below). The last few of these photographs were taken by Pape, after Glueck's camera was damaged.

2. Photographs of objects, largely sculpture, and of the site, with five digit numbers of the form 18.123, etc.
Beginning 15, 18, or 20, on 5 × 7 inch glass plates or 4 ¾ × 6 ½ inch film. These were taken at both Khirbet et-Tannur and in the Palestine Archaeological Museum and always include a scale. They were taken by the Museum's photographer S. J. Schweig. Although these are Palestine Archaeological Museum negative numbers, the large photograph file compiled by E. Vogel (see below) includes negatives (or duplicate negatives) of many of them, including glass plates. Schweig also took the formal wide angle shots of the site.

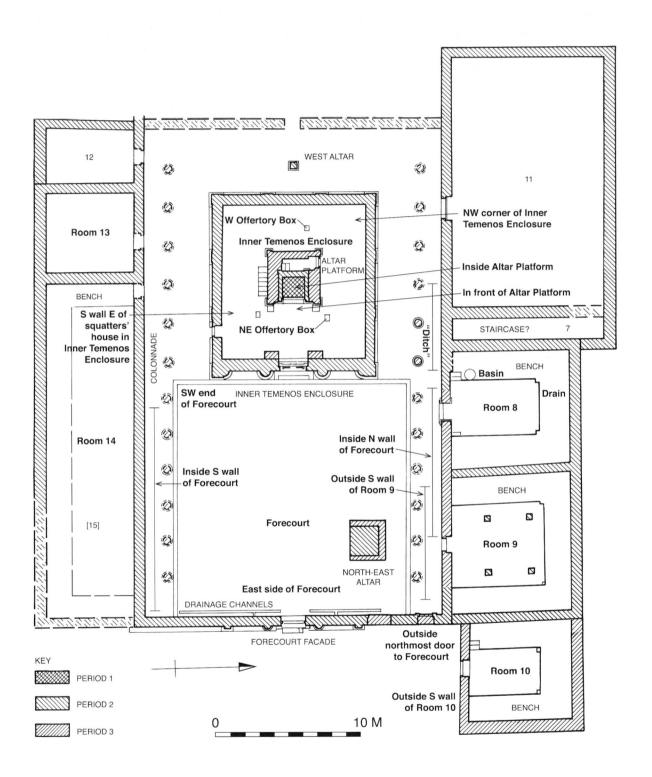

FIG. 6.3   *Khirbet et-Tannur, plan with nomenclature used for find-spots of pottery sherds in the Glueck Archive, Semitic Museum, Harvard University.*

3. Photographs of the additional stone sculpture from Khirbet-Tannur which came to light in 1951, by Richmond Brown for the Department of Antiquities of the Hashemite Kingdom of Jordan.

4. Photographs of additional details of the sculpture in Cincinnati Art Museum by F. van Houten Raymond taken in 1962. Most of these have a tape measure in inches in them.

B. Glueck's Albums of Prints, I to III, and Numbers of the Form II-3b, etc.

Glueck glued prints, especially the Palestine Archaeological Museum images of the sculpture and formal wide-angle views of the site, into three black albums, which he annotated. These provide the numbering system I-1a, etc. The Roman numeral refers to the number of the album and the Arabic numeral to the page number, while "a" or "b," etc. indicates the photograph on the page (as there are usually two), sometimes with an additional one added on the facing page and labeled "c." If there is more than one object in a photograph, then they have superscript Arabic numbers. Thus II: 3b[1] (given here as II-3b-1) is Album 2, page 3, photograph b, object 1. These numbers became the main working numbers of Glueck and Vogel for identifying these photographs as well as the objects in them, especially in Vogel's file mentioned below. The Palestine Archaeological Museum negative numbers are visible at the edges of the prints in this album, but the album numbers replace them in Vogel's file.

C. Eleanor Vogel's Photograph File

When Glueck and Vogel were working on the material for publication in *Deities and Dolphins*, Vogel compiled a large file (which filled three filing cabinet drawers) which included the multiple prints of the photographs made in order to obtain the best results for the plates for the book, and often typed 8½ × 11 inch record sheets for the objects or images. The photographs of the objects were filed by the numbering system from Glueck's albums (I-2a, etc.), along with their negatives. However,

Vogel added additional prints to these, also using those numbers as a way of identifying the objects. Consequently, on occasion, images of the same object from more than one negative ended up with the same number. In addition, she filed selected photographs of the excavation and site, which all had numbers in the 100s, by their numbers in sequence, as in 609, 610, 721, etc. Usually she filed the negatives of these with their prints, although occasionally these negatives are in the relevant negative holder (see Section A, no. 1, above). Thus, the file contains images from the Palestine Archaeological Museum, Glueck, the Department of Antiquities of the Hashemite Kingdom of Jordan, and the Cincinnati Art Museum.

Records in Jerusalem, Amman, and Cincinnati

Records in the Rockefeller Museum in East Jerusalem include some Palestine Archaeological Museum photographic prints, two very brief reports Glueck wrote after both seasons for the Department of Antiquities of Transjordan, and a copy of the Division Lists with Palestine Archaeological Museum numbers. The Rockefeller also has record cards of objects which were sent to Amman in 1951.

Jordan Archaeological Museum, the Department of Antiquities in Amman, and its store in Amman have record cards, including some which are duplicates of those in the Rockefeller. We decided not to attempt to use the Jordanian Department of Antiquities record cards to find the sculpture, because of our lack of success with the pottery.

According to the late Glenn Markoe, there are no substantial records in the Cincinnati Art Museum.

Numbering System for Glueck Archive Units

When we began work on the non-architectural remains from Glueck's excavation in 2002, they were stored in the Semitic Museum in four (slightly larger than wine-carton-sized) storage boxes labeled: Box 4-A, Box A, Box 47, and Box 48. Within these boxes there were plastic bags containing

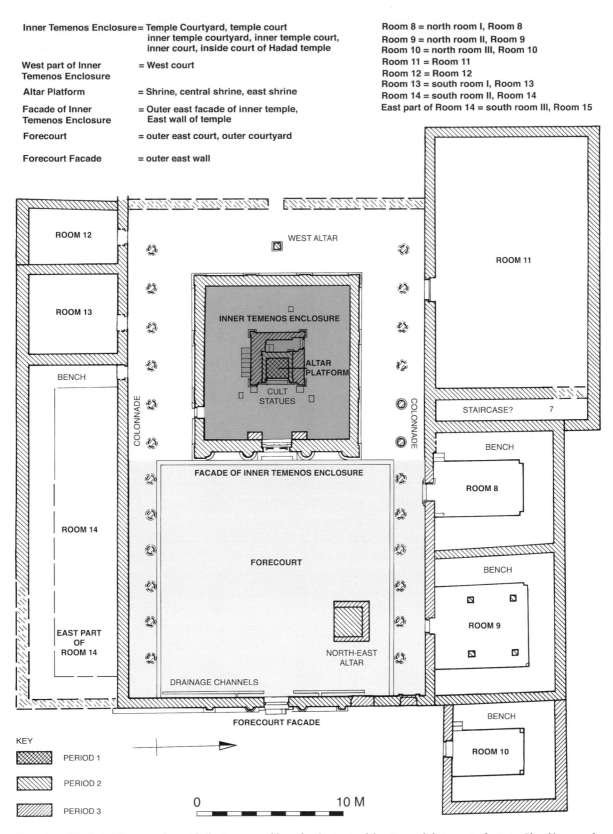

Inner Temenos Enclosure = Temple Courtyard, temple court
                          inner temple courtyard, inner temple court,
                          inner court, inside court of Hadad temple

West part of Inner   = West court
Temenos Enclosure

Altar Platform   = Shrine, central shrine, east shrine

Facade of Inner   = Outer east facade of inner temple,
Temenos Enclosure   East wall of temple

Forecourt   = outer east court, outer courtyard

Forecourt Facade   = outer east wall

Room 8 = north room I, Room 8
Room 9 = north room II, Room 9
Room 10 = north room III, Room 10
Room 11 = Room 11
Room 12 = Room 12
Room 13 = south room I, Room 13
Room 14 = south room II, Room 14
East part of Room 14 = south room III, Room 15

ROOM 12

ROOM 13

BENCH

ROOM 14

EAST PART
OF
ROOM 14

COLONNADE

WEST ALTAR

INNER TEMENOS ENCLOSURE

ALTAR
PLATFORM

CULT
STATUES

FACADE OF INNER TEMENOS ENCLOSURE

FORECOURT

NORTH-EAST
ALTAR

DRAINAGE CHANNELS

FORECOURT FACADE

COLONNADE

ROOM 11

STAIRCASE?   7

BENCH

ROOM 8

BENCH

ROOM 9

BENCH

ROOM 10

KEY

PERIOD 1

PERIOD 2

PERIOD 3

0   10 M

FIG. 6.4   *Khirbet et-Tannur, plan with the terms used here for the parts of the site, and their equivalents in Glueck's journal.*

sherds and sometimes glass, bone, charred grains, charcoal, and metal. In addition, some objects were stored separately, labeled 20-A-1, etc., which included the alloy sealing ring, copper *spatula*, Seleucid coin of Antiochus III, some nearly complete lamps, and some glass.

The packing inventories for the sixty-two boxes of Glueck's material, largely from Tell el-Kheleifeh, sent to the Semitic Museum in 1976 following Glueck's death in 1971, provide further information. They indicate that Box 4 included Khirbet et-Tannur "sacks of debris, charcoal, shards, etc." As Box 20 included "Khirbet et-Tannur objects: lamps, glass, 1 coin, ring, cosmetic pick, etc.," the objects labeled 20-A-1, etc. were those from Box 20. Box 47 contained "Khirbet et-Tannur Debris;" and Box 48 "Khirbet et-Tannur misc. pottery and sacks of shards." Thus, as Box 59 contained "Khirbet et-Tannur Debris," it would appear to be Box A.

The bags in Box 4-A were all numbered with a number of the form 4-A-1, 4-A-2, etc., and nearly always with an indication of the location from where they came, and sometimes the date they were collected. The bags in Box A were not numbered by Glueck, but were given numbers by Carrie Duncan and J. S. McKenzie in April 2002. Most of the bags in this box have the locations in which they were found given by Glueck and sometimes the date. The two exceptions are two large bags, Box A nos. 12 and 13, which are largely body sherds and for which no location or date is given. Box A bag 13 contained a noticeable number of lamp fragments. The bags in Box 48 were numbered by Duncan and McKenzie. Each of the bags in Box 48 was already labeled "Debris" (Box 48, bags 1-14), except for two bags (Box 48, bags 15-16) labeled from Room 14 and which seem to have been grouped together because they contain pieces which join.

Glueck often recorded the find-locations on the sherds themselves. Where the sherds are so labeled, they do accord with the label on their bag. However, Glueck had placed the sherds in brown paper bags which have rotted. Usually (possibly when they were re-boxed in the Semitic Museum on July 21, 1994, or before) these were placed in plastic bags, so that they stayed together, as those in Box 4A. As the term "debris" is sometimes writ-

ten on individual sherds by Glueck, it specifically means that there was no context for these sherds when he collected them.

However, Box 47 contained bags with sherds mixed together from a number of different locations, as indicated by the labels on the sherds themselves. Most of the sherds in these bags were labeled. Because it is not clear if there is some other reason why these sherds were grouped together in these bags, their new bag numbers were chosen to reflect these bags. For example, Box 47 bag 19 contained a noticeable number of lamp sherds. Thus, each bag was numbered (1, 2, etc.) by Duncan, in March–April 2002. After this, she sorted the sherds from each of these bags by find-location and grouped them together in bags, each of which was given a bag number to which a letter of the alphabet was added (hence 1A, 1B, 2A, 2B, etc.).

For easier study, in April 2002, Duncan grouped the bags for each Glueck Archive (GA) Unit together within larger bags by Locus number (established by McKenzie, see below). Within these bigger bags, they were kept in their GA Unit bags so that the sherds were not mixed together. This means that all sherds with identifiable find-locations now have a Locus number. Those sherds for which it has not been possible to identify Glueck's exact find-location (due to a lack of clarity, or clerical errors in the room numbers) have not been given Loci numbers. Samples of glass, organic remains, and metals, which had been in these bags, are now stored separately in the Semitic Museum.

In this volume the term "Glueck Archive Unit" (= GA Unit) is used to refer to the above Box and bag numbers, with the punctuation simplified to avoid confusion and to facilitate digital searching, e.g., 4A-01 is Box 4A bag 1; 48-01 is Box 48 bag 1; 47-01A is Box 47 bag 1A; with 20-A01, etc., for the groups of objects from Box 20.

The numbering format of the bags from Box 4-A (4-A-1, etc.) and of the objects stored separately (20-B-1, etc.) suggests that there had been an inventory for these numbers, now lost. However, the fact that fragments of Lamp 32, previously photographed together by Glueck, were in both 20-B01 and 20-B06 suggests that at least some subdivisions of Box 20 are of no significance.

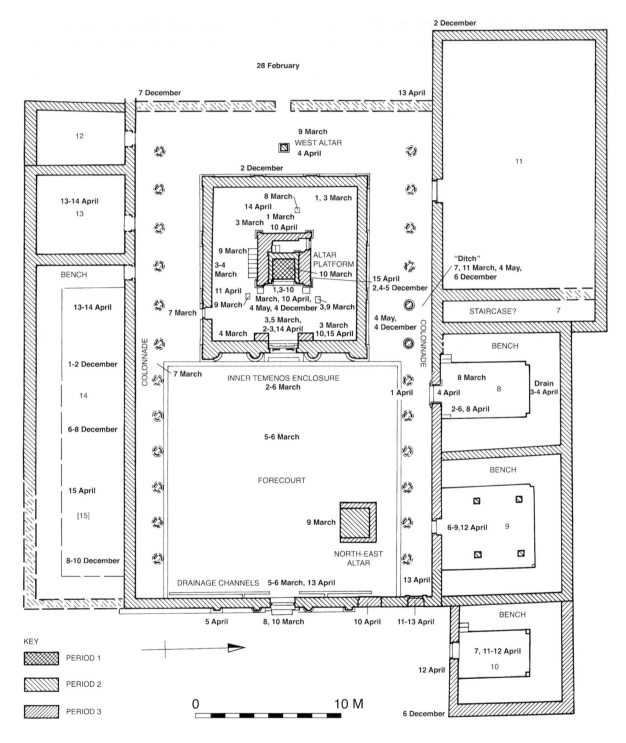

FIG. 6.5 *Khirbet et-Tannur, plan with dates when areas are mentioned in Glueck's journal.*

The relative proportions of sherds in the Glueck Archive seem to suggest that Glueck collected all of what he found rather than only diagnostic shapes.

If the pottery in the bags is taken as a whole, there are the expected relative number of body sherds to rims and bases (Stephan Schmid, pers. comm.).

Furthermore, there are many tiny body sherds which would not have been collected unless an attempt was being made to collect everything.

Loci and Standardization of Names of Find-Locations

The main source of Glueck's excavation records for the above material is his excavation journal (GJ). However, find-locations are also mentioned in his registration book (GR), which includes notable objects but not sherds. Many locations are marked on individual pot sherds or bag labels.

Because Glueck only discovered the shape of the temple complex as he excavated it (in the order of the dates marked on fig. 6.5), there is potential confusion from the terms he used at different stages of the excavation for the locations that were being excavated (given in fig. 6.4). This arose because they began with the Altar Platform, with the niche for the statue of the god at the front, which they called the "shrine." They then moved outwards to discover the shape of the Inner Temenos Enclosure and finally the Court around it, and east to the Forecourt, and the rooms on its north, and then those on its south. Thus, for example, Glueck refers to the Inner Temenos Enclosure as: temple courtyard, temple court, inner temple courtyard, inner temple court, inner court, and inside court of Hadad temple. The Forecourt was referred to as outer east court and outer courtyard. Similarly, the numbering system for the rooms along either side of the Court was changed. Thus, "north room II" became "Room 8," "north room III" became "Room 9," and "south room II" became "Room 14," etc. He sometimes referred to the east part of Room 14 as "Room 15" (e.g., fig. 6.1). Because in the end he did not find traces of a dividing wall, which he had expected, he also later used the single term Room 14. It has been retained here, along with "the east part of Room 14."

Thus, it was necessary for McKenzie to go through the excavation journal (GJ) and the labels on the pottery to clarify the locations meant by Glueck, sometimes helped by the dates they were excavated. She then gave each location a single number, the "Locus" in this volume. This infor-

mation is presented on four plans: Glueck's plan, drawn by C. S. Fisher, which shows his final room numbers and the areas covered by paving (fig. 6.1); fig. 6.2 gives the Loci numbers; fig. 6.3 gives the standardized name used here for each location; fig. 6.4 gives that name, plus all Glueck's names for each location; and fig. 6.5 gives the dates Glueck mentions excavating each area.

McKenzie has listed this information, grouping the bags of sherds by the Loci she had established, in Table 6.1. In the first column is her Locus number. In the second column is the Location, consisting firstly of her standardized name for the location, followed by Glueck's name for it in quotation marks opposite the number of the bag so labeled. The date it was excavated appears in the third column. If this date appears on the bag of sherds, then it is repeated. If the date can be inferred from some detail, it is put in brackets. The fourth column gives the GA Unit number (explained above, *Numbering System for Glueck Archive Units*). The fifth column indicates the types of finds from that particular GA Unit: pottery sherds, lamps, metal, glass, bones, grains, charcoal, etc.

Because of confusion possibly arising from Glueck's varied names for the locations, annotated copies of his excavation journal (GJ) and registration book (GR) have been included in the present volume (Chs. 7–8).

Note

1 There are at least 12 pieces in the Glueck Archive which are apparently gypsum, but they are sufficiently chipped and worn that it is not possible to determine their original function – if from wall-veneer, or vessels, or both. Approximate dimensions: north-east offertory box, Locus 3, Unit 4A-11, 2.5 × 1.0 × 0.8 cm. Outside northmost door to Forecourt, Locus 19, Unit 4A-09: 3.7 × 1.7 × 1.6 cm; Unit 20-B09: 2.9 × 1.2 × 1.0 cm and 1.9 × 0.9 × 0.8 cm. "Debris", Unit 47-13L: 8.4 × 5.8 × 1.5 cm and 4.9 × 4.5 × 1.7 cm; Unit 48-05: 4.0 × 3.7 × 1.7 cm; 2.4 × 1.8 × 0.9 cm; 2.8 × 1.3 × 1.2 cm; 2.9 × 1.8 × 1.6 cm; 3.3 × 1.7 × 1.4 cm. Provenience unknown, Unit A-12: 2.8 × 1.0 × 0.7 cm.

Table 6.1   Pottery sherds, pots, lamps, glass, metal, bones, and grains at Khirbet et Tannur (by context).

Explanation/Key

Locus numbers
Marked on fig. 6.2 by J. S. McKenzie.

Location, date excavated
Locations in quotation marks are Glueck's names on pottery sherd(s) and/or the bag containing the finds. Names of these locations are marked on figs. 6.3–4, and the dates they were excavated on fig. 6.5.

Glueck Archive Unit
The Glueck Archive (GA) Unit refers to the numbers of the box and bag in which they were in the Semitic Museum, Harvard University, in April 2002 (before work on the analysis of the finds began, as explained above). Where there is no GA Unit and they are in Glueck's list of pottery (GP) or his registration book (GR) those numbers are given.

Abbreviations for types of finds (for other abbreviations, see pp. xvii–xviii)
B = Bones, all in GA.
C = Charcoal, all in GA.
G = Grain or offering cakes, all in GA.
Gl = Glass with catalogue number (= GA glass number), all in GA.
L = Lamp with catalogue number (= GA lamp number when in GA). If not in GA, then GR no. (or GP no.) given in Glueck Archive Unit column. Lamps are in GA, unless otherwise indicated.
M = Metal (iron, unless coins or otherwise stated) with catalogue number (= GA metal number). Iron all in GA.
P = Pottery. All sherds are in GA. Complete or partially complete vessels are not.
Pl = Plaster, in GA.
R = Rock samples (apparently gypsum), in GA.
* = not in Semitic Museum.

Other locations excavated, according to GJ – but no labelled sherds in GA:

Central east doorway to Forecourt	8 March
In front of Forecourt facade	5 April
SE offering box	9 March
Room 12	7 December

LOCUS	LOCATION	DATE EXCAVATED, IN 1937	GLUECK ARCHIVE UNIT	TYPES OF FINDS
1	W part of Inner Temenos Enclosure "NW corner of temple and NW corner of temple courtyard, also from west side of court"	4 March	4A-05	B, G, C
	SW corner of temple platform	3 March	GR 27	L 33*
2	NW corner of Inner Temenos Enclosure	3 March	4A-23	P
	"NW corner of temple courtyard"	3 March	4A-27	M 06
			47-01C	P
			47-13G	P
			GR 28	L 29
	"burnings and vegetable matter from NW corner of court of temple"	3 March	part of 4A-18	G

Table 6.1 (cont.)   Pottery sherds, pots, lamps, glass, metal, bones, and grains at Khirbet et Tannur (by context).

Locus	Location	Date excavated, in 1937	Glueck Archive Unit	Types of finds
3	NE offertory box, with lid "break in pavement of temple courtyard"	3 March	4A-11	P, B, G, C, R
4	W offertory box "in floor storage basin, west inner court of shrine"	8 March	4A-10	P, B, G, C
5	Inside S wall of Inner Temenos Enclosure, E of squatters' house in Inner Temenos Enclosure	3 March	4A-06	P
	"inside S wall E of squatters' house"		47-01D	P
	"inside wall east of squatters' house"		47-13D	P
6	In front of Altar Platform; E part of Inner Temenos Enclosure	1, 3, 9–10 March		
	"in front of east shrine"	(3 or 10 March)	4A-01	B, G, C, M 05
	"in front of main shrine"		4A-25	P, L 40
			47-07E	P
	"grains of wheat from SE end of altar"	4 March	Part of 4A-18	G
	SE corner of Inner Temenos Enclosure	4 March	Part of 4A-18	Gl 08, Gl 09
	east part of Inner Temenos Enclosure	4 March	GR 39	L 37*
6A	Inner Temenos Enclosure doorway In front of Inner Temenos Enclosure "outside N inner court"	5 March	4A-07	C (doors), M 02 (apparently from door hinge)
	In N door socket	6 March	A-07	M 01 (door hinge)
7	Inside Altar Platform	10 March		
	"chamber in east shrine"		4A-20	B, C
	"bottom of east shrine"		4A-24	P, B
8	Forecourt	5-6 March		
	"main court"		4A-21	P
9	SW end of Forecourt	2-6 March		
	"SW end of outer east court"		4A-12	P
			4A-14	P
		7 March	4A-22	M 03
	"SW end of outer east court"	7 March	20-B13	Gl 01, Gl 21
10	Inside S wall of Forecourt	5–6 March		
	"inside S wall of main court"		4A-13	P, Gl 23
	"inside S wall of main outer court"		No number	P
11	E side of Forecourt	4–6 March		
	"east side of large east court"		4A-15	P
			4A-16	P

Table 6.1 (cont.) Pottery sherds, pots, lamps, glass, metal, bones, and grains at Khirbet et Tannur (by context).

Locus	Location	Date excavated, in 1937	Glueck Archive Unit	Types of finds
12	Outside S wall of room 9 "outside S wall of N room II" [i.e., to S of room 9 up to N door in facade of forecourt]	13 April	4A-02 4A-28 A-01	P P P
13	Inside N wall of Forecourt "inside N wall of main court"	5–6 March	4A-08 47-01B 47-05C 47-07D 47-13C	P P P L 38 P
14A	"Ditch" [N of N wall of Inner Temenos Enclosure] "ditch N of N. outer wall of Temple" "ditch on N side of N side court" "NE end of N ditch"	7,11 March, 4 May, 6 December (6 December) (6 December)	 4A-03 4A-17 4A-19 20-B11 47-05E	 P P P, L 15, Gl 10, Gl 11 P P
14B	S of "Ditch" [see dig journal 11 Mar.] " 'balatah' floor on N side of N outer courtyard" [GJ 11 March seems to indicate from under *balatah* floor]	11 March (11 March) (11 March)	 47-13B 47-20B	 P P
15	Room 8 "N room I"	8 Mar, 2–6, 8 April (3 April – drain, 4 April – entrance, 2 April – basin) 2 April	 47-07F 47-07I 47-13H A-05 [Misplaced] A-14 GR 72	 P P P P P L 42*
16	Room 9 "N room II" "SW end of N room II" SW corner of room 9 SW corner of room 9 Room 9	6–9 April (9 April) (7 April) 9 April 9 April	 47-11B 47-13I A-03 A-10 A-11 GR 80 20-B01 20-B02	 P P, L 47 P P P, Gl 29 L 18* L 12 L 44

Table 6.1 (cont.)   Pottery sherds, pots, lamps, glass, metal, bones, and grains at Khirbet et Tannur (by context).

Locus	Location	Date excavated, in 1937	Glueck Archive Unit	Types of finds
17	Room 10 "N room III"	7,11–12 April, 6 December	47-07G	P
			47-13F	P
			A-02	P
			A-09	P
			GP 10	P*
			GP 06	P 84 (flask)*
	"Inside west wall of north room III"		47-07F	P
	"SE corner of n. room III"		No number	P 42 (fine ware plain bowl fragment)
18	Outside S wall of room 10 "outside N room III"	12 April	47-01I	P
19	Outside northmost door to Forecourt	4 March, 11–13 April		
	"outer courtyard, outside temple courtyard at n.e. end"	4 March	GR 32	P 125
			GR 33	P 124
	"outside east wall near north end"	(11 April)	4A-09	P, R
		11 April	47-05B	P
		11 April	47-15	P
	"outside east outer wall near the north end"		20-B09	Gl 03, Gl 06, Gl 07, Gl 18, Gl 19, Gl 20, Gl 22, R
	"outside east outer wall near edge of platform near north end"		GP 08	P 24 (painted bowl fragments)*
			No number (=JAM J1472)	P 26 (painted bowl fragments)*
20	Room 13 "S room I"	13–14 April		
		(13 or 14 April)	47-01E	P
		14 April	47-01K	L 01
		(13–14 April)	47-05F	P
		(14 April)	47-09A	P
		(14 April)	47-10A	P
		13–14 April	47-13E	P
		(13 April)	47-14A	P

Table 6.1 (cont.)   Pottery sherds, pots, lamps, glass, metal, bones, and grains at Khirbet et Tannur (by context).

LOCUS	LOCATION	DATE EXCAVATED, IN 1937	GLUECK ARCHIVE UNIT	TYPES OF FINDS
21	Room 14 "S room II", "room 14" (Room 14 was excavated going west to east. "South room III", sometimes called "room 15" is the east part of Room 14, as no dividing wall was found)	13–14 April, 1, 6–8 December 9–10 December – SE corner 10 Dec.– east wall		
		13 April	47-01F	L 21
		(6–7 December)	47-01G	P
		(6 December)	47-03	P
		(6 December)	47-05A	P
			47-06A	P
		(7 December)	47-07A	P
			47-09B	P
			47-11A	P
		(6 December)	47-12A	P
		(6 December)	47-13D	P
			47-16A	P
		(7 December)	47-20C	P
			47-21	B
			48-15	P
			48-16	P
		(7 December)	A-06	Gl 02, Gl 13, Gl 14, Gl 15, Gl 16, Gl 25, Gl 26, Gl 27, Gl 28
			A-16	P
			No box/bag no.	L 39
		13 April	47-13J	P
		(14 April, 7 Dec)	20-B12	Gl 04
		15 April	20B-04	L 05
		15 April	20-B05	L 06
			20-B06	L 34
	"S room II"		20-B03	P (small base)
	"Room 15"	15 April	GP 12	L 04*
			47-01H	P
		7 December	20-B15	M 08 (alloy ring)
		8 December	20-B15	M 09 (copper *spatula*)
		10 December	GR 94	P 47 (bowl)*
	"Debris" of "room 15"	(*DD* 183)	GP 16	L 43*

Table 6.1 (cont.)   Pottery sherds, pots, lamps, glass, metal, bones, and grains at Khirbet et Tannur (by context).

Locus	Location	Date excavated, in 1937	Glueck Archive Unit	Types of finds
–	"Debris" (according to Glueck labels, i.e., no provenience)			
	"Debris" written on individual sherds		20-B08	P (base)
			47-01J	P, L 02
			47-05H	P
			47-07J	P
			47-13L	P, R
			47-19	L 08, L 09, L 13, L 14, L 20, L 23, L 46, L 48
	In bags labeled "debris" (but not written on individual sherds)		48-01	P
			48-02	P
			48-03	P
			48-04	P, L 10
			48-05	P, L 28, R
			48-06	P
			48-07	P
			48-08	P
			48-09	P
			48-10	P
			48-11	P
			48-12	P
			48-13	P
			48-14	P
–	Provenience unclear			
	"Room II"		47-07B	P
	"Room 3" [=room 10 or 15]		47-05G	P
			47-07C	P
			47-13K	P
			20-B12	Gl 05
	"room III or VII"		A-15	P
	"8 room II" [probably S room II = Room 14]	13 April	A-08	Gl 12, Gl 17
	"8-room II" and "N. room II"		47-01F	P
	"room 6"		47-05D	P
	room 6		4A-26	P
	"E. court and outside to north"		47-01A	P
	"N. room w side"		4A-26	P, Gl 24
	"NE end of portico outside ne. corner of temple courtyard"		47-06B	P
	"N. east end of portico outside ne. corner of temple courtyard"		47-20A	P

Table 6.1 (cont.)   Pottery sherds, pots, lamps, glass, metal, bones, and grains at Khirbet et Tannur (by context).

LOCUS	LOCATION	DATE EXCAVATED, IN 1937	GLUECK ARCHIVE UNIT	TYPES OF FINDS
–	Provenience unknown		20-B01	L 07
			20-B01 and 20-B06	L 32
			20-B02	L 41
			20-B04	L 05
			20-B07	L 30
			47-01H	P
			47-01K	P
			47-02	1 fragment of mortar 1 fragment of ?sculpture
			47-05I	P
			47-06C	P
			47-07H	P
			47-08	P
			47-10B	P
			47-12B	M 07
			47-12C	P
			47-13M	P
			47-14B	P
			47-16B	P
			47-17	P
			47-18	P
			47-20D	P
			48-17	P
			A-12	P, L 22, L 26, R
			A-13	P, L 16, L 17, L 19, L 24, L 25, L 31, L 35, L 36, L 45, worked bone
			A-17	P, L 11, L 27
			A-18	P
			GP 02	P 72 (casserole)*
			GP 05	P 126 (cooking pot)*
			GP 23	L 03*
			GP 34	P (half painted bowl with pomegrates)* M 10 (coin)
		1 March	20-B15	P (cooking pot)*
		4 March	GR 33	M 11 (coin)*
		5 April	No number	M 12 (coin)*
		5 April	No number	
		5 April	GR 74	M 14, M15 (?coins)*
		6 December		
			GR 85	M 13 (coin)*
			No number	P 23 (fragments of painted bowl with palmettes)*

Chapter 7

Glueck's Excavation Journal

edited by Judith S. McKenzie

Introduction

Although field records from an excavation would not normally be reproduced in a final report, it has been decided to publish an edited copy of Glueck's excavation journal (GJ) here, for a number of reasons. It is the main detailed record of the excavation, but because Glueck changed the nomenclature of the various parts of the building as he gained a greater knowledge of its design, sometimes it is difficult to be certain to what he is referring. Every attempt has been made to do so accurately here, but other scholars should have first-hand access to this account to judge for themselves. (Journal references in the present work are cited by the date of the journal entry, e.g., GJ 3 March.)

The journal is also of historical and methodological interest. It was written in 1937 and it is now apparent, as a result of our work, that Glueck was ahead of his time in the types of samples collected and his records – although we have most, but probably not absolutely all, of either. The excavation journal provides a glimpse of his methodology and thought processes – both how he tackled problems and how he was trying to solve them while he was excavating and afterwards. The journal shows how,

while he was excavating, Glueck was trying to work out the relative phases of the building, and how he attempted to use the pottery he was finding in order to do this. The journal reveals the order in which he excavated the site and how his understanding of it changed as he went along and discovered more about it.

Editing and Annotation System

There were three copies of Glueck's excavation diary in the Glueck Archive: the original copy, handwritten in the field, a typescript, labeled "Study Copy," and its carbon, labeled "Copy for 162 Glenmary," his home in Cincinnati, Ohio. All three copies have some annotations in common, but the main differences seem to be between those added to the Glenmary copy and to the Study copy. As the annotations on the Glenmary copy seem to be the most complete, it has been used here, then checked against the handwritten and the Study copies, and any further annotations, which are later (undated) thoughts, have been added. The main annotations in Glueck's handwriting on the Study copy were copied onto the Glenmary copy by Eleanor Vogel; then Glueck added further comments to it. She also copied important later annotations onto the original hand-written copy. His marginal notes highlighting what is being discussed are not included here. The lists he sometimes gives of some photographs, and the measurements for the Court paving stones have not been included, as these are incomplete.

As Glueck's understanding of the design of the complex evidently increased as the excavation proceeded, he changed the names he used for the different parts of it, as mentioned. This is the main potential source of confusion when reading the journal. The various names for each part of the site are given in fig. 6.4, the standardized names used for them in fig. 6.3, and the dates they were excavated in fig. 6.5. Consequently, these standardized names, and some corrections or clarifications, have been inserted in square brackets [ ] here. Most abbreviations in Glueck's text itself have not been corrected or standardized, to avoid unwittingly introducing errors. Glueck's own additions of his new room numbers and other minor corrections or clarifications by him – written on the typed copies – are given in curved brackets ( ), which he also occasionally uses in the diary. His later thoughts (which are not dated) are inserted in curly brackets { }. The figure references here have been inserted by the editor (J. S. McKenzie). Figure numbers of the form 16, 363, etc., refer to the figures in *The Nabataean Temple at Khirbet et-Tannur, Jordan,* Vol. 1: *Architecture and Religion.* Annual of ASOR 67.

KHIRBET ET-TANNUR DIARY
FEBRUARY 26 TO MARCH 11,
MARCH 30 TO APRIL 16, MAY 3 TO 4,
NOVEMBER 27 TO DECEMBER 11, 1937

February 26, 1937

Left Jerusalem 8:30 am Ylias Tutunjian driving Ford, and I the Dodge. Arrived Amman 11:30 am. Saw Harding and Ali Abu Ghosh, who are to come to Kh. et-Tannur on Sunday, Feb. 28. Met Peake Pasha and his wife above Qatrani. Harding secured 3 tents for us, and with Peake's permission we took his tent from the police at Kerak, where I saw Bahajet Bey. Slept at Manazir. I phoned Jerusalem.

February 27

Arrived at Kh. et-Tannur at 9 am. We are putting up tents. Arranged for workmen, local and otherwise, for water boys for our camp and the laborers' camp.

February 28

We started with 15 men today, including one water boy and one watchman. We made trial digs on the west side of the hill to provide a clear dumping place. Nothing was found in these trenches. We then started moving stones from the west side of the main mound and almost reached the centre of the mound. Someone has been making some soundings before us, including someone who tried to make a rude plaster-cast of an inscription. Several decorated stones were found, including another small "fish" Atargatis with her head broken off, and the side of the stone adorned with a vine and leaf ornament.

The workmen are moving their tent from the bottom of the hill to the top of the hill.

Harding and his man Hasan 'Awâd arrived this evening in their car, and also Ali Abu Ghosh with Dr Graham, Roger Graham, Mr Wood, Mr Nichols, and Mr Kerr in Graham's car.

March 1

17 men working today [for names of workmen, see Vol. 1, Ch. 1, Appendix 1.1]. We cleared the western half of the main Hadad room and Hadad is completely exposed (Vol. 1, figs. 82–83). He has 2 feet visible, and on right also is a young bull, but much damaged. He is, as is now apparent, represented in a sitting position. We discovered numerous heads (e.g., fig. 245b), busts in this room which are listed in record book. The other members of the staff have been tracing walls. Harding took charge of workmen this afternoon. We have 2 water boys now, one for the works and one for our camp. The Hadad figure is not in position. We are putting on additional men tomorrow.

March 2

We put on additional men today, most of whom were put at work clearing stones on east side of temple [Inner Temenos Enclosure]. A tremendous relief of Atargatis [the Vegetation Goddess] (fig. 160) which must have stood above east entrance of temple [Inner Temenos Enclosure], where 2 large ornamented stones which were above the entrance also, we have now moved. A large, fairly intact, eagle relief [acroterion] (figs. 164-65) was removed from debris on east side of temple, and also a much-damaged Hadad relief. In the n. east corner of the west half is a broken Atargatis bust. From near centre of east side of the temple is a 3 panelled altar with a Hadad and 2 Tyche figures with a Greek inscription [the Alexander Amrou altar] (fig. 10.4a–d). It is an incense altar stand. The oil or incense remains are still visible (fig. 10.4a).

NDROS	NΔPOC
AMRO	AMPO
V	V

The front of the east gate [doorway of the Inner Temenos Enclosure] of the Hadad temple is cluttered up with stones of a fallen arch [? from around the Vegetation Goddess panel], some of them having fallen in position.

The top of the temple [?] was evidently of rolled mud mixed with straw; we found a piece of it. There was evidently also very delicate plaster work.

A fine stone with a double thunderbolt came up from debris on east side of temple gate [Inner Temenos Enclosure] (fig. 166).

I sent Ylias and Mr Kerr to Amman today for new supplies, baskets, tools and money. We employed 47 men today. Harding's dog is known as Lachish and the local dog as el-Aban [Atarah was Glueck's dog].

March 3

Sherds coming up from n.e. inside corner of temple court [Inner Temenos Enclosure]. Nabataean inscription found outside s.e. corner of temple court [the La'abān inscription] (fig. 9.1a–b).

Many of the stones inside the temple court are heavily coated with plaster resulting from water seeping through. There must have been a strong earthquake. Much of the inside walls may have been covered with plaster, there being some fine plaster work in small separate fragments still remaining. Many of the stones were plastered (cemented) together. Other stones were probably burned to lime by the fire. An unfinished head from inside n.e. corner of the temple courtyard.

In centre of n. inside of temple courtyard [Inner Temenos Enclosure] there is burning on floor [from its doors; see below March 5 and April 2, 3]. Also in s.w. corner of inside temple courtyard [Inner Temenos Enclosure].

Harding finding bits of wheat grain, complete wheat grains from behind Hadad statue, and some pieces of burned metal (?). The wheat was probably brought as an offering to Hadad and Atargatis.

In n.e. side of temple court [Inner Temenos Enclosure] is a fairly square break offering chamber [north-east offertory box] (figs. 397–99) in the stone-block pavement (which encircles the central altar). In it Hassan is finding bits of fine (bird?) eggshell, fragments of Nabataean pottery, charcoal and grains.

On n.w. corner of inner temple courtyard [Inner Temenos Enclosure] are numerous wheat (?) grains, bits of charcoal, and pieces of iron (?) band (fig. 13.6).

A complete Nab. lamp [South Jordan slipper lamp] found at s.w. corner of shrine [Altar Platform] (fig. 17.33). This is the third lamp found. There must have been numerous lamps brought to the shrine. Numerous bits of charcoal and grains of wheat found on west side of shrine also. The spout still shows burning.

A number of parts of pillars [columns] fallen beyond s.w. corner of shrine.

Steps are showing up beyond east wall of shrine [Altar Platform], a part evidently of a massive entrance [of the Inner Temenos Enclosure], above which the huge Atargatis relief stood [Vegetation Goddess] (fig. 160).

At southwest corner of inside court [Inner Temenos Enclosure] of Hadad temple, and extending to near centre of west side of courtyard is a squatters' room, made by piling up drums of pillars [columns] to form a room (figs. 322–23). On north side of this room is a small, stone lined fireplace which the squatters made (figs. 324–25).

A terrific windstorm, which has started blowing in the morning, increased so in intensity after the whistle for work at 1:30 pm, that we had to call a halt for the day.

March 4

Front steps on east side of temple appearing very clearly.

Nabataean inscription in 3 parts [it is not clear to what he is referring] found on south side of south wall. There may be other parts yet.

One large Helios figure with two clear torches found in debris at s.e. end of temple (fig. 129). It is of Kh. Mesheirfeh type. Clearing on s. and e. and n. sides of temple.

Two fairly complete jugs [pots] found in outer courtyard [Forecourt], outside temple courtyard [Inner Temenos Enclosure] at n.e. end (figs. 18.30, no. 124; 18.31, no. 125).

Small reclining animal figure (fig. 89) from debris on south side of inner temple courtyard [Inner Temenos Enclosure].

Small complete bust in relief of woman between columns found in front of s.e. corner of building. Right half of head from inside s.e. corner of temple court [Inner Temenos Enclosure] (fig. 201).

Part of front upper part of statue, with left breast and armor-like dress on left side visible, with most of Medusa-like head, in centre of bottom, evidently bet. 2 breasts (fig. 290). Found in debris in front of east steps.

Bits of glass from s.e. corner of inner court (Ch. 15, nos. 8–9; fig. 15.1, no. 8).

A piece of copper, fragments of a glass vessel (the Nabatateans did make glass!) a piece of bone (was it part of a sacrifice?), and a complete Nab. lamp [South Jordan slipper lamp] found in inner east court [Inner Temenos Enclosure] back of steps (fig. 17.37).

The thunderbolt of Hadad is double-arrow-headed, the upper arrow having been broken off.

The broken head of an eagle was found in court-yard outside east step [the head of the eagle grappling a snake] (fig. 158). 1 1/2 Nab. lamps found in e. inner court [Inner Temenos Enclosure] back of steps.

March 5

A well executed stone ornamented with wreaths and Medusa-like head, the nose of which has been broken off (fig. 284). It was found in front of east steps. The other half of this stone was found yesterday. The back and tail of a lion (fig. 90) was found at east end of outer court [Forecourt].

The doorway [of Inner Temenos Enclosure] is now open, with 3 steps leading up to it from the east (fig. 93). There were iron door sockets still left in place at either end of the main sill. There is an outer sill slightly above it, with a peculiar notch for sliding doors in it (fig. 13.1), with remnants of iron door posts in it (figs. 13.2–3). The main doorway was evidently burned down, to judge from the ashes on the sill, and the burned stones on either side. The present entrance is a secondary construction and has to be removed before the stones belonging to the main entrance become visible.

The inner shrine [Altar Platform] shows a primary construction of fine stones covered by a rougher secondary construction, to which the steps leading to the top of the shrine on the south side belong (figs. 53, 60).

The entire outer court is paved.

Broken iron nail found in debris outside inner north court of temple (fig. 13.4).

Only a few, large, ribbed Nab. jugs and bowls found. A number of pieces of sigillata found in various isolated places. Numerous fine painted and rouletted sherds found around Khirbeh but very few inside. A number of complete lamps found inside. Some of the sigillata looks as if it might be imported, and some as if it were natively manufactured, although it would be impossible to tell the difference with certainty. There are also reddish sigillata sherds of a definite Nabataean type.

March 6

A Greek inscription, broken, from near east end of outer east court [Forecourt] (fig. 308).

A lintel with 2 intact heads (fig. 263) from in front of east wall of temple [Inner Temenos Enclosure], near north end.

A capital with one small intact head (figs. 266–67, 271a–b) from in front east wall of temple [Inner Temenos Enclosure] near north end.

A number of feet and one head from in front east wall of temple [Inner Temenos Enclosure] near south end.

It is particularly interesting to see how the backs of the stones were cut and measured with lines to insure proper cutting.

There are evidently porticos which surround 3 sides of temple [Inner Temenos Enclosure] with exception of east front side. The floors of these porticos are covered with *balatah*. At edge of *balatah* is a trench, extending apparently on all three sides, filled with debris and broken sherds.

The entire outer east court [Forecourt] seems originally to have been paved.

March 7

Fired about 23 men last night. For today's finds consult record book. A number of bits of glass coming up from various places (figs. 15.1, nos. 1 and 21; 15.2, no. 1; Vol. 1, fig. 404b), and also several bits of sigillata. There is almost a complete vessel of fine painted ware in the ditch on the north side, the pieces of which Harding is getting together [apparently the half bowl with pomegranates and palmettes, figs. 18.5*; 18.5, no. 21].

Digging in the ditch on the north side of the court outside the north inner court of the shrine, revealed that it is full of rubbish, containing fine painted sherds, and that apparently this rubbish goes under the pavement of the court and under the temple proper. The conclusion would be that the entire temple is a secondary construction built over earlier Nabataean debris. It is a fact that the only sherds and vessels found in the temple proper and above the *balatah* of the courtyard are of the coarser, black, and to an extent ribbed type. Most of the painted sherds found seem to be on the outside of the main building complex.

On the south side, squatters have built a hut at the east end of the pavement (fig. 320), which

reaches to the east end of the front of a line parallel with the east front of the entrance to the temple-courtyard. Here it is noticeable that there is a break, caused by squatters, in this end of the south courtyard outside the south wall of the temple courtyard south wall; the south landing continuing to the east end of the large outer courtyard and then descending two steps to the pavement of the large outer court, most of the stones of which have disappeared. The general appearance of all the destruction is that of an earthquake.

There appear then to be four construction periods.

A. The original one containing the debris with the fine painted sherds in it, and also some sigillata.
B. The primary part of the present standing shrine [Altar Platform] and walls, indicated by the fine nature of the stones, and the masons' lines on the back of them.
C. The secondary temple construction as evidenced by the construction around the primary part of the shrine, and heavy carved stones.
D. The squatters' buildings.

{Later annotation:
Periods
1a. rude stamped floor at bottom of N ditch.
1.   A – original shrine I.
2.   A–B fine painted pottery, just preceding paved floor which preceded Shrine II.
3.   B Fine floor of cut stone blocks.
4.   B Shrine II.
5.   C Shrine III.
6.   D Squatters' period.}

March 8

In centre of west court [of Inner Temenos Enclosure] is a small storage bin [west offertory box], on which a special lid stood (figs. 397, 401). In it were found bones (fig. 395), charcoal, bits of grain, etc. It is back of central shrine.

The east gate of the outer east court [Forecourt], which is on a line with the east gate of the inner temple court [Inner Temenos Enclosure] is being cleared. The path leading east from it is on a direct line with the path which leads partly through cut rock down the east, northeast slope of the hill.

We let all the men go except about 10 this evening.

Dr Fisher arrived. Harding left this morning having taken a number of numbered stones with him.

We commenced excavating 2 rooms on north side of hill, after cleaning the stones from the north side of the hill. In the west one of these north rooms [Room 8] is a gate leading into the west end of the outer east court [Forecourt] (fig. 280). In this room also is a round stone basin (fig. 281), in which there seems to be remains of cement.

Coarse pottery has been coming up from these north rooms also, and none of the fine pottery, or rather very little of it. It would seem definitely from this place that the fine pottery is BC and the coarse pottery is the end of this period and beginning of AD.

March 9

We are working with ten men and boys today, on cleaning up the court of the temple [Inner Temenos Enclosure]. The primary inner shrine [Altar Platform] is covered by the coarser backing of the walls built around it to which the steps on the south side leading to the top of the platform lead (figs. 53–55).

As one enters the outer east court [Forecourt] from the east, on the right, on the n. side, are the remains of an altar stand, which also seems to show two constructions (figs. 179, 188, 233).

The base of the main Hadad figure has been found, and cracked by the heat (of sacrifices?).

The main Hadad figure (fig. 86) has plaster on both narrow sides, indicating it was set in somewhere.

The peculiar base in the west inner court of the temple, which is bevelled only on the west side is probably an altar pedestal (figs. 10.2–3a; Vol. 1, fig. 177).

We removed Hadad figure, found a dowel (sceptre) behind it (figs. 84–85), parts of a water (?) basin, and several ornamented bits.

In front of shrine [Altar Platform] on east side, about 2 stones removed from it, we found 2 more storage basins [offertory boxes] at the n. and s. ends of the east front of the shrine (figs. 398–400), smaller than the storage basin we found in the

west court [west part of Inner Temenos Enclosure] immediately back of the shrine (fig. 401). In these 2 storage basins were charcoal, bones (fig. 395) and bits of grain (fig. 12.2), evidently sacrifices, or reserve sacrifices to the deities. They were covered with stone lids with holes in the centre to which evidently iron hooks were fastened by which they were lifted up. There are spaces on the lower side of these lids to anchor the hooks. Only one such lid has been found thus far on the n. side in front of the east end of the central shrine (figs. 398–99). The basin [the north-east offertory box] is particularly full of grains of wheat, offerings to the gods of fertility who sometimes had sheaves of wheat as symbols of their fertility-giving powers. There were 2 altar stones which filled the centre of the shrine, steps on the west side in between 2 other walls which are secondary to the primary construction (figs. 56–57). The steps on the west side belong to the primary construction.

Dr Fisher has been moving stones for later typing and working out nature of walls. Dr Graham, Mr Wood and Mr Kerr left today.

March 10

In cleaning the inner shrine [Altar Platform], looking from the east, one can see (under paved floor), a secondary floor of lime laid over debris, at a height of approximately two courses above the floor (fig. 33a). It is a floor simply over debris to give a basis for other debris stones above it. The secondary (or tertiary) builders had filled up this little room completely to make a platform, on which in the case of each shrine evidently the deities (or deity) stood.

We found a nail in front of east shrine [Altar Platform], which may have been in some wooden construction [? from burnt doors]. We found some bones and charcoal in front of this shrine also, perhaps from sacrifice on 2 small altars (?) at n. and s. ends of east shrine.

The present west outer wall of the shrine [Altar Platform] was once covered with a lime plaster facing (plaster made of lime, bits of red pottery and water) and is secondary to the main inner shrine which it surrounds. It is also of the same construction as the present door antae at the east gate of the temple court [Inner Temenos Enclosure]. The main east wall of the temple court seems to belong, however, to the inner, finely worked temple shrine. [i.e., Phase 2 not 3.]

In the inner shrine [Altar Platform] behind the main figure, when it had been removed, we found under the pounded lime floor [of Altar 1] (fig. 33b) rubbish consisting of burned bones for the most part – sacrifices brought to Hadad who was in position just in front.

In back of the original west wall of inner Shrine [Altar Platform], and between the outer secondary west wall is a small room, entered by a door from the north side near the west end (fig. 56). On the original west outer wall of the original shrine are remnants of two steps which originally led to the top of the platform of the original shrine (fig. 57). The little room back of this wall and between the outer west secondary shrine wall was plastered, before it became filled with debris.

The outer west secondary wall, which is similar in stones to the stones of the secondary door jambs at the east entrance to the shrine court [Inner Temenos Enclosure], was also plastered.

The main entrance to the outer east court [Forecourt] had two [half-]columns on either side.

The Wadi on the north side of Kh. et-Tannur is the Wadi Ain Nimr, which joins the Wadi el-Hesa below Hamam el-Barbita. The Wadi el-Aban joins the Wadi Ain Nimr, leaving Kh. et-Tannur surrounded by wadis, and commanding a view all around, on the west the hills of Palestine appearing above the cut of the end of the Wadi el-Hesa, the Wadi el-Aban extending to the s.s.e. and then to the s.s.w., the Moabite plateau across the Wadi Hesa to the north and the upper extension of Wadi el-Hesa to the east. Aineh is clearly visible to the east.

In the east front of the east shrine [Altar Platform] where the bones were found, there were several sherds of Nab. Roman rough type, and one sherd which could not be much earlier than the 3rd or 4th century AD. Some of the debris blew in, or was packed in then at a later date. In this debris was also found a fragment of a small, burnt stone, altar basin (fig. 10.10a–b).

In front of the east walls of the shrine [Altar Platform], are lines on the stones of the floor, in-

dicating that something or other rested on them at one time, which is altogether missing now.

Paid off all the workers today. We had about 10 of the best working and cleaning up corners, etc. Dr Willoughby visited us today.

March 11

We are packing preparatory to leaving camp for a few days. Hassan and I went up to the site this morning to do some small odd jobs. I brought back a number of small heads with me to see if any would fit on any of the headless bodies we had. One of them indeed, of the type with the hair-knot, did fit exactly on to the body of one of the winged Tyches [Nikes] (fig. 140). The head is no. 62, and was found buried, while the Tyche body was found in the debris outside the site on the east side. The body being on the surface was considerably worn while the head being buried was much better preserved.

In the ditch on the north side near the east end, where the fine Nabataean sherds were found, we dug down through more burned soil, to a rude stamped lime floor (mixed with small stones), on which was another Nabataean sherd. This floor with the burned earth on top of it goes straight under the present existing *balatah* floor, which extends to the present north wall of the shrine-wall.

To test this further we opened up several blocks in this n. *balatah* (s. of the n. ditch) and found underneath it nothing but burned earth, in which sherds from BC to AD times. The bottom of this is also a rude stamped floor. All this indicates that this n. *balatah* floor is certainly not primary. The sherds in this second opening in the n. outer *balatah* floor are the same as the debris sherds found inside the shrine [Altar Platform]. This n. *balatah* floor is considerably lower than the *balatah* floor around the shrine, however, on which the primary and secondary shrine is built. {Later annotation: ?!? ?!?} Inasmuch, however, as shrine II is built above the *balatah* of the inner shrine court [Inner Temenos Enclosure], this secondary construction of the shrine may belong to approximately the same period as the construction of the secondary north *balatah* floor.

March 30

Left Jerusalem in Dodge with Helen Glueck, Dr Fisher, Mr Pape, Mr Schweig. Slept in Amman.

March 31

Borrowed 6 blankets from Hotel Philadelphia. Arrived in el-Aban at 3 pm. Ylias had had a car breakdown the day before, and so camp was not made on the top of the hill, although most of the stuff had been brought up. One tent was set up, with Fisher, Pape and Schweig sleeping in it. Helen and I slept in sleeping bags in inner temple court. Atarah [Glueck's dog] slept by us.

April 1

Putting up tents. A very strong east wind this morning. On the way down from Jerusalem and Amman we passed groups of storks resting on their way north.

Fisher and Pape have been measuring stones. Schweig has been photographing. We have commenced clearing debris in front of room (Room 8) at n.w. corner of outer east court [Forecourt].

April 2

Opening n. room no. 8 (Room 8) at n.w. of outer east court. At s.w. end of this room is a staircase (?). A small torch found in this room, in addition to the eagle's head (fig. 292). This room I shall call room "I." The entire floor seems to have been covered with burned material. Some of the pottery is burned. At the s.w. end of the room, part of the room which turned out to be Room 8 is a secondary stone vat inserted into the main west cross wall [the front wall of the triclinium bench] (figs. 210, 281). The basin seems to have been filled originally with lime. Several bits of glass, and some burned bones were found. Several thoroughly burned stones were found.

The floor west of main doorway [of Inner Temenos Enclosure] to inner east shrine [Altar Platform] shows burning, as if the wooden door of the temple had fallen on the floor and burned there.

It is a very windy and hazy day. The air is full of dust making it difficult to work.

April 3

It rained a bit last night, and has continued very windy and dusty today, making work difficult and photography impossible. Back of the north wall of north room "I" (Room 8) at n.w. corner of outer east court [Forecourt], we have been finding quantities of fine Nabataean sherds. Evidently the well paved north room is later than the rubbish it was built against (?). This north room slopes to the north, and has a drain in the bottom centre of its north wall (figs. 29, 210).

The opening in the north wall of the n. room "I" (Room 8) leads in a widening "V" to what may originally have been a canal (?). This ditch was full of debris containing numerous fine Nabataean sherds.

It is to be noticed that left side of "leaf-Artemis" [the Vegetation Goddess] (fig. 160) has been burned, having apparently fallen thus into the fire, which burned the main doorway and discoloured the floor behind it.

April 4

Continued excavating north room "I" (Room 8). The debris containing masses of fine Nabataean sherds mixed with sherds going into the Roman and even Byzantine periods continued on all 3 sides. The entrance is on the south side (fig. 211). The drain opening on the north side continues straight through the rubbish and the rubbish wall behind it to the north down the slope of the hill. It would seem that the people who built the room with its fine stones [the triclinium benches] (figs. 210–11, 281) (which seem to be of the same general type as the stones of the main central shrine) put the rubbish (containing the fine Nabataean sherds) behind it, and also built the rubble wall [the actual walls of the room] which extends on all three sides (figs. 212–13). This confirms what seems to have been established from the main shrine, where the fine sherds came from the ditch, and were under the pavement.

The altar-stand [West Altar] on the west side of the west temple wall is curiously made of 2 halves resting on 2 halves. The upper 2 halves have a wedge cut out between them with a cut block closing the outside of the opening on the south side (fig. 10.2).

April 5

Helen and Schweig returned to Jerusalem today with Ylias. They left from below at about 8:30 am.

We completed n. room "I" (Room 8) at n.w. corner of outer east court [Forecourt]. The drain runs through the rubble wall n. of it. Not yet sure about the nature of this rubble wall [of the room], but it seems to be built after the fine room [the triclinium bench], which was backed against a rubble wall of its own (fig. 212). Between this rubble wall was an empty space {later annotation: Empty space – could a triclinium foundation have filled it originally? By the same token, could triclinium foundations and benches have occupied symmetrical empty spaces around well-paved floor of inner, raised walled shrine area? [of Inner Temenos Enclosure]} which the second rubble wall people? filled in and which contains mixed sherds including fine Nabataean sherds. {Later annotation: Those Nabataean sherds may have been cleaned out when paving of Room 8 was laid.}

In north room "I" (Room 8) at west end a coin was found with 2 cornucopiae and a head visible (fig. 13.11a–b).

In back of steps on n. side another coin was found. (Room 8).

We dug the front of the outer east wall, which goes down for several inches, and has been rebuilt several times. I am not yet certain about its phases, and it requires further study.

We also commenced tracing steps on n. side near west end, which may have led down to cistern.

April 6

Finished north room "I" (Room 8) and commenced on north room "II" (Room 9) (figs. 214–15). Also traced n.e. angle of outer wall; and commenced opening up w. room on south side [Room 12].

April 7

Digging north room "II" (Room 9) which seems to be better preserved than north room "I" (Room 8). Two pillars built of separate stones (fig. 215) (DD pl. 118a–b). Also digging north room "III" (Room 10) (figs. 217–18).

Baramki, Waechter, and Abis (?) visited us for a short time this afternoon on their way to Petra.

Fisher and Pape working on their plans.

Most of a broken Nabataean lamp recovered from north room "II" (Room 9); also a lion's head, of very friable sandstone (fig. 87) [from the female cult statue, see also April 8 and 12], a foot, and 2 birds' (?) feet.

I found a small Nabataean altar among the stones on the west side of the building complex.

Harding, Miss Caton-Thompson, Iliffe, Hassan, spent the night here. They brought the PAM [Palestine Archaeological Museum] truck, with two other men, to take away big stones.

Dr Graham, Dr Thompson, Mr Freeman, and Mr Roundtree (?) also spent the night here. Our equipment had to be stretched a bit.

April 8

Père Savignac, Père Abel, and Père [space] came up to visit us this morning. Père Savignac has worked out our inscription [the La'abān inscription] (fig. 9.1a–b), which is dedicated to Haretat [Aretas], king of the Nabataeans, and his wife Huldu (?) and is dated to the year 2, i.e., to 7 BC – which gives us the date of the first temple. The other temples date to the rest of the 1st century AD. All our visitors left this morning.

North Room no. "I" (Room 8) is evidently built on burned level of first Nabataean complex. A burned level is visible below its floor level. The burned level can be seen in the ditch behind the wall of the inner face of the room. This proves conclusively, I now think, that this present paved room belongs at least to period II, and that the fine pottery belongs to after period I, because the rubble in the ditch around the room [the triclinium bench] contains fine Nabataean pottery, (as well, however, as Roman pottery). {Later annotation:

Nabataean pottery. Fine pottery belongs to period following Period I and preceding paved floor which preceded Period II Shrine [Altar Platform]. The ability to cut the fine paving stones of Period II had developed at the same time fine, painted Nabataean pottery developed, but was laid down after painted Nabataean pottery had appeared.}

The workmen have been unable to move the big stones. We are therefore breaking off the backs of these stones, and have moved a large number of them down the hill.

It rained this afternoon, and we had to call off work.

The burned level I mentioned above, appears all over [? in Rooms 8 and 9], wherever we get down low enough to see it. It is thus visible on the outside of the west wall beyond the west wall of the north room.

We reached the floor of n. room no. 2 (Room 9) (fig. 215). It is paved with rubble packed down hard and mixed with lime, and seems never ? to have had the fine stone floor that number "I" (Room 8) has. It [Room 9] has, however, 4 pillars which evidently supported a flat roof. The pillars, square in form and built on 3 stones on each side (*DD* pl. 118a–b), with parts of pillars gone, were once covered with a plaster covering, of which only some fragments remain. It was in this room (Room 9) that we found the sandstone lion's head (fig. 87) [from the female cult statue, see also April 7 and 12].

April 9

Hannah Tango and his companion left with the PAM [Palestine Archaeological Museum] truck full of our stones for Amman; they left about 6 am.

It rained hard last night, and at 7 am we could see the water advancing down the Wadi el-Aban, and then down the Wadi el-Hesa. In the Wadi el-Aban it lasted for only about an hour, and then the wadi was dry again.

There is a burned layer, near the bottom of n. room no. "II" (Room 9). The bottom of the s. wall of north room "II" (Room 9) is so burned near the s.w. end of the room that the flint has been burned and crumbles when touched. In the burned dirt, in the southwest corner of the room we found 2 lamps,

one intact [the eagle lamp] and one almost intact [a wheel-made round lamp] (figs. 17.12 and 17.18).

The skies are covered with black clouds and it will probably rain again today.

The scheme of n. rooms "I" (Room 8) and "II" (Room 9) is becoming clear. The rough outside walls which go down to the rock bottom may well have belonged to Period I {later annotation: or III}. Inside these walls were set the smaller, well paved rooms, whose roofs were supported by four square pillars. The 3 stones forming the square sides of each section of a pillar [in Room 9] were held together by a lime plaster core and were based on a block, set in a hole in the rock and bonded ? by smaller stones (*DD* pl. 118a–b). The foundation of the four walls of the inside rooms [i.e., the walls of the triclinium benches] consisted of stones which rested on top of the burned level of the previous room of Period I. Between this inner face and the deep outer wall of Period I, {later annotation: III ?} the people of Period II put debris which is filled with Nabataean sherds and sherds of well into the 1st century [to fill in the triclinium bench].

North room "III" (Room 10) (figs. 217–18) is smaller than the other 2 north rooms. At the n.w. end of the outer old wall of this room, there seems to be steps leading up from outside, the bottom step consisted of a reused stone [these seem to be stones re-used when the wall was rebuilt (fig. 283)]. (Perhaps these steps led to top of n. room "III" (Room 10) of Period II?)

I should like Fisher to make a cross section of one of these rooms (*DD* plan F).

It blew terribly this morning, the wind coming from the west. It seems impossible to work this afternoon. We got into the bell-tent (Fisher, Pape, Atarah and I) and listened to the wind beating against it. The air was filled with dust. Then the rain started, and has been coming down in sheets ever since. The mist is around us, and from our eerie point, the scene looks like Scotland must on a stormy afternoon.

April 10

It rained and hailed last night as I have rarely experienced. There was lightning and thunder which must have come from Hadad, the lightning and thunder god of Kh. et-Tannur and the locality. Ylias who was with Hassan in Iliffe's small tent, which Iliffe left behind him, came into our tent, leaving Hassan alone. I certainly thought our tent would go, but it held up. During the night we could hear the water thundering down the Wadi el-Hesa, and this morning there is a stream of water again in the Wadi el-Aban. I paid off the workmen this morning, because it is probably going to rain all day today also. We have 2 or 3 days more work here, and can always get workmen if necessary. They appear out of the air, so to speak.

April 11

It blew so hard that it began to wear away the face of Hadad, so we covered him with canvas. The rain and wind continued all day yesterday, making it further impossible to work. The wind finally became so strong, that to save the bell-tent from being ripped to pieces on its exposed position, we had to take it down, and set it up on the fairly level field below the foot of Jebel et-Tannur. I also walked to the police station, and left the plans there for safe-keeping and phoned Jerusalem. All, or much, of the night, we could hear the surplus flood waters thundering down the Wadi el-Hesa, which by this morning is much quieter. The water has disappeared again from the Wadi el-Aban.

This morning the weather seems to be clearing up. We have begun working again with a small party. We are clearing what is evidently a gateway at the east end of the north platform of the outer east court [Forecourt] (figs. 272–73), just in front of old, no. I west wall of n. room "III" (Room 10). At the s.w. corner of n. room "III" (Room 10) is a flight of steps [in the triclinium bench, leading to its top] similar to those visible in the same corner in north room "I" (Room 8).

We also lifted 4 stones in the back of the west wall of the inner shrine [Altar Platform], finding a burned level beneath the stones, which were joined together with plaster. Beneath this burned level, resting apparently on a rubble foundation of an earlier floor, and beneath this earlier floor level, we are finding Nab. pottery, mostly fine, and bones.

[Judging by *DD* 128, this is the West Sounding; see also 14 April] (figs. 42, 44a, 45a, 46–48; location marked on fig. 40.) Further investigation has shown that about 20 cm below the present floor, there is a rough, mostly flint floor belonging to the first period. Above this first floor back of the west wall is a burned level about 5 cm thick. We tested and obtained the same results from the hole in the floor on the n.e. side of the inner temple court [Inner Temenos Enclosure in the North-east Sounding; see also 15 April] (figs. 41–43, 44d, 45d; location marked on fig. 40), and from a hole we made by lifting 2 stones on the s. side of the inner temple court [Inner Temenos Enclosure], immediately west of the west side gate [in the South Sounding] (figs. 43, 44b, 45b; location marked on fig. 40). Examining also the inner side of the east front of the shrine (I) [Altar Platform], we found that the bottom inner stones also rested on the flint *balatah* first floor [in the East Sounding] (figs. 44c, 45c; location marked on fig. 40). {Later annotation: Fine Nabataean pottery. Nabataean pottery found beneath early floor level, over which was rubble foundation for flagstone level of floor on which Shrine II rested, with a burning between the last two. [He gives a sketch drawing of South Sounding done after the excavation, in which he misinterprets it based on his journal entry, as also in *DD* 128. Compare with Fisher's drawing made during the excavation: fig. 44b.]}

Then we examined the inner core of the shrine [Altar Platform], and found that it is the *first* shrine, its smooth outer face having been plastered and built against by the finer *second* shrine, which in turn was built against by the larger *third* shrine (figs. 55, 59), to which period the "Fish goddess" (fig. 250), etc. belongs, and Artemis [the Vegetation Goddess] (fig. 160), and which was the greatest building period in the history of the site.

April 12

The weather has become definitely nice again, enabling us to work properly, without being plagued by excessive wind and dust, and by rain. We have completed the excavation of n. room "III" (Room 10) (fig. 218), and are excavating now in front of its south wall (figs. 36–37). Removing the stones which blocked up the gateway (fig. 192) at the n.e. end of the outer east court [Forecourt], it becomes apparent that there is a clear gateway, and that at least the second flight of the platform was built after the time the steps were made (figs. 272–73), and that the people who built the platform running along the n. side of the outer east court were the ones who stopped up the n.e. gate in order to make it level with the outer east wall. {Later addition: This might show that the foundation of the outer E wall belonged to Period I. (?)}

The walls of n. room "II" (Room 9) do not bind into its south wall, the upper part of which at least is later than the other 3 walls. There are 4 pillars in this room (figs. 214–15).

In n. room "III" (Room 10) which is smaller than the other 2 n. rooms, there is a flight of steps in the s.w. corner (fig. 218) (*DD* pl. 119a–b) as in the same corner of n. room no. I (Room 8). The outer s. wall of room "III" (Room 10) belongs to period III. It runs into a north–south cross wall at its east end which evidently precedes the building of n. room "III" (Room 10) (figs. 36–37). The stones have now been cleared from the gateway of the n.e. end of the outer east court [Forecourt] (fig. 272).

Harding returned today, walking and riding on horseback from Tafileh.

Found part of a small incense altar outside s. wall of n. room "III" (Room 10) near east end.

Harding found that one piece of sandstone fitted to head of lion from n. room "II" (Room 9), and that the small feet also belong to this complex (fig. 87). A single foot was found in connection with it, which may belong to a Hadad figure. [All from the female cult statue; see also April 7, 8 and 12.]

Harding found a fragment of a winged Tyche of the type on our round altar at the bottom of the n.e. dump heap.

On s. outside (rebuilt) wall of n. room "III" (Room 10) one reused stone is visible with the Nabataean 45° angle cutting on it (fig. 36). The s.-west half of this wall, west of the steps leading into n. room "III" (Room 10) is built of stones of period "III," and this wall is *not* bonded into e. outer wall of n. room "II" (Room 9) (fig. 216). The east half of s. wall of n. room "III" (Room 10) east of steps

leading into this room is a rebuilt wall resting on a rubble wall. Against it, (or perhaps this wall has cut through it) is a rough n-s cross wall. North room "III" (Room 10) has been reused by squatters, who seem to have dragged round pillars [column drums] into it. Its e. inner wall [front of the triclinium bench] has been much repaired, perhaps by squatters (fig. 218).

At bottom of outer east wall near north end is a well laid, well cut layer of stones, from which the steps at the n.w.? end lead up. The rest of this outer east wall towards its n. end is much broken.

April 13

Removed stones in outer east wall near gate at n.e. end of outer east wall [of Forecourt], and found stones belonging to another pavement or gate.

Examined west extension of n. wall bounding ditch on north side of outer n. court, and traced its extension on rock bottom till it turns to meet outermost n. wall. {Later annotation: ?}. There seems to be no west cross-wall across outer west end [of the Court around Inner Temenos Enclosure] beyond west altar and broken west pavement on west side of west wall of shrine.

We cleaned down in front of n. room "II" (Room 9) to gate at n.e. end of n. platform, till we reached the burning on the floor and the stones on which the foundation, well cut, 3rd period stones belong. They run along a stone and rubble foundation. Inner room "II" (Room 9) [i.e., the triclinium benches] belongs to period II, as does probably the entire east court [Forecourt], and the first flight of steps of the platform. The second gate in the outer east wall [of the Forecourt] going from n. to s. may also be period II (figs. 189–90). The top of the inner face of the outer east wall seems to have been rebuilt by period III, with many stones from period II.

This second gate from n. to s. has 3 large well cut, flat stones, with plaster between them, the n. one resting in a special jamb (fig. 188). I have just had removed the stones blocking this second doorway on the inner side of the outer east wall [of the Forecourt] (fig. 189), and it is obvious that the stones built against the channel are also secondary.

One possible explanation of 2 gateways, going into main outer east court [Forecourt], aside from n.e. gateway leading into platform (figs. 192, 272), is that the main gateway was used only for ceremonial reasons, and kept locked otherwise.

Excavating two of the rooms s. side nearer west end. No cont. walls found going towards the west, where there seems to have been an open court. In s. room II (Room 14) a small bird's head was found, carved only on left side of face (fig. 291).

The three n. rooms are no. II period, some partly rebuilt. With regard to the top layer of the platform on n. side of outer east court [Forecourt], which seems to come after gate on n.e. side (figs. 272–73), and after entrance of room II (Room 9) we must take into considerations that fact that it may be a secondary II, because it seems to be of the same type of stone as the first layer of the platform. The stones of the floor of the outer east court [Forecourt] seem to be built against it, that is the lower base of this platform. The burnt level goes under the second flight of the platform and is a little above the first flight.

South room no. II (Room 14) has been almost completely excavated. It shows only the rough walls characteristic of Period I of the n. side. There is no inner room [triclinium benches] of Period II set into it, as on n. side. S. Room I (Room 13) to the west of it is smaller, and apparently also has only rough rubble walls (fig. 221).

Burned grain has been turning up in s.e. corner of s. room II (Room 14) {later annotation in study copy: 15}. Perhaps it was a storeroom for the temple.

Every now and then in all the rooms bits of glass are found.

April 14

Cleared s. rooms I (Room 13) and II (Room 14), finding mixed sherds in them, including Nab. and sigillata and glass. The rooms had 2 burned levels each, one near the top and one near the very bottom. They go steeply down hill, and surrounded by rude rubble walls. It requires further study to determine what period these rough south rooms belong.

We have determined that shrine III [Altar Platform III] rests on pavement II, upon which also pavement II [? shrine II] rests (figs. 58–59). Shrine I rests on its own pavement. Shrine 3 and 2 and probably one have their own type of dressing. Shrine 3 was plastered on outside.

We have cleaned gates [threshold] of shrine, and it seems that the outer gate [threshold of Inner Temenos Enclosure] belongs to shrine II, and the inner gate [threshold] somewhat below it to shrine III (fig. 13.1). The stones between this inner gate and actual altar are blackened, showing where large door of shrine III of inner gate [of Inner Temenos Enclosure] fell and burned and blackened the earth.

Removing the stones from the rough floor below the fine floor in the west court w. of west wall of shrine III [Altar Platform], we found that they went down for a considerable distance before reaching rock bottom [in the West Sounding, see 11 April] (figs. 42, 44a, 45a, 48; location marked on fig. 40), and that there were several mixed sherds among them – the conclusion being that the foundation had been laid by the builders of the fine *balatah* floor, beneath which was a burning consisting of grain. Did the builders of floor of period II lay out an offering of a layer of grain all over the floor before they put in the stones of the actual floor? The stone foundation going way down may also simply have been to bring level up for main floor.

In s. room I (Room 13) we found remains of what looks like a multi-mouthed lamp, and which may be the remains of an offering bowl. When the bowl was full, it flowed over. Several sigillata sherds were also found in south room I (Room 13).

The two storage basins [offertory boxes] set in the floor in front of the shrine [Altar Platform] are separate stone boxes set in the floor (figs. 398–400). They are still water-proof, having gathered half full of water since the last rain.

April 15

Working on s. room III (Room 15) [the east half of Room 14] which seems to be like fine rooms on n. side. The two south rooms I (Room 13) (fig. 222) and II (Room 14) are poorly built of small stone rubble with larger, reused limestone blocks among them. {Later annotation: Rebuilt}

The Nabataean capitals belonged to the east front of the wall of shrine II and to the outer east wall of it? having been displaced by the Corinthian type of capitals. It is to be noticed that some of the stones, used in shrine III, have been reused and recut, and redressed from stones belonging to shrine and temple complex II.

The Fortuna (Tyche) goddesses belonged to Shrine II.

Dug part of south room III (Room 15) [the east part of Room 14]. It is also sloping down hill steeply but is a part of a long, narrow room, narrowing down to the east {later annotation: ?}, which is well built, faced with finely cut stones of the period apparently of II (figs. 225–28). We also ran a sounding down in the n. east side of the inner temple court [Inner Temenos Enclosure] to see how far down the rough foundation floor below the *balatah* floor went [apparently a continuation of the North-east Sounding; see also 15 April] (figs. 42–43, 44d, 45d; location marked on fig. 40). Will take the measurements tomorrow.

We also cleared the n. side of inner shrine II [Altar Platform] and made visible its fine n. face (fig. 236). It is also seen that the *balatah* flooring runs under the n. wall of inner shrine III [Altar Platform].

From s. room III (Room 15) [the east part of Room 14] a number of peculiar lamps were found and even a Umm Rasas type of Byzantine sherd, and also rough and also somewhat fine painted Nabataean sherds.

We tore down the front of inner shrine II (fig. 237), which Harding wants to set up in Jerusalem [shipped to Cincinnati Art Museum]. We also removed the debris between shrine II and III on the n. side, and saw that the stones of the pavement also on this side go beneath the n. wall of shrine III (figs. 58–59, 237).

April 16

Harding went down to the police-post yesterday to 'phone to Amman and see if he could get the PWD to repair the road sufficiently so that we could get through Tafileh, where Harding had left his car. His call was effective, and they have been working on the road. Early this morning it began to rain slightly, so I decided to strike camp and make for Tafileh. By the time I paid off the workmen it was 1 pm. We got to Tafileh, returned with Harding's car to the crossroads, crossed over to Jurf ed-Derawish, and then north to Qatrani, arriving in Amman at 10 pm. The lights of the Ford burned out, and we had to go very slowly – the Ford being put in position between the Dodge and Harding's car.

April 17

Arrived in Jerusalem at noon.

May 3

Ylias Tutunjian and I left Jerusalem at 6:30 am and arrived at Amman at 9:05 am. Kirkbride and Harding and Hassan had already left. Just below Dhat Ras we caught up with them, Harding's Ford having gotten a broken spring just by Dhat Ras. We stayed behind him till he crawled into el-Aban. There, below the hill we found Hassan and the PAM [Palestine Archaeological Museum] truck, with camp set up, about ready to bring in the last, third load of stones. One man, alone, had brought the Hadad figure (fig. 86) down the mountain, with two others supporting him.

An airplane flew low over el-Aban the day before and dropped a streamer marked "Please return to B FLT 14 sqd Jess Meltaimie 9801."

May 4

Kirkbride got another car and has gone on to Maan. Harding and Hassan have returned to Jerash. The PAM truck has returned with the third and last load to Amman.

This morning I walked around Jebel Tannur looking unsuccessfully for tombs. This afternoon I am taking a few extra measurements. I have Mohammed ibn Salim doing some digging in the trench on the n. side where the fine Nab. bowl was found.

[List of measurements of paving stones of Forecourt]

In the ditch on the n. side where the fine bowl

came from, masses of fine Nab. sherds are coming up in the burned mass of earth, but also a glazed Arabic sherd, and a piece of sigillata, and several coarse pieces.

The small Room 13 on the s. side may be taken as an example of the Rooms 1 (Room 14) and 2 (Room 15) on the south side, except that in this case the inner core of the room [the triclinium benches] has been preserved [in Room 14] (fig. 226). {Later annotation: ?} In rooms I (Room 14) and II (Room 15) this fine inner core has disappeared. The floor of III (Room 13) is also on a slope (figs. 219–20). {Later annotation, marginal note: ?} [He seems to have gotten the room numbers mixed up.]

Kirkbride suggested something very reasonable last night – that the Nabataeans got to Damascus and the Jebel Druze through the Wadi Sirhan, and did not have to touch the territory of the cities of the Decapolis.

Photographed another stone with diagonal Nab. cutting which makes 2 of this type discovered thus far. It is sandstone, and probably belongs to the earliest period. {Later annotation: ?!?}

The s. entrance of the main inner shrine has a stone on its east side, which shows the same Nab. diagonal cutting as mentioned above. These cuttings are in the w. face of the east side of the doorway. On the e. face of the w. side of the doorway can be seen the hole for the bolt. (See drawing on p. 112, MS) [There is no drawing on p. 112. Hence later annotation: ?].

After removing the base stones in front of s.e. side of shrine II [Altar Platform], it is clearly seen that shrine II as well as shrine III rest in the same pavement. (See [top] drawing in MS on p. 113.)

It is now seen that the wall of II is definitely built over pavement and over base of wall of I too. It may be that shrine II, at least its front, was rebuilt even in Period II.

It would appear that some of the stones in the pavement in front of the shrine belong to Period III, because the one s. of the n. pilaster base at the n.e. front of shrine has been cut to fit against its base.

The bottom stone of the east side of the now standing portion of shrine II is cut over another stone, which may originally have been the border base of shrine I (fig. 58). Anyway, the pavement

fits up against this border base. A ground plan of the east front n.n. side now looks as follows: (See [lower] drawing, p. 113, MS).

November 29

Left Jerusalem in Dodge with S. V. McCasland, C. S. Steinbeck, and W. Reed. Stopped at Tell Mustâh on way. Spending night at Hotel Philadelphia. Ylias arrived here last night and left for Kh. Tannur this morning.

November 30

Left Amman 9 am. Arrived Tannur at 3 pm. Ylias had already put up the PWD tent and my personal one. We set up a third kitchen-tent.

December 1

Two men working on Room 14; will have to wait till end of Ramadan to get a proper force.

[List of photograph references].

Double headed corner stone – on one side a mutilated Hadad? bust, with a winged, lotus-like lightning bolt on left shoulder (figs. 122–23). The left wing of lightning bolt at bottom of lotus-like top of bolt is clear, and complete; the lower half of the right wing is lost in the top of the left shoulder near the neck. There is a torque around the neck, with a lion's head at each end, both heads being held together by a fibula (almost effaced). The lion's head at the left end of the torque on the left breast is still fairly clear. The other lion's head has been almost completely worn away. The fold of the himation thrown over the left shoulder is visible. Most of the chest and the right breast are bare. However, only apparently so. Above the torque, and around the neck is visible the line of the close-fitting tunic, over which then the himation is placed. The twirls in the torque are visible above the right shoulder. The hair too has been destroyed except part of its outline on the left side of the head. This Hadad figure must have faced the east {later annotation: west (?)} [east is correct] side of the south end of the east facade of the inner raised temple [Inner Temenos Enclosure]. This double-headed stone was found near this corner. On the right side the torque goes all the way back to the inside of the block from which the head emerges, and on the left side the raised edge of the himation goes all the way back. There is thus no place for women's long curly-locks, and this is additional proof that a male figure is represented here. There are traces of a beard on the lower left side of the face.

[List of photograph references].

On s. side of this double-headed stone is Tyche-Atargatis, with horn of plenty on right side (fig. 124). The top of the horn is broken off, but at the bottom of the top the egg-dart design is clear. She is dressed in a loosely-hung garment, of an almost transparent nature, with a himation flung over the left shoulder and breast. The twisted double curls are still retained on either side of the head; those on the right side being damaged. The face has been damaged beyond all recognition, and the top of the head completely broken off. The long side of this side of the stone measures 74 cm, the short side measures 54. The length of the Hadad side measures 77 cm; the width measures 54 cm. The length of thunder-bolt is 15 cm. The spread of wings at their top is 12 cm. The length of left wing is 8 cm.

December 2

Removed 3 stones of n. wall of shrine 3 [Altar Platform], showing clearly that pavement went under this wall (fig. 237). It quite obviously runs under all of the walls of shrine 3. The pavement also apparently runs under n. wall of shrine 2. There was a layer of plaster between the stones of n. wall of shrine 3 which were removed (fig. 59). {Later annotation: (Was plaster between stones of Shrine II or I?)}

The outer face of walls of shrine 3 were plastered, and perhaps painted. Traces of plaster, and small sections of plaster are still visible on w. outer wall of shrine 3.

The plaster on the inside of the doorway entering into small room between w. outer walls of shrines 2 and 3 seems to have been painted red.

The paving blocks of floor back of (w) of w. wall of shrine 3 are set in plaster or between sides and

on to bottom of each stone. This is true of all the paving blocks in the inner raised court [Inner Temenos Enclosure].

A section was cut through outer west wall of inner temple courtyard [Inner Temenos Enclosure] (fig. 177). The paving blocks jut against inner e. side of the outer west wall, which was obviously rebuilt at a period in the latter (?) part of era of shrine and temple 3. The wall has been set in some places on the inner side through the inner raised pavement which juts against it. That is, the inner e. face of the outer w. wall of inner temple court is sunk below the edge of the paving blocks which jut against it (fig. 42). In its present condition this wall is later than the pavement, but there must have been earlier walls {later annotation: of Period IIIA and Period II} built against or respectively over the pavement. {Later annotation: (?) (The II Period outer wall could also have been built over pavement.)}

The blocks of the pavement w. of the outer west wall [Inner Temenos Enclosure] jut against the wall. The outer w. ledge goes under the wall, and is an integral part of the wall. The wall is formed of the flat stone on the inner face, of the ledge stone and stretchers on outer face, with some smaller stones and debris between inner and outer stones proper of wall. They are set in heavy plaster.

The double headed corner piece from n.e. end of outer east facade of inner temple: The north side had a Tyche bust with a broken horn of plenty on her left side (fig. 126). The top of the horn is broken off. On her left side, her curls come down inside of edge of horn. (The horn of plenty on her left side matches horn of plenty on right side of Tyche on s. face of s.e. corner of inner temple) (fig. 124). The upper part of the neck and the entire face and head have been broken off. The neck is also enclosed with the tunic, leaving bare a V shaped section.

The east face of this corner stone also has a Tyche (?) with a mural (?) crown, part of which is still visible on the lower left side of her head (figs. 122, 125). It looks something like a ladder-like affair (fig. 363), and apparently represents the turrets of a city wall. On her left shoulder is a broken object, with 2 thin parallel walls supporting a broken box-like structure, the 2 sides and the front side being broken off (fig. 125). Her face has been damaged beyond recognition. Her hair falls down in single locks on her head, with her himation covering her head. She has the same soft folding dress as the Tyche (on the other side) at the s.e. corner. The object on the left shoulder may represent an altar supported on walls, something like the inner altar of the shrine. The length of Tyche w. object side is 79 cm, the depth is 54 cm. The length of n. side is about same originally; the depth – 54 cm.

[List of photograph references]

The outer n. wall of Room 11 is made of very large, rude flint blocks. There are flint blocks in the repaired part of the outer east wall near its south end. There are also some flint blocks in the rough walls behind the fine walls of the triclinia on the n. side. Part of the east wall of Room 11 is also made of large flint blocks.

Some of the fine stones in Room 14 have cuttings on face of typical stones of period 3. The fine stones of w. end of this room are in a trench sunk into the rock. The n. wall of this room is later than period 3.

December 3

A clear sunny day. We went to Kh. edh-Dherih. Immediately below e.s.e. side of temple, the Wadi el-'Aban makes approximately s-n bend, which the Nabataeans dammed up. The s. wall of the dam with its large limestone blocks is still largely intact. The n. wall of the dam, about 50 m below it, is largely destroyed.

From Kh. Dherih to our camp below Kh. Tannur is 4 miles. From Kh. Dherih one can see the volcanic (?) black pt. on n. side of W. Hesa, but not Kh. Tannur itself.

[List of photograph references].

December 4

We pulled down the stones on the east half of north wall of shrine 2 [Altar Platform], and found that the pavement went not only under the north wall of shrine 3, but also under the north wall of shrine 2, and went up to the ledge of shrine 1, bordering the bevelled edge of base of the n. wall of shrine 1 (figs. 58–59, 237). Whenever the pavement was built, it was built before the n. wall of

shrine 2 was placed on it. The outer face of the n. wall of shrine 1 is well cut, the stones of this wall (as of all of shrine 1, being held together by a thick layer of lime-plaster) and it is not impossible that the pavement bordering it was laid at the time it was built and therefore belongs to it. Indeed the raised ledge bordering the n. side of shrine 1 (i.e., the east half) (fig. 31) seems to call for an abutting pavement, whether or not it was the present pavement. This raised ledge probably goes all the way around shrine 1, but the bevelled edge does not (?). It may have belonged to a pilaster base, similar to the kind found in the same relative position in shrines 2 and 3.

By tearing down the front stones of shrine 2 on east side near south end and by tearing out one of the stones of the south wall of shrine 1 near east end, the same ledge, and bevelled stone above it was found as on the n. side of shrine 1. In addition, here, the bevelled stone is bevelled on the south side and on the east side also, the east bevelled edge of a stone of shrine 1 on the east side which is partly broken off giving thus the east front of the east wall of shrine 1, which then had a bevelled stone above a lower base extending beyond it all along the east side of shrine 1. A granite (?) block faced this base, and it is perhaps on this block that the original Hadad and Atargatis stood. {Later annotation: ???}

While tearing down the north wall of shrine 2, we found that this n. wall which appears so nice on the outside was of rather shoddy construction. One thing, however, this wall shows, namely, that the first shrine was so holy, that every attempt was made in the two main, successive rebuildings or rather additions to preserve the first shrine. Thus the first stone pulled down on the n. side near the east end, showed that an attempt had been made to cut the lower inside of this stone to fit over the base and over the bevelled ledge of the n. side of shrine 1 near the east end (fig. 58). Then this attempt was abandoned, and a smaller cut was made to fit the lower inside edge of this "2" period stone merely over the base of shrine 1. Meanwhile a hole was left where the original cut had been made. To fill it up, a smaller slab of stone was plastered into the base, and the larger stone of 2 period then fitted over this inserted piece, and the rest of it fitted roughly over the base. A thick layer of plaster filled out the empty spaces. It is surprising that a stone so finely cut on the outside, should be so poorly cut on the inside. The contractor figured evidently that no one would ever examine his work, but he was wrong. Continuing to pull down the stones of the n. wall of shrine 2, we found more work of the same shoddy character. The outside face was made of a slab [space] long, and [space] thick, at its thickest end. At one end it tapers down to [space] cm in thickness. The distance from the outer face of the n. wall of shrine 1, to the inner side of this stone, which is [space] cm high, and the 3rd row from the bottom varies from [space] cm to [space] cm. In the intervening space the contractor put in a thick, solid mass of lime plaster, and small stones (fig. 59). This was his procedure throughout.

The point is visible on the floor, where the bottom edge of the first row of shrine 1 was put on a lime-plaster layer between it and the stone paving. The people who built shrine 3 never saw this part of the pavement.

December 5

Pulled down rest of n. wall of shrine 2 [Altar Platform], revealing all of n. wall of shrine 1 (fig. 237). Only one stone with moulding, above one stone of ledge, which undoubtedly at one time fronted the entire north front. A base-ledge probably also went around the other 2 sides. At the present time, however, it is evident that the pavement under 2 on west side juts directly against the west wall of no. 1. The east side of no. 1 had a base-ledge, and also a stone front with a moulding above it, of the same type as the moulding stone on the n. side. This stone shows lines of Nabataean cutting on top of it. There were 2 stones with the moulding on the n. side of shrine 1, the first one nearest to the east side missing. The rest of the base ledge on the n. side of shrine 1 is missing, the place where it had been being filled up with small stones and plaster under the blocks of the n. wall of 2 built over it and against the n. wall of 1. The base of the bevelled base of the pilaster of Period II at n.w. corner was laid on 2 flat broken stones, hewn, which in turn rested on the pavement-blocks under them

which jutted against the empty space where the base ledge of the n. wall of 1 had been, and against part of the block to the north of this block. The flat hewn 2 stones under the pilaster-base at the n.w. corner had been shoddily hewn. At the time of making, one corner of it had broken off. It was filled with plaster. The other piece was only partly hewn. (see drawing) {Later annotation: ?}.

The question arises as to whether the moulding stones on the n.e. corner of the n. side of 1 (fig. 31) and on the s.e. and e. corner of 1, do not belong to a sub-1 period, and represent an earlier shrine, or parts of an earlier altar, which were rebuilt into shrine 1. It is evident, that each succeeding building was meticulously careful to preserve as much of the preceding structure as possible. The moulding on n. wall of 1 should have, it seems, if it had belonged originally to 1 gone along the entire length of n. wall of 1, whereas actually it breaks off abruptly, with no bevelling sloping into the wall. The similar stone on s.e. corner is bevelled on s. and e. sides. Furthermore, the builders of shrine 1 seem to have built from the west to the east, as is noticed in the lowest row. A long stretcher goes from w. to e. along n. wall, and then a small block had to be stuffed in to meet the edge of the bevelled stone on n. side of 1. At some time or other this small block was smashed, and it attests to the sacredness with which each stone was held, that the fragments of this small block were put back in place with thick layers of plaster between them.

December 6

Began working in Room 14 with a gang of 13. A number of pillar drums have been found in it, and several well-cut blocks of the same type as in the n. and s. walls of this room. A Roman (?) coin was found on the s. side near the centre of the total length of the room, and a broken stone torch. There is a thick layer of burning in this room about a foot beneath the surface and varying from 1 to 6 inches in thickness. A number of arch. fragments, and lumps of lime-plaster.

We are also digging the old cross-wall running n.-s. from s. end of Room 10 (figs. 36–37; location marked on fig. 29). After a short distance it broke off completely, the debris around and in front of it containing Nabataean and Roman sherds.

In the ditch on n. side of outer n. wall of temple enclosure [Inner Temenos Enclosure], we have found Nabataean and Roman sherds, including sigillata and one glazed Mediaeval Arabic.

In Room 14, Nab., Roman (including sigillata) and early Byz (?) sherds are turning up. The room contains nothing thus far but debris.

We dug from west edge of broken pavement outside w. wall of temple, going westward in order to attempt to find outer west wall of outer west court. No luck. A small, one shallow stone deep small wall was encountered, which may have served in post-Nab. times as a corall. It was 2 stones wide (see drawing) (marked on fig. 29).

December 7

Twenty boys and men working today. All working in Room 14, which is filled with masses of debris, and as we proceed farther eastward in the room there are but few and practically no traces of burning. Late Nab. Roman and early Byz. sherds, however, continue to be found, including fine glass (Ch. 15, nos. 2, 13–16, 25–28; figs. 15.1, nos. 2, 13–14; 15.2, no. 13). A small perfect, bronze ring (figs. 13.7a–13.8) was found on the s. side near the east end of the room. There are also fine painted and rouletted sherds; also small animals' bones and animals' teeth; a piece of blue faience; a lump of charcoal.

The rear west wall [of the court] cannot be found, but it ought to extend at farthest on same line as west of Room 12 (fig. 219), and as far as well-cut stones of s. wall of Room 11 (marked on fig. 29).

December 8

Reed's cold became worse last night, and so this morning I decided to send him, together with McCasland and Steinbeck, back to Jerusalem. They left at 10:30 am, with Ylias driving the Dodge. I sent Mohammed ibn Za'rûr down from the hill to guard the camp, while I remained on the hill. I am alone in camp tonight, with Mohammed on guard.

It was a foul, windy day, the wind coming from the east, and half blinding the workmen with the

sand it blew in their eyes. Room 14 continues to extend eastward, and will probably be found to blank the entire south side of the temple complex. As we are nearing the east end of the outer court, the floor of Room 14 slopes down sharply to the east (figs. 227–28). Its north wall, which is really in part the south wall of the outer east-court rises to a number of courses high ([space]) (figs. 229, 231). It can be seen how the outer east court [Forecourt] floor had evidently to be built up in order to make it fairly flat, because if the east end of the east court slopes the way the east end of Room 14 does, it required considerable building up. We shall have to move a dump heap to get to the very east end of Room 14. We have been able to trace almost the entire length of the outer, large, strongly built, flint-block wall of Room 14, which is spaced about the same distance from its fine inner wall (fig. 227) as Rooms 8–9. It is the continuation of the outer wall of Rooms 12 and 13 (fig. 219).

I forgot to mention that the fine inner s. wall [edge of bench] of Room 14 (fig. 227) is also, as the room slopes to the east, based higher and higher on a rough stone wall foundation. Near its eastern end, only the rough stone wall foundation remains (fig. 232). The room is still near its east end filled with debris, indeed it becomes thicker as we get nearer to its east end. It yields quantities of Nab.-Roman pottery; another stone torch; a bronze *spatula* (fig. 13.9a–b), a pottery figurine of an animal that looks all the world as if it had been handed down from Edomite times (fig. 405a–d). It is crude enough to be similar in type of construction to the crude Edomite figurines of goddesses published by Harding in the last *PEFQS* [*Palestine Exploration Quarterly* 1937]. As sacred a place as Jebel Tannur was in all probability venerated also in EI [Early Iron] times. All EI remains have been destroyed or effaced by the massive reconstruction of the hilltop. If all of the Nabataean construction were removed, some EI vestiges might be found underneath it.

December 9

The cold east wind continued blowing this morning, and all the boys struck, and after I had paid them off went home to Tafileh. It was just as well, because their usefulness at the dig was just about over. One of the local men also quit. The other five men went up to the hill and spent all day removing the dump-heap on the s.e. corner of Room 14. They almost finished, and also cleared some new ground in the s.e. corner of Room 14. At the present, it is apparent that the outer east wall of the outer east court extends farther than we thought it did, and Fisher's plan will have to be changed. The east cont. of the inner south wall of Room 14 has not yet been found, and in this case, as well as in the case of the cont. of the outer east-wall, it may be impossible to find the right-angle at which supposedly they originally met, or perhaps a tangent wall connected them. At the point where they perhaps once met at a right-angle, or where a tangent line connected them, the hillside goes down at about an 80° angle.

While digging in what may either have been the bottom of the dump-heap or the previously undisturbed soil in Room 14, another Zeus-Hadad head was found, with its nose smashed off (fig. 329) (*DD* 183, pl. 127). The back of its head is gone, but otherwise it is intact. It is related in general appearance and impression to the Parthian ? version of the Zeus-Hadad head, which we found previously. It is, however, much smaller. In addition, a part of the draped left shoulder and breast of a woman's figure was found in the dump-heap, similar to the piece previously found. Also there was found the top fragment of the head of some figure.

Ylias and C. Pape arrived this evening at 6:05 pm having left Jerusalem at 8:20 am this morning. Ylias arrived with the others in Jerusalem last night at 6:00 pm.

December 10

We finished Room 14 today. The east end of inner wall is broken off, and the outer wall was broken off several metres farther back. At the very east end of the room, squatters had built a tiny little room, in the west wall of which was a pillar drum (figs. 320, 326). This room seems to have been used as a fireplace. The debris showed a considerable burnt layer near the bottom. The east wall of Room 14 is a solid extension of the east wall of the outer

east court [Forecourt]. A tangent row of fallen building blocks connects this section of the east wall with the remaining foundation of the inner s. wall of Room 14. This tangent row seems to have been built by squatters also. At one time, the east end of Room 14 may have been rectangular, but the steep hillside on which the east and south ends was possibly built must have fallen away, taking these portions of the walls with them. In the little squatters-room, we found a complete Nab. Roman, slightly ribbed bowl (Ch. 18, fig. 18.11, no. 47).

We cleared the lines of the walls on all the sides of the temple-complex, wherever necessary. The actual digging is now finished.

Pape started measuring up Room 14, with my assistance.

I left my camera on the ledge of the temple when I went down for lunch. Returning, I noticed that someone had meddled with it, and apparently ruined it. It is unserviceable now. In the squabble which ensued among the 6 who had been on top of the hill, during which the 5 from Tafileh accused the one from La'aban, Mohammed ibn Salim Za'rûr of La'aban tried to knife Mohammed Suleiman of Tafileh. I got my hands over the hands of both, and finally got the knife away from Mohammed Suleiman, who with the help of his gang had gotten it away from Mohammed ibn Salim Za'rûr. I believe it was Mohammed Suleiman of Tafileh who ruined my camera.

December 11

Spent the day on the hill helping Pape measure. A strong east-wind blowing all day. Pape took some photographs for me, but the wind shook the camera so, that it was impossible to get good results (fig. 232). In the morning I had paid off the five remaining men. Only Mohammed ibn Salim Za'rûr remains. Tomorrow morning we are breaking camp for Jerusalem.

December 12

Left Kh. Tannur at 9 am with the Dodge very heavily loaded. Brought back the PWD tent to the museum at 'Amman. Arrived in Jerusalem at

6:30 pm, with only partly broken spring. During our entire stay at Kh. Tannur, with the exception of the winds, the weather has been extremely nice.

[On the last page, there is a plan giving the room numbers from 7 to 14.]

[Notes on two small sheets, tucked in at the end of the hand-written journal pages:]

[Sheet 1:]
The outer stones of the podium {later annotation: (= altar?)} [North-east Altar], in the outer east court [Forecourt], are finer than the inner stones which are rougher. There seem to be two building periods at least in this podium (fig. 179). The inner podium has a clear cut outer face on all sides.

The much larger building blocks in Room 9 as compared with those in Room 8, seem to indicate that it was not built in the same period, and was probably built later.

The outer east rubble extension wall over part of which the s.e. corner of Room 10 is built is only one layer deep; it is built of boulders (figs. 36–37).

The n. wall of Room 11 is built of rough flint blocks. The west wall is built of flint blocks and flint rubble. The e. cross wall of Room 11, only the south third of which is intact, is built of flint and limestone rubble as are the other cross-walls on the n. side of the temple-complex. There are about 3 distinct levels in Room 14.

[Sheet 2:]
There are two distinct floor levels in Room 14, marked by the drops in the level of the ground as the room drops steeply to the east. The 2 levels are marked also by a break, approximately in the middle, of the rows of building blocks on the north side of Room 14 (figs. 229–30). In the west half of the n. wall of this room are a number of blocks cut in the style of Period "3." The blocks in the east half of the n. wall are, on the whole, longer than those on the west half. The blocks at the very east end of the n. wall are also cut in the manner of Period 3 (fig. 232).

Chapter 8

Glueck's Registration Book

edited by Judith S. McKenzie

The registry of objects excavated at Khirbet et-Tannnur is recorded on eight pages in front of the book which was then used as the 1938 Tell el-Kheleifeh Registration Book. Not every single object was given a registration number, as the discovery of some is only recorded in his excavation journal. The find-locations of some finds, such as pottery sherds, glass, and bones, were recorded only on the find itself or the brown paper bag in which it was placed. Glueck does seem to have tried to record the findspot of each find in at least one of these places. His annotations (M) or (A), after the object number, refer to the object having been assigned to the American School (A) or the Palestine Archaeological Museum (M). (He had sometimes ticked these, indicated here by underlining, and sometimes he put a question mark instead.)

The content of the entries is reproduced in full here, but it should be noted that some of the descriptions are misleading, in the light of further knowledge about the objects. When it has been possible to determine to which object a description refers, figure numbers in the present work are given, and clarifications in square brackets [ ]. Figure numbers of the form 1–500 refer to Vol. 1 here.

March 1, 1937

West side of main room [Inner Temenos Enclosure] of temple of Hadad.

1. (<u>A</u>) Relief of grain goddess Atargatis of same type as presumably found by Abdullah Rihani. The fishes are broken off (??), on left side of shell is a single ear of wheat (?), which was broken off from relief found by Abdullah Rihani. Near also is the vine design on left of main relief panel. Another difference is that the dress is different, the diamond like neck band of the dress being absent in this one. (fig. 244)

2. (<u>A</u>) The front side of a male (?) head, broken off of some relief or other. The right ear is half broken off. The hair is waved and curled. It seems to come directly from Palmyra or Dura, so far as general type is concerned (fig. 245b).

3. (?) An Atargatis (?) head broken off of a relief. It is of another type than the "fish-goddess" thus far known.

4. (<u>M</u>) Complete bust of Atargatis on a half-broken relief [the small cult statue]. No. 3 may belong to a relief of this type. She is wearing a loosely draped dress, which fits up around

bottom of neck. Around top of dress reaching to neck is a heavy necklace fastened in front by a brooch. It may be a part of the dress. Both hands are broken off. The bottom of the left-hand has a hole drilled into it, into which a hand once fitted (fig. 88).

5.   (?) A separate small hand, which may belong to bust no. 4. The index finger is broken off. The fingers are curled, and evidently once held some object (fig. 152).

6.   (A) An Atargatis relief set in a circular panel, the bottom part of which is broken off [the Zodiac Tyche upper block]. There is a crown over her wavy hair, which falls down the sides of her head in two long tresses. Over her right shoulder is a moon. Extending above her left shoulder is a trident-like scepter. The outer rim of the panel encircling the goddess is divided at the present into eleven panels, the bottom two of which are broken. There are small figures and animals of the zodiac (!) filling the panels (figs. 91, 357–58).

7.   (A) Upper half of a winged dragon (?) [eagle], the upper body part of which is broken off. A life-like snake is crawling over it, its head is intact (fig. 158).

7a.   (A) The bottom part of the dragon [eagle] showing its feet, and the bottom part of the tail of the snake. There are 5 small stone pieces, which belong to the dragon complex. On back of it are plaster remains, as on back of no. 7. It was set into a panel (fig. 158).

8.   (A) A lion's head almost completely intact (fig. 208a–b).

9.   (?) A small stone libation (?) stand and basin.

10.   (?) Fragment of stone basin.

10a. Fragment of stone basin.

10b. Fragment of stone basin, and part of no. 10.

11.   (A) Small curved pillar [incense altar] with ornamented capital, with 2 intact Ionic-like adornments, 1 damaged, and one broken off (fig. 10.13a–b).

12.   (M) Small stone stand, broken.

12a. Fragment of no. 12.

13.   Fragment of stone basin.

14.   Fragment of stone basin.

15.   Fragment of ornamented stone.

16.   (?) Broken foot (?) of a throne (?).

17.   Small broken lamp (fig. 17.41).

18.   Coin [Seleucid] (fig. 13.10a–b).

18a. (A) Hadad – cleared but not in position. He is in seated posture. On left side young bull, on right side another much damaged. The right arm is broken off. Over left is thunder bolt. Head crowned with polos (fig. 86).

March 2

19.   (M) 3 panelled incense stand with Greek inscription   A
                                              NDROS
                                              AMRO
                                                V
      It has 2 Tyche (?) and one Hadad panel. Found in debris of east gate (?) [main doorway of Inner Temenos Enclosure] of Hadad temple. Two inscribed fragments belonging to it, numbered 19a and b. The top of the basin shows oil or incense remains and stains (fig. 10.4a–d).

20.   (?) Broken feminine figure from northeast corner of temenos.

21.   (M) Almost intact eagle relief [acroterion], found on east side of east gate (?) of Hadad [main doorway of Inner Temenos Enclosure] (figs. 164–65).

22.   (M) Huge Atargatis relief found on east side of debris of east gate (?) [main doorway of Inner Temenos Enclosure] of Hadad Temple. Several separate ornamented stones belong to this relief panel. Leaf goddess (fig. 160).

23.   Small broken Nabataean lamp (fig. 17.32).

March 3

24.   (M) Nabataean [La'abān] inscription from outside s.e. corner of temple courtyard [Inner Temenos Enclosure] (fig. 9.1a–b).

25.   (M) An unfinished head from inside n.e. corner of temple courtyard [Inner Temenos Enclosure], in debris (fig. 305).

26.   (M) Ornamented stone with double thunderbolt from debris outside east gate (?) of temple-courtyard [Inner Temenos Enclosure] (fig. 166).

27. Complete small Nabataean lamp from south-west corner of courtyard of Hadad shrine (fig. 17.33).

March 4

28. Complete small Nabataean lamp from north-west corner of courtyard [Inner Temenos Enclosure] of Hadad shrine (fig. 17.29).
29. (A) Four parts of Nabataean inscription from debris outside south wall, near east end.
30. (M) Small reclining animal sculpture with head broken off; found in debris on s. outside of temple courtyard [Inner Temenos Enclosure] (fig. 89).
31. (?) Bust relief of woman, bet. 2 small columns, found in debris at s.e. corner of temple bldg; pick scar on left cheek.
32. Broken black jug [cooking pot], found in debris on n. outside of temple courtyard near east end (fig. 18.31, no. 125).
33. Broken black jug [pot], found in debris on n. outside of temple courtyard near east end (figs. 18.30*, 18.30, no. 124).
34. (A)[in Amman] Right half of head, from s.e. corner of inside temple court (fig. 201).
35. (M) Fragment of bust, with left breast visible, and most of Medusa-like head bet. it and other breast which is not retained (fig. 290).
36. Small fragments of glass from s.e. corner of inner court.
37. (M) Fairly intact Zeus head from debris in main court in front of east steps.
38. Broken Nabataean lamp, a piece of copper, and a piece of bone in centre of inner east court back of steps; all in bag no. 38.
39. Complete Nabataean lamp from inner east court [Inner Temenos Enclosure] back of steps (fig. 17.37).
40. (A) Half of head of eagle, from debris in east inner court back of steps (fig. 158).
41. (A) Stone ornamented with wreaths, and slightly damaged Medusa-like head, found outside front east steps. cf. no. 35 (fig. 284).
42. Stone belonging to no. 41 (fig. 284).
43. Broken iron nail found outside north inner court (fig. 13.4).

44. (A) Model house (?) or temple (?) [incense burner] from n.w. end of large east court [Forecourt] (fig. 10.9a–c).

March 6

45. (?) Intact head of a relief, from front of east wall of temple [Inner Temenos Enclosure facade] near debris.
46. Fragment of Greek inscription from near east end of east outer court [Forecourt] (fig. 308).
47. (M) Lintel with 2 rosettes and 2 small figures in relief intact, from east side of temple [Inner Temenos Enclosure] near north end (fig. 263).
48. (A) Capital with one small intact figure on it, from in front east side of temple [Inner Temenos Enclosure facade] near north side (figs. 267, 271a).
48a. A similar, better preserved capital found in front of east temple near south wall, with small head broken off is numbered 48a (figs. 266–67, 269).
49 and 49a. (A) (Helios?) Face and head in 2 parts found in separate places in front of east temple wall [Inner Temenos Enclosure facade] near south end. This head may belong to pieces with small Medusa-like head in centre, see no. 35 [From Helios bust] (fig. 129).
50. (M) Head of woman [Nike] with hair in top knot, from in front of east court wall [Inner Temenos Enclosure facade] near south end (fig. 141).
51 and 51a. (A) Two parts of front of woman of no. 35, found in front of east wall of temple [Inner Temenos Enclosure facade] near south end.
52. (A) Back and tail of lion (?) found near east end of east court (fig. 90).
53. (A) A hand found in front of east wall of temple [Inner Temenos Enclosure facade] near s. end (fig. 153).
54. (M) A single foot on a base [a globe], found in front of east wall of temple [Inner Temenos Enclosure facade] near s. end (fig. 156).
55. (M) [in CAM] Left half of head found in southeast corner of outer east court [Forecourt] (fig. 204).

56. (M?) [in CAM] A single foot found in front of east wall of temple [Inner Temenos Enclosure facade] near south end (fig. 157).

57. (A) A single foot found in front of east wall of temple [Inner Temenos Enclosure facade] near south end (fig. 205).

57a. [in CAM] Leg belonging to no. 57 (fig. 205).

58. (M) Two broken feet on base [a globe] found in front of east wall of temple [Inner Temenos Enclosure facade] near south end (fig. 155).

59. (A) Two broken feet on base [a globe] found in front of east wall of temple [Inner Temenos Enclosure facade] near south end (fig. 140).

60. Iron from door socket at north end of upper door sill of east gate of temple [Inner Temenos Enclosure] (figs. 13.1–13.2). One piece shows a screw hole in it.

61. (A) [in Amman] Broken body of Tyche (?) with legs showing through dress, found near northeast end of outer east court [Forecourt] (probably fig. 201).

March 7

62. (A) Feminine head, like no. 50, top-knot broken off, found in south court outside temple near east end (fig. 140).

63. (M) Bearded head in front of east wall of temple court [Inner Temenos Enclosure facade], near south end.

March 8

64. (M) Large almost intact head of Hadad, off of some decorative stone, found in debris in front of southeast corner of outer wall of inner temple court [Inner Temenos Enclosure], on top of landing leading along south side of outer east court [Forecourt].

64 a and b.   Parts of hair of no. 64.

March 9

65. (A) Altar pedestal with winged Tyches, found in debris in front of east wall of temple shrine [Altar Platform] (fig. 10.5a–d).

March 10

66a–c.   (A) Three pieces of one finely hewn stone piece used as a dowel (?) or as a scepter – found in debris back of original position of main Hadad relief (figs. 84–85).

67a–b.   (?) Two parts of basin found in debris of shrine back of where main Hadad relief stood [in Altar 1].

68. Fragment of small, burned, stone altar, found in debris inside shrine [in Altar 1], together with burned bones (fig. 10.10a–b).

April 1

69. (A) Eagle's head in debris in front of entrance of north room [Room 8] at n.w. corner of outer east court [Forecourt]. It is carved in detail only on right side of head (fig. 292).

April 2

70. Top of small torch. Locus as above.

71. (A) Mold – debris in n.e. corner of outer east court (fig. 13.12).

72. Small, complete Nabataean lamp from north room [Room 8] at n.w. corner of outer east court (fig. 17.42).

73. (X) Large stone basin, (locus as above), set originally on pillar (?) (fig. 211, visible at south end of west bench) [whereabouts unknown in 2010].

April 5

74. (?) Coin [of Aretas IV] from w. end of north room 1 [Room 8] at n.w. end of outer east court (fig. 13.11a–b).

75. Coin from back of steps leading down n. from near w end of n. wall of n. court.

April 7

76. (A) Lion's head of sandstone from north room II [Room 9] on n. side of outer east court [from female cult statue] (fig. 87).

77. (?) Small Nabataean altar from debris on west side of temple complex.

78. (<u>A</u>) Friable sandstone with remnants of 2 feet of a lion, locus as no. 76 (belongs to no. 76) (fig. 87).

79. (<u>A</u>) Fragment of friable sandstone with remnants of one foot on it; locus as above (fig. 87).

April 9

80. Lamp from s.w. corner of n. room "II" [Room 9], with eagle (fig. 17.18).

81. Slightly broken lamp from s.w. corner of room "II" [Room 9] (fig. 17.12).

April 11

82. (A) Fragment of small incense altar from outside s. wall of n. room II [Room 10].

April 13

83. (<u>M</u>) Small bird's head, carved only on left side of face, from s. room II [Room 14], s. of s. shrine wall [in Cincinnati, according to annotations in Glueck's photograph album II] (fig. 291).

84. (A) Small fragment of face showing right eye, nose, part of left eye, and part of mouth [in Cincinnati, according to annotations in Glueck's photograph album II] (fig. 151).

December 6

85. (A) Roman (?) coin from Room 14.

86. Broken stone torch from Room 14.

December 7

87. Bronze ring from Room 14 (fig. 13.7a–b).

88. (M) Small broken stone receptacle from Room 14.

December 8

89. Bronze *spatula* from near n.e. end of Room 14 (fig. 13.9a–b).

90. Broken stone torch from s.e. end of Room 14.

91. Animal pottery figurine from n.e. end of Room 14 (fig. 405a–d).

December 9

92. (<u>A</u>) Parthanized (?) Zeus-Hadad head (fig. 329) (*DD* 183, pl. 127).

93. (A) Fragment of left draped shoulder of fem. stone figure.

December 10

94. Complete Nab.-Roman bowl from Room 14a (fig. 18.11, no. 47).

Chapter 9

The Nabataean Inscriptions

by John F. Healey

INTRODUCTION

This volume provides an opportunity for a review of the epigraphic remains recovered from the temple of Khirbet et-Tannur (Ḥirbet et-Tannūr), with the benefit of modern photography and incorporating some corrections which have been made to the earliest readings. The original drawings made by R. Savignac and J. T. Milik do, however, remain fundamental.

There are four Nabataean inscriptions (see in summary Healey 2001: 60–61). Three were published by Savignac in 1937 (with corrected reading of the first by Savignac and J. Starcky in 1957). The fourth item was published by Milik in 1958. The numbering given here is new and has the advantage of collocating the material as two pairs of texts, for reasons which will become clear.

These inscriptions are associated with the sanctuary in the late 1st century BC, when it had an altar for burnt offerings in an open air enclosure along with some adjoining rooms. Nabataean worship at the site had begun by the late 2nd century BC, but the main construction phase of the sanctuary (Period 2) was not until the first half of the 2nd century AD. This was followed by renovations in

the 3rd century (Period 3), with worship continuing there until the earthquake of AD 363.

DISCUSSION

1. The Laʻabān Inscription

Fig. 9.1a; Vol. 1, fig. 38. Drawing of inscription: fig. 9.1b (= Savignac 1937: pl. 9.2).
Savignac 1937: 405–8 (no. 1), pl. 9; Glueck 1965: 512–13 and pl. 194d; Hackl et al. 2003: 217–18.
Palestine Archaeological Museum no. M38.1235. Whereabouts unknown 2011. Limestone.
Locus: found outside south-east corner of Inner Temenos Enclosure (GJ March 3, 1937); GR no. 25.

A building inscription on a stone block, recessed within a border or cartouche which is 36 × 15 cm (the complete stone is 60 × 20 cm). There are four lines of writing.

1. *dy bnh nṭyrʼl br*
2. *zydʼl rʼš ʻyn lʻbn ʻl ḥyy ḥrtt*
3. *mlk nbṭw rḥm ʻmh wḥyy ḥldw*
4. *ʼtth bšnt 2*

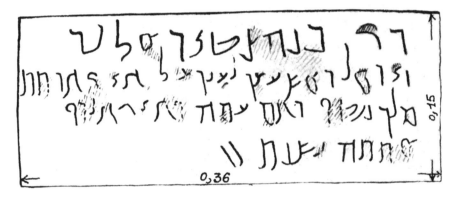

FIG. 9.1A–B   *No. 1. La'abān Inscription.*

1. Which Naṭīr'el son of Zayd'el,
2. head of the La'abān spring, built for
   the life of Aretas,
3. king of the Nabataeans, lover of his
   people, and (for) the life of Ḥuldu,
4. his wife, in the year 2

Epigraphy

The script (as copied in the facsimile of Savignac)
is untidy and irregular (note the letter {b} appearing in three different forms; {h} with and without
an upper projection on the top right). It could not
be precisely dated if it were not for the date which
is given in the inscription itself, but the letter-
forms have parallels in other inscriptions from
Petra and Ḥegrā (Healey 1993: 292–97).

2. The Naṭīr'el Inscription

Fig. 9.2a. Drawing of inscription: fig. 9.2b (=
Glueck 1965: pl. 195b).
Savignac 1937: 409–10 (no. 3); Glueck 1965: 513–14
and pl. 195a–b.
Cincinnati Art Museum no. 269. Limestone.
Locus: provenience unknown. Visible, prior to the
excavation, in GA photo 392.

A building inscription set within a *tabula ansata*,
the main dimensions of which are 25 × 20 cm (ears
extra; the complete stone is 42 × 24 cm, th. 23 cm).
The last of the four lines is completely lost, though
it probably contained a date; line 3 is restored on
the basis of knowledge of the conventional title of
Aretas IV.

Fig. 9.2a–b
*No. 2. Naṭīrʾel Inscription
(CAM 269).*

1. *(dy) bnh nṭyrʾl br*
2. *(zydʾ)l ʿl ḥyy ḥr(tt)*
3. *(mlk nbṭw rḥm) ʿm(h)*
4. *(bšnt) ......*

1. (Which) Naṭīrʾel son of
2. (Zaydʾ)el built for the life of Are(tas
3. king of the Nabataeans, lover of his) people,
4. (in the year) ......

Epigraphy

The copy made by Savignac (reproduced in Glueck 1965) does not provide much evidence of the script. The few clear letter-forms (e.g., in *bnh*) are consistent with a date in the reign of Aretas IV (see below).

Comment on nos. 1 and 2

Nos. 1 and 2 share the same formulaic elements and belong to the *ʿl ḥyy ...*, "for the life of ...," genre of inscriptions studied in great detail by K. Dijkstra (1995). The typical inscription of this type (found in Nabataea, Palmyra, Hatra, and Edessa) dedicates a generous act (like Greco-Roman euergetism) to the welfare of a higher official, often a ruler. The thing dedicated may be a small object or part of a building. Clearly the use of the verb *bnh* here, meaning "build," as opposed to the more common verb *ʿbd*, meaning "make," implies that what is being referred to is part of the building or at least something that needed to be constructed on the spot, such as an altar-base or stairway, though, as noted by Dijkstra (1995: 66–67), the small size of the inscriptions suggests that neither referred to the whole building complex, but rather to a small part of it. Thus nos. 1 and 2 should be considered together, because they refer to specific elements in the building programme at Khirbet et-Tannur.

The failure of both inscriptions to mention the character of the structure being dedicated has parallels in other contemporary Aramaic inscriptions. A number of such inscriptions are discussed by J. Naveh (2002), though he does not mention these Khirbet et-Tannur examples. Usually the beginning of the inscription with the relative pronoun ("Which so-and-so built / made …") creates no problem because it is obvious to the original readers what is being referred to. Such formulae are used, for example, on silver bowls offered to deities: the inscription is *on* the bowl and therefore there is no need to begin with "This is the bowl — which so-and-so offered …." It was probably obvious in the Khirbet et-Tannur temple, too. (It is interesting to compare similar dedications at Palmyra, where a great variety of architectural terms appear in dedications of parts of buildings.)

The dedicant in both cases is the same person, Naṭīrʾel son of Zaydʾel. The absence of his title in no. 2 cannot be taken to have any significance in terms of his status at the time the inscription was drawn up; we cannot conclude that he had not yet become "head of the Laʿabān spring." He would have been a very well-known figure locally and his title could be omitted in a short inscription.

The nature of this office needs little comment. The use of *r'š* or *ryš*, "head," in administrative titles is attested elsewhere in Nabataean (Stiehl 1970; al-Najem and Macdonald 2009); it appears that Naṭīrʾel was in charge of the spring associated with the Wādī Laʿabān and he probably had connections with Khirbet edh-Dharih (Ḥirbet eḏ-Ḏarīḥ). An official in charge of an important spring is also attested in the Palmyrene inscriptions (Savignac and Starcky 1957: 216–17; Dijkstra 1995: 67, fn. 48; al-Muheisen 2009: 173; see Healey 2013).

No. 1 is specifically dated to the second year of Aretas IV, which places the inscription in 8 or 7 BC. The mention of Aretas' first wife, Ḥuldu, is interesting at this date in the context of what seems

to have been a contentious transfer of power when Obodas III died. It is a widely held view that Aretas' claim to the throne was based in part at least on the status of Ḥuldu, who was probably the daughter of Obodas. He himself was not Obodas' son and was challenged for the throne by another member of the royal family, Syllaeus. The naming of Ḥuldu in inscriptions (from Puteoli: Hackl et al. 2003: 116–18; and Wādī Ramm: Hackl et al. 2003: 284–85) and on coins may have been important ways of confirming Aretas' legitimacy (Zayadine 1999: 52; al-Fassi 2007: 39–41).[1]

There might, therefore, be some significance in the fact that Ḥuldu is not mentioned in no. 2. Maybe Aretas' position was no longer in doubt, and maybe the inscription comes from later in his reign, when Šaqīlat is named as his wife (e.g., in the Baalshamin dedication of AD 15/16 from Wādī Mūsā: Hackl et al. 2003: 274–78; Healey 2009: no. 3). Šaqīlat's name replaces that of Ḥuldu on the coinage in Aretas' 27th year (AD 18/19) (Meshorer 1975: 55–56).

Whatever about this, there is no doubt that both inscriptions belong within the same time frame of Aretas' reign, 9 BC to AD 40, and this dating is important in the context of trying to understand the architectural history of the site.

3. The Qōs Stele

Fig. 9.3a; Vol. 1, figs. 39a, 334a–335. Drawing of inscription: fig. 9.3b (= Savignac 1937: pl. 9.3). Savignac 1937: 408–9 (no. 2), pls. 9.3, 10; Glueck 1965: 514–15 and pls. 196–97; also Milik 1958: 236–38; McKenzie 2003: 187, fig. 196. Cincinnati Art Museum no. 268. Limestone. Locus: provenience unknown.

A dedicatory inscription on a (horned?) stone stele (h. 40 cm, 32 cm from the point where the stele was above ground level, w. 20 cm, th. 13 cm).

1. *(d)y ʿbd qsmlk*
2. *lqs ʾlh*
3. *ḥwrwʾ*

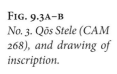

Fig. 9.3a–b
No. 3. Qōs Stele (CAM 268), and drawing of inscription.

1. Which Qōsmalik made
2. for Qōs, the god of
3. Ḥōrawā (or: Ḥawarawā).

Epigraphy

The three lines are quite clear, at least in the copy of Savignac, but the script is crude and irregular (note {s} and {ʾ}). Although there is no date, the script is consistent with a date late in the 1st century BC (Milik 1958: 237 and fn. 1, comparing this with the first Tell Šuqāfiyyah inscription of 48/44 BC and one from Sīʿ of 2/1 BC [*CIS* II, no. 163]; see also Starcky 1956: 522, fig. 2).

4. The Matīʿel Altar

Figs. 9.4a–b, 10.6a–b; Vol. 1, fig. 39b. Drawing of inscription: figs. 9.4c (= Milik 1958: 238 fig. 1), 9.4d (= Savignac in Glueck 1965: pl. 194c).
Milik 1958: 237–38 and fig. 1; Glueck 1965: 510 and pl. 194a–c. Ch. 10, below, altar no. 6.
Cincinnati Art Museum no. 228. Limestone.
Locus: provenience unknown. Taken from the site by ʿAbdullah Rīhānī Bey, prior to the excavation.

A dedicatory inscription on an altar of the following dimensions: h. 47 × w. 22 × d. 22 cm.

1. *dy qrb mtyʿl*
2. *(b)r(?)......(ʿw)tʾl*
3. *lḥwrwy*

1. Which Matīʿel
2. son of (?) .... (ʿAw)tʾel offered
3. for the Ḥawarawite.

Epigraphy

It may be noted that the word *qrb* appears to have been added later, to correct an omission: it is written more finely and in smaller lettering below the word *dy* (see Milik 1958: 238, fn. 2). The second line cannot really be read; the transliteration here follows Milik (fig. 9.4c). The ligature at the end of line 3 between the final {w} and {y} is unusual, but the sequence of {w}+{y} is in any case rare and the reading seems assured (Milik 1958: 238, fn. 2). It may be noted, however, that Savignac's drawing (fig. 9.4d) implies a reading of *ltwdtʾ*, "for thanksgiving, as a thank-offering" (as in Jewish Aramaic *tōḏeṭā*) (see Glueck 1965: 510).

The script is compatible with a date in the late 1st century BC, as in the case of no. 3, with some letter-forms similar to those of the earlier tomb inscriptions at Ḥegrā (Healey 1993: 292–97).

Comment on nos. 3 and 4

The fact that the other two inscriptions from Khirbet et-Tannur also begin with the relative pronoun suggests that this was characteristic in that

FIG. 9.4A   *No. 4. Matīʿel Altar (CAM 228).*

FIG. 9.4B   *No. 4. Matīʿel Altar (CAM 228), detail of inscription.*

FIG. 9.4C   *No. 4. Matīʿel Altar (CAM 228), inscription, drawing by J. T. Milik.*

FIG. 9.4D   *No. 4. Matīʿel Altar (CAM 228), inscription, drawing by R. Savignac.*

region. This usage is much less common elsewhere in Nabataea. Naveh (2002: 308) mentions *CIS* II, no. 174: *dy qrb nṭr'l* on an altar from Boṣrā.

In the case of no. 4 there is no doubt as to what is being dedicated, since the inscription is found on an altar. In the case of no. 3 there is no such helpful evidence, but we may note that in neither of these inscriptions is the verb *bnh*, "build," used (as it is in nos. 1 and 2). Instead we have *'bd*, "make," and the much less common *qrb*, "offer, dedicate." The clear implication of these verbs is that we are dealing with individual objects for which the verb "to build" would be inappropriate.

The other quite startling common feature of nos. 3 and 4 is the fact that no. 3 is clearly dedicated to the Edomite god Qōs, while no. 4 is *probably* dedicated to the same deity (on Qōs in Nabataean religion, see Healey 2001: 126–27; for Qōs at Boṣrā see the inscription published in Milik 1958: 235–41 [no.3] and pl. XIXa).

We may note that the name of the god Qōs appears also in the personal name Qōsmalik in no. 3. Qōs names are rare in Nabataean. F. al-Khraysheh notes *qws'dr* in Sinai (*CIS* II, 923) and *qsntn* at Ḥegrā (*CIS* II, 209), drawing attention also to Liḥyanite Qōs names (al-Khraysheh 1986: 158, 161).[2]

The other common element in nos. 3 and 4 is the appearance in slightly different forms of the name Ḥōrawā; this is the vocalization normally provided, but of course it is far from certain and Ḥawarawā is also possible (see below and note that Milik described the vocalization as arbitrary: Milik 1958: 238).

In no. 3 the name appears in the phrase *'lh ḥwrw'*. Comparison with other Nabataean usage would suggest that Ḥōrawā could be a personal or tribal name.[3] There are dozens of such divine titles, "god of so-and-so," especially from the Ḥawrān (Hauran) area (Healey 2010). However, the personal name *ḥwrw'* is otherwise unknown in Nabataean and other related Aramaic dialects (though *ḥwrw* is attested in Nabataean; see n. 3 here). The "god of …" formula occasionally appears with a place name rather than a personal name. Thus we have Dushara described at Petra as "the god of Madrasa" (*'lh mdrs'*) and "god of Manbatu" (*'lh mnbtw*), and at 'Avdat and al-Jawf as "the god of Gaia" (*'lh

g'y') (for details see Healey 2001: 89–91). In other instances the formula used is "the god(dess) who is in …" (*'lh' / 'lht' dy b-*). For example, one of the inscriptions from Tell Šuqāfiyyah in Egypt refers to "Dushara, the god, who is in Daphne" (*dwšr' 'lh' dy bdpn'*) (Healey 2001: 91).

In the case we are dealing with here, the geographical interpretation is made almost certain by the fact that in no. 4, the god who is the recipient of the dedication of the altar is described as *ḥwrwy*, probably "the Ḥōrawite / Ḥawarawite" (so Milik 1958: 237–38, though note the alternative reading above). Morphologically this is an adjective of the *nisbah* form typical of Aramaic and other Semitic languages. It essentially means "related to Ḥōrawā / Ḥawarawā." (One might have expected a final *alif*: **ḥwrwy'*, as in *tymny'*, "Taymanite:" Healey 1993: no. 12: 2.)

The question naturally then arises over the identity of this place. Starcky listed a number of possibilities (1968: 209, including fn. 11). Could it be the ancient name of Khirbet et-Tannur itself? This is possible and it was the preferred understanding of Milik (1958: 238 — etymology *ḥrw*, "burn").

However, there must be a suspicion that these dedications refer to the prime location of the Qōs cult as being elsewhere (Starcky 1968: 209, fn. 11). There are a number of Nabataean inscriptions referring to the place where the deity in question is worshipped and they are not normally set up in that place itself, e.g., "the god of Gaia" in 'Avdat and al-Jawf and "the god who is in Daphne" in Tell Šuqāfiyyah (above). Even without that evidence, one might ask why the location would need to be specified if Ḥōrawā / Ḥawarawā is Khirbet et-Tannur.

Looking for another possible identification leads most obviously to Auara / Aὔαρα (Ptolemy's *Geography*) / Hauarra (*Tabula Peutingeriana*) / Hauare (*Notitia Dignitatum*), which has been identified as al-Ḥumaymah, 60 km north of Aqaba (see Wenning 1987: 99; Graf 1992; Oleson 2010: 50–57). Now confirming this identification of al-Ḥumaymah with Auara is a Latin inscription from al-Ḥumaymah which appears to contain the abbreviated name of the site, HAV(ARRAE) (see Oleson et al. 2002: 113–16 and pl. 4, inscription no. 4, line 7; Oleson et al. 2003: 47–48).

Starcky (1968: 209, fn. 11) seems to have been the first to mention the possibility that *ḥwrw'* at Khirbet et-Tannur is to be identified with Auara, but the suggestion has been subsequently ignored. The only difficulty seems to be the additional syllable, *-wā*, at the end. This does not, however, rule the identification out, especially since the possibility that the god of al-Ḥumaymah was Qōs has been argued on other grounds (Graf 1992: 75). Hence the suggestion that the Ḥōrawā / Ḥawarawā of the Khirbet et-Tannur inscriptions is to be located at al-Ḥumaymah is seductive. It is not, however, certain and more evidence would be desirable![4]

A Note on the Khirbet et-Tannur Script

The crudeness of the script in the inscriptions from Khirbet et-Tannur led Starcky (1966: col. 930) to place them alongside inscriptions from the Ḥawrān area in a group of what we might call "provincial" scripts not subject to the stylization and standardization which the script used in Petra underwent. They are more archaic in character and can be compared with the earlier scripts found at Petra in inscriptions such as the Aṣlaḥ inscription (*RES* §1432, dated 96–95 BC) and the inscription of the statue of Rabbel I (*CIS* II, no. 349, probably c. 67 BC). Starcky's point is that there was a great variety of scripts in use when Aramaic came again to the fore in the post-Seleucid era. In some major centres (such as Petra and Palmyra, and one could add Edessa) standard "national" scripts came into existence. In remoter areas, older script-forms persisted.

NOTES

1   Note, however, that the queen's portrait appears already on coins of Obodas III, though she is not named (Meshorer 1975: 33–35).

2   Al-Khraysheh 1986 only covers names which appear in *CIS*. Negev 1991 is more comprehensive, but lists our *qsmlk* under *'bdqwsmlk* (no. 823) and reads *qs'lh* in no. 3 as a personal name (no. 1028). For *qws'dr* and *qsntn* see Negev's nos. 1013 and 1035.

3   So Savignac 1937: 409: "the god of *Ḥwrw*", followed by the letter {'} used as an abbreviation for *'mn'*, "architect, sculptor", referring for the personal name to occurrences at Ḥegrā (Healey 1993: nos. 5: 11; 7: 8; 9: 5; al-Khraysheh 1986: 78–79). See also

Glueck 1965: 514–15. This division of line 3 into two parts is rightly rejected by Milik (1958: 237).

4   The thorough discussion of D. F. Graf (1992) is focused on al-Ḥumaymah and the explanation of the name *'bd'lḥwr* in an inscription and similar names in Thamudic script. In accordance with his argument, there can be little doubt about the origin of the name of Auara in the Semitic root ḤWR, meaning "white," or at least it was so understood secondarily: see Uranios / Stephen of Byzantium on the foundation legend of Auara (Graf 1992: 73; Vattioni 1992: 131 32; Hackl et al. 2003: 596).

References

Abbreviations

CIS   *Corpus Inscriptionum Semiticarum* (followed by volume and inscription number)
RES   *Répertoire d'Épigraphie Sémitique*

Dijkstra, K.
1995   *Life and Loyalty. A Study in the Socio-Religious Culture of Syria and Mesopotamia in the Graeco-Roman Period Based on Epigraphical Evidence.* Religions in the Graeco-Roman World 128. Leiden.

al-Fassi, H. A.
2007   *Women in Pre-Islamic Arabia: Nabataea.* British Archaeological Reports, International Series 1659. Oxford.

Glueck, N.
1965   *Deities and Dolphins.* New York, NY.

Graf, D. F.
1992   "The 'God' of Ḥumayma." Pp. 67–76 in *Intertestamental Essays in Honour of Józef Tadeusz Milik*, ed. Z. J. Kapera. Cracow. [reprinted in D. F. Graf, Item VII in *Rome and the Arabian Frontier: from the Nabataeans to the Saracens.* Variorum Collected Studies Series CS 594. Aldershot and Brookfield, VT. 1997.]

Hackl, U.; Jenni, H.; and Schneider, Ch.
2003   *Quellen zur Geschichte der Nabatäer: Textsammlung mit Übersetzung und Kommentar.* Novum Testamentum et Orbis Antiquus 51. Freiburg and Göttingen.

Healey, J. F.
1993   *The Nabataean Tomb Inscriptions of Mada'in Salih.* Journal of Semitic Studies Supplement 1. Oxford.
2001   *The Religion of the Nabataeans: A Conspectus.* Religions in the Graeco-Roman World 136. Leiden.
2009   *Aramaic Inscriptions and Documents of the Roman Period.* Textbook of Syrian Semitic Inscriptions 4. Oxford.

2010   "The Nabataean 'God of the Fathers.'" Pp. 45–57 in *Genesis, Isaiah, and Psalms: A Festschrift to Honour Professor John Emerton for his Eightieth Birthday*, eds. K. J. Dell, G. Davies, and Yee Von Koh. Vetus Testamentum Supplement 135. Leiden.
2013   "Water in Nabataea and Palmyra: From Everyday Realities to Imagination." Pp. 85–89 in *Man and Environment in the Arab World in Light of Archaeological Discoveries,* eds. A. R. al-Ansary, Kh. I. al-Muaikel, and A. M. Alsharekh. Riyadh.

al-Khraysheh, F.
1986   *Die Personennamen in den nabatäischen Inschriften des Corpus Inscriptionum Semiticarum.* Marburg.

McKenzie, J. S.
2003   "Carvings in the Desert: The Sculpture of Petra and Khirbet et-Tannur." Pp. 169–95 in *Petra Rediscovered, Lost City of the Nabataeans,* ed. G. Markoe. New York, NY.

Meshorer, Y.
1975   *Nabataean Coins.* Qedem 3. Jerusalem.

Milik, J. T.
1958   "Nouvelles inscriptions nabatéennes." *Syria* 35: 227–51.

al-Muheisen, Z.
2009   *The Water Engineering and Irrigation System of the Nabataeans.* Irbid, Jordan.

al-Najem, M., and Macdonald, M. C. A.
2009   "A New Nabataean Inscription from Taymā'." *Arabian Archaeology and Epigraphy* 20: 208–17.

Naveh, J.
2002   "Appendix C: The Relative Pronoun Opening Short Aramaic Inscriptions and the Body of the Bar-Kokhba Letters." Pp. 380–82 in *The Documents from the Bar Kokhba Period in the Cave of Letters. Hebrew, Aramaic and Nabatean-Aramaic Papyri,* eds. Y. Yadin, J. C. Greenfield, A.

Yardeni, and B. A. Levine. Judean Desert Studies. Jerusalem.

Negev, A.
1991   *Personal Names in the Nabatean Realm.* Qedem 32. Jerusalem.

Oleson, J. P.
2010   *Humayma Excavation Project, 1: Resources, History and the Water-Supply System.* American Schools of Oriental Research Archaeological Report 15. Boston, MA.

Oleson, J. P., et al.
2002   "New Dedicatory Inscriptions from Humayma (Ancient Hawara), Jordan." *Zeitschrift für Papyrologie und Epigraphik* 140: 103–21.
2003   "Preliminary Report of al-Ḥumayma Excavation Project, 2000, 2002." *Annual of the Department of Antiquities of Jordan* 47: 37–64.

Savignac, R.
1937   "Le Dieu nabatéen de Laʿaban et son temple." *Revue biblique* 46: 401–16.

Savignac, R., and Starcky, J.
1957   "Une Inscription nabatéenne provenant du Djôf." *Revue biblique* 64: 195–217.

Starcky, J.
1956   "Inscriptions archaïques de Palmyre." Pp. 509–28 in *Studi orientalistici in onore di Giorgio Levi della Vida II.* Publicazioni dell'Istituto per l'Oriente 52. Rome.

1966   "Pétra et la Nabatène." Cols 886–1017 in *Dictionnaire de la Bible,* ed. H. Cazelles et al. Supplément 7. Paris.
1968   "Le Temple nabatéen de Khirbet Tannur: à propos d'un livre récent." *Revue biblique* 75: 206–35.

Stiehl, R.
1970   "A New Nabataean Inscription." Pp. 87–90 in *Beiträge zur Alten Geschichte und deren Nachleben: Festschrift für F. Altheim zum 6. 10. 1968,* eds. R. Stiehl and H. E. Stier. Berlin.

Vattioni, F.
1992   "Sui toponimi e le loro etimologie in Stefano di Bisanzio." *Studi epigrafici e linguistici* 9: 127–38.

Wenning, R.
1987   *Die Nabatäer – Denkmäler und Geschichte.* Novum Testamentum et Orbis Antiquus 3. Freiburg and Göttingen.

Zayadine, F.
1999   "Pétra, le Sīq." *Dossiers d'archéologie* 244: 46–53.

Chapter 10

The Altars

by Andres T. Reyes and Judith S. McKenzie

INTRODUCTION

The altars from the Khirbet et-Tannur sanctuary range from the main Altar Platform for burnt offerings to tiny incense altars.[1] The main Altar Platform (no. 1) was used for burnt offerings of meat and grains, but also had a niche for the cult statues built into the front of it in Period 2. On either side, in front of this, there were two altars turned upside-down and re-used as plinths (fig. 10.1). These apparently supported the two incense altars decorated with a male figure (in the form of Zeus) and a figure holding a torch, respectively, between engaged columns and Nikes (nos. 4–5). The one inscribed with the name "Alexander Amrou" had carbonized remains on it which chemical analysis revealed were of incense. In the Forecourt there is a second large altar, the North-east Altar, presumably for burnt offerings (no. 2), as on the main altar. To the west of the Inner Temenos Enclosure, there is a smaller altar, the West Altar, decorated with a thunderbolt (no. 3).

The remaining altars are all for incense and are made of limestone. These include some which were set against walls, but their original exact location is unknown (nos. 4–5, 7). There are also smaller free-standing examples, each of which is unique at the site. These include a house-shaped one with perforated sides (no. 9) and one in the form of an Ionic capital with corner volutes (no. 13). There is also a very small one with triangular legs (no. 10), like cubical (cube-shaped) examples in Petra and related to earlier examples at Tell el-Kheleifeh from Iron Age II.

DISCUSSION

The practice of burning incense was common in the Near East, and Strabo (16.4.26) had noted it was typical among the Nabataeans (King and Stager 2001: 346–48 on different types of incense). Like the Alexander Amrou altar (no. 4), some of the smaller altars (nos. 10, 11, and 12) had traces of burning, with the deposit surviving in no. 10 chemically identified as incense. It is sometimes assumed that the small sizes of many of these altars (e.g., no. 10 with a width of 0.12 m) show that they were dedicatory, not functional, especially because it is not usual to find traces of burning on such finds (King and Stager 2001: 345; Chambon et al. 2002: 86, no. 120). Thus, the signs of incense burning at Khirbet et-Tannur constitute impor-

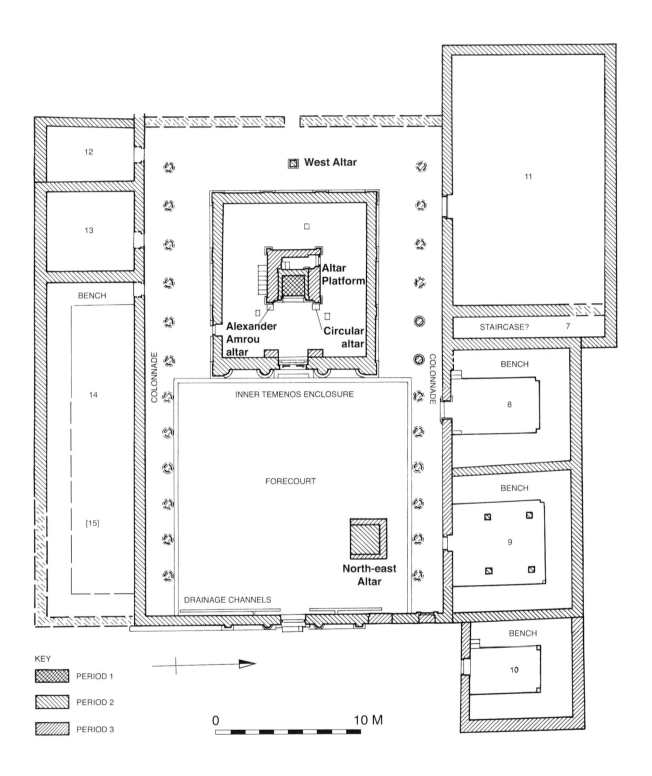

FIG. 10.1   *Khirbet et-Tannur, plan, with altars indicated.*

tant evidence for Nabataean and Near Eastern practice.

Hassell has advanced the theory that such altars reflect not ritual practice by authorities of a sanctuary, but rather individual use. They may be indicators of long-distance desert trade, in which a merchant arriving at the sanctuary would make an offering to the local deities bringing his own altar (Hassell 2005: 157–60). Such a theory could explain the different shapes and styles of the altars found at Khirbet et-Tannur. Celebrants presumably stood around the individual altars, and Healey has suggested that "circumambulation," probably around the main altar, may have played a part in certain rituals (Healey 2001: 163).

Most typical of the Nabataean altar types are nos. 6 and 7, with a horn on each corner. Both examples are now damaged. The height of such horned altars is normally double their width, but that is untrue of no. 7, the height of which is only a third greater than its width. Examples from Petra and Hegra (Medain Saleh) are similar (Starcky 1966: 1007; Patrich 1990: 92–93). Other Nabataean horned altars are known from the Ḥawrān (Hauran) (e.g., Dentzer-Feydy 2003: 103, pl. 76, no. 214).

The horned altar, however, has a long history in Near Eastern religion and is not unique to the Nabataeans. The Bible, for example, mentions horned altars in the times of David and Solomon (I Kings 1:50–51 and 2:28), to which those fearing for their lives could cling for refuge. Amos 3:14 refers to "punishment" of the altars of Bethel when the horns of the altar break and fall to the ground. Accordingly, King and Stager (2001: 339) suggest that the horns were stylised representations of the deity, and their deliberate removal was tantamount to desecration. A horned altar from the late 12th century BC is known from Megiddo (Loud 1948: pl. 254, nos. 1–2; with evidence for the dating in Lamon and Shipton 1939: 7) and other archaeological examples are recorded from Dan in the 9th century BC and Arad in the 9th or 8th century (Aharoni 1974: 2–6; Biran 1974: 106–7; Mazar 1992: 494–96; Gitin 1989: 52–67, for other examples from Israel and Judah).

The Nabataean inscription on the Matī'el altar (no. 6) makes clear that the altar itself was a dedicated object, rather than simply an object used for worship. The excavators at Khirbet edh-Dharih suggest a plain altar from that site, similar in height to no. 6 (0.48 m), could have been used for the sacrifice of small animals, perhaps pigeons (Chambon et al. 2002: 69, no. 86). It is possible that the West Altar (no. 3), from its size (c. 0.6 × 0.5 m), was used for such offerings. Chicken bones were found at Khirbet et-Tannur, but not those of smaller birds (see Ch. 11).

The plain corner pillars and simple cornice on the Matī'el altar (no. 6) show some classical influence already in evidence by the late 1st century BC. This is stronger, over a century later, on the Alexander Amrou altar (no. 4) which is, in style, a classical version of the basic Nabataean horned altar. Its sculptural style, combining classical and Nabataean elements, is analogous to its inscription, which combines a Greek name (Alexander) and a Semitic one ('Amr). The horns on the corners have become acroteria, and on each side pilasters frame classical figures (cf. Bowerman 1913: 29–30, no. 21; 51–52, no. 70). Like no. 5, it was carved in the first half of the 2nd century AD (in Period 2).

Nos. 5 and 8 are also classical in inspiration, but circular in form, rather than rectangular. Altars of circular or semi-circular shape are attested from the Classical and Hellenistic periods (cf. Pausanias 5.14.5; Yavis 1949: 153–54). Compare, too, a hexagonal altar of the 1st century AD from the Ḥawrān (Hellenkemper Salies 1981: pls. 66–67).

No. 13, in the shape of an Ionic capital, is completely classical in inspiration. The type of this Ionic capital, characterised by four corner volutes, is relatively rare but is the form commonly used in architecture at Petra (McKenzie 1990: pl. 49a–d; 2001: 102 on origins, figs. 12–13). Similar in conception is an altar from southern Syria in the shape of a stylised Corinthian capital (Dentzer and Dentzer-Feydy 1991: 123–24, pl. 7, no. 367).

As it has a pediment, no. 9 is related to other altars with architectural features. It resembles a house-model with a pitched roof, but is unusual in having drilled holes along its back and sides. It also has a small recess in the ridge of its "roof." It is related to *naiskoi* – altars built to resemble shrines – known from the Ḥawrān belonging the 3rd and

4th centuries AD (cf. examples listed in Augé and Linant de Bellefonds 2004: 427). Arnaud notes unprovenanced *naiskoi* from the Ḥawrān also used as altars similar to no. 9 (Arnaud 1986: 375, objects listed under 1.5). Examples from the Ḥawrān have a cup-like space above the "roof" of the altar for the placing of incense. The recess on the top of no. 9 would have served a similar purpose. One of Arnaud's examples (his no. 9) is open on the front, with a niche carved on each side and the back. It has drilled holes on the two sides (Arnaud 1986: 385, no. 9, faces C and D) that recall the drilled holes on the Khirbet et-Tannur altar. There is no evidence for a niche on the Khirbet et-Tannur example.

Plain small altars have a long history in the Near East, and Hassell has noted their continuity at Tell Jemmeh in Palestine from the latter half of the 7th century to the middle of the 4th century BC (Hassell 2005: 152). Nos. 10 and 11 are small cubical altars. They are plain in appearance and usually on squared legs, but no. 10 rests on triangular, rather than square, legs.

Patrich warns that the identification of such finds as altars cannot be absolutely certain, since such an object may be a *mwtb* or "the symbol of a worshipped deity" (Patrich 1990: 92–93; cf. Healey 2001: 158–59). But traces of burning and incense on no. 10 confirm its identification as an incense altar. It comes from the earliest phases at Khirbet et-Tannur, having been found in the Period 1 main altar. Traces of burning are also found in some of the small cubical altars from Tell el-Kheleifeh (such as excavation Registry no. 396 = *DD* pl. 193e, top left; excavation Registry nos. 885 and 11072, in the Semitic Museum, Harvard University).[2]

The Edomites used similar cubical altars, with examples recorded from the site of 'En Hazeva and assigned to the 7th or 6th century BC (Cohen and Yisrael 1995: 26–27, 37). Incense altars with similar triangular legs are known from Petra (*DD* 425, pl. 193d). Nos. 10 and 11 at Khirbet et-Tannur also argue, therefore, for continuity into the Nabataean period. No. 12, which is unusually deep, may be related to nos. 10 and 11 in its plainness. It has the taller proportions of the more classical altars, but was carved without legs. It is related too to ex-

amples of terracotta incense altars from 'En Hazeva, which are less tall, but are also plain and without legs (Cohen and Yisrael 1995: 27).

The incense altars at Khirbet et-Tannur cover the full period of worship at the site, as they range from the simple cubical altar of the 2nd (or early 1st) century BC to those with Nabataean and classical features of the late 1st century BC, first half of the 2nd century AD, and 3rd/4th century. Considered chronologically, the incense altars indicate a development from an early plain style to an increasingly classical style. This parallels the development of the main altar which was initially plain (2nd/1st century BC), before gaining classical decoration in Period 2 (first half of the 2nd century AD; Vol. 1, fig. 75), which became more elaborate in Period 3 (3rd century AD; fig. 234). The Alexander Amrou altar (no. 4) was still in use in the mid-4th century in front of the main Altar Platform when both were covered by rubble in the major damage which brought worship at the sanctuary to an end.

Catalogue

For abbreviations see pp. xvii–xviii.

In Situ *Altars*

1. Main Altar Platform

Vol. 1, figs. 30–33b, 41–43, 53–61, 75–76, 234–37, 321, 333, 380.
See also Vol. 1, pp. 47–49, 65, 137–46, 164, 221, 236.

The main altar was used for burnt offerings of sheep or goat, young cattle, and grains (Chs. 11 and 12). It had three main building phases, and final repair (as described in Ch. 2). The first phase was an approximately square altar (1.45 × 1.38 m, h. c. 1.75 m). The remains of burnt bones were found in this, including in the lower part under the pounded lime floor (fig. 33a), which was approximately two courses above the floor (GJ 10 March). This first altar was repaired a number of times. The bones would have been dropped into the cavity of it through a slot in the top.

In the second phase (Period 2, first half of the 2nd century AD), the altar was enlarged around

FIG. 10.2 *No. 3. West Altar,* in situ *base, with repaired paving, looking north-west.*

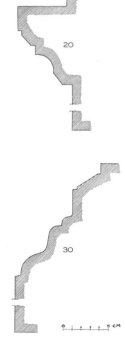

FIG. 10.3A *No. 3. West Altar, showing depth of foundation, view to west wall of Inner Temenos Enclosure.*

FIG. 10.3B *No. 3. West Altar, profile drawing of crown and base mouldings.*

the south, west, and north sides and given a flight of stairs on the west side so that the top could be reached. The cult statues were placed in the new decorative niche at the front of it (fig. 75). This was at the same time (Period 2) that the main construction of the rest of the sanctuary was undertaken (the Inner Temenos Enclosure, the colonnaded Court, and rooms off it).

In the third phase (Period 3, probably in the 3rd century), in association with other repairs after an earthquake, the Altar Platform was further expanded around three sides and decorated at the front with the pilasters with personifications of the zodiac and other decoration (fig. 234). It was given a new staircase, beginning on the south side, to the top where there would probably have been an altar on top of the platform. After a further earthquake, which also damaged the colonnades of the Court, the steps of the Altar Platform were repaired using column drums. That it was still used for burnt offerings in its final phase, up to the mid-4th century, is indicated by the discovery of burnt bones in the Inner Temenos Enclosure and carbonized wheat behind the male cult statue, buried under the collapse caused by the AD 363 earthquake.

2. North-East Altar

Vol. 1, figs. 178–79, 402. *DD* pl. 91.
GJ 4 April; FAN p. 8.

The altar in the north-east corner of the Forecourt is large enough to have been used for burnt offerings of animals. It only survived at the level of its foundations. The first (surviving) version of it was 2.0 m square. After the paving around it was *in situ*, it was subsequently enlarged by 0.45 m on the north, east, and west sides indicating that it faced south onto the Forecourt.

3. West Altar

Figs. 10.2–10.3b; Vol. 1, figs. 177, 403. *DD* 155, 512, pl. 114a–c.
Dimensions, excluding mouldings: l. 0.58 m; w. 0.485 m (FFN).

The West Altar is only slightly larger than the incense altars from in front of the main Altar

Platform, so that it could have been used for small burnt food offerings or incense. It stands on two blocks which go below the level of the paving which Glueck considered was repaired to accommodate it, although he considers this was probably a repair in Period 3 (*DD* 155). It was decorated on the west side with a thunderbolt motif in a bevelled frame. The plinth was decorated with a cyma recta and an astragal, and the altar crowned with a cavetto between two bevelled mouldings (fig. 10.3b).

Incense Altars Engaged against Walls

4. Alexander Amrou Altar

Figs. 10.4a–d, 364. *DD* 125, pls. 187a–b, 188a–b.
Limestone. h. 0.55 m; w. 0.31 m; d. 0.29 m.
Locus: found near the centre of the east side of the Altar Platform. GR no. 19; GJ 2 March. JAM no. J.3263, M38.1220.

This altar is decorated on three sides with figures framed by pilasters. On the front, a partially draped male holds a sceptre in his right hand and a thunderbolt in his left hand. On each side, there is a Nike (winged Victory) holding a wreath and a palm, and with her hair in a top-knot. On the front between the horns/acoteria decorated with palmettes is an inscription: [ALEXA]NDROS AMROU (NΔPOC AMPOV), i.e., "Alexander, son of 'Amr," which combines a classical name with a Semitic one. Traces of burnt frankincense or similar compound survived in the recess at the top (Chemist's report 30 July 1938): "The fragrant odours developed by the burning of the [black] stuff on a platinum foil were similar to that of frankincense (*olibanum*). … The big altar has an appreciable amount of charred incense, that provides an indication of incomplete burning and a sufficient explanation of the greasy appearance of the stone around the remnants of the incense, where the resin of frankincense has been melted and re-solidified without being burnt." The altar was thoroughly cleaned for the exhibition *Petra: Lost City of Stone* in 2003, removing most of the black deposit.

The back face is plain and unfinished, indicating that this altar stood against a wall. Presumably because it was found near the centre of the east side of

FIG. 10.4A   *No. 4. Alexander Amrou altar, showing incense remains on top.*

FIG. 10.4B   *No. 4. Alexander Amrou altar, front, with figure of god.*

the Altar Platform (GJ 2 March), Glueck (*DD* 125) suggested that it stood on one of the two plinths in front of the niche for the cult statues. From its size, it would appear to have stood on the south one (CAM no. 246) (Vol. 1, figs. 53, 321), i.e., beside the male cult statue, while no. 5 below (which is slightly larger), would have stood on the slightly larger north plinth beside the goddess (fig. 10.1). These plinths themselves are upside-down old altar bases sunk into the paving (*DD* 125).

5. Circular Altar

Fig. 10.5a–d. *DD* 447, pl. 189a–b.
Limestone. h. 0.38 m; w. 0.33 m; d. 0.27 m; w. of right-hand panel 0.24 m; w. of left-hand panel 0.27 m; h. of right-hand figure 0.255 m.

Locus: found in debris in front of the Altar Platform. GR no. 65. CAM no. 212.

This altar of an asymmetrical circular shape is broken at the back. There appears to be a hollowed-out indentation at the back. It has two panels between engaged columns. The defaced figure on the left, with feet broken off, has a halo behind traces of a radiate crown and is holding a torch in its right hand (attributes of the Greek sun god Helios). The long thin object in its left hand is damaged. This figure is wearing long sleeves and a cloak (both sometimes worn by Helios), but it is also wearing the female attire of a peplos like the Nike (winged Victory) beside it. This Nike is holding up a wreath in her left-hand (with her arm held across her chest) and a palm in her right hand. This composition is identical to the Nike on the

FIG. 10.4C *No. 4. Alexander Amrou altar, left-hand side, with Nike.*

FIG. 10.4D *No. 4. Alexander Amrou altar, right-hand side, with Nike.*

left-hand side of the Alexander Amrou altar (fig. 10.4c), which also has similar treatment of the feet (frontal and side on). On this one, her head and part of her wreath are damaged.

This altar was found in debris in front of the Altar Platform (GR 9 March no. 65). It is highly probable that it was made at about the same time as the Alexander Amrou altar (no. 4 above) for the north plinth (fig. 58) beside the female cult statue (fig. 10.1). Both of these altars appear to date to Period 2. However, as the plinths on which they stand are in front of the Period 3 decoration (fig. 234), they would have been re-installed after the Period 3 extensions to the Altar Platform.

Glueck (*DD* 509, pl. 190a) suggests that the fragment of the Nike in fig. 287 (CAM no. 280) came from a similar round altar, which its size (h. 0.15 m, w. max. 0.22 m) suggests is possible.

6. Matīʿel altar

Figs. 9.4a–d, 10.6a–b; Vol. 1, fig. 39b. *DD* 509–10, pl. 194a–c. Ch. 9, above, inscription no. 4.
Limestone. h. 0.47 m; w. 0.22 m; th. 0.22 m.
Locus: provenience unknown. Removed by ʿAbdullah Rīhānī Bey, prior to excavation. CAM no. 228.

FIG. 10.5A–D   *No. 5. Circular altar (CAM 212): a. back (broken surface) and left-hand side; b. left-hand panel, with female figure holding torches; c. right-hand panel, with Nike; d. right-hand panel and back.*

FIG. 10.6A–B   *No. 6. Matīʿel altar (CAM 228): a. front and right-hand side; b. left-hand side and back.*

Horned altar with plain columns (without capitals) on corners and three inscribed lines, instead of mouldings, along the top and two along the bottom. Below the bottom band it is slightly recessed. The top is broken so that the two horns above the inscription are broken off, as is part of a third horn. The panel between the columns on the left-hand side is inscribed in Nabataean: "Which Matīʿel son of (?) … (ʿAw)tʾel for the Ḥawarawite." This inscription, which indicates the altar itself was an offering, is dated to the late 1st century BC (see Ch. 9, inscription no. 4). It had a recessed basin in the top (with no traces of burning).

This altar was recovered from the site by ʿAbdullah Rīḥānī Bey, as it was photographed by Glueck at Rīḥānī Bey's house in Tafileh in 1936

where he also photographed the "Fish Goddess" (GA photos. 356–59).

7. Small Horned Altar

Fig. 10.7. *DD* 510, pl. 192b.
Limestone. h. 0.36 m; w. 0.24 m; th. 0.18 m.
Whereabouts unknown February 2010.
Locus: provenience unknown. PAM no. M38.1219.

Small rectangular altar with horns carved in relief and a classical moulding round the base and a concave moulding below the horns. There was a circular depression in the top, apparently with no trace of burning (*DD* 510). Part of the top, including two horns, is broken away. The back is plain and not worked, indicating that it was placed against a wall.

FIG. 10.8 *No. 8. Fragment of small circular altar, with pilasters (CAM 290).*

← FIG. 10.7 *No. 7. Small horned altar.*

Free-Standing Incense Altars

8. Fragment of Small Circular Altar with Pilasters

Fig. 10.8. *DD* 509, pl. 191c.
Limestone. h. 0.21 m; w. 0.33 m; th. 0.085 m.
Locus: provenience unknown. CAM no. 290.

Fragment of a small circular altar with pilasters. The left-hand pilaster had a smaller niche inside it (of which the top of the right-hand pilaster survives). The top and bottom of the altar are broken away, as is over half of one side.

9. House-Shaped Perforated Incense Burner

Fig. 10.9a–c. *DD* 511–12, pl. 192a.
Fine limestone. h. 0.205 m; w. 0.18 m; l. 0.23 m; th. of perforated sides 0.04 m; diam. of holes 0.075 m. Locus: found in the north-west end of the Forecourt. GR no. 44. CAM no. 237.

Glueck, and Joe Greene (pers. comm.), considered CAM no. 239 probably comes from it (h. 0.10 m, w. 0.10 m, d. of solid portion 0.04 m, d. of perforated portion 0.03 m, diam. of holes 0.075 m).

This is the top and part of the sides of an incense burner shaped like a house (or casket/sarcophagus) with a gabled roof (or lid). It seems to have been open at the front and with holes drilled in recessed panels in the sides and back. There is a recess in the top, in the "ridge of the roof" and with no signs of burning, which was probably for unburnt incense.

10. Small Plain Square Incense Altar with Four Triangular Legs

Fig. 10.10a–b. *DD* 511, pl. 193b.
Limestone. h. 0.105 m; w. 0.12 m; d. 0.065 m.
Locus 7: found inside the Altar Platform with burnt bones. GR no. 68; GJ 10 March. CAM no. 291 (previously PAM no. 38.1218).

This small square incense altar had plain sides with an incised line c. 0.01 m below the top. It had a triangle cut into each side to create the legs. A deep square basin with curved sides was cut in the top. One half of the altar is broken off. It retains blackening from fire and was also reddened by fire to a considerable depth below the surface. The traces of burning are from "incense of an oleoresinous

FIG. 10.9A–C *No. 9. House-shaped perforated incense burner (CAM 237): a. back view, showing recess in ridge of roof; b. right-hand side view; c. back and right-hand side from below.*

variety," which when heated produced odours similar to frankincense (Chemist's report 30 July 1938).

This altar is like examples made of clay and stone found in Petra (*DD* pl. 193d centre and right). Half its size, the Petra examples have similar legs, and one has a similar incised line below its rim. They were also found in the Petra "Great Temple" (D. G. Barrett, pers. comm.). They are related to earlier examples from the Iron Age at Tell el-Kheleifeh (*DD* pl. 193e; Roche 1999: 66). The Khirbet et-Tannur example is described by Glueck as found in the Altar Platform with burnt bones, but it is not clear if this was in the sealed layer below the pounded lime floor with the earliest pottery at the site (probably 2nd century BC; see Ch. 18, p. 209).

11. Small Low Square Incense Altar with Cross-Pattern

Fig. 10.11a–b. *DD* 510–11, pl. 193c.
? sandstone; h. 0.035 m; w. 0.07 m.
Locus: provenience unknown. PAM no. M38.2242; whereabouts unknown February 2010.

This low altar has a deep rectangular basin and low feet. It has a decoration of two diagonally placed crosses on the sides. One side and two feet

are broken away. The inside has slight traces of reddening from burning within.

12. Deep Basin Incense Altar

Fig. 10.12. *DD* 510, pl. 192c.
Limestone. h. 0.20 m; w. 0.17 m; th. 0.16 m.
Locus: provenience unknown. CAM no. 279.

This completely plain, roughly cut, incense altar has a deep basin in the top, blackened by fire.

FIG. 10.10A–B *No. 10. Small plain square incense altar with triangular legs (CAM 291), with remains of incense visible in (a).*

FIG. 10.11A–B *No. 11. Small low square incense altar, with cross-pattern.*

FIG. 10.12 *No. 12. Deep basin incense altar (CAM 279).*

FIG. 10.13A–B   *No. 13. Incense altar, shaped like an Ionic capital with corner volutes (CAM 232), with slight circular recess for incense visible in (b).*

FIG. 10.14A–B   *No. 14. Four-legged square base of ? small altar (CAM 234), from above and underside.*

13. Incense Altar Shaped Like Ionic Capital

Fig. 10.13.a–b. *DD* 229, pl. 191a.
Fine limestone. h. 0.23 m; w. max. 0.16 m.
Locus: provenience unknown. GR no. 11. CAM no. 232.

Incense altar in the form of an Ionic column. There is a circular depression, c. 0.08 m in diameter, in the top. The capital has four corner volutes, of which one is broken and one damaged. The column splays out in a slow curve towards the bottom which is broken off.

Possible Incense Altar

14. Four-Legged Square Base ? of Small Altar

Fig. 10.14a–b. *DD* 511, pl. 193a.
Limestone. w. 0.180 m; th. 0.185 m; h. 0.115 m.
Locus: provenience unknown. CAM no. 234.

Stand with a classical moulding and four square legs (0.06 m square) of which one is broken off. On the top side, there are three circular depressions on three corners. On the fourth corner, there is a 1 cm high base of a pillar which is apparently broken off.

Notes

1   We are grateful to the late Glenn Markoe for checking dimensions and details of the altars in Cincinnati Art Museum.
2   We are grateful to Hannah Wellman for collating the records of incense altars, and possible ones, from the records of Glueck's Tell el-Kheleifeh excavations and objects in the Glueck Archive in the Semitic Museum, Harvard University. Excavation Registry no. 7090 there, made of "silty chalk" with a circular hollow, seems to be a small mortar.

References

Aharoni, Y.
1974   "The Horned Altar of Beer-sheba." *Biblical Archaeologist* 37: 2–6.

Arnaud, P.
1986   "Les Naiskoi en Syrie Méridionale." Pp. 373–86 in *Hauran I: recherches archéologiques sur la Syrie du Sud à l'époque hellénistique et romaine, deuxième partie*, ed. J.-M. Dentzer. Paris.

Augé, C., and Linant de Bellefonds, P.
2004   "Naiskoi." P. 427 in *Thesaurus Cultus et Rituum Antiquorum I*. Los Angeles, CA.

Biran, A.
1974   "An Israelite Horned Altar at Dan." *Biblical Archaeologist* 37: 106–107.

Bowerman, H. C.
1913   *Roman Sacrificial Altars*. Lancaster, PA.

Chambon, A.; al-Muheisen, Z.; Janif, M. M.; and Villeneuve, F.
2002   *Khirbet edh-Dharih: des Nabatéens au premier Islam*. Amman.

Cohen, R., and Yisrael, Y.
1995   *On the Road to Edom: Discoveries from 'En Hazeva*. Jerusalem.

Dentzer, J.-M., and Dentzer-Feydy, J.
1991   *Le Djebel al-'Arab*. Paris.

Dentzer-Feydy, J.
2003   "Mobilier cultuel." Pp. 103–104 in *Hauran II: les installations de Si' 8*, eds. J. Dentzer-Feydy, J.-M. Dentzer, and P.-M. Blanc. Beirut.

Gitin, S.
1989   "Incense Altars from Ekron, Israel, and Judah: Context and Typology." *Eretz-Israel* 20: 52–67.

Hassell, J.
2005   "A Re-examination of the Cuboid Incense-
       burning Altars from Flinders Petrie's
       Palestinian Excavations at Tell Jemmeh."
       Levant 37: 133–62.

Healey, J. F.
2001   *The Religion of the Nabataeans: A Con-
       spectus*. Religions in the Graeco-Roman
       World 136. Leiden.

Hellenkemper Salies, G.
1981   *Die Nabatäer*. Bonn.

King, P. J., and Stager, L. E.
2001   *Life in Biblical Israel*. London and
       Louisville, KY.

Lamon, R. S., and Shipton, G. M.
1939   *Megiddo I*. Chicago, IL.

Loud, G.
1948   *Megiddo II*. Chicago, IL.

Mazar, A.
1992   *Archaeology of the Land of the Bible:
       10,000–586 B.C.E.* London and New York,
       NY.

McKenzie, J. S.
2001   "Keys from Egypt and the East: Observa-
       tions on Nabataean Culture in the Light
       of Recent Discoveries." *Bulletin of the
       American Schools of Oriental Research*
       324: 97–112.

Patrich, J.
1990   *The Formation of Nabataean Art*.
       Jerusalem.

Roche, M.-J.
1999   "Khirbet et-Tannûr et les contacts entre
       Édomites et Nabatéens. Une nouvelle ap-
       proche." *Transeuphratène* 18: 59–69.

Starcky, J.
1966   "Pétra et la Nabatène." Cols. 886–1017 in
       Dictionnaire de la Bible, ed. H. Cazelles et
       al. Supplément 7. Paris.

Yavis, C. G.
1949   *Greek Altars: Origins and Typology*. Saint
       Louis, MO.

Chapter 11

The Animal Bones

by Sarah Whitcher Kansa

INTRODUCTION

The animal bone assemblage from the 1937 excavations at Khirbet et-Tannur, in the Glueck Archive in the Semitic Museum, Harvard University, consists of a small number of highly fragmented, burnt, and ashy bones. The degree of burning is such that many bones are porous and powdery and have lost many of their diagnostic features. Nevertheless, the assemblage provides some insights into the use of space and selection of taxa in ritual activities which took place at this Nabataean sanctuary from the 2nd century BC through to the mid-4th century AD. The full dataset is published and available for download in Open Context (Kansa 2013).

METHODS

The author analyzed the animal bones from Khirbet et-Tannur at the Zooarchaeology Laboratory of the Peabody Museum at Harvard University. Dr Richard Meadow, the director of the Zooarchaeology Laboratory, generously provided workspace and access to the laboratory's extensive skeletal reference collection which includes specimens from a variety of Near Eastern fauna sufficient for the comparative needs of this project.

Every bone and tooth fragment from Khirbet et-Tannur received an identification number. These numbers were documented on an Excel spreadsheet, along with a detailed record of taxon, element, fragment size, side, age, and burning. Identifications were made using the skeletal reference collection. Measurements were taken, where possible, according to von den Driesch (1976).

Data presented here are based on NISP (Number of Identified Specimens). Due to the highly fragmentary state of the assemblage, no elements were found to articulate or pair. NISP statistics do not reflect the actual number of animals represented by this assemblage. Instead, NISP counts are best suited for determining the relative proportion of various types of taxa, elements, and frequency of observed cut marks, burning, etc. For comparison, MNI (Minimum Number of Individuals) counts are used on a contextual level. Sheep and goat bones are notoriously difficult to distinguish. For this reason, the majority of the sheep and goat bones are included in the broader category "sheep/goat." When diagnostic parts were present, the distinction was made following morphological and metri-

73

cal criteria described by Boessneck et al. (1964), Boessneck (1969), and Prummel and Frisch (1986).

RESULTS

The Khirbet et-Tannur sanctuary assemblage contained 255 fragments, the majority of which (73%) came from Locus 7 (inside the Altar Platform).[1] Of these 255 fragments, 57 were identifiable to species and element (Table 11.1). The remaining 80% of the fragments were only identifiable to a size category (Table 11.2). A 20% identification rate is not surprising, given that the amount of burning has caused the bones to be highly friable and fragmented. In fact, over 200 bones, or 80% of the assemblage, are burnt (Vol. 1, fig. 394) and consist of fragments less than one quarter of the original bone size. The average length of the 255 fragments is less than three centimeters, and the average weight is 1.7 grams.

Table 11.1 lists the 57 bones identified to genus and/or species and element. The assemblage is dominated by sheep (*Ovis aries*) and goat (*Capra hircus*), which together make up 84.1% of the identified portion of the assemblage. Goats are almost twice as numerous as sheep. Notably, at Khirbet edh-Dharih there were twice as many goats as sheep (Lepetz, unpublished report), while in the Nabataean levels at ez-Zantur in Petra sheep were twice as common as goats (Studer 2007: 254). At Khirbet et-Tannur five identified cattle (*Bos taurus*) bones make up 8.8% of the assemblage, and four bird bones make up 7.1%. The only bird species identified is chicken (*Gallus gallus*). Sex could only be determined for one bone in the entire assemblage, a female chicken lacking a spur on the tarsometatarsus. The sheep/goat and cattle bones in the assemblage contained none of the diagnostic features commonly used to determine sex (such as horn core size or pelvis morphology).

In cases where bones could not be identified to genus and/or species and element, they were assigned to a general size class, such as "large mammal" (see Table 11.2). However, in light of the very narrow range of taxa present in the identified portion of the assemblage (predominantly sheep/goat and cattle), it is likely that most of these unidentified fragments come from these taxa as well. It is possible that other taxa, such as gazelles, donkeys, pigs, and camels were part of this assemblage but have not been identified due to the highly fragmented nature of the material. Indeed, a much wider range of taxa was found 70 km to the south, in the Nabataean capital Petra in the ez-Zantur excavation, a fact perhaps explained by the much larger assemblage (5,148 identified bones of mammals, birds, and fish) (Studer 1996). However, it is also likely that the range of taxa exploited at

Table 11.1   Identified taxa at Khirbet et-Tannur.

TAXON	COMMON NAME	NISP	PERCENT
Bos taurus	Cattle	5	8.8
Ovis aries / Capra hircus	Sheep / Goat	32	56.1
Ovis aries	Sheep	6	10.5
Capra hircus	Goat	10	17.5
Gallus gallus	Chicken	3	5.3
Other bird	Bird	1	1.8
Total		57	100

Table 11.2 Unidentified bone fragments from Khirbet et-Tannur.

Size group	NISP	Percent
Large mammal	38	19.2
Large ungulate	6	3.0
Medium-large mammal	2	1.0
Medium-large ungulate	1	0.5
Medium mammal	120	60.6
Medium ungulate	26	13.1
Small-medium mammal/bird	5	2.5
Total	198	100

Khirbet et-Tannur is restricted due to the ritual nature of the site. If animals or animal parts were brought to the site as offerings, non-food animals such as camels and donkeys may not have been considered appropriate in this context. The relative proportions of the three dominant species at Khirbet et-Tannur are notably similar to those found at the Edomite site of Busayra, where there were 85.8% sheep and goat combined, and 10.4% cattle (Bienkowski 2002: 471).

No pig bones were found at Khirbet et-Tannur, and though this may be owing to the site's location in a hot, arid environment, other factors may account for their absence, especially as a small quantity of them was found at nearby Khirbet edh-Dharih (Lepetz, unpublished report). Indeed, though the faunal assemblage from the "Great Temple" at Petra produced a mere 2% pig bones during the Nabataean period, the subsequent Roman and Byzantine periods produced 13%, suggesting that dietary preferences, social, or economic factors may account for the exploitation of pigs rather than just environmental conditions. At the "Great Temple," it was concluded that pigs were not a typical component of the "Nabataean diet" at Petra, which was characterized by species suitable to mobile lifestyles, such as goats and camels (Kansa, in press).

The absence of fish remains in the Khirbet et-Tannur assemblage is of interest and was also observed at nearby Khirbet edh-Dharih (Lepetz, unpublished report). In Late Roman (4th-century) levels at ez-Zantur in Petra, fish made a significant contribution to the diet (their bones comprised 11% of the animal bone assemblage). However, in Nabataean contexts at ez-Zantur, fish made up a mere 2% of the animal bone assemblage, leading the authors to question whether this reflects an insignificant contribution of fish to the Nabataean economy or another factor such as sampling bias (Desse-Berset and Studer 1996; Studer 2007: 253 figs. 1, 262–63). At the "Great Temple," we see the opposite pattern, where Nabataean contexts contained 5.2% fish remains and Roman less than 2%. The complete absence of fish remains from the Khirbet et-Tannur assemblage supports the low numbers of fish at ez-Zantur, but may also result from collection strategies, destruction of tiny fish bones with burning, or a preference for only certain types of animals as offerings. At the Monastery of St Aaron on Jabal Haroun, near Petra, the fact that in the late 5th and 6th centuries half of the bones found are from fish, especially parrotfish, is related to the function of that site (Studer 2001: 385; 2002: 169–70).

The Contexts

The Khirbet et-Tannur animal bones come from seven different contexts, each with a corresponding Locus number (locations marked on fig. 6.2) and Glueck Archive Unit number (see Table 11.3). The places these samples were found were focused inside the Inner Temenos Enclosure, including the Altar Platform and two of the in-floor offertory boxes (Vol. 1, figs. 395, 398–99, 401), and Room 14. The whereabouts of the specimens from two further areas where Glueck mentions in his excavation journal (GJ) finding bones is unknown, as these are not in the Glueck Archive: burnt bones in Room 8, a triclinium (GJ 2 April), and bones under the back of the Altar Platform beneath the earlier floor level (GJ 11 April).

The site produced an NISP of 255, counting all fragments, none of which were observed to pair or

Table 11.3   Minimum Number of Individuals at Khirbet et-Tannur (by context).

LOCUS	LOCATION	GLUECK ARCHIVE UNIT	DATE IN EXCAVATION JOURNAL, 1937	NISP	MNI	MNI PER TAXON, ELEMENT USED
1	W part of Inner Temenos Enclosure	4A-05	4 March on label	15	1	1 *Ovis/Capra,* femur
3	NE offertory box	4A-11	3 and 8 March	5	2	1 *Ovis/Capra,* radius; 1 Bird, long bone
4	W offertory box	4A-10	8 March (also on label)	14	3	2 *Ovis/Capra,* humerus; 1 *Gallus gallus,* tarso-metatarsus
6	In front of Altar Platform	4A-01	?10 March	3	1	1 *Ovis/Capra,* mandible
7	Inside Altar Platform	4A-20	10 March (also on label)	184	6	4 *Ovis/Capra,* calcaneus; 2 *Bos taurus,* petrous (cranial bone)
7	Bottom of inside Altar Platform	4A-24	10 March	1	1	1 *Gallus gallus,* tibiotarsus
21	Room 14	47-21	7 December	33	4	3 *Ovis/Capra,* astragalus; 1 *Gallus gallus,* radius

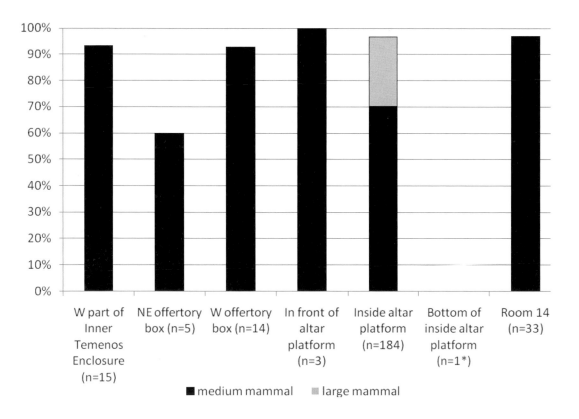

FIG. 11.1 *Distribution of medium-sized and large-sized mammal bones in different contexts at Khirbet et-Tannur. (Note: "Medium mammal" counts include sheep and goats; "large mammal" counts include cattle.*
* The sole specimen from this context is a chicken leg bone.)

Table 11.4   Identified bones at Khirbet et-Tannur (by context).

Locus	Location	Glueck Archive Unit	No. of bones Identified	Total in context	% Identified
1	W part of Inner Temenos Enclosure	4A-05	1	15	7%
3	NE offertory box	4A-11	3	5	60%
4	W offertory box	4A-10	14	14	100%
6	In front of Altar Platform	4A-01	2	3	67%
7	Inside Altar Platform	4A-20	22	185	12%
7	Bottom of inside Altar Platform	4A-24	1	1	100%
21	Room 14	47-21	14	33	42%

articulate. The state of fragmentation of the bones prohibited refitting; however, it is likely that many of these fragments came from the same bones. As a result of the poor preservation, there is an overall MNI of only 18 individuals, a number that certainly would be higher if the bones were not so highly fragmented.

All the contexts are dominated by sheep and goat. Fig. 11.1 shows the proportions of medium mammal (including sheep/goat and medium ungulate) in each context. For all but one context (Locus 7), medium mammal bones make up nearly 100% of the assemblage (those from Loci 3 and 6 should be disregarded because of small sample size).

A few interesting observations can be made about Locus 7, which contained the majority of the bones in the assemblage (73%). Locus 7 represents two contexts of bones recovered from the Altar Platform: 184 bones come from GA Unit 4A-20, inside the Altar Platform "under the pounded lime floor" (GJ 10 March) (visible in Vol. 1, fig. 33), and one bone (a chicken tibiotarsus) comes from GA Unit 4A-24, the bottom of the Altar Platform. To facilitate discussion, these two contexts from Locus 7 are considered together.

Given that the majority of the assemblage comes from Locus 7, we would expect Locus 7's MNI to be higher, but this context actually has the lowest percentage of identifiable bones (Table 11.4). This is

owing to the poor preservation and high fragmentation of the bones in this context due to burning. In fact, the context contained a large amount of ashy powder from the crumbling bones. The MNI would certainly be higher in this context if more bones were identifiable to taxon, element, and side.

Locus 7 is the only context that shows notable differences with the other contexts. As mentioned above, all contexts except for Locus 7 contain nearly exclusively sheep/goat and medium mammal bones (presumably also sheep/goat). However, while Locus 7 contains about 70% sheep/goat and medium mammal, the remaining 30% is almost all cattle and large mammal. This is the only context containing cattle bones and, just as significantly, all the bones for which age could be determined are from calves (see *Kill-Off Patterns* below). The presence of cattle bones *only* in the Altar Platform suggests a special role for cattle in the ritual activities at Khirbet et-Tannur. Further indication of the importance of cattle is found in the representation of a young bull beside the cult statue of the god, which stood in the niche in front of the Altar Platform (Vol. 1, figs. 75, 86).

Kill-Off Patterns

Zooarchaeologists commonly use two methods to determine the age of death of animals, tooth

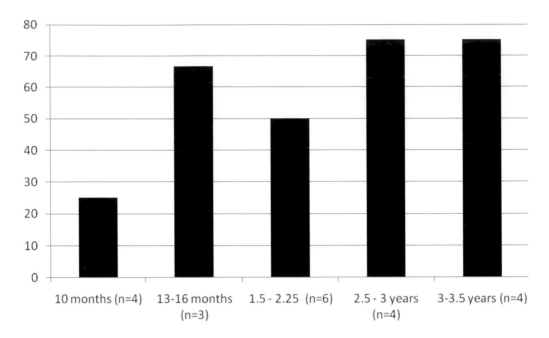

FIG. 11.2 *Sheep/goat age of death at Khirbet et-Tannur (showing percent killed within each age category).*

eruption and wear, and fusion stages. This study relies on the latter method. While less informative than tooth eruption and wear, it is required in this case in light of the near absence of mandibles, maxillae, and loose teeth in the Khirbet et-Tannur assemblage. Animals reach skeletal maturity at more or less predictable rates. Specifically, the ends of bones (epiphyses) affix, or "fuse," to the shaft at different stages in the animal's growth. By observing the state of fusion, we can tell if an animal was younger or older than a certain age at the time of death.

Fig. 11.2 shows the numbers of fused and unfused bones for sheep and goat from all contexts at Khirbet et-Tannur. Five different age categories are shown, and the black bars represent the percent of animals killed at that age or younger for each age group (i.e., the black bars represent the percent of unfused bones in each age category). The kill-off patterns show that nearly all the specimens are from young animals, with very few animals surviving into adulthood, in contrast to the Nabataean levels at ez-Zantur in Petra (Studer 2007: 254–56). In each age category, unfused bones are nearly twice as common as fused bones. Although this is

a very small sample size, the predominance of juveniles is interesting because of the fragmentary state of the assemblage. With this state of preservation we would expect to find fewer juveniles and more adults because adult bones are more durable, and this differential preservation should over-represent adults in the assemblage.

While there are very few cattle bones in the Khirbet et-Tannur assemblage, those present are all from calves. If we lump together the "large ungulate" bones (which are most likely cattle, as there is no other large ungulate identified in the assemblage), all eight bones for which age could be determined are unfused, including a distal humerus, a bone that fuses very early, within the first eighteen months (Silver 1969). The MNI for cattle is two, based on two complete left petrous bones (part of the cranium). It is possible, therefore, that the cattle bones at the site represent only two individuals.

Unfortunately, a larger sample of bones and teeth is needed to determine the time of the year during which these offerings were made. For example, we know that the calf with the unfused distal humerus was killed before reaching eighteen months of age,

Table 11.5 Burning on bones from Khirbet et-Tannur.

Locus	Location	Glueck Archive Unit	No. of Burnt Bones	Total no. of Bones	% of Bones Burnt
1	W part of Inner Temenos Enclosure	4A-05	14	15	93%
3	NE offertory box	4A-11	0	5	0%
4	W offertory box	4A-10	0	14	0%
6	In front of Altar Platform	4A-01	0	3	0%
7	Inside Altar Platform	4A-20	179	184	97%
7	Bottom of inside Altar Platform	4A-24	0	1	0%
21	Room 14	47-21	18	33	55%

but we cannot determine when exactly during those first eighteen months it was killed.

Body Part Representation

Dividing the carcass up into head, back, forelimb, hindlimb, and feet for the primary taxa, it is clear that all body parts are present across the assemblage. However, there are slightly lower numbers of cranial bones, teeth, and toes than would be expected if whole animals were present. This is not surprising, as fragile cranial bones and tiny toes probably did not survive the burning and subsequent fragmentation. However, teeth are very durable with a high mineral component and should have survived burning. Loose teeth are also more numerous when compared to the other elements of the skeleton, so we would expect them to be present. Their low representation suggests that: (1) in modern times, teeth were not collected by the archaeologists, or (2) in ancient times, teeth were either destroyed in the fire or some offerings were selected carcass parts rather than whole animals.

Interestingly, the small number of cattle bones from the site include three petrous bones. The petrous, a very hard cranial bone, is more likely to survive burning and crushing than other bones

and is commonly found in cremation remains (Mays 1998: 214). The presence of petrous bones would lead us to assume that whole calves (not just meaty parts) were taken to the altar complex on the hoof. However, in addition to the preserved petrous bones, we would also expect to find many cattle teeth (they are even harder than the petrous and far more numerous). On the contrary, of the eleven cattle and large ungulate bones, there is only one tooth fragment, an unexpected observation that cannot be explained by this small assemblage.

Burning

Of the Khirbet et-Tannur assemblage 83% has burning. Of the burnt bones 75% are burnt to a light grey-blue or white color, indicating that they were in contact with a hot fire (Shipman et al. 1984). Burning occurs differentially in the different contexts (Table 11.5). There is no burning on the few bones from Loci 3, 4, and 6. Loci 3 and 4 are the north-east and west offertory boxes, respectively. Locus 6 is in front of the Altar Platform.

However, nearly all the bones from Loci 1 and 7 are burnt (fig. 394). These loci correspond to the Altar Platform and the Inner Temenos Enclosure, respectively. It is, therefore, not surprising that the highest burning is seen on the Altar Platform and the second highest in the area around the Altar Platform. Burning, which destroys the organic component of bone, makes the bone highly friable and difficult to identify. It is not surprising, then, that Loci 1 and 7 have the highest percentage bones that could not be identified to genus/species and element, with 12% and 7%, respectively, compared to an average of 67% across the rest of the contexts (Table 11.4).

Nearly all the burning on the Khirbet et-Tannur bones was to the most advanced state, calcination. Of the burnt bones 74% are calcined or partly calcined, indicating that the bones were in direct contact with fire. Bone burnt to this extreme is very brittle and easily turns to powder (Stiner et al. 1995), an observation made on the Locus 7 material.

Butchery and Fragmentation

Related to their high amount of burning, Loci 1 and 7 also have the highest fragmentation. Of bones in these two contexts, 90% and 100% respectively, are less than one quarter complete, compared to an average of 60% for all other contexts.

All bones have jagged breaks, indicating they were broken after they were dry. This is not surprising, given the way bone becomes so friable when it is burnt. The bones were probably mostly broken after deposition, upon excavation, and in transport, storage, and analysis. No fresh breaks or cut marks could be observed that would indicate that these animals were butchered.

DISCUSSION

The animal bone assemblage from Khirbet et-Tannur, while small, permits some interesting observations on the role of animals in a Nabataean sanctuary context. Not surprisingly, the evidence points to non-subsistence activities involving animals. However, in order for an animal bone deposit to stand out as special (as compared to the "mundane" refuse of daily meals), it must meet certain and numerous criteria regarding location, context, and modification. Some of the criteria used by zooarchaeologists when exploring the

role of animals in ritual include: (1) animal bones found in association with human remains; (2) whole animals, or articulated portions of animals; (3) selection of a particular side; (4) selection of a particular sex; (5) a narrow range of species; (6) selection of a particular age; (7) selection of particular body parts (criteria based on Horwitz 1987).

The first three criteria cannot be met with this assemblage. There were no identified human bones in association with any of these remains. Additionally, there is no evidence that whole or articulated parts of animals were present in the assemblage. Finally, there is no preference for side: the assemblage produced exactly 37 left and 37 right-sided bones. The fourth criterion, a narrow range of sex, cannot be determined because of the highly fragmented nature of the assemblage; no bones could be determined to be male or female except for one female chicken bone.

The Khirbet et-Tannur assemblage meets the last three criteria. There is a narrow range of species, specifically sheep/goat, cattle, and chickens, common sacrificial animals of this period (Toplyn 1994: 236). The Khirbet et-Tannur assemblage also shows a selection of specific ages. Kill-off of sheep/goat and cattle is clearly focused on juvenile animals. This preference for young animals probably has to do with the specific type of rite being performed in the sanctuary. Toplyn (1994: 236) points out that a particular size, age, or state of health was not required of animals for sacrifice during this period, and probably had more to do with the type of rite being performed. This choice of young animals at Khirbet et-Tannur may also reflect the needs of the community, where young males were chosen for sacrifice because they were less valuable than animals of optimal meat weight or older females kept for milk or wool. A similar assemblage has been identified in the faunal remains from a Nabataean context at the "Great Temple" at Petra (Kansa, in press), where a high occurrence of burning and fragmentation was associated with an extremely narrow range of species (over 90% sheep/goat) and specific body parts (meat-bearing limb bones). These assemblages contrast with that of the Edomite site of Busayra, where only half of the animals had been killed by age three (Bienkowski 2002: 471).

One of the most compelling features of the Khirbet et-Tannur assemblage is the spatial difference in cattle bone distribution in the altar (Locus 7, GA Unit 4A-20) compared with the rest of the sanctuary. As mentioned above, bones from the altar context are highly fragmented and nearly all of them (97%) are burnt to such an extent that it is evident they were exposed directly to fire. Cattle bones are *only* present in the inside of the Altar Platform. This is a statistically significant observation (as determined by a chi-square test of observed and expected cattle bones found at the Altar Platform and away from the platform, with $\alpha = .05$). This result is even more significant because the bones in the altar area are highly fragmented and unidentifiable, much more so than in the rest of the site. Therefore, if cattle were present (even in low numbers) in the non-altar area, we would expect to easily identify them since the bones are better preserved there.

This clear and significant spatial patterning in the Khirbet et-Tannur assemblage, taken together with the high occurrence of burning in this context, the preference for young animals, and the narrow range of species, provides convincing evidence that this assemblage did, indeed, come from a sanctuary context in which the community undertook non-subsistence activities.

Key Observations

Key observations made on the animal bones from the Nabataean sanctuary at Khirbet et-Tannur include:

- The assemblage shows a very limited range of taxa, with a preponderance of sheep and goat bones and a handful of specimens from cattle and chickens.
- The majority of the bones show heavy burning, indicating direct contact with fire.
- No butchery marks were observed on the bones; however, there is a high degree of fragmentation due to burning that has probably destroyed any evidence of pre-burning butchery.
- The assemblage is dominated by young animals.
- The assemblage, though small, shows marked spatial patterning, with a concentration of cattle bones in the Altar Platform, indicating that cattle played a special role in the rites being performed in this sanctuary.
- There is a surprising lack of cranial and mandibular bones, particularly teeth, which are highly recognizable even when fragmented and would have survived better than most postcranial elements. This suggests that animals may not always have been brought to the sanctuary on the hoof (with the possible exception of cattle). The shortage of toe bones might not be as a result of their lack of survival, but perhaps combined with the shortage of cranial bones and teeth suggest that the sheep and goats were slaughtered either outside the temple complex or that their carcasses were carried up the mountain.

Note

1   After this analysis was completed a few further bones were found, but they do not significantly change the results, as none was of particular interest when examined by the author. These included: GA Unit 48-01 (no provenience) one burnt bone; Unit A-06 (Room 14) one partially burnt bone; Unit A-17 ("Ditch" north of north wall of Inner Temenos Enclosure) four not burnt bones; Unit A-16 (Room 14) one burnt bone and one not burnt bone. Glueck also mentions (GJ 7 December) finding in Room 14 "small animals' bones and animals' teeth," which apparently are not in the Glueck Archive.

Table 11.6   Condensed table of identified animal bones from Khirbet et-Tannur.*

* This condensed table contains the 90 specimens for which "element" could be identified. It does not contain specimens identified as "long bone" or "axial" fragments.

BONE NO.	LOCUS	GA UNIT	LENGTH (MM)	WEIGHT (G)	NISP	TAXON	COMMON NAME	BONE	SKEL AREA	PART	% PRESERVED	SIDE	PROX FUSED?	DIST FUSED?	AGE	SEX
1	21	47-21	78	7.2	1	Ovis/Capra	sheep/goat	radius	upper forelimb	dist shaft	half	L		n		
2	21	47-21	35.4	3.3	1	Capra hircus	goat	phalanx 1	feet	C	complete		n			
3	21	47-21	34.1	2.2	1	Ovis aries	sheep	phalanx 1	feet	nC	75% complete		n			
4	21	47-21	19.9	1.3	1	Ovis/Capra	sheep/goat	metatarsal	feet	dist frag	less than 25%	NA		y		
5	21	47-21	34.9	5.3	1	Capra hircus	goat	metacarpal	feet	dist shaft	25-49%	L		y		
6	21	47-21	44.2	7.9	1	Capra hircus	goat	metacarpal	feet	dist shaft	25-49%	R		y		
7	21	47-21	29.1	4.2	1	Capra hircus	goat	astragalus	feet	nC	75% complete	R				F
8	21	47-21	30.1	4.5	1	Ovis aries	sheep	astragalus	feet	nC	75% complete	R				
9	21	47-21	29.3	4.2	1	Ovis aries	sheep	astragalus	feet	C	complete	L				F
10	21	47-21	20.7	1.6	1	Ovis/Capra	sheep/goat	astragalus	feet	plantar lateral frag	25-49%	R				
11	21	47-21	63.4	0.7	1	Gallus gallus	chicken	radius	upper forelimb	C	complete	L	y	y		
12	21	47-21	25.3	1.9	1	Ovis/Capra	sheep/goat	maxillary tooth	head	M1 or M2		L			adult	
13	21	47-21	29.6	0.7	1	Ovis/Capra	sheep/goat	mandibular tooth	head	Incisor		L				
14	21	47-21	53.2	3.8	1	Ovis/Capra	sheep/goat	mandible	head	artic condyle	less than 25%	R				
34	6	4A-01	NA	0.9	1	Ovis/Capra	sheep/goat	tooth	head	many frags of M?	25-49%	NA				
36	6	4A-01	NA	1.4	1	Ovis/Capra	sheep/goat	mandible	head	ascending ramus frag (behind M3)	less than 25%	L				
37	3	4A-11	55.8	4.2	1	Ovis/Capra	sheep/goat	mandible	head	diastema and I2, I3, C	less than 25%	R			Incisors' root tips are not quite closed	
38	3	4A-11	34.5	2.4	1	Ovis aries	sheep	phalanx 1	feet	nC	75% complete			y		
39	3	4A-11	89.1	4.5	1	Ovis/Capra	sheep/goat	radius	upper forelimb	shaft frag	less than 25%	L				
40	3	4A-11	30.9	0.1	1	Bird	bird	long bone		shaft frag						

BONE NO.	CUT	GNAW	BURNT	OTHER MODIFICATIONS	ARTIC	COMMENTS	M1	M2	M3	M4	M5	M6
1				surface is exfoliating, weathered-looking				SD= 12.7	DD= 7.4		Bd= 26.1(u)	
2			grey				GL= 35.4(u)	Bp= 13.1(u)	Bd= 12.9			
3							GL= 32.8(u)	Bp= 11.3(u)				
4			grey and white									
5											Bd= 28	
6			grey brown								Bd= 27.3	
7			grey and white				GLl= 29.1					
8			grey and white				GLl= 30.3	GLm= 29.6	Bd= 19.3			
9			grey and white				GLl= 29.3	GLm= 27.4	Bd= 19.3			
10			grey and white									
11							GL= 63.4	SD= 3.2	Bp= 5.4	Bd= 6.8		
12												
13												
14			grey brown				condyle =19.8					
34												
36				eroded- looks weathered								
37												
38							GL= 33		Bd= 11.3	SD= 9.2		
39												
40				root etching on shaft								

Table 11.6 (cont.)   Condensed table of identified animal bones from Khirbet et-Tannur.

BONE NO.	LOCUS	GA UNIT	LENGTH (MM)	WEIGHT (G)	NISP	TAXON	COMMON NAME	BONE	SKEL AREA	PART	% PRESERVED	SIDE	PROX FUSED?	DIST FUSED?	AGE	SEX
42	4	4A-10	32.6	7.6	1	Ovis aries	sheep	astragalus	feet	nC	75% complete	R				
43	4	4A-10	62.2	1.6	1	Ovis/Capra	sheep/goat	metatarsal	feet	shaft	half	L		n	young- very small, but mtIII&IV are fused	
44	4	4A-10	78.6	1.9	1	Ovis/Capra	sheep/goat	ulna	upper forelimb	shaft frag	25-49%	L				
45	4	4A-10	57.8	0.9	1	Gallus gallus	chicken	tarsometatarsus	feet	dist shaft	75% complete	L				F (no spur)
46	4	4A-10	36.4	12.8	1	Capra hircus	goat	tibia	upper hindlimb	prox shaft (and unfused epiphysis)	25-49%	L	n			
47	4	4A-10	53.9	19.9	1	Capra hircus	goat	femur	upper hindlimb	dist shaft	25-49%	L		y		
48	4	4A-10	63.4	3.1	1	Ovis/Capra	sheep/goat	rib	back	shaft frag	25-49%	NA				
49	4	4A-10	72.5	8.9	1	Capra hircus	goat	humerus	upper forelimb	shaft	half	L				
50	4	4A-10	67.3	5.1	1	Capra hircus	goat	humerus	upper forelimb	dist shaft	half	R		n		
51	4	4A-10	31.6	4.8	1	Ovis/Capra	sheep/goat	humerus	upper forelimb	dist frag	less than 25%	L		y		
52	4	4A-10	31.8	5.3	1	Ovis/Capra	sheep/goat	humerus	upper forelimb	dist frag	less than 25%	R		y		
53	4	4A-10	27.6	3.5	1	Ovis/Capra	sheep/goat	femur	upper hindlimb	prox frag (caput frag)	less than 25%	L	y (caput)			
54	4	4A-10	30.7	1.7	1	Ovis/Capra	sheep/goat	atlas	back	frag of left prox artic region	less than 25%				young- bone very porous and light	
55	4	4A-10	24.9	0.6	1	Ovis/Capra	sheep/goat	vertebra/cervical	back	caudal epiph	less than 25%			n		
56	1	4A-05	25.4	1.5	1	Ovis/Capra	sheep/goat	femur	upper hindlimb	dist epiph frag (medial epicondyle)	less than 25%	R		n		
58	1	4A-05	16.1	0./	1	Medium ungulate	Medium ungulate	astragalus	feet	caudal frag	less than 25%	R				
59	1	4A-05	12.6	0.3	1	Medium ungulate	Medium ungulate	tibia	upper hindlimb	dist frag	less than 25%	L				
71	7	4A-24	74.1	1.8	1	Gallus gallus	chicken	tibiotarsus	upper hindlimb	shaft	half	R				
75	7	4A-20	25.8	0.9	1	Ovis/Capra	sheep/goat	horn core	head	frag of tip	less than 25%	NA				
189	7	4A-20	43.8	1	1	Medium ungulate	Medium ungulate	mandible	head	angle and artic condyle	less than 25%	R				
190	7	4A-20	21.1	0.8	1	Ovis/Capra	sheep/goat	tibia	upper hindlimb	prox epiph frag (lateral)	less than 25%	L	n			

BONE NO.	CUT	GNAW	BURNT	OTHER MODIFICATIONS	ARTIC	COMMENTS	M1	M2	M3	M4	M5	M6
42	poss cut mark on plantar-caudal	rodent gnawing on borders of medial side					GLl= 32.8	GLm= 30.9	Bd= 19.8			
43		heavy roden gnawing all over shaft					SD= 6.3	DD= 6.3				
44												
45							Bd= 11.7	SD= 4.9				
46									Bp= 44.1			
47										Bd= 40		
48												
49				areas of root etching on shaft				SD= 10.8				
50		rodent gnawing on shaft						SD= 9.8	Bd= 23.3(u)			
51	sliced/chopped cleanly along distal epicondyles			root etching on trochlea								
52		rodent gnawing on all borders of distal										
53	caput sliced? cleanly off						DC= 19.3					
54												
55												
56			dark grey partial									
58			grey and white									
59			grey and white									
71							SD= 5.4					
75			grey and white									
189			white									
190			grey									

Table 11.6 (cont.)　　Condensed table of identified animal bones from Khirbet et-Tannur.

BONE NO.	LOCUS	GA UNIT	LENGTH (MM)	WEIGHT (G)	NISP	TAXON	COMMON NAME	BONE	SKEL AREA	PART	% PRESERVED	SIDE	PROX FUSED?	DIST FUSED?	AGE	SEX
191	7	4A-20	13.4	0.4	1	Medium ungulate	Medium ungulate	tibia	upper hindlimb	dist shaft frag (lateral)	less than 25%	R		n		
192	7	4A-20	22.2	1.5	1	Ovis aries	sheep	tibia	upper hindlimb	dist epiph	less than 25%	L		n		
193	7	4A-20	30.4	1.3	1	Medium ungulate	Medium ungulate	tibia	upper hindlimb	dist shaft	25-49%	R		n		
194	7	4A-20	40.1	1.7	1	Ovis/ Capra	sheep/ goat	tibia	upper hindlimb	dist shaft frag (lateral)	less than 25%	L		n		
195	7	4A-20	73.6	17.3	1	Capra hircus	goat	horn core	head	body frag		L				
196	7	4A-20	34.1	1.3	1	Ovis/ Capra	sheep/ goat	innominate	upper hindlimb	acetab and isch frag	less than 25%	R	very small- prob not fused			
198	7	4A-20	23.1	0.2	1	Medium ungulate	Medium ungulate	rib	back	shaft frag	less than 25%	NA			small- prob young sh/g	
200	7	4A-20	24.8	1.1	1	Ovis/ Capra	sheep/ goat	radius	upper forelimb	dist epiph frag (medial)	less than 25%	R		n		
201	7	4A-20	20.8	0.5	1	Ovis/ Capra	sheep/ goat	radius	upper forelimb	dist epiph frag (medial)	less than 25%	L		n		
202	7	4A-20	39.2	1.5	1	Medium ungulate	Medium ungulate	scapula	upper forelimb	spine frag	less than 25%	R				
209	7	4A-20	14.7	0.3	1	Ovis/ Capra	sheep/ goat	tarsal	feet	centroquartal (medial portion)	25-49%	R				
210	7	4A-20	12.9	0.1	1	Ovis/ Capra	sheep/ goat	tarsal	feet	pisiform	complete	R				
211	7	4A-20	39.3	1.5	1	Medium ungulate	Medium ungulate	scapula	upper forelimb	spine and body frag	less than 25%	R				
212	7	4A-20	14	0.4	1	Medium ungulate	Medium ungulate	radius	upper forelimb	dist epiph frag (lateral)	less than 25%	R		n		
213	7	4A-20	15.2	0.6	1	Ovis/ Capra	sheep/ goat	carpal	feet	radial carpal (cranial half)	half	L				
214	7	4A-20	19	1.1	1	Medium- large ungulate	Medium- large ungulate	lateral malleolus	feet	nC	75% complete	R				
215	7	4A-20	36.7	2	1	Medium ungulate	Medium ungulate	humerus	upper forelimb	shaft frag	less than 25%	L				
216	7	4A-20	30.3	1.3	1	Medium ungulate	Medium ungulate	humerus	upper forelimb	dist shaft frag (medial)	less than 25%	L		n		
217	7	4A-20	16.1	0.6	1	Medium ungulate	Medium ungulate	humerus	upper forelimb	dist epiph frag	less than 25%	L		n		
218	7	4A-20	14.2	0.3	1	Medium ungulate	Medium ungulate	humerus	upper forelimb	dist epiph frag	less than 25%	R		n		
219	7	4A-20	21.5	1	1	Medium ungulate	Medium ungulate	humerus	upper forelimb	dist shaft frag	less than 25%	R		n		
222	7	4A-20	24.6	1.3	1	Ovis/ Capra	sheep/ goat	astragalus	feet	nC	75% complete	R				

BONE NO.	CUT	GNAW	BURNT	OTHER MODIFICATIONS	ARTIC	COMMENTS	M1	M2	M3	M4	M5	M6
191			white									
192			white				Bd= ca.22.2	Dd= ca.18.6				
193			white			very small- could be gazelle	Bd= 18.4(u)	Dd= 13.6(u)				
194			grey and white									
195			grey and white	twisted								
196			grey and white									
198			white									
200			grey									
201			white									
202			grey and white									
209			grey									
210			white									
211			white									
212			grey and white									
213												
214			grey			possibly deer						
215			grey and white									
216			white									
217			white									
218			black									
219			grey									
222			grey and white					GLm= 24.6				

Table 11.6 (cont.)   Condensed table of identified animal bones from Khirbet et-Tannur.

BONE NO.	LOCUS	GA UNIT	LENGTH (MM)	WEIGHT (G)	NISP	TAXON	COMMON NAME	BONE	SKEL AREA	PART	% PRESERVED	SIDE	PROX FUSED?	DIST FUSED?	AGE	SEX
223	7	4A-20	46.9	2.7	1	*Capra hircus*	goat	calcaneus	feet	cranial portion (prox broken off)	half	R				
224	7	4A-20	28.7	0.9	1	Medium ungulate	Medium ungulate	calcaneus	feet	prox	half	R	n			
225	7	4A-20	22.2	0.7	1	Medium ungulate	Medium ungulate	calcaneus	feet	prox	25-49%	R	n			
226	7	4A-20	23.2	0.6	1	Medium ungulate	Medium ungulate	calcaneus	feet	prox	25-49%	R	n			
227	7	4A-20	24.5	0.9	1	Medium ungulate	Medium ungulate	calcaneus	feet	prox	half	L	n			
228	7	4A-20	22	0.8	1	Medium ungulate	Medium ungulate	calcaneus	feet	prox	25-49%	L	n			
229	7	4A-20	17.7	0.6	1	Medium ungulate	Medium ungulate	calcaneus	feet	prox	25-49%	L	n			
230	7	4A-20	17.8	0.6	1	Medium ungulate	Medium ungulate	calcaneus	feet	prox	25-49%	L	n			
231	7	4A-20	17.8	0.8	1	Medium ungulate	Medium ungulate	femur	upper hindlimb	prox-caput	less than 25%	R	n			
232	7	4A-20	16.9	0.6	1	Medium ungulate	Medium ungulate	femur	upper hindlimb	prox-caput	less than 25%	L	n			
233	7	4A-20	23.7	1.1	1	*Ovis/ Capra*	sheep/ goat	humerus	upper forelimb	dist frag	less than 25%	R		y		
234	7	4A-20	31.3	0.7	1	*Ovis/ Capra*	sheep/ goat	cranium	head	zygomatic frag		L				
235	7	4A-20	24.7	0.5	1	Medium ungulate	Medium ungulate	mandible	head	coronoid process	less than 25%	R				
236	7	4A-20	12.5	0.1	1	Medium ungulate	Medium ungulate	cranium	head	palate frag		NA				
237	7	4A-20	23.4	1.7	1	*Ovis/ Capra*	sheep/ goat	cranium	head	petrous		R				
239	7	4A-20	39	8.8	1	*Bos taurus*	cow	cranium	head	petrous		L				
240	7	4A-20	34.3	4.1	1	*Bos taurus*	cow	cranium	head	petrous frag		L				
241	7	4A-20	39	6.2	1	*Bos taurus*	cow	cranium	head	petrous frag		R				
242	7	4A-20	27.5	1.4	1	Large ungulate	Large ungulate	vertebra/ cervical	back	cranial portion of centrum	less than 25%		n			
243	7	4A-20	56	10.5	1	Large ungulate	Large ungulate	calcaneus	feet	prox (volar) portion of shaft and prox epiph	25-49%	R	n			
244	7	4A-20	37.9	3.5	1	Large ungulate	Large ungulate	tibia	upper hindlimb	prox epiph frag	less than 25%	R	n			

11. The Animal Bones   89

BONE NO.	CUT	GNAW	BURNT	OTHER MODIFICATIONS	ARTIC	COMMENTS	M1	M2	M3	M4	M5	M6
223												
224			black				Bp=7.2(u)					
225			grey				Bp=8.1(u)					
226			white				Bp=7.3(u)					
227			grey and white				Bp=7(u)					
228			white				Bp=7.9(u)					
229			white				Bp=8.1(u)					
230			grey and white									
231			white									
232			grey and white									
233												
234			white									
235			white									
236												
237			grey and white									
239			grey and white		might pair w/ 241							
240			grey and white		might pair w/ 241							
241			grey and white		might pair w/ 239 or 240							
242			white									
243			grey and white				Bp=18.9(u)					
244			white									

Table 11.6 (cont.)   Condensed table of identified animal bones from Khirbet et-Tannur.

BONE NO.	LOCUS	GA UNIT	LENGTH (MM)	WEIGHT (G)	NISP	TAXON	COMMON NAME	BONE	SKEL AREA	PART	% PRESERVED	SIDE	PROX FUSED?	DIST FUSED?	AGE	SEX
245	7	4A 20	53.2	6.3	1	*Bos taurus*	cow	humerus	upper forelimb	dist epiph frag	less than 25%	L		n		
246	7	4A-20	34.1	3.4	1	*Bos taurus*	cow	radius	upper forelimb	dist epiph frag (medial)	less than 25%	L		n		
247	7	4A-20	37.2	2	1	Large ungulate	Large ungulate	humerus	upper forelimb	prox epiph frag	less than 25%	NA	n			
252	7	4A-20	23.4	0.6	1	Medium ungulate	Medium ungulate	mandible	head	alveolus frag	less than 25%	NA				
254	7	4A-20	31.3	2.7	1	Large ungulate	Large ungulate	tibia	upper hindlimb	dist shaft frag	less than 25%	NA		n		
255	7	4A-20	28.4	1.4	1	Large ungulate	Large ungulate	radius	upper forelimb	dist epiph frag	less than 25%	L		n		

Table 11.7   Table of all identified animal bones from Khirbet et-Tannur.*

* The complete dataset presented here is also available as a downloadable table in Open Context: http://dx.doi.org/10.6078/M7NK3BZZ.

BONE NO.	LOCUS	GA UNIT	LENGTH (MM)	WEIGHT (G)	NISP	TAXON	COMMON NAME	BONE	SKEL AREA	PART	% PRESERVED	SIDE	PROX FUSED?	DIST FUSED?	AGE	SEX
1	21	47-21	78	7.2	1	*Ovis/Capra*	sheep/goat	radius	upper forelimb	dist shaft	half	L		n		
2	21	47-21	35.4	3.3	1	*Capra hircus*	goat	phalanx 1	feet	C	complete		n			
3	21	47-21	34.1	2.2	1	*Ovis aries*	sheep	phalanx 1	feet	nC	75% complete		n			
4	21	47-21	19.9	1.3	1	*Ovis/Capra*	sheep/goat	metatarsal	feet	dist frag	less than 25%	NA		y		
5	21	47-21	34.9	5.3	1	*Capra hircus*	goat	metacarpal	feet	dist shaft	25-49%	L		y		
6	21	47-21	44.2	7.9	1	*Capra hircus*	goat	metacarpal	feet	dist shaft	25-49%	R		y		
7	21	47-21	29.1	4.2	1	*Capra hircus*	goat	astragalus	feet	nC	75% complete	R				F
8	21	47-21	30.1	4.5	1	*Ovis aries*	sheep	astragalus	feet	nC	75% complete	R				
9	21	47-21	29.3	4.2	1	*Ovis aries*	sheep	astragalus	feet	C	complete	L				F
10	21	47-21	20.7	1.6	1	*Ovis/Capra*	sheep/goat	astragalus	feet	plantar lateral frag	25-49%	R				
11	21	47-21	63.4	0.7	1	*Gallus gallus*	chicken	radius	upper forelimb	C	complete	L	y	y		

BONE NO.	CUT	GNAW	BURNT	OTHER MODIFICATIONS	ARTIC	COMMENTS	M1	M2	M3	M4	M5	M6
245			grey and white									
246			white									
247			grey and white									
252			white									
254			grey and white									
255			black and grey partial									

BONE NO.	CUT	GNAW	BURNT	OTHER MODIFICATIONS	ARTIC	COMMENTS	M1	M2	M3	M4	M5	M6
1				surface is exfoliating, weathered-looking				SD= 12.7	DD= 7.4		Bd= 26.1(u)	
2			grey				GL= 35.4(u)	Bp= 13.1(u)	Bd= 12.9			
3							GL= 32.8(u)	Bp= 11.3(u)				
4			grey and white									
5												Bd= 28
6			grey brown									Bd= 27.3
7			grey and white				GLl= 29.1					
8			grey and white				GLl= 30.3	GLm= 29.6	Bd= 19.3			
9			grey and white				GLl= 29.3	GLm= 27.4	Bd= 19.3			
10			grey and white									
11							GL= 63.4	SD= 3.2	Bp= 5.4	Bd= 6.8		

Table 11.7 (cont.)   Table of all identified animal bones from Khirbet et-Tannur.

BONE NO.	LOCUS	GA UNIT	LENGTH (MM)	WEIGHT (G)	NISP	TAXON	COMMON NAME	BONE	SKEL AREA	PART	% PRESERVED	SIDE	PROX FUSED?	DIST FUSED?	AGE	SEX
12	21	47-21	25.3	1.9	1	*Ovis/Capra*	sheep/goat	maxIllary tooth	head	M I or M2		L			adult	
13	21	47-21	29.6	0.7	1	*Ovis/Capra*	sheep/goat	mandibular tooth	head	Incisor		L				
14	21	47-21	53.2	3.8	1	*Ovis/Capra*	sheep/goat	mandible	head	artic condyle	less than 25%	R				
15	21	47-21	51.2	0.9	1	Medium mammal	Medium mammal	rib	back	body frag	25-49%	NA				
16	21	47-21	32.8	0.9	1	Medium mammal	Medium mammal	rib	back	body frag	less than 25%	NA				
17	21	47-21	23.8	0.5	1	Medium mammal	Medium mammal	axial		frag	less than 25%					
18	21	47-21	17.7	0.2	1	Medium mammal	Medium mammal	axial		frag	less than 25%					
19	21	47-21	24.7	1.1	1	Medium mammal	Medium mammal	long bone		frag	less than 25%					
20	21	47-21	16.2	0.7	1	Medium mammal	Medium mammal	long bone		frag	less than 25%					
21	21	47-21	66.1	4.5	1	Medium mammal	Medium mammal	long bone		frag	less than 25%					
22	21	47-21	47.5	3	1	Medium mammal	Medium mammal	long bone		frag	less than 25%					
23	21	47-21	29.5	1.8	1	Medium mammal	Medium mammal	long bone		frag	less than 25%					
24	21	47-21	29.8	1.2	1	Medium mammal	Medium mammal	long bone		frag	less than 25%					
25	21	47-21	27.3	0.7	1	Medium mammal	Medium mammal	long bone		frag	less than 25%					
26	21	47-21	16.1	0.1	1	Medium mammal	Medium mammal	long bone		frag	less than 25%					
27	21	47-21	29	1.1	1	Medium mammal	Medium mammal	long bone		frag	less than 25%					
28	21	47-21	33.4	0.6	1	Medium mammal	Medium mammal	long bone		frag	less than 25%					
29	21	47-21	18.5	0.4	1	Medium mammal	Medium mammal	long bone		frag	less than 25%					
30	21	47-21	15.3	0.4	1	Medium mammal	Medium mammal	long bone		frag	less than 25%					
31	21	47-21	17.5	0.4	1	Medium mammal	Medium mammal	long bone		frag	less than 25%					
32	21	47-21	21.3	0.4	1	Medium mammal	Medium mammal	long bone		frag	less than 25%					
33	21	47-21	16.9	0.5	1	Medium mammal	Medium mammal	long bone		frag	less than 25%					
34	6	4A-01	NA	0.9	1	*Ovis/Capra*	sheep/goat	tooth	head	many frags of M?	25-49%	NA				
35	6	4A-01	NA	2.3	1	Medium mammal	Medium mammal	long bone		frags	less than 25%	NA				

BONE NO.	CUT	GNAW	BURNT	OTHER MODIFICATIONS	ARTIC	COMMENTS	M1	M2	M3	M4	M5	M6
12												
13												
14			grey brown				condyle =19.8					
15												
16												
17												
18												
19												
20			black and grey partial									
21												
22												
23			grey									
24			grey									
25												
26												
27			grey									
28			black partial									
29			grey (inside) and white (outside)									
30			black									
31			black									
32			black and grey partial									
33			grey partial									
34												
35												

Table 11.7 (cont.)   Table of all identified animal bones from Khirbet et-Tannur.

BONE NO.	LOCUS	GA UNIT	LENGTH (MM)	WEIGHT (G)	NISP	TAXON	COMMON NAME	BONE	SKEL AREA	PART	% PRESERVED	SIDE	PROX FUSED?	DIST FUSED?	AGE	SEX
36	6	4A-01	NA	1.4	1	*Ovis/Capra*	sheep/goat	mandible	head	ascending ramus frag (benind M3)	less than 25%	L				
37	3	4A-11	55.8	4.2	1	*Ovis/Capra*	sheep/goat	mandible	head	diastema and I2, I3, C	less than 25%	R			Incisors' root tips are not quite closed	
38	3	4A-11	34.5	2.4	1	*Ovis aries*	sheep	phalanx 1	feet	nC	75% complete		y			
39	3	4A-11	89.1	4.5	1	*Ovis/Capra*	sheep/goat	radius	upper forelimb	shaft frag	less than 25%	L				
40	3	4A-11	30.9	0.1	1	Bird	bird	long bone		shaft frag						
41	3	4A-11	20.1	0.1	1	Small mammal/ bird	Small mammal/ bird	rib?		shaft frag						
42	4	4A-10	32.6	7.6	1	*Ovis aries*	sheep	astragalus	feet	nC	75% complete	R				
43	4	4A-10	62.2	1.6	1	*Ovis/Capra*	sheep/goat	metatarsal	feet	shaft	half	L		n	young- very small, but mtIII&IV are fused	
44	4	4A-10	78.6	1.9	1	*Ovis/Capra*	sheep/goat	ulna	upper forelimb	shaft frag	25-49%	L				
45	4	4A-10	57.8	0.9	1	*Gallus gallus*	chicken	tarsometatarsus	feet	dist shaft	75% complete	L				F (no spur)
46	4	4A-10	36.4	12.8	1	*Capra hircus*	goat	tibia	upper hindlimb	prox shaft (and unfused epiphysis)	25-49%	L	n			
47	4	4A-10	53.9	19.9	1	*Capra hircus*	goat	femur	upper hindlimb	dist shaft	25-49%	L		y		
48	4	4A-10	63.4	3.1	1	*Ovis/Capra*	sheep/goat	rib	back	shaft frag	25-49%	NA				
49	4	4A-10	72.5	8.9	1	*Capra hircus*	goat	humerus	upper forelimb	shaft	half	L				
50	4	4A-10	67.3	5.1	1	*Capra hircus*	goat	humerus	upper forelimb	dist shaft	half	R		n		
51	4	4A-10	31.6	4.8	1	*Ovis/Capra*	sheep/goat	humerus	upper forelimb	dist frag	less than 25%	L		y		
52	4	4A-10	31.8	5.3	1	*Ovis/Capra*	sheep/goat	humerus	upper forelimb	dist frag	less than 25%	R		y		
53	4	4A-10	27.6	3.5	1	*Ovis/Capra*	sheep/goat	femur	upper hindlimb	prox frag (caput frag)	less than 25%	L	y (caput)			
54	4	4A-10	30.7	1.7	1	*Ovis/Capra*	sheep/goat	atlas	back	frag of left prox artic region	less than 25%				young- bone very porous and light	
55	4	4A-10	24.9	0.6	1	*Ovis/Capra*	sheep/goat	vertebra/ cervical	back	caudal epiph	less than 25%			n		

BONE NO.	CUT	GNAW	BURNT	OTHER MODIFICATIONS	ARTIC	COMMENTS	M1	M2	M3	M4	M5	M6
36				eroded- looks weathered								
37												
38							GL= 33		Bd= 11.3	SD= 9.2		
39												
40				root etching on shaft								
41												
42	poss cut mark on plantar-caudal	rodent gnawing on borders of medial side					GLl= 32.8	GLm= 30.9	Bd= 19.8			
43		heavy roden gnawing all over shaft					SD= 6.3	DD= 6.3				
44												
45							Bd= 11.7	SD= 4.9				
46									Bp= 44.1			
47										Bd= 40		
48												
49				areas of root etching on shaft				SD= 10.8				
50		rodent gnawing on shaft						SD= 9.8	Bd= 23.3(u)			
51	sliced/chopped cleanly along distal epicondyles			root etching on trochlea								
52		rodent gnawing on all borders of distal										
53	caput sliced? cleanly off						DC= 19.3					
54												
55												

Table 11.7 (cont.)　Table of all identified animal bones from Khirbet et-Tannur.

BONE NO.	LOCUS	GA UNIT	LENGTH (MM)	WEIGHT (G)	NISP	TAXON	COMMON NAME	BONE	SKEL AREA	PART	% PRESERVED	SIDE	PROX FUSED?	DIST FUSED?	AGE	SEX
56	1	4A-05	25.4	1.5	1	Ovis/Capra	sheep/goat	femur	upper hindlimb	dist epiph frag (medial epicondyle)	less than 25%	R		n		
57	1	4A-05	21.2	1.1	1	Medium mammal	Medium mammal	long bone		frag	less than 25%					
58	1	4A-05	16.1	0.7	1	Medium ungulate	Medium ungulate	astragalus	feet	caudal frag	less than 25%	R				
59	1	4A-05	12.6	0.3	1	Medium ungulate	Medium ungulate	tibia	upper hindlimb	dist frag	less than 25%	L				
60	1	4A-05	10.1	0.1	1	Small mammal/bird	Small mammal/bird	long bone		frag	less than 25%					
61	1	4A-05	24.2	0.4	1	Medium mammal	Medium mammal	long bone		frag	less than 25%					
62	1	4A-05	16.2	0.4	1	Medium mammal	Medium mammal	long bone		frag	less than 25%					
63	1	4A-05	17	0.1	1	Medium mammal	Medium mammal	long bone		frag	less than 25%					
64	1	4A-05	14.1	0.2	1	Medium mammal	Medium mammal	axial		frag	less than 25%					
65	1	4A-05	10.9	0.1	1	Medium mammal	Medium mammal	axial		frag	less than 25%					
66	1	4A-05	11.3	0.1	1	Medium mammal	Medium mammal	axial		frag	less than 25%					
67	1	4A-05	11.3	0.2	1	Medium mammal	Medium mammal	axial		frag	less than 25%					
68	1	4A-05	9.5	0	1	Medium mammal	Medium mammal	axial		frag	less than 25%					
69	1	4A-05	12.3	0.1	1	Medium mammal	Medium mammal	long bone		frag	less than 25%					
70	1	4A-05	10.4	0	1	Medium mammal	Medium mammal	axial		frag	less than 25%					
71	7	4A-24	74.1	1.8	1	Gallus gallus	chicken	tibiotarsus	upper hindlimb	shaft	half	R				
72	7	4A-20	23.2	0.8	1	Medium mammal	Medium mammal	axial		frag	less than 25%					
73	7	4A-20	37.7	0.8	1	Medium mammal	Medium mammal	axial		frag	less than 25%					
74	7	4A-20	11.4	0.2	1	Small mammal/bird	Small mammal/bird	axial		frag	less than 25%					
75	7	4A-20	25.8	0.9	1	Ovis/Capra	sheep/goat	horn core	head	frag of tip	less than 25%	NA				
76	7	4A-20	18.3	0.4	1	Medium mammal	Medium mammal	axial		frag	less than 25%					
77	7	4A-20	24.2	1.1	1	Medium mammal	Medium mammal	axial		frag	less than 25%					

BONE NO.	CUT	GNAW	BURNT	OTHER MODIFICATIONS	ARTIC	COMMENTS	M1	M2	M3	M4	M5	M6
56			dark grey partial									
57			white									
58			grey and white									
59			grey and white									
60			grey and white									
61			black									
62			grey and white									
63			grey and white									
64												
65			grey and white									
66			grey and white									
67			white									
68			white									
69			black partial (inside)									
70			black partial									
71							SD= 5.4					
72			grey and white									
73			white									
74			grey and white									
75			grey and white									
76			white									
77			white									

Table 11.7 (cont.)   Table of all identified animal bones from Khirbet et-Tannur.

BONE NO.	LOCUS	GA UNIT	LENGTH (MM)	WEIGHT (G)	NISP	TAXON	COMMON NAME	BONE	SKEL AREA	PART	% PRESERVED	SIDE	PROX FUSED?	DIST FUSED?	AGE	SEX
78	7	4A-20	18.5	0.5	1	Medium mammal	Medium mammal	axial		frag	less than 25%					
79	7	4A-20	16.9	0.5	1	Medium mammal	Medium mammal	axial		frag	less than 25%					
80	7	4A-20	22.9	0.9	1	Medium mammal	Medium mammal	axial		frag	less than 25%					
81	7	4A-20	16.7	0.3	1	Medium mammal	Medium mammal	axial		frag	less than 25%					
82	7	4A-20	14.4	0.4	1	Medium mammal	Medium mammal	axial		frag	less than 25%					
83	7	4A-20	27.4	0.8	1	Medium mammal	Medium mammal	axial		frag	less than 25%					
84	7	4A-20	23.8	0.6	1	Medium mammal	Medium mammal	axial		frag	less than 25%					
85	7	4A-20	13.5	0.5	1	Medium mammal	Medium mammal	axial		frag	less than 25%					
86	7	4A-20	20.9	0.6	1	Medium mammal	Medium mammal	axial		frag	less than 25%					
87	7	4A-20	20.1	0.4	1	Medium mammal	Medium mammal	axial		frag	less than 25%					
88	7	4A-20	21.5	0.6	1	Medium mammal	Medium mammal	axial		frag	less than 25%					
89	7	4A-20	24.9	0.8	1	Medium mammal	Medium mammal	axial		frag	less than 25%					
90	7	4A-20	17.4	0.4	1	Medium mammal	Medium mammal	axial		frag	less than 25%					
91	7	4A-20	30.3	0.8	1	Medium mammal	Medium mammal	axial		frag	less than 25%					
92	7	4A-20	27.9	0.6	1	Medium mammal	Medium mammal	axial		frag	less than 25%					
93	7	4A-20	20.7	0.7	1	Medium mammal	Medium mammal	axial		frag	less than 25%					
94	7	4A-20	24.5	0.6	1	Medium mammal	Medium mammal	axial		frag	less than 25%					
95	7	4A-20	19	0.6	1	Medium mammal	Medium mammal	axial		frag	less than 25%					
96	7	4A-20	23.5	0.6	1	Medium mammal	Medium mammal	axial		frag	less than 25%					
97	7	4A-20	22.8	1.2	1	Medium mammal	Medium mammal	axial		frag	less than 25%					
98	7	4A-20	15	0.5	1	Medium mammal	Medium mammal	axial		frag	less than 25%					
99	7	4A-20	21.6	0.1	1	Medium mammal	Medium mammal	axial		frag	less than 25%					
100	7	4A-20	17.3	0.5	1	Medium mammal	Medium mammal	axial		frag	less than 25%					
101	7	4A-20	35	0.9	1	Medium mammal	Medium mammal	axial		frag	less than 25%					

BONE NO.	CUT	GNAW	BURNT	OTHER MODIFICATIONS	ARTIC	COMMENTS	M1	M2	M3	M4	M5	M6
78			grey and white									
79			grey and white									
80			white									
81			grey and white									
82			white									
83			grey and white									
84			grey									
85			white									
86			grey									
87			grey									
88			white									
89			white									
90			white									
91			brown and grey									
92			white									
93			white									
94			white									
95			grey and white									
96			grey and white									
97			grey and white									
98			grey and white									
99			white									
100			grey and white									
101			dark grey									

Table 11.7 (cont.)   Table of all identified animal bones from Khirbet et-Tannur.

BONE NO.	LOCUS	GA UNIT	LENGTH (MM)	WEIGHT (G)	NISP	TAXON	COMMON NAME	BONE	SKEL AREA	PART	% PRESERVED	SIDE	PROX FUSED?	DIST FUSED?	AGE	SEX
102	7	4A-20	19.8	0.6	1	Medium mammal	Medium mammal	axial		frag	less than 25%					
103	7	4A-20	40.7	1.1	1	Medium mammal	Medium mammal	axial		frag	less than 25%					
104	7	4A-20	16.5	0.5	1	Medium mammal	Medium mammal	axial		frag	less than 25%					
105	7	4A-20	22.8	1	1	Medium mammal	Medium mammal	axial		frag	less than 25%					
106	7	4A-20	17.3	0.4	1	Medium mammal	Medium mammal	axial		frag	less than 25%					
107	7	4A-20	31.3	0.6	1	Medium mammal	Medium mammal	axial		frag	less than 25%					
108	7	4A-20	21.1	0.4	1	Large mammal	Large mammal	axial		frag	less than 25%					
109	7	4A-20	26.3	1.1	1	Large mammal	Large mammal	axial		frag	less than 25%					
110	7	4A-20	25.7	1.5	1	Large mammal	Large mammal	axial		frag	less than 25%					
111	7	4A-20	28.7	0.7	1	Large mammal	Large mammal	axial		frag	less than 25%					
112	7	4A-20	25.7	1.4	1	Large mammal	Large mammal	axial		frag	less than 25%					
113	7	4A-20	34.7	2.2	1	Large mammal	Large mammal	axial		frag	less than 25%					
114	7	4A-20	31.2	1.9	1	Large mammal	Large mammal	axial		frag	less than 25%					
115	7	4A-20	35.3	2	1	Large mammal	Large mammal	axial		frag	less than 25%					
116	7	4A-20	25.9	1.2	1	Large mammal	Large mammal	axial		frag	less than 25%					
117	7	4A-20	28.3	2.1	1	Large mammal	Large mammal	axial		frag	less than 25%					
118	7	4A-20	24.7	0.9	1	Large mammal	Large mammal	axial		frag	less than 25%					
119	7	4A-20	27.8	2.6	1	Large mammal	Large mammal	axial		frag	less than 25%					
120	7	4A-20	29	0.7	1	Large mammal	Large mammal	axial		frag	less than 25%					
121	7	4A-20	33.9	1.3	1	Large mammal	Large mammal	axial		frag	less than 25%					
122	7	4A-20	20.1	0.5	1	Large mammal	Large mammal	axial		frag	less than 25%					
123	7	4A-20	22.1	0.8	1	Large mammal	Large mammal	long bone		shaft frag	less than 25%					
124	7	4A-20	26.4	1.3	1	Large mammal	Large mammal	long bone		shaft frag	less than 25%					
125	7	4A-20	21.3	0.8	1	Large mammal	Large mammal	long bone		shaft frag	less than 25%					

BONE NO.	CUT	GNAW	BURNT	OTHER MODIFICATIONS	ARTIC	COMMENTS	M1	M2	M3	M4	M5	M6
102			grey and white									
103			grey and white									
104			grey and white									
105			white									
106			grey and white									
107			grey and white									
108			grey and white									
109			grey and white									
110			grey and white									
111			white									
112			white									
113			grey and white									
114			grey and white									
115			white									
116			grey and white									
117			white									
118			grey and white									
119			grey and white									
120			white									
121			grey and white									
122			brown and grey									
123			grey									
124			grey and white									
125			grey and white									

Table 11.7 (cont.)   Table of all identified animal bones from Khirbet et-Tannur.

BONE NO.	LOCUS	GA UNIT	LENGTH (MM)	WEIGHT (G)	NISP	TAXON	COMMON NAME	BONE	SKEL AREA	PART	% PRESERVED	SIDE	PROX FUSED?	DIST FUSED?	AGE	SEX
126	7	4A-20	41.5	2.3	1	Large mammal	Large mammal	long bone		shaft frag	less than 25%					
127	7	4A-20	28.9	1	1	Large mammal	Large mammal	long bone		shaft frag	less than 25%					
128	7	4A-20	32.5	2	1	Large mammal	Large mammal	long bone		shaft frag	less than 25%					
129	7	4A-20	25	2.5	1	Large mammal	Large mammal	long bone		shaft frag	less than 25%					
130	7	4A-20	29	1.1	1	Large mammal	Large mammal	long bone		shaft frag	less than 25%					
131	7	4A-20	28.9	2	1	Large mammal	Large mammal	long bone		shaft frag	less than 25%					
132	7	4A-20	37	2.6	1	Large mammal	Large mammal	long bone		shaft frag	less than 25%					
133	7	4A-20	27.4	1.4	1	Large mammal	Large mammal	long bone		shaft frag	less than 25%					
134	7	4A-20	30.6	2.3	1	Large mammal	Large mammal	long bone		shaft frag	less than 25%					
135	7	4A-20	43.3	2.8	1	Large mammal	Large mammal	long bone		shaft frag	less than 25%					
136	7	4A-20	42.6	3	1	Large mammal	Large mammal	long bone		shaft frag	less than 25%					
137	7	4A-20	42.6	5.3	1	Large mammal	Large mammal	long bone		shaft frag	less than 25%					
138	7	4A-20	32.4	3.3	1	Large mammal	Large mammal	long bone		shaft frag	less than 25%					
139	7	4A-20	29.3	1.8	1	Large mammal	Large mammal	long bone		shaft frag	less than 25%					
140	7	4A-20	24	3	1	Large mammal	Large mammal	long bone		shaft frag	less than 25%					
141	7	4A-20	48.6	6.4	1	Large mammal	Large mammal	long bone		shaft frag	less than 25%					
142	7	4A-20	44.6	6.6	1	Large mammal	Large mammal	long bone		shaft frag	less than 25%					
143	7	4A-20	57.1	8.9	1	Large mammal	Large mammal	long bone		shaft frag	less than 25%					
144	7	4A-20	63.6	4.1	1	Medium mammal	Medium mammal	long bone		shaft frag	less than 25%					
145	7	4A-20	50	1.9	1	Medium mammal	Medium mammal	long bone		shaft frag	less than 25%					
146	7	4A-20	22.8	0.7	1	Medium mammal	Medium mammal	long bone		shaft frag	less than 25%					
147	7	4A-20	30.1	1.2	1	Medium mammal	Medium mammal	long bone		shaft frag	less than 25%					
148	7	4A-20	43.2	2	1	Medium mammal	Medium mammal	long bone		shaft frag	less than 25%					
149	7	4A-20	30.7	1.6	1	Medium mammal	Medium mammal	long bone		shaft frag	less than 25%					

BONE NO.	CUT	GNAW	BURNT	OTHER MODIFICATIONS	ARTIC	COMMENTS	M1	M2	M3	M4	M5	M6
126			white									
127			white									
128			grey									
129			white									
130			white									
131			white									
132			grey and white									
133			grey and white									
134			white									
135			white									
136			grey and white									
137			grey and white									
138			grey and white									
139			grey and white									
140			white									
141			grey and white									
142			grey and white									
143			white									
144			white									
145			grey									
146			white									
147			white									
148			white									
149			grey									

Table 11.7 (cont.)   Table of all identified animal bones from Khirbet et-Tannur.

BONE NO.	LOCUS	GA UNIT	LENGTH (MM)	WEIGHT (G)	NISP	TAXON	COMMON NAME	BONE	SKEL AREA	PART	% PRESERVED	SIDE	PROX FUSED?	DIST FUSED?	AGE	SEX
150	7	4A-20	18.5	0.8	1	Medium mammal	Medium mammal	long bone		shaft frag	less than 25%					
151	7	4A-20	32	0.5	1	Medium mammal	Medium mammal	long bone		shaft frag	less than 25%					
152	7	4A-20	24	0.8	1	Medium mammal	Medium mammal	long bone		shaft frag	less than 25%					
153	7	4A-20	31.4	1.5	1	Medium mammal	Medium mammal	long bone		shaft frag	less than 25%					
154	7	4A-20	20.5	0.2	1	Medium mammal	Medium mammal	long bone		shaft frag	less than 25%					
155	7	4A-20	24.2	0.7	1	Medium mammal	Medium mammal	long bone		shaft frag	less than 25%					
156	7	4A-20	43.3	1.2	1	Medium mammal	Medium mammal	long bone		shaft frag	less than 25%					
157	7	4A-20	18.8	0.6	1	Medium mammal	Medium mammal	long bone		shaft frag	less than 25%					
158	7	4A-20	18.5	0.5	1	Medium mammal	Medium mammal	long bone		shaft frag	less than 25%					
159	7	4A-20	21.9	1.3	1	Medium mammal	Medium mammal	long bone		shaft frag	less than 25%					
160	7	4A-20	37.6	1.9	1	Medium mammal	Medium mammal	long bone		shaft frag	less than 25%					
161	7	4A-20	26.4	1	1	Medium mammal	Medium mammal	long bone		shaft frag	less than 25%					
162	7	4A-20	27.4	0.8	1	Medium mammal	Medium mammal	long bone		shaft frag	less than 25%					
163	7	4A-20	20.2	0.6	1	Medium mammal	Medium mammal	long bone		shaft frag	less than 25%					
164	7	4A-20	31	1.1	1	Medium mammal	Medium mammal	long bone		shaft frag	less than 25%					
165	7	4A-20	30	0.9	1	Medium mammal	Medium mammal	long bone		shaft frag	less than 25%					
166	7	4A-20	17.2	0.6	1	Medium mammal	Medium mammal	long bone		shaft frag	less than 25%					
167	7	4A-20	30	1.9	1	Medium mammal	Medium mammal	long bone		shaft frag	less than 25%					
168	7	4A-20	23.2	0.9	1	Medium mammal	Medium mammal	long bone		shaft frag	less than 25%					
169	7	4A-20	29.9	0.8	1	Medium mammal	Medium mammal	long bone		shaft frag	less than 25%					
170	7	4A-20	23.3	0.7	1	Medium mammal	Medium mammal	long bone		shaft frag	less than 25%					
171	7	4A-20	22.6	0.5	1	Medium mammal	Medium mammal	long bone		shaft frag	less than 25%					
172	7	4A-20	34.9	0.9	1	Medium mammal	Medium mammal	long bone		shaft frag	less than 25%					
173	7	4A-20	25.2	0.5	1	Medium mammal	Medium mammal	long bone		shaft frag	less than 25%					

BONE NO.	CUT	GNAW	BURNT	OTHER MODIFICATIONS	ARTIC	COMMENTS	M1	M2	M3	M4	M5	M6
150			grey and white									
151			white									
152			grey									
153			white									
154			grey and white									
155			grey and white									
156			grey									
157			grey and white									
158			grey									
159			white									
160			brown and grey									
161			brown and grey									
162			white									
163			grey and white									
164			grey and whIte									
165			grey and white									
166			grey									
167			grey and white									
168												
169			grey and white									
170			grey and white									
171			grey and white									
172			grey and white									
173			grey									

Table 11.7 (cont.)   Table of all identified animal bones from Khirbet et-Tannur.

BONE NO.	LOCUS	GA UNIT	LENGTH (MM)	WEIGHT (G)	NISP	TAXON	COMMON NAME	BONE	SKEL AREA	PART	% PRESERVED	SIDE	PROX FUSED?	DIST FUSED?	AGE	SEX
174	7	4A-20	20.5	0.7	1	Medium mammal	Medium mammal	long bone		shaft frag	less than 25%					
175	7	4A-20	22.7	0.6	1	Medium mammal	Medium mammal	long bone		shaft frag	less than 25%					
176	7	4A-20	25.2	1	1	Medium mammal	Medium mammal	long bone		shaft frag	less than 25%					
177	7	4A-20	25.6	0.5	1	Medium mammal	Medium mammal	long bone		shaft frag	less than 25%					
178	7	4A-20	31.4	0.8	1	Medium mammal	Medium mammal	long bone		shaft frag	less than 25%					
179	7	4A-20	17.4	0.8	1	Medium mammal	Medium mammal	long bone		shaft frag	less than 25%					
180	7	4A-20	26.5	0.6	1	Medium mammal	Medium mammal	long bone		shaft frag	less than 25%					
181	7	4A-20	15.4	0.4	1	Medium mammal	Medium mammal	long bone		shaft frag	less than 25%					
182	7	4A-20	32.3	0.4	1	Medium mammal	Medium mammal	long bone		shaft frag	less than 25%					
183	7	4A-20	27.1	0.3	1	Medium mammal	Medium mammal	long bone		shaft frag	less than 25%					
184	7	4A-20	11.4	0.3	1	Medium mammal	Medium mammal	long bone		shaft frag	less than 25%					
185	7	4A-20	23	0.6	1	Medium mammal	Medium mammal	long bone		shaft frag	less than 25%					
186	7	4A-20	21.6	0.3	1	Medium mammal	Medium mammal	long bone		shaft frag	less than 25%					
187	7	4A-20	25.8	0.6	1	Medium mammal	Medium mammal	long bone		shaft frag	less than 25%					
188	7	4A-20	27.9	0.4	1	Medium mammal	Medium mammal	long bone		shaft frag	less than 25%					
189	7	4A-20	43.8	1	1	Medium ungulate	Medium ungulate	mandible	head	angle and artic condyle	less than 25%	R				
190	7	4A-20	21.1	0.8	1	*Ovis/Capra*	sheep/goat	tibia	upper hindlimb	prox epiph frag (lateral)	less than 25%	L	n			
191	7	4A-20	13.4	0.4	1	Medium ungulate	Medium ungulate	tibia	upper hindlimb	dist shaft frag (lateral)	less than 25%	R		n		
192	7	4A-20	22.2	1.5	1	*Ovis aries*	sheep	tibia	upper hindlimb	dist epiph	less than 25%	L		n		
193	7	4A-20	30.4	1.3	1	Medium ungulate	Medium ungulate	tibia	upper hindlimb	dist shaft	25-49%	R		n		
194	7	4A-20	40.1	1.7	1	*Ovis/Capra*	sheep/goat	tibia	upper hindlimb	dist shaft frag (lateral)	less than 25%	L		n		
195	7	4A-20	73.6	17.3	1	*Capra hircus*	goat	horn core	head	body frag		L				
196	7	4A-20	34.1	1.3	1	*Ovis/Capra*	sheep/goat	innominate	upper hindlimb	acetab and isch frag	less than 25%	R	very small- prob not fused			

BONE NO.	CUT	GNAW	BURNT	OTHER MODIFICATIONS	ARTIC	COMMENTS	M1	M2	M3	M4	M5	M6
174			grey and white									
175			white									
176			grey and white									
177			dark grey									
178			brown and grey									
179			white									
180			grey									
181			grey									
182			brown and grey									
183			white									
184			grey and white									
185			black and grey									
186			grey									
187			white									
188			white									
189			white									
190			grey									
191			white									
192			white				Bd= ca.22.2	Dd= ca.18.6				
193			white			very small- could be gazelle	Bd= 18.4(u)	Dd= 13.6(u)				
194			grey and white									
195			grey and white			twisted						
196			grey and white									

Table 11.7 (cont.)   Table of all identified animal bones from Khirbet et-Tannur.

BONE NO.	LOCUS	GA UNIT	LENGTH (MM)	WEIGHT (G)	NISP	TAXON	COMMON NAME	BONE	SKEL AREA	PART	% PRESERVED	SIDE	PROX FUSED?	DIST FUSED?	AGE	SEX
197	7	4A-20	45.7	0.3	1	Small mammal/ bird	Small mammal/ bird	rib	back	shaft frag	25-49%	NA				
198	7	4A-20	23.1	0.2	1	Medium ungulate	Medium ungulate	rib	back	shaft frag	less than 25%	NA			small- prob young sh/g	
199	7	4A-20	21.4	0.1	1	Small mammal/ bird	Small mammal/ bird	rib	back	shaft frag	less than 25%	NA				
200	7	4A-20	24.8	1.1	1	Ovis/Capra	sheep/goat	radius	upper forelimb	dist epiph frag (medial)	less than 25%	R		n		
201	7	4A-20	20.8	0.5	1	Ovis/Capra	sheep/goat	radius	upper forelimb	dist epiph frag (medial)	less than 25%	L		n		
202	7	4A-20	39.2	1.5	1	Medium ungulate	Medium ungulate	scapula	upper forelimb	spine frag	less than 25%	R				
203	7	4A-20	17.3	0.8	1	Medium mammal	Medium mammal	humerus	upper forelimb	dist frag	less than 25%	NA				
204	7	4A-20	19.7	0.8	1	Medium mammal	Medium mammal	humerus	upper forelimb	dist frag	less than 25%	NA				
205	7	4A-20	17	0.6	1	Medium mammal	Medium mammal	rib	back	shaft frag	less than 25%	NA				
206	7	4A-20	22.1	0.4	1	Medium mammal	Medium mammal	rib	back	shaft frag	less than 25%	NA				
207	7	4A-20	25.4	0.3	1	Medium mammal	Medium mammal	rib	back	shaft frag	less than 25%	NA				
208	7	4A-20	27	0.9	1	Medium mammal	Medium mammal	vertebra/ lumbar	back	postzyg frag	less than 25%					
209	7	4A-20	14.7	0.3	1	Ovis/Capra	sheep/goat	tarsal	feet	centroquartal (medial portion)	25-49%	R				
210	7	4A-20	12.9	0.1	1	Ovis/Capra	sheep/goat	tarsal	feet	pisiform	complete	R				
211	7	4A-20	39.3	1.5	1	Medium ungulate	Medium ungulate	scapula	upper forelimb	spine and body frag	less than 25%	R				
212	7	4A-20	14	0.4	1	Medium ungulate	Medium ungulate	radius	upper forelimb	dist epiph frag (lateral)	less than 25%	R		n		
213	7	4A-20	15.2	0.6	1	Ovis/Capra	sheep/goat	carpal	feet	radial carpal (cranial half)	half	L				
214	7	4A-20	19	1.1	1	Medium- large ungulate	Medium- large ungulate	lateral malleolus	feet	nC	75% complete	R				
215	7	4A-20	36.7	2	1	Medium ungulate	Medium ungulate	humerus	upper forelimb	shaft frag	less than 25%	L				
216	7	4A-20	30.3	1.3	1	Medium ungulate	Medium ungulate	humerus	upper forelimb	dist shaft frag (medial)	less than 25%	L		n		
217	7	4A-20	16.1	0.6	1	Medium ungulate	Medium ungulate	humerus	upper forelimb	dist epiph frag	less than 25%	L		n		
218	7	4A-20	14.2	0.3	1	Medium ungulate	Medium ungulate	humerus	upper forelimb	dist epiph frag	less than 25%	R		n		

BONE NO.	CUT	GNAW	BURNT	OTHER MODIFICATIONS	ARTIC	COMMENTS	M1	M2	M3	M4	M5	M6
197			grey and white									
198			white									
199			white									
200			grey									
201			white									
202			grey and white									
203			grey and white									
204			grey partial									
205			white									
206			white									
207			white									
208			grey									
209			grey									
210			white									
211			white									
212			grey and white									
213												
214			grey			possibly deer						
215			grey and white									
216			white									
217			white									
218			black									

Table 11.7 (cont.)   Table of all identified animal bones from Khirbet et-Tannur.

BONE NO.	LOCUS	GA UNIT	LENGTH (MM)	WEIGHT (G)	NISP	TAXON	COMMON NAME	BONE	SKFI AREA	PART	% PRESERVED	SIDE	PROX FUSED?	DIST FUSED?	AGE	SEX
219	7	4A-20	21.5	1	1	Medium ungulate	Medium ungulate	humerus	upper forelimb	dist shaft frag	less than 25%	R		n		
220	7	4A-20	30.8	1.5	1	Medium-large mammal	Medium-large mammal	vertebra/ lumbar	back	centrum frag	less than 25%			n		
221	7	4A-20	11.6	0.1	1	Medium mammal	Medium mammal	vertebra/ lumbar	back	prezyg frag	less than 25%					
222	7	4A-20	24.6	1.3	1	*Ovis/Capra*	sheep/goat	astragalus	feet	nC	75% complete	R				
223	7	4A-20	46.9	2.7	1	*Capra hircus*	goat	calcaneus	feet	cranial portion (prox broken off)	half	R				
224	7	4A-20	28.7	0.9	1	Medium ungulate	Medium ungulate	calcaneus	feet	prox	half	R	n			
225	7	4A-20	22.2	0.7	1	Medium ungulate	Medium ungulate	calcaneus	feet	prox	25-49%	R	n			
226	7	4A-20	23.2	0.6	1	Medium ungulate	Medium ungulate	calcaneus	feet	prox	25-49%	R	n			
227	7	4A-20	24.5	0.9	1	Medium ungulate	Medium ungulate	calcaneus	feet	prox	half	L	n			
228	7	4A-20	22	0.8	1	Medium ungulate	Medium ungulate	calcaneus	feet	prox	25-49%	L	n			
229	7	4A-20	17.7	0.6	1	Medium ungulate	Medium ungulate	calcaneus	feet	prox	25-49%	L	n			
230	7	4A-20	17.8	0.6	1	Medium ungulate	Medium ungulate	calcaneus	feet	prox	25-49%	L	n			
231	7	4A-20	17.8	0.8	1	Medium ungulate	Medium ungulate	femur	upper hindlimb	prox-caput	less than 25%	R	n			
232	7	4A-20	16.9	0.6	1	Medium ungulate	Medium ungulate	femur	upper hindlimb	prox-caput	less than 25%	L	n			
233	7	4A-20	23.7	1.1	1	*Ovis/Capra*	sheep/goat	humerus	upper forelimb	dist frag	less than 25%	R		y		
234	7	4A-20	31.3	0.7	1	*Ovis/Capra*	sheep/goat	cranium	head	zygomatic frag		L				
235	7	4A-20	24.7	0.5	1	Medium ungulate	Medium ungulate	mandible	head	coronoid process	less than 25%	R				
236	7	4A-20	12.5	0.1	1	Medium ungulate	Medium ungulate	cranium	head	palate frag		NA				
237	7	4A-20	23.4	1.7	1	*Ovis/Capra*	sheep/goat	cranium	head	petrous		R				
238	7	4A-20	18.8	0.5	1	Large mammal	Large mammal	tooth	head	root frag, position indeterminate		NA				
239	7	4A-20	39	8.8	1	*Bos taurus*	cattle	cranium	head	petrous		L				
240	7	4A-20	34.3	4.1	1	*Bos taurus*	cattle	cranium	head	petrous frag		L				

BONE NO.	CUT	GNAW	BURNT	OTHER MODIFICATIONS	ARTIC	COMMENTS	M1	M2	M3	M4	M5	M6
219			grey									
220			white									
221			white									
222			grey and white					GLm= 24.6				
223												
224			black				Bp= 7.2(u)					
225			grey				Bp= 8.1(u)					
226			white				Bp= 7.3(u)					
227			grey and white				Bp= 7(u)					
228			white				Bp= 7.9(u)					
229			white				Bp= 8.1(u)					
230			grey and white									
231			white									
232			grey and white									
233												
234			white									
235			white									
236												
237			grey and white									
238			grey and white									
239			grey and white	might pair w/ 241								
240			grey and white	might pair w/ 241								

Table 11.7 (cont.)   Table of all identified animal bones from Khirbet et-Tannur.

BONE NO.	LOCUS	GA UNIT	LENGTH (MM)	WEIGHT (G)	NISP	TAXON	COMMON NAME	BONE	SKEL AREA	PART	% PRESERVED	SIDE	PROX FUSED?	DIST FUSED?	AGE	SEX
241	7	4A-20	39	6.2	1	*Bos taurus*	cattle	cranium	head	petrous frag		R				
242	7	4A-20	27.5	1.4	1	Large ungulate	Large ungulate	vertebra/cervical	back	cranial portion of centrum	less than 25%		n			
243	7	4A-20	56	10.5	1	Large ungulate	Large ungulate	calcaneus	feet	prox (volar) portion of shaft and prox epiph	25-49%	R	n			
244	7	4A-20	37.9	3.5	1	Large ungulate	Large ungulate	tibia	upper hindlimb	prox epiph frag	less than 25%	R	n			
245	7	4A-20	53.2	6.3	1	*Bos taurus*	cattle	humerus	upper forelimb	dist epiph frag	less than 25%	L		n		
246	7	4A-20	34.1	3.4	1	*Bos taurus*	cattle	radius	upper forelimb	dist epiph frag (medial)	less than 25%	L		n		
247	7	4A-20	37.2	2	1	Large ungulate	Large ungulate	humerus	upper forelimb	prox epiph frag	less than 25%	NA	n			
248	7	4A-20	31.7	2.3	1	Large mammal	Large mammal	axial		frag	less than 25%					
249	7	4A-20	18.7	0.3	1	Medium mammal	Medium mammal	vertebra/indeterminate	back	frag	less than 25%					
250	7	4A-20	20.8	0.6	1	Medium mammal	Medium mammal	vertebra/indeterminate	back	frag	less than 25%					
251	7	4A-20	25.7	1.5	1	Medium-large mammal	Medium-large mammal	long bone		epiph frag	less than 25%	NA				
252	7	4A-20	23.4	0.6	1	Medium ungulate	Medium ungulate	mandible	head	alveolus frag	less than 25%	NA				
253	7	4A-20	24.5	1.4	1	Medium mammal	Medium mammal	cranium	head	maxilla frag		NA				
254	7	4A-20	31.3	2.7	1	Large ungulate	Large ungulate	tibia	upper hindlimb	dist shaft frag	less than 25%	NA		n		
255	7	4A-20	28.4	1.4	1	Large ungulate	Large ungulate	radius	upper forelimb	dist epiph frag	less than 25%	L		n		

BONE NO.	CUT	GNAW	BURNT	OTHER MODIFICATIONS	ARTIC	COMMENTS	M1	M2	M3	M4	M5	M6
241			grey and white		might pair w/ 239 or 240							
242			white									
243			grey and white				Bp= 18.9(u)					
244			white									
245			grey and white									
246			white									
247			grey and white									
248			black and white partial									
249			grey									
250			white									
251			grey and white									
252			white									
253			grey and white									
254			grey and white									
255			black and grey partial									

Appendix 11.1 — Worked Bone

by Judith S. McKenzie

There is one small piece of worked bone (not ivory) in the Glueck Archive (fig. 11.3). It is probably a piece of inlay as would be set into a wooden object, such as a box. It is nearly triangular in shape and is flat on one side, with a cushion-shaped cross-section. It is 1.7 cm long, and 1.0 cm wide, with a maximum thickness of 0.5 cm. It has a black substance on parts of the edge of it, with traces of this on the flat side. This appears to be bitumen, or a similar substance, which was used as an adhesive. It has no provenience (Unit A-13).

FIG. 11.3 *Flat side of piece of bone inlay, with remains of an adhesive.*

REFERENCES

Bienkowski, P.
2002   *Busayra: Excavations by Crystal-M. Bennett 1971–1980.* Oxford.

Boessneck, J.
1969   "Osteological Differences between Sheep (*Ovis aries* Linné) and Goats (*Capra hircus* Linné)." Pp. 331–58 in *Science in Archaeology* (2nd edition), eds. D. Brothwell and E. S. Higgs. London.

Boessneck, J.; Müller, H.-H.; and Teichert, M.
1964   "Osteologische Unterschiedungsmerkmale zwischen Schaf (*Ovis aries* Linné) und Ziege (*Capra hircus* Linné)." *Kühn-Archiv* 78: 1–129.

Desse-Berset, N., and Studer, J.
1996   "Fish Remains from ez Zantur (Petra, Jordan)." Pp. 381–87 in *Petra – Ez Zantur I. Ergebnisse der Schweizerisch-Liechtensteinischen Ausgrabungen 1988–1992*, eds. A. Bignasca et al. Terra Archaeologica 2.

Monographien der Schweizerisch-Liechtensteinischen Stiftung für archäologische Forschungen im Ausland [SLSA / FSLA]. Mainz.

Driesch, A. von den
1976   *A Guide to the Measurement of Animal Bones from Archaeological Sites.* Peabody Museum Bulletin 1. Cambridge, MA.

Horwitz, L. K.
1987   "Animal Offerings from Two Middle Bronze Age Tombs." *Israel Exploration Journal* 37: 251–55.

Kansa, S. Whitcher
2013   "Khirbet et-Tannur Zooarchaeology." Open Context. Http://dx.doi.org/10.6078/M7NK3BZZ.
in press   "Food Production and Procurement at Petra's Great Temple: Report on Faunal Analyses from the 1995–2004 Excavations." In *The Petra Great Temple III:*

Architecture and Material Culture, ed. M. S. Joukowsky, Journal of Roman Archaeology Supplement. Portsmouth, RI.

Lepetz, S.
unpublished report   "Étude des ossements animaux des contextes liés au fonctionnement du sanctuaire de Dharih (IIe – milieu IVe siècle – Jordanie)." Unpublished draft of an internal report, Jordanian and French Archaeological Project at Dharih.

Mays, S.
1998   *The Archaeology of Human Bones.* London.

Prummel, W., and Frisch, H. J.
1986   "A Guide for the Distinction of Species, Sex, and Body Side of Sheep and Goat." *Journal of Archaeological Science* 13: 567–77.

Shipman, P.; Foster, G.; and Schoeninger, M.
1984   "Burnt Bones and Teeth: An Experimental Study of Color, Morphology, Crystal Structure, and Shrinkage." *Journal of Archaeological Science* 11: 307–25.

Silver, I. A.
1969   "The Ageing of Domestic Animals." Pp. 283–302 in *Science in Archaeology* (2nd edition), eds. D. Brothwell and E. Higgs. London.

Stiner, M. C.; Kuhn, S.; Weiner, S.; and Bar-Yosef, O.
1995   "Differential Burning, Recrystallization, and Fragmentation of Archaeological Bone." *Journal of Archaeological Science* 22: 223–37.

Studer, J.
1996   "La Faune romaine tardive d'ez Zantur, à Petra." Pp. 359–75 in *Petra – Ez Zantur I. Ergebnisse der Schweizerisch-Liechtensteinischen Ausgrabungen 1988–1992*, eds. A. Bignasca et al. Terra Archaeologica 2. Monographien der Schweizerisch-Liechtensteinischen Stiftung für archäologische Forschungen im Ausland [SLSA / FSLA]. Mainz.
2001   "Observations on the Animal Bones from Jabal Haroun." In J. Frösén et al., "The 1998–2000 Finnish Harun Project: Specialized Reports." *Annual of the Department of Antiquities of Jordan* 45: 384–86.
2002   "City and Monastery: Animals Raised and Consumed in the Petra Area." Pp. 167–72 in *Petra – A City Forgotten and Rediscovered*, eds. J. Frösén and Z. Fiema. Helsinki.
2007   "Animal Exploitation in the Nabataean World." Pp. 251–72 in *The World of the Nabataeans*, ed. K. D. Politis. Stuttgart.

Toplyn, M.
1994   Meat for Mars: Livestock, *Limitanei*, and Pastoral Provisioning for the Roman Army on the Arabian Frontier (AD 284–551). Unpublished PhD dissertation, Harvard University. Cambridge, MA.

Chapter 12

The Plant Remains

by Wilma Wetterstrom

INTRODUCTION

In 1937, when Nelson Glueck worked at Khirbet et-Tannur, archaeologists had not yet taken much interest in plant materials left behind by ancient inhabitants. Systematic sampling and study would not come until much later in the 1950s and 60s. Glueck, however, had the wisdom to pluck snatches of burnt grains and charcoal as he encountered them during the course of his excavations. He bagged and recorded the samples, and they eventually ended up in the basement of the Semitic Museum, Harvard University, along with other Khirbet et-Tannur materials in the Glueck Archive. Although these archaeobotanical samples fall far short of modern standards for a plant assemblage, they nonetheless offer a window, albeit narrow, onto activities at this Nabataean sanctuary, from the 2nd century BC through to the mid-4th century AD. Consisting of wheat grains, charcoal, and a charred amorphous material (burnt bread?), this tiny assemblage sheds light on the ritual activities at the shrine. The wheat grains were most likely offerings burnt on the altar. The charred amorphous material may be fragments of offering bread/cakes. The charcoal fragments suggest that the altar fires were probably fueled by a variety of woods and shrubs that may have been collected in the area.

METHODS

The six samples in the collection were taken during the excavations in 1937 from various locations (Loci marked on fig. 6.2) within the Inner Temenos Enclosure, including the Altar Platform (Vol. 1, figs. 30, 33a–b, 53, 333), two of the offertory boxes (figs. 49, 397–99, 401), and behind the cult statue (fig. 83) (see Table 12.1).

They consist of a mixture of grains and/or charcoal and, in four cases, possible burnt bread (see Table 12.2). These various components were separated out from each sample and examined using a reflected light microscope at 7 to 50 × magnification. The specimens were identified to the extent possible using reference material from publications and my own collection.

Following current conventions, the materials were measured or counted. But it is not clear how useful the quantitative data are, given the fact that no systematic sampling procedures were used at the site. Moreover, Glueck's excavation journal (GJ) suggests that he was taking what were essentially

Table 12.1   Carbonized plant remains from Khirbet et-Tannur (by context).

Locus	Location	Glueck Archive Unit	Date in excavation journal, 1937	Grains (G), "Vesicular material" (V), or Charcoal (C)
1	NW and W parts of Inner Temenos Enclosure	4A-05	3 March (On label: 4 March)	G; V; C
3	NE offertory box	4A-11	3 and 9 March	G; V; C
4	W offertory box	4A-10	8 March (Also on label)	G; V; C
6	In front of Altar Platform	4A-01	3 and 10 March	V; C
6	SE end of Altar Platform (behind cult statue)	4A-18	3 March (On label: 4 March)	G
7	Inside Altar Platform	4A-20	(On label: 10 March)	C

"grab bag" samples in some cases. He mentions, for example, that the north-east offertory box (fig. 49) (Locus 3; GA Unit 4A-11) "is particularly full of grains of wheat" (GJ 8 March). Yet, the packet at the Semitic Museum held only two grains. Apparently, Glueck collected little of the grain, or it was lost during the intervening seventy-plus years between the excavation and this study.

Glueck also noted two locations with considerable quantities of burnt grains that did not turn up among the Glueck Archive materials. In the south-east corner of Room 14, there was so much burnt grain that Glueck thought, "Perhaps it was a store room for the temple" (GJ 13 April). Below the paving of the Inner Temenos Enclosure surrounding the Altar Platform burnt grain was so abundant that he asked, "Did the builders of the floor of period II lay out an offering of a layer of grain all over the floor before they put in the stones of the actual floor?" (GJ 14 April). All of these grains were either lost or never collected. He also mentions burnt wood from the roof in the ashes on the floor of Room 8 (Glueck 1965: 181).[1]

Nonetheless, the counts provided here at least give the reader some sense of the amount of mate-

rial at hand and the quantities on which conclusions have been based.

Results

Cereals

Three types of cereals were found: barley and two wheats. The latter were identified as emmer wheat (*Triticum dicoccum* Schübl) (fig. 12.1) and as a free-threshing wheat (fig. 12.2), probably durum (*Triticum durum*), but they were difficult to sort out because the grains, all charred, had suffered some distortion during burning. In a well-preserved state, their morphology is fairly distinct: emmer, a hulled wheat, has elongated, spindle-shaped grains with a flat dorsal surface, while free-threshing wheats have a rounded appearance. Unfortunately, upon charring cereal grains may expand and even explode like popcorn, depending on the conditions under which they burn. Spindles can blow up into roly-poly spheroids. Thus many of the grains were difficult to identify to species and in the end some of those marked free-threshing might in fact be emmer. Some grains simply could not be identified

Table 12.2   Types of carbonized plant remains at Khirbet et-Tannur.

Locus	Location	Glueck Archive Unit	Emmer Wheat Grains	Free-Thresh. Wheat Grains	Unident. Wheat Grains	Barley Grains	Cereal Grain Fragm. (ml)	Vesicular Material* (gm)	Char-coal (gm)
6	In front of Altar Platform	4A-01	–	–	–	–	–	9	2.5
1	NW and W parts of Inner Temenos Enclosure	4A-05	80	25	8	–	1.6	73	4.0
4	W offertory box	4A-10	48	20	–	1	1.0	15	7.6
3	NE offertory box	4A-11	2	–	–	–	1.0	1	4.5
6	SE end of Altar Platform (behind cult statue)	4A-18	13	6	–	–	< 0.5	–	–
7	Inside Altar Platform	4A-20	–	–	–	–	–	–	0.8
Totals			143	51	8	1	c. 3.6	98	19.4

* Vesicular material: charred amorphous chunks fraught with holes. May be burnt bread.

with any certainly at all and were labeled simply wheat (*Triticum* sp.) grains (fig. 12.3) or cereal grain fragments (fig. 12.4).

The definitive diagnostic traits that distinguish hulled from the free-threshing wheats are found in the rachis and glume bases (the central axis of the cereal head and the stem to which the glumes, or hulls, enclosing the grain are attached). None of this material, however, appears in the samples collected, as discussed below. Thus we can only observe that despite the poor condition of the grains, it appears that there are some free-threshing wheats. Both emmer and durum were common cereals of the ancient world, emmer being the older (Zohary et al. 2012: 24, 41, 45) and hardier plant (van der Veen 2007: 985). Free-threshing wheats, on the other hand, had the advantage of being easier to process. The naked grains break free from the rachis and glumes when the cereal is threshed (hence "free-threshing"), whereas, with

FIG. 12.1 *Charred emmer wheat grains from the north-west and west part of the Inner Temenos Enclosure.*

FIG. 12.2 *Charred grains of free-threshing wheat from the west offertory box.*

FIG. 12.3 *Unidentified wheat grains from the north-west and west part of the Inner Temenos Enclosure. Because of their poor conditions these specimens cannot be definitively identified as emmer or free-threshing wheat.*

FIG. 12.4 *Cereal grain fragments from inside Altar Platform.*

FIG. 12.5 *Barley grain from the west offertory box, the only barley specimen in the collection.*

emmer, a hulled cereal, the spikelet (a packet with grains enclosed in glumes) must be arduously pounded to free the grain (Nesbitt and Samuel 1996: 41, 50; D'Andrea and Haile: 2002: 206–7). Early in the fourth millennium BC, free-threshing wheats eclipsed hulled wheats in the Near East and became the dominant cereal types, except in Egypt (Nesbitt and Samuel 1996: 75).

If the rounded grains are indeed free-threshing wheats, they are probably durum (*Triticum durum* Desf.) rather than the other common free-threshing wheat, bread wheat, *Triticum aestivum*. But we have no way to be sure since the grains are not sufficiently different to separate the two. Nor do we have any rachis material, as noted above, which is the only element among archaeological remains that can be used to distinguish the two (Hillman et al. 1996: 202–3). Durum seems to be a more probable identification as durum wheats are generally adapted to Mediterranean climates, whereas bread wheats are most common at sites in cooler continental Europe (van Zeist and Bakker-Heeres 1982: 199). However, Hillman et al. (1996: 198–99) point out that identification based on geographical and ecological considerations alone is not justified since all wheats can in fact have wide ecological ranges. Whatever the free-threshing wheat may be, emmer was clearly the main cereal at Khirbet et-Tannur.

Charlène Bouchaud (pers. comm. October 2010) has observed that emmer wheat (*Triticum dicoccum*) as the dominant grain at Khirbet et-Tannur contrasts with finds from related sites. She notes that at el-Lejjun (Crawford 2006), southern Syria (Willcox 2003), Udhruh (Neef 1987), ez-Zantur (Karg 1996), and Khirbet edh-Dharih (Bouchaud 2007) *Triticum dicoccum* is very scarce, with *Hordeum vulgare* dominant, followed by *T. aestivum/durum*. Consequently, she suggests that emmer wheat was used in rituals at Khirbet et-Tannur for religious reasons.

The poor condition of the wheat grains indicates that they probably burnt under oxidizing conditions (Boardman and Jones 1990), which sheds light on the way in which they were used at the shrine. Grains burnt as an offering in open flames on the altar would have been exposed to such conditions. This probably was the case for the grains found around the Altar Platform and in the offertory boxes. Those in GA Unit 4A-05, found in the north-west and western parts of the Inner Temenos Enclosure (Locus 1), are probably also offerings.

As mentioned, Glueck recorded in his excavation journal that burnt grains were abundant under the paving of the Inner Temenos Enclosure surrounding the Altar Platform (but no samples were included in this study). However, these grains were probably burnt on the altar(s) of the earlier phases of the site. A sense of the quantity of grain below the paving is conveyed by Glueck's observation, mentioned above, that beneath it "was burning consisting of grain. Did the builders of floor of period 2 lay out an offering layer of grain all over the floor before they put in the stones of the actual floor?" (GJ 14 April).

Barley (*Hordeum vulgare* L.) was represented by a single grain that can probably be dismissed as an incidental. Found in the sample from GA Unit 4A-10, the west offertory box (fig. 12.5; Vol. 1, fig. 401), it occurred with 68 wheat grains. In markets in the Near East today it is not unusual to find an occasional stray barley grain mixed in a sack of wheat and vice versa. However, without systematic sampling of the site we cannot be certain that barley was not used here. Barley could have

Table 12.3   Identified charcoal remains at Khirbet et-Tannur.

Locus	Location	Glueck Archive Unit	Quantity (gm)	No. of Types	Largest in cm	Smallest in cm	Conifer	cf. Acacia	cf. Tamarix	Diffuse porous	Ring porous	Comments
6	In front of Altar Platform	4A-01	2.5	1	2 × 1.2 × 1	0.8 × 0.5 × 0.5	×					
1	NE and W parts of Inner Temenos Enclosure	4A-05	4	5	2 × 0.6 × 1.5	0.3 × 0.15 × 0.1	×	×	×	×		2 types of diffuse porous wood
4	W offertory box	4A-10	7.6	3	4.5 × 2.5 × 3.5			×	×	×		
3	NE offertory box	4A-11	4.5	5	2 × 1.8 × 1	1.2 × 0.5 × 0.4	×	×		×		Charcoal includes small sticks
6	SE end of Altar Platform	4A-18	–									
7	Inside Altar Platform	4A-20	0.8	1	2 × 1 × 1		×					Found with 13 oz of burned bone, 1 piece
Total			19.4									

been fed to sacrificial animals that came in on the hoof (although the bones suggest that they were not slaughtered inside the complex, see Ch. 11). Barley was, and still is, an important fodder plant (Zohary et al. 2012: 52).

One striking feature of the cereals at Khirbet et-Tannur is that they are extraordinarily "clean." There were no field weeds, which are ubiquitous in cereal harvests with traditional agriculture. Nor were there any by-products of cereal processing: rachis segments, glumes, and glume bases. All of these contaminants – weeds and cereal by-products – are removed through a series of cleaning operations that include winnowing, coarse- and fine-sieving, and hand-picking (Hillman 1981; 1984). The last remaining contaminants are usually not removed until just before the grain is prepared for consumption, and even then the batch may not be completely devoid of a stray weed seed or two. Although the total sample from Khirbet et-Tannur is very small, we would expect to see a few weed seeds or glume bases. Perhaps Glueck and his workmen selectively picked up only cereal grains? This is unlikely given that the small grains and

Fig. 12.6 *Coniferous wood charcoal from the north-west and west part of the Inner Temenos Enclosure (see caption to fig. 12.7 for more information about the charcoal).*

contaminants would have been difficult to pluck out of their sediment matrix without forceps and probably a hand lens. On the contrary, the grain-laden samples are a mixture of cereals, bits of charcoal, and burnt bread (?) along with sediments, suggesting that the whole sample was scooped or swept up and placed in a container. Thus the grains probably were meticulously cleaned in antiquity – a food fit for the gods – supporting the notion that they were indeed offerings and not, say, grains that accidentally burnt in storage.

Charcoal

The charcoal (see Table 12.3) was presumably the fuel burnt in the sacrificial fires on the main altar. All the pieces are quite small (as can be seen in figs. 12.6, 12.7a–e) as would be expected if fuel were used frugally. For example, the largest piece is only 4.5 × 3.5 × 2.5 cm. Among the remaining pieces the largest dimension is 2 cm.

Although there is little more than a handful of charcoal bits (c. 19 gm, less than an ounce), some six or seven types of wood are represented. They

include a coniferous wood (fig. 12.6), specimens that might be *Acacia* and *Tamarix* (fig. 12.7a–b), a couple of different diffuse porous woods (one might possibly be poplar or willow) (fig. 12.7c), as well as a ring porous type. The latter term refers to a wood in which annual growth rings are evident and the pores or vessels cluster in the early stages of the ring. In the diffuse porous wood (fig. 12.7e), on the other hand, the pores are scattered throughout the growth of the annual ring. Identification beyond this level is difficult because the pieces of wood are so very small. Definitive identification of the possible *Acacia* and *Tamarix* would require further study.

Even without any definitive identifications, the wood collection is still telling. Six or more wood types is a great deal of variety in less than an ounce of charcoal. All of the pieces appear to be from wood with relatively small diameters: small branches, twigs (fig. 12.7e), and sticks. It appears that priests or pilgrims to Khirbet et-Tannur picked up whatever woody material they could find, probably on their way to the site. The Bdūl bedouin of Petra in the early 1980s would collect firewood, and carry

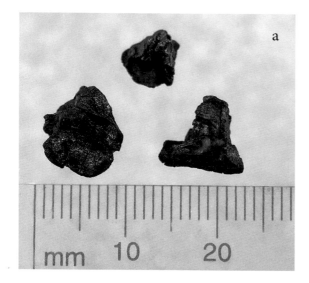

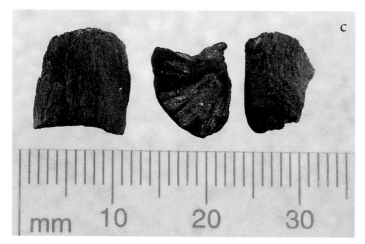

FIG. 12.7 *Even though the total quantity of charcoal in the assemblage is very small, six or seven species are represented, suggesting that the pilgrims collected whatever they could find in the environment to use as fuel, perhaps gathering woody material as they made their way to the site. At the shrine they used their fuel frugally, probably burning most of it to ash, leaving only small bits behind. The pieces, as can be seen when comparing the specimens to the scales in the photos, are mostly under 2 mm long. The photos do not show the tangential surfaces, which are the most useful for identification (at higher magnifications), but are presented here to give a sense of the size and variety of charcoal fragments in the collection.*

a–b. Charcoal fragments, probably acacia or tamarisk, from the north-east offertory box (a) and west offertory box (b).

c. Fragments of charred diffuse porous wood from the north-east offertory box.

d. Charcoal fragments, wood with wide rays from the north-east offertory box. Rays run perpendicular to the long axis of the tree from the center outward, carrying nutrients.

e. Charred twigs of a diffuse porous woods from the north-east offertory box.

it on their donkeys, from as far away as half a day's walk if going there for other reasons, e.g., to Wādī Sabra (J. S. McKenzie, pers. comm., 2010). The immediate environment of Khirbet et-Tannur today is devoid of vegetation, but the wadis at the base of the mountain probably supported some perennial shrubs and trees in the past, as observed today 7 km away at Khirbet edh-Dharih near the spring, 'Ain al-La'abān. The Wādī al-Hasā is a major drainage system with abundant springs and a long history of human habitation going back to the Neolithic (Hill 2000). Farming and pastoralism has undoubtedly degraded the area, leaving some portions of the wadi barren as it is here today. In the past some sections of the wadi may have periodically been denuded and its soils depleted, but then regenerated when left fallow. In a survey of site distribution, Hill (2000) found that settlements shifted about within the wadi over time, suggesting that the inhabitants moved back and forth between degraded and rejuvenated habitats. Today in southern Jordan, poplar, willow, *Tamarix,* and palms grow in wadis, while *Acacia* and a few shrubs are found beyond the wadis. Juniper grows in the open woodlands at higher elevations (Baierle et al. 1989; Danin 1995).

FIG. 12.8 *"Vesicular material" from in front of Altar Platform. These amorphous bits of charred material may be burned bits of offering cakes/breads.*

"Vesicular Material"

These are small, amorphous chunks of charred material fraught with cavities of various shapes and sizes (fig. 12.8). Dr Joseph Greene (pers. comm., 2004) suggested that the material might have come from offering cakes/breads. To test this idea, several informal experiments were carried out. Three types of bread were first carbonized with indirect heat in an oven. They included a conventional light white bread, a heavy "loaf" made by mixing whole wheat flour with a little water, and a "batter loaf" made of white flour and water. After charring in the oven, none of the breads was

a very good match for the vesicular material. But then the chunks were moved into the flame of a gas range where they ignited. Before they could combust completely to ash they were extinguished and examined. The bits of heavy loaf produced something most like the archaeological samples. The irregular pattern of pores and the somewhat bubbled surface were very similar. The other two breads were too light and airy to be a good match. A heavy loaf is what we would expect to have seen at Khirbet et-Tannur if offering cakes/breads were in fact part of the ritual at the shrine. Emmer wheat has little gluten, the protein that produces elastic strands needed for bread to rise (Percival 1921). As a result, emmer makes a dense, heavy loaf. More work would be necessary to confirm that the vesicular material actually is burnt bread fragments, but these experiments are suggestive.

If these charred bits are indeed burnt offering breads or cakes, they raise a question about how the cakes were made and used. Since an open flame was required in the experiments to mimic the features of the ancient specimens, does this mean that the bread was tossed into the flames on the altar? Or were pieces of bread dropped in the fire? Another possibility is that these cakes were baked on site in an open flame and accidentally burnt. Were they perhaps ash-cakes, "… piles of loaves baked in embers," as described in the *Epic of Gilgamesh* (quoted in Stager 2000: 7)? Or were the cakes baked in moulds, known throughout the Mediterranean, from the 4th century BC onward (Karageorghis 2000)? The burnt bits may have been dough that was extruded around the outer edges of the mould and charred when the bread was baked in an open fire. But it is also possible that these limited experiments did not cover the range of possible situations that may have created the burnt fragments. For example, indirect heat higher than what was used in the experiments, or applied over a longer period, may also have achieved the effect. This would then raise another set of questions about how the breads were made and used at Khirbet et-Tannur.

Conclusions

Since there are no written records about sanctuaries such as Khirbet et-Tannur, the miniscule plant

assemblage offers valuable insights into religious practices at this shrine. It appears that scrupulously cleaned grains were given up as offerings in the open flames of the altars. The fuel that kept the altars lit came from shrubs and trees – perhaps acacias, tamarisk, poplars, willows, juniper, and assorted shrubs – gathered within the vicinity of the shrine. Or, if the area had been denuded at this time, possibly carried some distance, collected by pilgrims en route. Offering cakes or bread may have been burnt on the altar in the flames, or scraps from them may have ended up in the fires. Unfortunately, this plant assemblage seems to be mute on another important element of the religious practices: the ritual meals that worshippers consumed in the triclinia at Khirbet et-Tannur. This study, however, is preliminary and further work might uncover clues to the ritual meals.

Note

1   After this study was complete, charcoal was found in GA Unit 4A-07 from Locus 6A, the upper threshold of the Inner Temenos Enclosure doorway. It possibly came from the doors.

References

Baierie, H. U.; Frey, W.; Jagiella, C.;
and Kuschner, H.
1989 "Die Brennstoffressourcen im Raum Fenana (Wadi Araba, Jordanien) und die bei der Kupfererzverhüttung verwendeten Brennstoffe." *Der Anschnitt* 7: 213–22.

Bouchaud, C.
2007 Les Relations hommes-plantes en contexte semi-aride aux périodes classiques et islamiques. Étude carpologique des sites de Bosra (Syrie) et Khirbet edh-Dharih (Jordanie). Unpublished thesis, Université Paris 1 Panthéon-Sorbonne. Paris.

Boardman, S., and Jones, G.
1990 "Experiment on the Effects of Charring on Cereal Plant Components." *Journal of Archaeological Science* 17: 1–11.

Crawford, P.
1987 "Food for a Roman Legion: The Plant Remains from el-Lejjun." Pp. 691–704 in *The Roman Frontier in Central Jordan, Interim Report on the Limes Arabicus Project, 1980-1985*, Vol. 2, ed. S. T. Parker. British Archaeological Reports, International Series 340. Oxford.
2006 "The Plant Remains." Pp. 453–61 in *The Roman Frontier in Central Jordan: Final Report on the Limes Arabicus Project, 1980-1989*, ed. S. T. Parker. Washington, DC.

D'Andrea, A. C., and Haile, M.
2002 "Traditional Emmer Processing in Highland Ethiopia." *Journal of Ethnobiology* 22.2: 179–217.

Danin, A.
1995 "Man and the Natural Environment." Pp. 24–37 in *The Archaeology of Society in the Holy Land*, ed. T. E. Levy. London.

Glueck, N.
1965 *Deities and Dolphins.* New York, NY.

Hill, J. Brett
2000 "Decision Making at the Margins: Settlement Trends, Temporal Scale, and Ecology in the Wadi al Hasa, West-Central Jordan." *Journal of Anthropological Archaeology* 19: 221–41.

Hillman, G.
1981 "Reconstructing Crop Husbandry Practice from Charred Plant Remains of Crops." Pp. 123–62 in *Farming Practice in British Prehistory*, ed. R. Mercer. Edinburgh.
1984 "Interpretation of Archaeological Plant Remains: The Application of Ethnographic Models from Turkey." Pp. 1–41 in *Plants and Ancient Man*, eds. W. van Zeist and W. A. Casparie. Rotterdam.

Hillman, G. C.; Mason, S.; de Moulins, D.;
and Nesbitt, M.
1996 "Identification of Archaeological Remains of Wheat: The 1992 London Workshop." *Circaea* 12.2: 195–210.

Karageorghis, V.
2000 "Another Mould for Cakes from Cyprus: A. The Mould and its Interpretation." *Rivista di studi fenici* 28: 3–5.

Karg, S.
1996 "Pflanzenreste aus den Nabatäischen und Spätrömischen Schichten." Pp. 355–58 in *Petra – Ez Zantur I. Ergebnisse der Schweizerisch-Liechtensteinischen Ausgrabungen 1988–1992*, eds. A. Bignasca et al. Terra Archaeologica 2. Monographien der Schweizerisch-Liechtensteinischen Stiftung für archäologische Forschungen im Ausland [SLSA / FSLA]. Mainz.

Neef, R.
1987 "Botanical Remains." P. 16 in *Udhruh, Caravan City and Desert Oasis. A Guide to Udhruh and its Surroundings*, ed. A. Killick. Romsey, Hampshire.

Nesbitt, M., and Samuel, D.
1996   "From Staple Crop to Extinction? The Archaeology and History of Hulled Wheats." Pp. 40–99 in *Hulled Wheat: Proceedings of the First International Workshop on Hulled Wheats*, eds. S. Padulosi, K. Hammer, and J. Heller. Rome.

Percival, J.
1921   *The Wheat Plant*. London.

Stager, L. E.
2000   "Another Mould for Cakes from Cyprus: B. In the Queen's Image." *Rivista di studi fenici* 28: 6–11.

van der Veen, M.
2007   "Formation Processes of Desiccated and Carbonized Plant Remains – the Identification of Routine Practice." *Journal of Archaeological Science* 34: 968–99.

van Zeist, W., and Bakker-Heeres, J. A. H.
1982   "Archaeobotanical Studies in the Levant. 1. Neolithic Sites in the Damascus Basin: Aswad, Ghoraifé, Ramad." *Palaeohistoria* 24: 165–256.

Willcox, G.
2003   "L'Économie végétale à Bosra et à Sī': résultats d'analyse de restes végétaux carbonisés des périodes romaine, byzantine, et islamique." Pp. 177–84 in *Hauran II: les installations de Sī' 8, du sanctuaire à l'établissement viticole*, eds. J. Dentzer-Feydy, J.-M. Dentzer, and P. Blanc. Beirut.

Zohary, D.; Hopf, M.; and Weiss, E.
2012   *Domestication of Plants in the Old World*, 4th edition. Oxford.

Chapter 13

The Metals

by Judith S. McKenzie, Elias Khamis, and Andres T. Reyes

INTRODUCTION

The dry conditions on the peak of Jabal et-Tannur meant that a few metal objects were recovered in the 1937 excavations of the Khirbet et-Tannur temple complex in relatively good condition.

The non-ferrous metal items include two Seleucid coins (of Antiochus III and IV), at least one Nabataean coin (apparently of Aretas IV), a copper *spatula* (c. 2nd–4th century AD), and a copper-tin-zinc alloy sealing ring (with a portrait head in a similar style to the royal portraits on Nabataean coins of the 1st to early 2nd century AD, but probably an example of non-royal Nabataean portraiture). The latter two objects and the coin of Antiochus III are in the Glueck Archive in the Semitic Museum, Harvard University. The whereabouts of the other coins (and their precise composition) are unknown.

Glueck also had the foresight to save some iron samples, although they are badly corroded, including one pivot hinge of the Inner Temenos Enclosure doors. Microstructural analysis of this hinge by Brian Gilmour (Ch. 14) revealed, surprisingly, that it is an exceptionally early (2nd to mid-4th century AD) example of ultra-high carbon steel, which made it particularly suitable to take the pressure of the weight of the heavy door when it was opened and closed.

Despite expensive hinges, the discovery of only a few nails and no metal sheeting suggests that these doors were painted or left plain, rather than metal clad. If metal sheeting had been salvaged soon after the destruction of the doors, then it is unlikely that the hinges would have been left. This suggests that no metal cladding was found because it was not used to decorate the doors. Evidence of iron-working in the nearby settlement of Khirbet edh-Dharih was found in a 3rd-century AD context (Villeneuve and al-Muheisen 2008: 1508).

CATALOGUE

The "GA metal" numbers indicate the number of metal object or sample in the Glueck Archive, Semitic Museum, Harvard University. Those numbers are the same as their catalogue numbers. The whereabouts of coins without a GA metal number were unknown in 2011.

For abbreviations, see pp. xvii–xviii.

FIG. 13.1   *Inner Temenos Enclosure steps, upper and lower door sills, with slots, facing north. The door hinge, no. 1, came from the cutting near the scale, on the top step, at the north end.*

Iron

1. Door pivot hinge. Figs. 13.2–3, 14.1–3b.
Locus 6A: Inner Temenos Enclosure upper threshold of doorway, north end; GA Unit A-07; GR no. 60; GJ 5 March. GA metal 1.
Door hinge: surviving h. 8.1 cm, w. c. 8 cm. Plus 12 fragments. Ultra-high carbon steel (see Ch. 14).

"Iron door socket" (pivot for hinge) from north end of upper door sill of Inner Temenos Enclosure (fig. 13.1) (*DD* pl. 100a–b), and flaked fragments. The largest piece was apparently originally approximately hemispherical in shape with a rod embedded into the top of it. At time of excavation, 6 March 1937, "one piece shows a screw hole in it," which is no longer visible. This was probably from the tongue which ran along from the top of the "hemisphere" (see fig. 14.1) and would have been embedded in the base of the door to stop the pivot block rotating in the door when it was opened and closed (see reconstruction in fig. 13.3).

FIG. 13.2   *No. 1. Door pivot hinge, top view.*

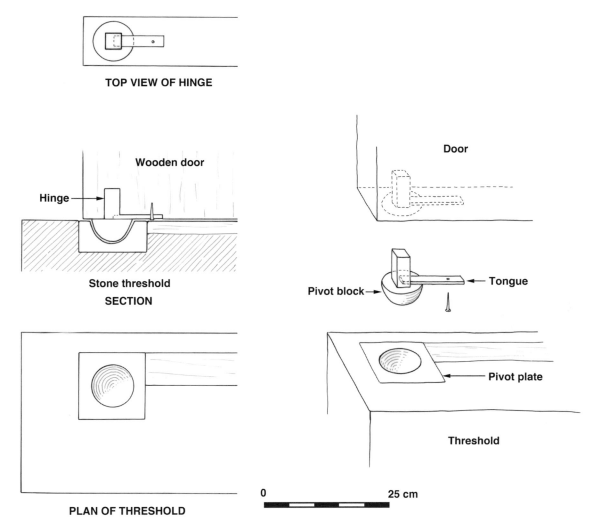

TOP VIEW OF HINGE

SECTION

PLAN OF THRESHOLD

Fig. 13.3 *Hypothetical reconstruction of door hinge in figs. 13.2, 14.1–3b.*

This was the pivot block (rotating on a metal pivot plate) from a pair of hinges for the two Inner Temenos Enclosure main doors which were each 0.43 m wide, 3.85 m high, and (based on the hinge block) probably c. 0.08 m thick. These wood doors must have been made either when the Inner Temenos Enclosure was built in Period 2 (in the first half of the 2nd century AD) or as part of a repair before the fire which destroyed them (apparently in association with the AD 363 earthquake). Based on the dimensions, Joseph Greene (pers. comm.) has calculated that each door would have weighed about 70 kilograms, if made of cedar or juniper.

The apprearance of the door and its pivot hinges can be visualised from Roman examples carved of rock, surviving on tombs such as at Beth She'arim, with similar pivot hinges, usually of stone (Avigad 1976: figs. 5.1–3, 37.1–4, 53, 55, pl. 18.1, bronze example: 48–50, fig. 21). The well-preserved examples for the Petra Church are later and more complex; however, the hemispherical pivot embedded in some of them was made of iron (Fiema and Kanellopoulos 2001: 122–25, figs. 135–46).

2.
Locus 6A: Inner Temenos Enclosure upper threshold of doorway; GA Unit 4A-07. GA metal 2.

Five large and 17 smaller pieces of iron. Apparently from the long tongue or band holding the bottom of the door. Pieces of charred timber,

apparently from the door, were also found in this unit.
Label: "Pieces of iron found 5 March."

3.
Locus 9: apparently south-west end of entrance to Forecourt; GA Unit 4A-22. GA metal 3.

More than 24 small flakes from something like no. 2 above.
Label: "Iron fragments found 7 March at SW end of entrance to east court."

4. *Nail.* Fig. 13.4.
Locus: "debris" outside Inner Temenos Enclosure; GA Unit 20-B14; GR no. 43; GJ 5 March. GA metal 4.
l. 3.8 cm; w. max. 1.0 cm.

Broken tip of slightly curved nail.
Label: "Broken iron nail from outside n. inner court. March 5."

5. *Nails.* Fig. 13.5.
Locus 6: in front of Altar Platform; GA Unit 4A-01. GA Metal 5.
Larger piece: l. 3.3 cm; w. 1.15 cm.
Smaller piece: l. 2.45 cm; w. 1.2 cm.

Apparently pieces of two nails, like no. 4 above.
Label: "Iron fragments (pieces of iron nail), bones and charcoal in front of the east shrine."

6. Fig. 13.6.
Locus 2: north-west corner of Inner Temenos Enclosure; GA Unit 4A-27; GJ 3 March. GA metal 6.
Curved piece: h. 3.7 cm; th. 1.25 cm. Short straight piece: h. 1.8 cm; diam. 1.2 cm. Longer straight piece: h. 3.3 cm; diam. max. 1.0 cm. Pointed piece: h. 1.2 cm; diam. 0.85 cm to 0.45 cm.

Pieces of a long piece of iron of a ? "band," or a hook, with a circular cross-section.
Label: "Metal band from northwest corner of temple courtyard. Mar 3."

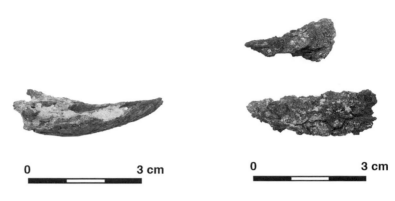

FIG. 13.4   *No. 4. Fragment of nail.*   FIG. 13.5   *No. 5. Fragments of nails.*

FIG. 13.6   *No. 6. Fragment of ? hook.*

7.
Locus: provenience unknown; GA Unit 47-12B. GA metal 7.

Three small pieces of iron.

Alloy and Copper Objects

8. *Sealing ring.* Figs. 13.7a–8. *DD* pl. 57j–k (= GA photo I-38c-d).
Locus 21: Room 14 on south side near the east end of the room; GA Unit 20B-15A; GR no. 87; GJ 7 December. GA metal 8.
h. max. 0.85 cm; diam. max. 2.0 cm; diam. min. 1.7 cm. Alloy of copper, zinc, and tin, with a trace of lead and/or arsenic (metal composition by Katherine Eremin).

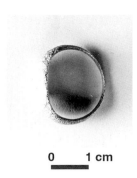

FIG. 13.7A   *No. 8. Sealing ring, actual size.*

→ FIG. 13.7B   *No. 8. Sealing ring, seal with head facing left.*

→→ FIG. 13.8   *No. 8. Sealing from sealing ring, with head facing right.*

Brass-coloured sealing ring, apparently with a small face, looking left, with a tall headdress. The back is worn thin from much wear.
Label: "[No.] 87 bronze ring from Room 14. 12/7/37." [= 7 December].

The ring has an oval bezel in one piece with the hoop, a shape well-attested from at least the Achaemenid period, when different types of metal-rings with engraved bezels proliferated in the Near East (Buchanan and Moorey 1988: 85). Found in Room 14, it cannot be dated closely from its context. Moorey remains uncertain "whether the changing shapes indicated the impact of Greek taste in the east, as is commonly argued, or whether it was a local development at present concealed by the absence of excavated evidence from the mature Iron Age in Anatolia and Syro-Phoenica" (Buchanan and Moorey 1988: 85). The continued lack of archaeologically well-documented comparanda from Near Eastern sites means that the ring from Khirbet et-Tannur can be dated in only the most general way, through the style and appearance of its device, rather than from its shape (Marshall 1907: xlv–xlix; Higgins 1980: 183; Zazoff 1983: 346–47 for attempts to isolate sequences of ring-shapes in the Greco-Roman period; Musche 1988: 218–37, 276–78 for a tentative chronology of

examples from the Near East, with pl. 78, no. 1.3.4 a ring of the 2nd century AD comparable to the one from Khirbet et-Tannur).

The device shows a profile head, facing right when seen in impression (fig. 13.8), cut along the long axis of the bezel, as is customary, rather than the short axis. The neck is long and slender, and the hair – or what may be a headdress – appears with vertically striated lines. The eye is represented by a simple dot. It belongs to a series of such heads from Greco-Roman times, popular from the late 1st through the 3rd centuries AD, showing portraits of the upper-class in profile (Zazoff 1983: 342–43, with pl. 110, no. 6, for a head with a slender neck and vertical striations above, dated to the first half of the 3rd century AD).

The head on the Khirbet et-Tannur example recalls not so much the aristocratic style of Greco-Roman rings, but the more summary appearance of kings on Nabataean coinage, an artistic medium closely related to glyptics. Compare, for example, the dotted eyes and vertically striated headdresses on a coin from Petra showing the heads of king Aretas IV (9 BC–AD 40) and his queen Shaqilat IV (*DD* 130, pl. 58). Also similar are the slender necks and vertical striations above heads on coins with the profile bust of Rabbel II (AD 70–106) (e.g.,

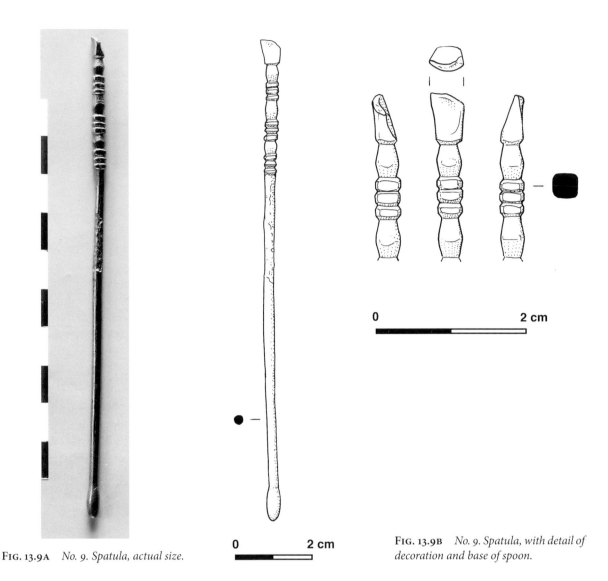

FIG. 13.9A   *No. 9. Spatula, actual size.*

0   2 cm

FIG. 13.9B   *No. 9. Spatula, with detail of decoration and base of spoon.*

Meshorer 1975: pl. 8, nos. 145 and H12). The style of the die-cutting of these coins, especially of Rabbel II, is close to that of the ring-portrait.

It goes beyond the evidence, however, to argue that the head from Khirbet et-Tannur must represent a king and that, therefore, the ring is a royal seal. Nor is it likely that the head is that of a god or goddess, though profile-heads of deities appear in glyptics of the time (e.g., Henig and MacGregor 2004: 36, no. 1.59, an "intaglio of red paste" with no provenance, showing "Helio-Sarapis" and assigned to the 2nd century AD). Since, in the Greco-Roman period, portraits on such rings are largely of the aristocracy, rather than of a ruler or emperor, it is more likely that the head shows a member of the

local upper class. If so, it is a unique example in Nabataean art of miniature non-royal portraiture.

9. *Copper* spatula. Fig. 13.9a–b. *DD* pl. 57 (= GA photo. I-38c). GA photo. I-38d.
Locus 21: Room 14, near north-east end; GA Unit 20B-15B; GR no. 89; GJ 8 December. GA metal 9. l. 12.70 cm; diam. max. 0.4 cm; diam. min. 0.2 cm. Copper with a trace of lead (metal composition by Katherine Eremin).

Spatula with a long rod with a round cross-section. One end terminates in a bulb-like projection. The other ends with the concave stump of a spoon-bowl which is broken off. The spoon's base is decorated with three groups of bead-and-reel pattern, with square cross-section. Preservation is good. Any patina has been thoroughly cleaned, leaving a copper-coloured surface.

Spatulae of a similar type originally have a lanceolate spoon with a ridge running the length of it and a bulb-like projection at the end of the handle. They usually date to the Roman and Byzantine periods and were decorated with a bead-and-reel decoration where the stick meets the spoon. This decoration was probably made by turning on a lathe. These *spatulae* were found in numerous sites both in Palestine and the Roman–Byzantine world. The missing parts could have been a bowl of a spoon, blade, or other parts used for cosmetic or surgical purposes. Most of these implements were used as small spoons (*spatulae*) that were mainly used for mixing and measuring an exact quantity of expensive powdered commodities — medical and cosmetic materials. Some were used as kohl sticks. The most common cosmetic spoon in the classical periods is the *spatula*, which is characterized by a small, elongated spoon shaped like a leaf. The bowl is broken off at its base — a feature known from similar implements found at numerous sites. The point where the bowl meets the handle of the *spatula* is relatively weak and has a tendency to break. Another feature of *spatulae* from the Roman and Byzantine periods is the decoration on the opposite end, which often terminates in a small bulb. Examples with surviving spoons, but with plain handles except for bead and reel decoration at the join with the spoons, were found at Khirbet edh-Dharih (al-Muheisen and Villeneuve et al. 2002: 41, nos. 40–42).

For Roman surgical, cosmetic spoons, probes, and their ancient names, see Bliquez 2003: 323–30. For similar *spatulae* from Jordan and Palestine, see Baramki 1932: pl. 9.9, 11 (first half of the 4th century AD); Needler 1949: pl. 18 (Roman); Crowfoot 1957: fig. 100, nos. 24–25 (2nd–3rd century AD); Colt 1962: 23, no. 7 (7th century AD or later); Yadin 1966: 149 (early Roman); Tushingham 1972: fig. 28, no. 17; pl. 35, no. 16 (Byzantine); Avigad 1976: fig. 9, pl. 73, no. 15 (mid-3rd century AD); Meyers 1981: pl. 9.6, nos. 21, 22 (AD 360–750); Clark et al. 1986: pl. 26, no. 2 (in 7th–8th century fill, but probably earlier); Berry 1988: 233, pl. 8-2, no. 38 (Roman);

Weber 1991: 230, fig. 3, no. 4 (Byzantine); Seligman et al. 1996: 53, fig. 17 (4th–5th centuries AD); Bliquez 1998: 87, figs. 2–4, nos. 12–13 (Roman). From the East Mediterranean, see, for example, Petrie 1927: pl. 23, no. 54 (Roman); Deonna 1938: fig. 252, pl. 74, no. 605 (Roman); Davidson 1952: 184, no. 1334, pl. 82 (probably Late Roman); Waldbaum 1983: nos. 640–42 (Late Roman to early Byzantine).

Coins

Seleucid coins

10. Coin of Antiochus III. Fig. 13.10a–b. *DD* 12, pl. 57e–f, h (= GA photos. I-38a-b; I-38d).
Locus: provenience unknown; GA Unit 20B-15C; GR no. 18. GA metal 10.
Diam. 1.3 cm. Copper and tin (bronze) with a trace of arsenic and/or lead (metal composition by Katherine Eremin).
(Description and comparanda based on notes by A. R. Bellinger, 1 March 1963, in GA.)

Bronze "half" of Antiochus III from Antioch on the Orontes (223–213 BC). Head of Apollo, Laureate. Circle of dots. Reverse: BASILE[OS] on right [ANT]IOCHOU on left. Apollo facing left holding arrow in his right hand and leaning on bow with left elbow. Left leg bent on left, outside mint mark for Antioch.

In February 2011, the coin was examined by Carmen Arnold-Biucchi, Damarete Curator of Ancient Coins of Harvard Art Museums, who confirmed Bellinger's identification, especially of the Antioch mint mark.

Comparanda: Newell 1941: 137, no. 1064, pl. 15. The dot below the mint mark is doubtful on the coin. Cf. p. 136, no. 1056, with mint mark for Antioch alone.

11. Coin of Antiochus IV. DD 12, 183.
Locus 21: east part of Room 14. Whereabouts unknown 2011.

Worn coin of Antiochus IV Epiphanes (c. 175–164 BC).

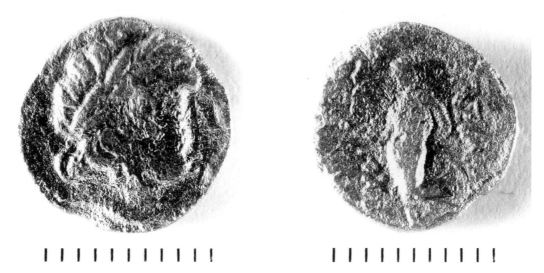

FIG. 13.10A–B   *No. 10. Seleucid coin of Antiochus III: a. obverse; b. reverse.*

FIG. 13.11A–B   *No. 12. Nabataean coin of Aretas IV: a. obverse; b. reverse.*

FIG. 13.12 *No. 17. Possible metal mould.*

Nabataean Coin

12. Coin of Aretas IV. Fig. 13.11a–b. *DD* 11-12, pl. 57a–d (= GA photo. I-37-a, I-37-b, I-37-c).
Locus 15: Room 8 at west end. Whereabouts unknown 2011.

Bronze coin of Aretas IV with crossed cornucopiae on the reverse. For basis of identification, see *DD* 11–12.

Unidentified Coins

13.
Whereabouts unknown 2011.
GJ 5 April: "In back of steps on n. side another coin was found."

14.
Locus 21: Room 14; GR no. 85. Whereabouts unknown 2011.
GJ 6 December: "A Roman (?) coin" was found on south side half way along Room 14.

15.
Locus 15: Room 8. Whereabouts unknown 2011.
GR no. 74: "? coin from w. end of north room I."

16.
Whereabouts unknown 2011.
GR no. 75: "? Coin from back of steps leading down from near w. end of n. wall of n. court."

Possible Metal Mould

17. Fig. 13.12. *DD* 227, 423, pl. 191d (= GA photo I-20b).
Locus: provenience unknown, GR no. 71.
Cincinnati Art Museum no. 289.
Limestone. h. 10 cm; l. 33 cm; th. 10 cm.

Traces of burning around edges of cavity. It does not look especially like a mould (Joe Greene, pers. comm. September 2011).

References

Avigad, N.
1976 *Beth Shea'rim: Report on the Excavations During 1953–1958, Vol. III: The Catacombs 12–23.* Jerusalem.

Baramki, D. C.
1932 "Note on a Cemetery at Karm al-Shaikh, Jerusalem." *Quarterly of the Department of Antiquities of Palestine* 1: 3–9.

Berry, W.
1988 "The Minor Objects." Pp. 227–56 in *Excavations at Jalame*, ed. G. D. Weinberg. Columbia, MO.

Bliquez, L. J.
2003 "Roman Surgical Spoon-probes and their Ancient Names (μήλη, μηλωτίς / μηλωτρίς, *specillum*)." *Journal of Roman Archaeology* 16: 323–30.

1998 "Two 'Sets' of Roman Surgical Tools from the Holy Land." *Saalburg Jahrbuch* 49: 83–92.

Buchanan, B., and Moorey, P. R. S.
1988 *Catalogue of Ancient Near Eastern Seals in the Ashmolean Museum*, Vol. 3. Oxford.

Clark, V. A.; Bowsher, J. M. C.; Stewart, J. D.; Meyer, C. M.; and Falkner, B. K.
1986 "The Jerash North Theatre: Architecture and Archaeology 1982–1983." Pp. 205–302 in *Jerash Archaeological Report 1981–1983*, ed. F. Zayadine. Amman.

Colt, H. D.
1962 *Excavations at Nessana (Auja Hafir, Palestine)*, Vol. 1. Princeton, NJ.

Crowfoot, G. M.
1957 "Roman Tombs: North Cemetery." Pp. 423–38 in *Samaria Sebaste*, Vol. 3: *The Objects from Samaria*, eds. J. W. Crowfoot, G. M. Crowfoot, and K. M. Kenyon. London.

Davidson, G. R.
1952 *Corinth*, Vol. 12: *The Minor Objects*. Princeton, NJ.

Deonna, W.
1938 *Délos*, Vol. 18: *Le Mobilier délien*. Paris.

Fiema, Z. T., and Kanellopoulos, C.
2001 "Appendix B: Observations on the Door Fittings." Pp. 122–26 in Z. T. Fiema, C. Kanellopoulos, T. Waliszewski, and R. Schick, *The Petra Church*. Amman.

Henig, M., and MacGregor, A.
2004 *Catalogue of the Engraved Gems and Finger-Rings in the Ashmolean Museum*, Vol. 2. Oxford.

Higgins, R.
1980 *Greek and Roman Jewellery*. 2nd edition. London.

Marshall, F.
1907 *Catalogue of the Finger Rings, Greek, Etruscan, and Roman in the Department of Antiquities, British Museum*. London.

Meshorer, Y.
1975 *Nabataean Coins*. Qedem 3. Jerusalem.

Meyers, E. M.
1981 *Excavations at Ancient Meiron Upper Galilee, Israel 1971–72, 1974–75, 1977*. Cambridge, MA.

al-Muheisen, Z.; Villeneuve, F.; et al.
2002 *Khirbet edh-Dharih, des Nabatéens au premier Islam*. Amman.

Musche, B.
1988 *Vorderasiatischer Schmuck zur Zeit der Arsakiden und der Sasaniden*. Leiden.

Needler, W.
1949 *Palestine Ancient and Modern: A Handbook and Guide to the Palestinian Collection of the Royal Ontario Museum*. Toronto.

Newell, E. T.
1941 *The Coinage of the Western Seleucid Mints*. New York, NY.

Petrie, F.
1927 *Objects of Daily Use*. London.

Seligman, J.; Zias J.; and Stark, H.
1996 "Late Hellenistic and Byzantine Burial Caves at Giv'at Sharet, Bet Shemesh." 'Atiqot 29: 43–62.

Tushingham, A. D.
1972 *The Excavations at Dibon (Dhībân) in Moab: The Third Campaign 1952–53*. Annual of the American School of Oriental Research 40. Cambridge, MA.

Villeneuve, F., and al-Muheisen, Z.
2008 "Le Sanctuaire nabatéo-romain de Dharih (Jordanie): nouvelles découvertes, 2001–2008." *Comptes Rendus de l'Académie des Inscriptions et Belles-Lettres*: 1495–1520.

Waldbaum, J. C.
1983 *Metalwork from Sardis: The Finds through 1974*. Cambridge, MA.

Weber, T.
1991 "Gadara of the Decapolis: Preliminary Report on the 1990 Season at Umm Qais." *Annual of the Department of Antiquities of Jordan* 35: 223–31.

Yadin, Y.
1966 *Masada: Herod's Fortress and the Zealots' Last Stand*. London.

Zazoff, P.
1983 *Die antiken Gemmen*. Munich.

Chapter 14

Ultra-High Carbon Steel Door Hinge: Microstructural Analysis

by Brian Gilmour

Introduction

Material recovered from the 1937 excavation of the ruined temple complex at Khirbet et-Tannur and stored in the Nelson Glueck Archive in the Semitic Museum, Harvard University, included very badly corroded iron fragments which were found in association with the charred collapsed remains of the pair of doors at the entrance to the Inner Temenos Enclosure, some of which Glueck saved despite their poor condition. The shape, size, and position of the largest fragment suggest that it was most likely the poorly-preserved remnant of the lower hinge belonging to the north door (found *in situ* in the upper threshold of the doorway, fig. 13.1). While some other pieces apparently came from it and other parts of the door, in their present condition they are almost completely unrecognisable as such. These doors would have been installed sometime between the construction of the doorway in Period 2 – the first half of the 2nd century AD – and when the doors were burnt in the mid-4th century. Although very poorly-preserved, it was clear that the hinge was of a distinctive type (pivot hinge) consisting of a long "tongue" – which had been attached to the lower part of the door – with a large (fist-sized) lump at one end (Ch. 13, Iron sample no. 1, fig. 13.2), this having once formed the main weight-carrying pivot assembly (as in fig. 13.3), now totally corroded and virtually unrecognisable.

Examination and Analysis

Despite the unpromising and fragmentary state of these remnants, one "set" of hinge fragments was submitted for analysis on the basis that it might yield some useful information about the style of hinge and the type of iron used. An initial examination showed that there was no surviving metallic iron in any of the fragments. This is to be expected for a long, relatively thin strip of iron forming the tongue, but rather surprising for the lump at the end (figs. 14.1–2), given that it was approximately 8 cm thick. As this temple site was in a very dry place, much slower corrosion of the iron might be expected and hence better survival of metallic iron especially at the lump/hinge axis end, but very careful examination of all the fragments including the lump, showed that no metal survived at all.

Another unusual aspect to the lump was the way it had corroded. Instead of a (however distorted) layered structural pattern to the corrosion – the result of homogenisation/consolidation of the original billet of bloomery iron used – a more radial pattern of deep corrosion fissures was evident in this case, and this is suggestive of a high carbon steel structure as opposed to one merely of iron.

The main hinge block (i.e., the lump) was then subjected to x-ray examination which revealed that there were two main axial orientations or directions to the main corroded but less fissured part of the block (fig. 14.3a–b). These were at right angles to one another, indicating that a part of a heavy iron pivot block – presumably originally embedded in the floor beneath the jamb of the door – still contained the thick iron pivot pin, that is, the part connected to the tongue which was fixed to the bottom of the door (in an arrangement like that in fig. 13.3).

One detached fragment from the heavily fissured part of the corroded hinge block was then mounted and examined metallographically (i.e., using reflected light microscopy). Instead of the usual amorphous or featureless structure – the end result of relatively rapid corrosion of iron in the ground – in this case some evidence of a relic ferrous metal structure survived (fig 14.4). A relic metal structure for any kind of iron only survives where corrosion in the ground is slow, as here was clearly the case because of the dry local burial conditions, and it can be enough to identify, if only approximately, the type of ferrous metal used.

In this case, the structure which survived in places was one which suggested the use of ultra-high carbon steel to make at least part (i.e., the part examined) of the fist-sized hinge block. The structure observed was one which showed traces of a relic grain structure partly marked by (black)

FIG. 14.1 *The main surviving part of the totally corroded and heavily fissured lower hinge block, with tongue, top view.*

FIG. 14.2 *Side view of the main hinge block in fig. 14.1, without tongue.*

corrosion voids left by the secondary corrosion of grain boundary iron carbide (cementite), plus some needle-like voids left by the secondary corrosion of needle-like cementite plates. The more amorphous infill in between this darker relic structure would appear to be what is left of the products of the primary (or first phase of) corrosion of the ferrous block forming this hinge block.

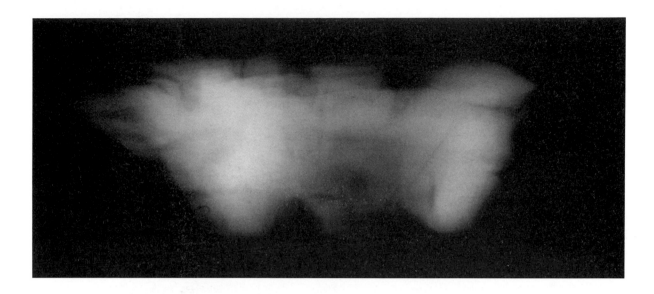

FIG. 14.3A–B   *X-ray image (original and inverted) showing the remains of the swivel pin projecting downwards from the end of the tongue into the lower locating steel block of the hinge.*

In other words, the primary corrosion products resulted from the decay of the infill of the ferrous grains, whereas the black voids were left after the much longer term corrosion of the material – most likely cementite – which once had both formed the surrounding material to each ferrous grain and formed a seemingly random pattern of occasional cementite plates scattered throughout the original section, i.e., this part of the hinge block. Although its survival was patchy (due to differential corrosion rates), this structure is consistent with the use of ultra-high carbon steel in this part of the hinge block at least. The distinctive deeply fissured appearance of the surviving iron hinge block is indicative of the use of ultra-high carbon steel to make the whole hinge pivot block. As this hemispherical pivot block would have rotated in a hemispherical recess in a metal plate recessed into in the end of the door threshold (see reconstruction in fig. 13.3), the question arises whether, in order to minimise wear, the metal plate would have also been made of ultra-high carbon steel.

DISCUSSION AND CONCLUSIONS

This entirely unexpected result suggests the use of ultra-high carbon steel with a carbon content in the region of 1.0–1.2% to make at least the

FIG. 14.4 *Polished section of a fragment from the lower hinge block showing traces of black voids left by the secondary corrosion of grain boundary and needles (plates) of iron carbide (cementite) within an amorphous ground-mass of greyish ferrous corrosion products from the primary corrosion of the matrix (in this case steel): thus a surviving relic ultra-high carbon steel structure. Field of view 0.9 mm wide.*

hinge block, and most likely the hinge tongue and pivot plate as well, of the lower hinge of the Inner Temenos Enclosure north door. Although difficult to work (compared to lower carbon iron or steel), this metal would have been very hard and resistant to wear and so actually very well-suited to its use for this type of hinge. Conceivably, there could possibly have been some kind of extra significance to the use of a very special steel here, but in any case its occurrence suggests that this type of special steel might have been rather better known and more widely used at this date (mid-2nd to mid-4th century AD) than previously suspected.

It may be significant that no non-metallic inclusions were observed amongst the otherwise relatively well-preserved relic ultra-high carbon steel structure. This would suggest the possibility that this was a crucible-made ultra-high carbon steel. This might seem fanciful, given our almost total lack of evidence so far, but this is not so. At least one recipe for crucible steel of this kind was known in the wider region by the 2nd century AD, when it was described by Zosimos of Panopolis (now Akhmim in southern Egypt), and there seems a distinct possibility that the technology was already then of some antiquity (A. Giumlia-Mair, pers. comm. 2012: research in progress).

To this can be added some snippets of evidence that have come from the recent reappraisal of a chapter on iron written (in a work on mineralogy) in Afghanistan by the Iranian scientist al-Biruni in the 11th century, together with mentions in pre-Islamic poetry which can generally be dated to the 4th–6th century and which relate to the Levantine region or further south. The upshot of these is that we can postulate with a fair degree of confidence that a crucible steel-making industry existed by the 6th century AD in the hilly Ḥawrān (Hauran) region of southern Syria c. 90 km (55 miles) south-south-east of Damascus, not far from the present Jordanian border.

The key to these references is the repeated mention of an area or group of villages referred to by the name Mashraf or Masharif which is in turn linked to Mashraf/Ḥawrān, and the connection with the 6th-century Ghassanid dynasty of that region (Hoyland and Gilmour 2006: 97–99, 164–65). Furthermore, the main ancient route from the Nabataean metropolis of Petra north to Damascus, the King's Highway, beside which the temple at Khirbet et-Tannur stood, passes through the Ḥawrān (c. 250 km/150 miles north of Tannur) where the city of Bosra was the Nabataean capital after AD 106 (map 1).

We need to be aware, however, that ultra-high carbon steel(s) can be expected to be of either bloomery (directly produced or smelted) or crucible (indirectly produced) origin. In the case of the Khirbet et-Tannur hinge, a crucible origin makes a lot of sense for two reasons. Firstly, there is the likelihood of crucible steel being available from the Ḥawrān, transported along the King's Highway. Secondly, the fact that this could be cast would make the manufacture – especially of the block or ball of the Tannur hinge (with its locating mortise) – a much more practical proposition than if it had to be forged as a solid lump, which would have been very difficult.

This is not the first time that a relic high carbon steel structure (in this case of probable bloomery origin) has been reported in an early ferrous artefact: a near eutectoid (0.8% carbon) steel structure was observed in a bronze hilted 'iron' dagger of c. 800 BC from Hasanlu, north-west Iran (Knox 1963: 43–45); analyses to look for evidence of this kind are extremely rare but can be very instructive.

High (approximately 0.5–1%) and ultra-high (approximately 1–2%) carbon steel is occasionally reported in early ferrous artefacts, such as a late Roman (approximately AD 315–40) ultra-high car-bon steel punch – with a carbon content approaching 2% – from Heeten, eastern Netherlands, from an ironworking site at which a partially ultra-high carbon steel bloom was also recovered (Godfrey and van Nie 2004: 1117–18, 1122, fig. 6).

But the apparent rarity of early artefacts made of high carbon and ultra-high carbon steel may have more to do with the rarity of metallographic analysis, and therefore recognition, as opposed to the actual former rarity of artefacts made of this alloy. However, they have occasionally been noted, as in the case of a relic ultra-high carbon steel structure seen in an almost completely corroded sword blade excavated in the late 1930s from a probable 9th-century AD level at Tepe Madraseh, Nishapur, in northern Iran (Allan 1982: 57–58), but not examined metallographically until the present author did so much more recently (Allan and Gilmour 2000: 55–56). In this example the needle-like relic cementite structure indicated a slightly higher carbon content (approximately 1.4–1.5%) compared to the Tannur hinge.

The results presented here further suggest that more metallographic investigations of early ironwork might be highly productive in terms of the identification of early specialized ferrous metalwork, even if it is very badly corroded and looks unpromising.

Unfortunately, although ancient low carbon bloomery iron often survives quite well, we cannot expect this degree of preservation in ultra-high carbon steel artefacts because the metal is much more active as far as corrosion is concerned, especially where the metal is of crucible (i.e., liquid) origin. The reason is exactly the same as why modern iron and steel of liquid origin corrodes much faster than early iron and that is essentially because early iron is much purer, in that it contains far less of the impurities which encourage the metal to corrode. But, as we can see here, relic structures often survive and can be used to identify the best of ancient steels, previously barely thought to exist.

REFERENCES

Allan, J.
1982 *Nishapur: Metalwork of the Early Islamic Period.* New York, NY.

Allan, J., and Gilmour, B.
2000 *Persian Steel: The Tanavoli Collection.* Oxford.

Godfrey, E., and van Nie, M.
2004 "A Germanic Ultrahigh Carbon Steel Punch of the Late Roman-Iron Age." *Journal of Archaeological Science* 31: 1117–25.

Hoyland, R., and Gilmour, B.
2006 *Medieval Islamic Swords and Swordmaking: Kindi's Treatise 'On Swords and their Kinds.'* Oxford.

Knox, R.
1963 "Detection of Iron Carbide Structure in the Oxide Remains of Ancient Steel." *Archaeometry* 6: 43–45.

Chapter 15

The Glassware:
Typological Analysis

by Margaret O'Hea

INTRODUCTION

There are over fifty glass fragments from the Nabataean sanctuary of Khirbet et-Tannur in the Glueck Archive in the Semitic Museum, Harvard University, which Nelson Glueck retrieved when excavating it in 1937. He had put some of the larger fragments aside, while others were found bagged with the pottery sherds. Of the at least twenty-nine glass vessels in the resultant assemblage, only eighteen are well-preserved enough to identify as types or their repeats.[1] The types are predominantly beakers (or beaker-like jars), small bowls, and flasks. Where identifiable, the glass types at Khirbet et-Tannur all fall comfortably into the 3rd century AD, perhaps as late as the early to mid-4th century – none is typologically purely Early Byzantine, but all have 4th-century relatives. It is therefore possible that use of glassware here was restricted to the last phase of the temple complex.

By the time he had excavated parts of all the rooms, Glueck mentions in his excavation journal (GJ) finding glass in all of them: "Every now and then in all the rooms bits of glass were found" (GJ 13 April). The loci with fragments large enough to collect are the Inner Temenos Enclosure (Locus 6),

the Forecourt (Loci 9 and 10), just outside it (Locus 19), and Room 14 (Locus 21) (see Table 15.1). Only one of the glass fragments collected comes from the three triclinia on the north side, Rooms 8, 9, and 10.

DISCUSSION

There is nothing to suggest, spatially or typologically, that the surviving glassware was directly related to libation or the pouring of perfumed oils. There are no glass balsamaria – tall-necked flasks for perfumed oils – of any type or from any period, despite their ubiquity in Syro-Palestine up to the very end of the 3rd century AD. However, at least one, and at most four, of the vessels indicated by the fragments could have been medium-sized flasks of forms which elsewhere appear in domestic assemblages, and which therefore could have been used in feasts as oil-flasks as much as for oil-based toiletry products. However, three of these vessels could equally be beakers, reinforcing the dominance of clearly identifiable beakers and small bowls in this repertoire. There are no glass lamps of any form, including the earliest conical and goblet forms. As glass lamps only came into common use within the 4th century, and are not

145

Table 15.1   Glass at Khirbet et-Tannur (by context).

Locus	Location	Glass Catalogue Number	Glass Type Number	MNE	Date in excavation journal, 1937 (and /or on label)	Glueck Archive Unit
6	SE corner of Inner Temenos Enclosure	8 and 9	5 (beaker)	2	4 March (also on label)	4A-18
9	SW end of Forecourt	1 21	1 (bowl) 13 (base re-used as lid)	1 1	7 March (also on label)	20-B13
10	Inside S wall of Forecourt	23	two unidentified joining body fragm.	1	This area 5/6, 9 March	4A-13
14A	Ditch N of N wall of Inner Temenos Enclosure	10 and 11	6 (beaker)	2	This area 7, 11 March, 4 May, 6 December	4A-19
16	SW end of Room 9	29	Unidentified base	1	This area 6–9 April	A-11
19	Outside northmost door to Forecourt	6 3 18 19 and 20 22 7	4 (small bowl or large beaker) 3 (small bowl or wide beaker) 11 (flask) 12 (flask) flask bowl	1 1 1 2 1 1	(on label: 11 April)	20-B09
21	Room 14	2 13 14 16 15 25, 26 and 27 28 4	2 (small bowl) 8 (beaker-jar) 9 (small bowl or large flask) squat beaker beaker unidentified rims unidentified base 3 (small bowl or wide beaker)	1 1 1 1 1 1 1	7 December (also on label) —	A-06 20-B12
? 21	Probably Room 14 ("8-room II")	12 17	7 (beaker) 10 (flask)	1 1	13–14 April (on label: 13 April)	A-08
?	"Rm 3"	5	3 (small bowl or wide beaker)	1	—	20-B12
—	Provenience unclear ("N room W side")	24	Unidentified body fragment	1	—	4A-26

yet attested archaeologically for pagan temples, this is unsurprising.

In the absence of any vessels that can be directly related to sacrifice or offerings, the glass might be expected to have been associated with ritual dining in the triclinia flanking the temple's Forecourt, although there are no plates, jug rims, or flagon/flask handles of any kind. Shallow glass platters were not common in mid- or Late Roman glassware anywhere, reflecting perhaps the taste in Late Roman pottery for shallow and deep bowls for dining, but trefoil-mouthed jugs and wine flagons would be expected in any Late Roman (3rd-century) or Byzantine domestic glass assemblage large enough to be statistically representative. Flagon handles, in particular, have a high survivability rate where originally present, and are easily identifiable, so their absence suggests a scarcity of this common type of glass wine-vessel on the site.

The presence of identifiable dining rooms at Khirbet et-Tannur (Vol. 1, figs. 30, 51, 210–15, 217–18, 227) and adjoining the temple in nearby Khirbet edh-Dharih (fig. 393) demonstrates that ritual dining took place in these Nabataean sanctuaries. Khirbet edh-Dharih also yielded glass vessels, but it remains unclear whether or not this glassware was used in symposia.

Glass vessels from the sanctuary complex at Khirbet edh-Dharih (dated from the second half of the 2nd to the 4th century AD) overlap in date with those from Khirbet et-Tannur. In the absence of a published trench concordance, however, it is not always clear which glass came from the temple at Khirbet edh-Dharih and which from buildings beyond its temenos, but the bulk of the glass represented in Dussart 2007: figs. 2–6, is said to have come from the temple (Dussart 2007: 208). Bowls – both shallow and deep – predominate, but beakers, flasks, and balsamaria are also well-attested, albeit not in the proportions seen in Roman funerary contexts. There are also a few small trefoil-mouthed jugs (Dussart 2007: fig. 6.8). It could, of course, be argued that the glass bowls and beakers at Khirbet edh-Dharih were left with food offerings for the gods, as could the much smaller number of flasks. But the broad overlap of glass vessel functions with that of Khirbet et-Tannur means that it is possible

that they were used for ritual dining at Khirbet edh-Dharih.

When Glueck discovered the first glass in the Inner Temenos Enclosure in the first week of the excavation, he gleefully noted "the Nabataeans did make glass!" (GJ 4 March). In fact, in 1936–37, Murray and Ellis had already retrieved Early Roman glass from the caves at Wādī Abu 'Olleqah, Petra, but it was only cursorily published three years later (Murray and Ellis 1940: 15, 26, pls. 14 and 36). Whether the Nabataeans before the Roman annexation of Arabia in AD 106 did, in fact, make their own glass is very much up for debate. Of the relatively small amount of early glass recorded from Nabataean Petra, very little can be attributed to a local Levantine production, rather than be identified by fabric and form as imports from Egypt or the Mediterranean world (Keller 2006: 183; O'Hea, in press). Most of these putative imports are decolourised and cut tableware. Whether the smaller proportion of naturally-hued blown glass was also imported in the 1st century from neighbouring Judaea or the Decapolis cannot be determined by either typology or scientific analysis; work by Swan and Marii on the glass from Petra can, at best, identify only these two broad groupings from the first two centuries AD (Marii 2007). There are no peculiarly Nabataean forms, for example, and compositional analysis to determine provenance of glass vessels can group glass into a shared "recipe" but not pinpoint where the glass was worked into vessels, since both the raw glass and its colourants could and did traverse the Mediterranean.

From the "Great Temple" Complex at Petra no glass has been identified either typologically or stratigraphically as purely 3rd century in date, and so it is not possible to make a direct comparison with the Khirbet et-Tannur vessels, although activity continued in the area of the "Great Temple," and its Lower "Temenos" until the late 5th or mid-6th century (Joukowsky 2007: 406–7). The late 1st- to early 2nd-century phases of the "Great Temple" site did, however, yield glass bowls, drinking vessels, and flagons. All of these are likely to have been imports from either the Mediterranean or from Egypt, and relatively high-value glass vessels. However, there is controversy over the function

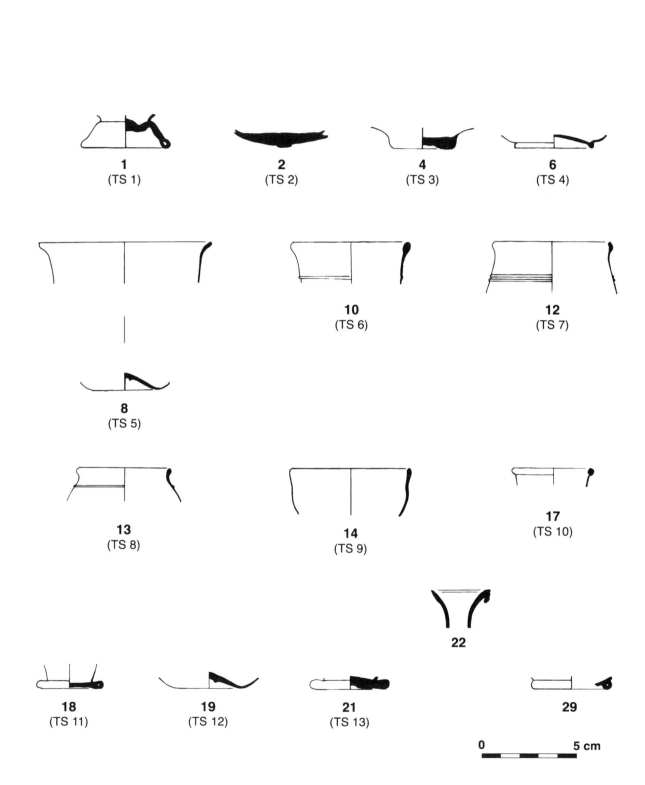

Fig. 15.1 *Profiles of glass, with catalogue and Type Series (TS) numbers.*

of the "Great Temple" in these earlier periods: it could be argued that the glass table and drinking wares from it were for feasts held by the royal and/or civic administration rather than purely cultic activity. There is no reason to assume any ancient clear-cut distinction between religious, royal, and civic ritual feasting, whether in terms of the nature and location of the feast or of the participants.

Whether calculated by weight or by MNE (Minimum Number Estimate), the dominant glass fabric at Khirbet et-Tannur is blue-greenish, as elsewhere in the Roman Levant. Only two identified vessels are greenish, and only one bluish glass vessel was retrieved. Roughly 13% (MNE 3) of the vessels were decolourised, but these may be under-represented as a percentage of the total weight because decolourised glassware in the 2nd and 3rd centuries was typically thin-walled and therefore could have a low survivability rate. Furthermore, the heyday of decolourised glass tableware was during the later 1st to early 2nd centuries, and this is missing entirely from the excavated corpus. The low number of vessels retrieved in Glueck's excavations here makes any statistical observation extremely tentative. (Only the bowl-base Type 4 was decolourised effectively; the other two vessels are under-decolourised or over-decolourised, the former shown by faint natural blue-greenish tinting and the latter by uneven pinkish mottling.)

Most glass from any site within what had been Nabataea dates from the Late Roman (3rd-century) or Byzantine periods – a point which holds true for all sub-regions in the Levant. It is mainly the ubiquity of low-cost, blown glass on all sites of the Levant which underpins the modern consensus that every major town of these periods probably had its own glass workshops. There is no reason to think that Roman or Byzantine Petra was any different. Indeed, recent work on 5th- to 6th-century glass from Petra has identified a characteristic occurrence of calcium phosphate and manganese oxide which is shared by blown glass vessels found at Petra and Deir 'Ain 'Abata, and bun-shaped ingots of glass used for mosaic-making in Petra's churches (Marii and Rehren, in press). Results of the chemical analysis (Ch. 16) suggest that the glass at Khirbet et-Tannur was produced in a local production centre, possibly even in Khirbet edh-Dharih, rather than in Petra.

CATALOGUE

All fabric colours are translucent, and all glass is blown. The catalogue numbers are the same as those on the glass fragments themselves (GA glass) in the Glueck Archive (numbered in June 2010) and used for the chemical analysis in Ch. 16. The chemical groups are those determined in Ch. 16. The Minimum Number Estimates (MNE) (i.e., of examples) are based on unassociated rim or base fragments. TS refers to Types Series.

For other abbreviations, see pp. xvii–xviii.

Possible Bowls

At least five, and at most seven, bowls are represented in the small assemblage from the temple. All are small bowls, whose functionality in terms of eating or drinking is impossible to determine. In addition to the six of Types 1–4 below, there were small body fragments of a thin-walled, greenish bowl with tubular trailed decoration (no. 7).

Type 1: Everted Small Bowl Rim and Folded Base

1. Figs. 15.1, no. 1; 15.2, no. 1; Vol. 1, fig. 404b.
Locus 9: south-west end of Forecourt; GA Unit 20-B13; GJ 7 March. GA glass 1.
Rim diam. 10 cm; base diam. 4.5 cm. Chemical group: outlier.

Everted fire-rounded rim, folded on self below slight, carinated ridge on steep body, very thin walled. Three, of seven, fragments join and taper to a narrow base (c. 2 cm), on high folded foot, centre kicked with reamer and small light pontil scar. Thin walled. Blue-greenish. Flaky iridescence.

MNE: 1. The type should be mid-3rd or early 4th century, as examples occur further east at mid-3rd century Dura-Europos (Clairmont 1963: 54, nos. 226–27). The form persisted, however, into the late 4th/5th century at Jalame (Weinberg and Goldstein 1988: 52, no. 97, fig. 4-12) and Pella (Hennessy et al. 1989: 433, fig. 11, no. 3).

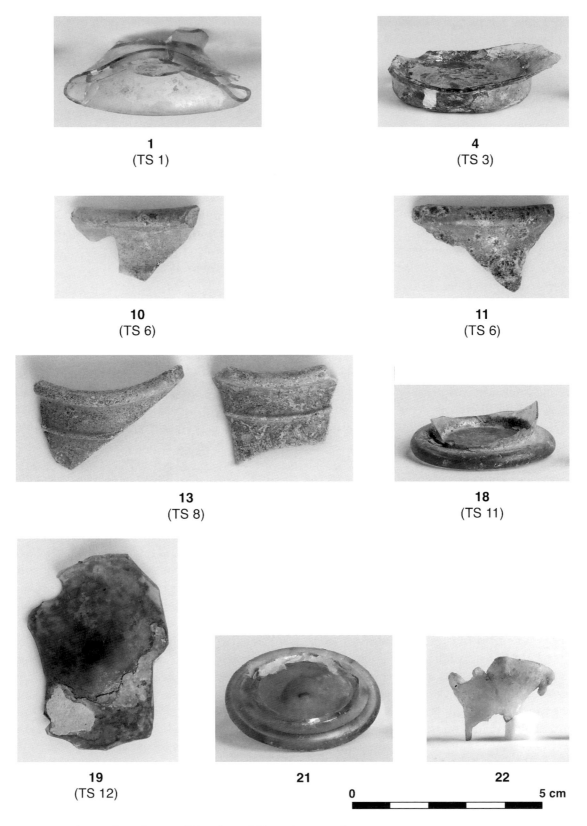

FIG. 15.2 *Glass, with catalogue and Type Series (TS) numbers, actual size.*

Type 2: Footed Bowl Base

2. Fig. 15.1, no. 2.
Locus 21: Room 14; GA Unit A-06; GJ 7 December.
GA glass 2.
Base diam. > 4 cm. Chemical group: Tannur 1.

Foot missing; rounded bowl base, thickened at centre. Small pontil blob still attached. Medium-thick; strongly blue-greenish. Enamel-like black weathering.

MNE: 1. This is too small for typological comparisons.

Type 3: Pad Base

3.
Locus 19: outside northmost door to Forecourt;
GA Unit 20-B09. GA glass 3.
Chemical group: Tannur 1.

4. Figs. 15.1, no. 4; 15.2, no. 4.
Locus 21: Room 14; GA Unit 20-B12. GA glass 4.
Chemical group: Tannur 1.

5.
Locus unclear: "Rm 3;" GA Unit 20-B12. GA glass 5.
Base diam. 4 cm. Chemical group: Tannur 1.

Wide low base, curving in to pad with solid pontil mark. Medium-thin walled. Dark blue-greenish. Enamel-like black hydration.

MNE: 3. As not much survives from any of these above the heel, it is possible that these belonged to small bowls or wide beakers. Pad bases developed in the 3rd century on both bowls and some beakers. A hybrid form from near Ben-Shemen dates from the late 2nd or 3rd centuries (Reich 1982: 3, fig. 3, pl. 5) but a bowl found in a 3rd-century building at Palmyra might be later, that is, Early Byzantine (Bylinksi 1995: 242, fig. 16, no. 1). Pad bases were commonest, however, on 4th- to early 5th-century beakers, such as those found at Jalame in the Galilee (Weinberg and Goldstein 1988: 61, no. 171, fig. 4-23) and at Pella. Unlike the Galilean examples, all three at Khirbet et-Tannur have sheared, solid pontil marks, which could be a regionalised variation in glass-working.

Type 4: Small Bowl or Large Beaker, Low Folded Ring-Base

6. Fig. 15.1, no. 6.
Locus 19: outside northmost door to Forecourt;
GA Unit 20-B09. GA glass 6.
Base diam. 4 cm. Chemical group: Tannur 2.

Wide low heel, curving in to low folded ring-base, thickened and centre exterior; negative pontil scar. Medium-thin walled. Decolourised, very faintly yellowish. White enamel-like weathering.

MNE: 1. This decolourised fabric is unusual; it could be an imported and/or decorated vessel.

Type Unclear

7.
Locus 19: outside northmost door to Forecourt;
GA Unit 20-B09. GA glass 7.
Chemical group: Tannur 2.

Three body fragments, two joining, of a thin-walled bowl, with tubular trailed decoration. Greenish.

Beakers and Flasks

As early as 1952, Vessberg published the possibility that many small, squat beakers could have functioned as jars for "salves and cosmetics," citing the series of painted mid-Roman glass lids from Cyprus which seemed to belong to these low, baggy vessels (Vessberg 1952: 120, on type A jars). They occur as late as the Severan period (Vessberg 1952: 120, 145–46). Later versions of the same, drooping forms with lid have been found at Hanita, datable to the 3rd–4th centuries (Barag 1978: 27–30).

Given the possibility that at least some examples of this baggy form functioned as jars rather than beakers, it remains to be asked what exactly could have been contained within them (ed.: also called sack-shaped beakers, e.g., for nos. 10–13, 19). Ointments aside, even the most traditional tumbler-shaped cup was on occasion shown functioning as a green olive- or fruit-jar at Herculaneum (*Soprintendenza per i Beni Archeologici delle Province di Napoli e Cuserta*, inv. 8610). An *olla* painted on the cubiculum of the Samnite House shows peppers in water (Scatozza-Höricht 1986: pl. 3). The 3rd-century food and wine bar at Ostia (I, II, 5) famously advertised its light refreshments by showing two glass tumblers (Bianchi-Bandinelli 1970: 401, pl. 71), one of which sits on its own stand, and which Meiggs (1973: 428) described as showing "olives in brine," although other foods have been suggested. Unlike the mid- to Late Roman series discussed by Vessberg and Barag, the murals do not show glass lids for glass food-containers. Lids are not represented in the small assemblage here either.

At Khirbet et-Tannur, Types 7–8 share with the earlier *olla* an inverted neck and wide body. It is perfectly plausible, if not provable, that the Nabataean beakers could have been used either for drinking wine, water, or other beverages, or were pickle/fruit jars for diners. Roman imperial images in mosaic and murals of glass drinking vessels tend to show sets – that is, decanters, ewers, or pitchers, as well as goblets or tumblers – in the one medium, as with silverware. In the absence of glass goblets or hemi-spherical drinking bowls, the only glass contenders for a group of drinking vessels here are the beakers, but there are no strap-handled flagons represented in this small assemblage, despite the robustness of glass flagon handle fragments. However, not much weight rests on this absence, since handle-less carafes were also used for wine, as seen on a late 2nd-century mosaic from Carthage which shows a servant carrying a wine-filled glass carafe, suspended by a leather or rope thong (Ceselin 1998: pl. 15, no. 3); it is unclear if it is trefoil-mouthed for pouring. At most, the Khirbet et-Tannur material might have contained one flask of similar proportions, surviving only as a neck 2 cm in diameter.

The possibility that the beaker forms at Khirbet et-Tannur were for food rather than drink, therefore, remains a valid but unverifiable hypothesis. It must be added that at the Faiyum town of Karanis, a baggy Late Roman (3rd-century) beaker had a cloth cover and was assumed to be used for cosmetics (Harden 1936: 132).

In addition to the seven beakers indicated below, another two beakers were identified. One was a simple everted rim fragment (no. 15), too small to take a profile or diameter, but likely to be a beaker rather than a larger bowl (roughly speaking, complete glass bowl-profiles seldom have rims smaller than 10 cm, whilst complete beakers are usually 6–9 cm in diameter). In addition, blue-greenish body fragments from a squat beaker (no. 16) with at least three small indentations were retrieved from Room 14 (Locus 21). Indented glass beakers have a long life-span, popular from Flavian times through to the 4th century, when indentations were typically longer, on tall forms. No rim or base could be associated with these undrawable fragments, making typological comparisons difficult, but the very short indentations are suggestive of the type of squat beaker excavated at Amathus Tomb 17, dated by a single coin of c. AD 140 to the late 2nd century on the assumption that the coin's wear implied about twenty years from mint-date to deposition (Vessberg 1952: 154–55). Needless to say, the beaker could have been later still, and a 3rd-century date would not go amiss.

Ovoid trailed beakers of the 3rd into 4th century in naturally-hued fabrics are commonplace throughout the Levant. At Petra, mid-3rd century examples come from domestic contexts at ez-Zantur (Keller 2007: 55, 221, fig. 16. VII.37c) but not the late 3rd- to early 4th-century baths annexed to the "Great Temple" Complex (O'Hea, in press). Cylindrical trailed beakers of the Early Roman period and at least one with ovoid or baggy body from the Late Roman or Early Byzantine periods were also retrieved from Khirbet edh-Dharih (Dussart 2007: fig. 5.5–7) but in greenish or olive-greenish fabrics – that is, naturally-hued glass.

There are also flasks represented in the temple assemblage and fragments of a flared neck (no. 22). Late Roman (3rd century) flasks typically no longer had the flat, folded rims of earlier unguentaria, but had either shallow or very steep and narrow funnel-mouths; the latter are best described as tall-mouthed, as they can be almost cylindrical, with or without a clearly-defined neck below. Tall-mouthed flasks can be decanter-sized, with rim diameters approximating those of beakers and Early Byzantine goblets, but those with rolled rims have a straight, sloping profile not usually found on contemporary beakers.

Type 5: Everted Beaker Rim (and Probable Base)

8. Fig. 15.1, no. 8.
Locus 6: south-east corner of Inner Temple Enclosure; GA Unit 4A-18; GJ 4 March. GA glass 8. Rim diam. 9 cm. Chemical group: Tannur 1.

Everted rim on upright wall. Thin walled. Four fragments, three non-joining. Possibly decolourised, faintly blue-greenish. Black on iridescent flaking.

9.
Locus 6: south-east corner of Inner Temple Enclosure; GA Unit 4A-18; GJ 4 March. GA glass 9. Chemical group: Tannur 1.

A simple, kicked base with pronounced pontil scar probably belongs to the type, but does not rejoin.

MNE: 2. This common form is late 3rd and 4th century (Pella type 30a), also found at Hanita (Barag 1978: 31), Nahariyah, Samaria-Sebaste, and Lohamei HaGeta'ot (Peleg 1991: 135).

Type 6: Small Tooled Beaker Rim

10. Figs. 15.1, no. 10; 15.2, no. 10.
Locus 14A: "Ditch" north of north wall of Inner Temenos Enclosure; GA Unit 4A-19. GA glass 10. Rim diam. 5.5 cm. Chemical group: Tannur 2.

Everted fire-rounded rim, curving in to upright wall. Single tooled ridge below carination. Medium walled. Strongly blue-greenish. Black on iridescent patches.

11. Fig. 15.2, no. 11.
Locus 14A: "Ditch" north of north wall of Inner Temenos Enclosure; GA Unit 4A-19. GA glass 11. Chemical group: Tannur 2.

Almost identical to no. 10 above.

MNE: 2. Clearly tooled, not trailed (with corresponding recess on internal wall), it nevertheless is similar to Jalame no. 196 (Weinberg and Goldstein 1988: 63–64, fig. 4-25) and a trailed beaker with pad base like Type 3 from Lohamei HaGeta'ot (Peleg 1991: 135, fig. 8, no. 13) where it was dated to the

early to mid-4th century by associated finds. This does not, however, preclude the Khirbet et-Tannur rim from being an earlier 3rd-century version.

Type 7: Everted Sagging Beaker Rim, Trailed

12. Fig. 15.1, no. 12.
Locus ? 21: probably Room 14 ("8-room II"); GA Unit A-08; GJ 13 April (date on label). GA glass 12. Rim diam. 6 cm. Chemical group: outlier.

Everted fire-rounded rim, gently curving to sagging beaker. Pair of fine trails added upper body. Probably decolourised, or faintly greenish, with contrasting trails in either strongly blue-greenish or mid-bluish. Thin walled. Flaky iridescence.

MNE: 1. This has parallels from Cyprus and elsewhere (Vessberg 1952: 10, pl. IV, Bii gamma) either with simple domed base or rolled foot.

Type 8: Everted Rim Convex Beaker-Jar, Trail-Decorated

13. Figs. 15.1, no. 13; 15.2, no. 13.
Locus 21: Room 14; GA Unit A-06; GJ 7 December. GA glass 13.
Rim diam. 5.5 cm. Chemical group: Tannur 2.

Everted fire-rounded rim, on very convex beaker/jar. Medium-thick walled. Single fine trail added below rim carination. Blue-greenish. Three fragments, non-joining. Enamel-like black hydration.

MNE: 1. Variant of Type 7.

Type 9: Simple Rim

14. Fig. 15.1, no. 14.
Locus 21: Room 14; GA Unit A-06; GJ 7 December. GA glass 14.
Rim diam. 6 cm. Chemical group: Tannur 2.

Simple fire-rounded upright rim, curving in to missing body. Medium walled. Bluish. Black on iridescence.

MNE: 1. Either from very small bowl, or large, tall-mouthed flask. This is the only vessel from the site which is certainly of a bluish fabric, but cannot be precisely dated typologically. (ed.: cf. 'Ein ez-Zeituna: Winter 2006: 80, fig. 2.22)

Type Unclear

15.
Locus 21: Room 14; GA Unit A-06; GJ 7 December.
GA glass 15.
Chemical group: Tannur 2.
  Simple everted rim fragment, likely to be from a beaker.

16.
Locus 21: Room 14; GA Unit A-06; GJ 7 December.
GA glass 16.
Chemical group: Tannur 2.
  Body fragments of a squat beaker with at least three small indentations. Blue-greenish.

Type 10: Tall-Mouthed Flask with Rolled Rim

17. Fig. 15.1, no. 17.
Locus ? 21: probably Room 14 ("8-room II"); GA Unit A-08; GJ 13 April (date on label). GA glass 17.
Rim diam. 4 cm. Chemical group: Tannur 2.
  Everted rim, rolled in, on straight steep mouth. Medium walled. Indeterminate fabric, probably blue-greenish. Black on iridescence.
  MNE: 1. This is from a large flask, probably of Late Roman (3rd-century) / Early Byzantine type. Tall-mouthed flasks have been interpreted as tableware (Vessberg 1952: 111), and could have functioned as small decanters or condiment containers.

Type 11: Flask Footed Base

18. Figs. 15.1, no. 18; 15.2, no. 18; Vol. 1, fig. 404c.
Locus 19: outside northmost door to Forecourt, but labelled "Debris;" GA Unit 20-B09. GA glass 18.
Base diam. 3.5 cm. Chemical group: Tannur 1.
  Narrow, tapering body with flat folded foot. Medium-thin walled. Strongly blue-greenish. No pontil mark. Iridescent patches.
  MNE: 1. variant of Jalame types 190 and 198 (Weinberg and Goldstein 1988: 63–64, fig. 4-24, pl. 4-10).

Type 12: Simple Kicked Base

19. Figs. 15.1, no. 19; 15.2, no. 19.
Locus 19: outside northmost door to Forecourt;

GA Unit 20-B09. GA glass 19.
Base diam. 4 cm. Chemical group: Tannur 1.
  Rounded heel, base lightly kicked with reamer; small pontil scar. Thin walled. Decolourised, faintly aubergine tint. Some flaking, removed.

20.
Locus 19: outside northmost door to Forecourt; GA Unit 20-B09. GA glass 20.
Chemical group: Tannur 2.
  Shape and colour as for no. 19 above, but smaller fragment.

MNE: 2. These could be from either flasks or sack-shaped beakers.

Type 13: Low Folded Base, Re-Used as Lid

21. Fig. 15.1, no. 21.
Locus 19: SW end of Forecourt; GA Unit 20-B13; GJ 7 March. GA glass 21.
Base diam. 3.5 cm.
  Thin walled body, mostly missing, on flat folded base, pushed slightly with reamer point within negative small pontil scar. Strongly greenish, almost lime. Flaky iridescence.
  MNE: 1. This has clearly been retouched, its walls chipped down to form a disc, perhaps for use as a lid, although it must be noted that it is too small to fit any of the glass beakers. This distinctively flat version of the folded foot on beakers may have become unusual by the late 4th century in the Galilee and Samaria (Weinberg and Goldstein 1988: 63, no. 193, fig. 4-24); the original vessel-form here could be either a beaker or a footed flask.

Non-Diagnostic Fragments

22. Figs. 15.1, no. 22; 15.2, no. 22.
Locus 19: outside northmost door to Forecourt; GA Unit 20-B09. GA glass 22.
Rim diam. 2 cm. Chemical group: related to HIMT glass.
  Three fragments, two joining, of flared flask neck, tapering to 1 cm diam. neck. Very hydrated.

23.
Locus 10: inside south wall of Forecourt; GA Unit 4A-13. GA glass 23.
Two very thin, joining, body fragments.

24.
Locus: provenience unclear ("N. room w side"); GA Unit 4A-26. GA glass 24.
One body fragment.

25.
Locus 21: Room 14; GA Unit A-06; GJ 7 December. GA glass 25.
Chemical group: Tannur 2.
Rim fragment.

26.
Locus 21: Room 14; GA Unit A-06; GJ 7 December. GA glass 26.
Very thin rim fragment.

27.
Locus 21: Room 14; GA Unit A-06; GJ 7 December. GA glass 27.
Very thin rim fragment.

28.
Locus 21: Room 14; GA Unit A-06; GJ 7 December. GA glass 28.
Chemical group: Tannur 2.
Thick base.

29. Fig. 15.1, no. 29.
Locus 16: south-west end of Room 9; GA Unit A-06. GA glass 29.
Base diam. 4 cm. Chemical group: Tannur 1.
Fragment of small bowl base, formed by tubular ring.

Notes

1   I am grateful to Dr J. McKenzie for inviting me to study the glass from Glueck's excavations, and to Dr J. Greene for facilitating my access to the material stored at the Semitic Museum.

Editors' comment:
The drawings are by Margaret O'Hea, except fig. 15.1, nos. 22 and 29, which are by Catherine Alexander of pieces discovered after this report was initially prepared. The catalogue numbers, loci information, Table 15.1, chemical groups (from Ch. 16), and the non-diagnostic fragments (nos. 22–29) have been added by the editors, who have made every effort not to introduce errors. The parallels, terminology used, and conclusions are the responsibility of the author who, regrettably, would not respond to peer-review comments, nor proofs.

Further comparanda may be found in Erdmann 1977 (Mezad Tamar); Gorin-Rosen 2002 (Burial Cave D at Hurfeish, 3rd century AD, with many complete vessels); Winter 2006 ('Ein ez-Zeituna); and Winter 2010 (Nahal Haggit in southern Carmel). These have been added to the bibliography by the editor. Additional recent bibliography may be found in Winter 2010. The author compares many of the vessels to those found at Jalame (Weinberg and Goldstein 1988). Most of the glass vessels there are dated to the second half of the 4th century AD, the time of the glass workshop at the site, except for several fragments found in earlier contexts. Much closer parallels for the earlier examples have been found at other sites, including in the Judean desert and those mentioned above (Winter 2006; 2010). The types at Jalame dated to the second half of the 4th century AD are later than the material from Khirbet et-Tannur and so only demonstrate the continuity of the shapes and not their earlier or original forms.

For discussion of the results of the chemical analysis, see Ch. 16 below.

REFERENCES

Barag, D.
1978   "Hanita Tomb XV," *'Atiqot* (English Series) 12: 1–58.

Bianchi-Bandinelli, R.
1970   *Rome, the Centre of Power*, trans. P. Green. London.

Bylinksi, J.
1995   "A IIIrd Century Open-Court Building in Palmyra. Excavation Report," *Damascener Mitteilungen* 8: 213–46.

Ceselin, F.
1998   "Il vetro in epoca romana: un bene suntuario? Risultato di un'analisi delle fonti iconografiche.» Pp. 131–38 in *Il vetro dall'antichità all'età contemporanea: aspetti tecnologici, funzionali e commerciali (atti 2e giornate nazionali di studio AIHV – Comitato nazionale italiano 14-15 dicembre 1996)*. Milan.

Clairmont, C.
1963   *The Glass Vessels. The Excavations at Dura-Europos, Final Report* 4, Part 5. New Haven, CT.

Dussart, O.
2007   "Fouilles de Khirbet ed-Dharih, III. Les Verres." *Syria* 84: 205–48.

Erdmann, E.
1977   "Die Glasfunde von Mezad Tamar (Kasr Gehainije) in Israel." *Saalburg Jahrbuch* 34: 98–146.

Gorin-Rosen, Y.
2002   "The Glass Vessels from Burial Cave D at Hurfeish." Pp. 140–66 in *Eretz Zafon – Studies in Galilean Archaeology*, ed. Z. Gal. Jerusalem.

Harden, D. B.
1936   *Roman Glass From Karanis*. Ann Arbor, MI.

Hennessy, J. B., et al.
1989   "Pella (Tabaqat Fahl)." Pp. 406–41 in *Archaeology of Jordan, II.2 Field Reports*, eds. D. Homès-Fredericq and J. B. Hennessy. Leuven.

Joukowsky, M. S.
2007   *The Petra Great Temple II: Archaeological Contexts of the Remains and Excavations*. Providence, RI.

Keller, D.
2006   *Die Gläser aus Petra. Petra – Ez Zantur III.1: Ergebnisse der Schweizerisch-Liechtensteinischen Ausgrabungen*. Terra archaeologica 5. Monographien der Schweizerisch-Liechtensteinischen Stiftung für archäologische Forschungen im Ausland [SLSA / FSLA]). Mainz.

Meiggs, R.
1973   *Roman Ostia*. Oxford.

Marii, F.
2007   Glass, Glass Cakes, and Tesserae from the Petra Church in Petra, Jordan. Unpublished PhD thesis, University College, London, Institute of Archaeology. London.

Marii F., and Rehren T.
in press   "Levantine Glass of Petra Characteristics." In *Annales du 18e congrès de l'association internationale pour l'histoire du verre, Thessaloniki*.

Murray, M., and Ellis, J. C.
1940   *A Street in Petra*. London.

O'Hea, M.
in press   "Chapter 15: The Glass 1998–2006." In *The Petra Great Temple III: Architecture and Material Culture*, ed. M. S. Joukowsky, Journal of Roman Archaeology Supplement. Portsmouth, RI.

Peleg, M.

1991 "Persian, Hellenistic and Roman Burials at Lohamei HaGeta'ot." *'Atiqot* (English Series) 20: 131–51.

Scatozza Höricht, L.

1986 *I vetri romani di ercolano*. Rome.

Vessberg, O.

1952 "Roman Glass in Cyprus." *Opuscula Archaeologica* 7: 109–65.

Weinberg, G. D., and Goldstein, S. M.

1988 "The Glass Vessels." Pp. 38–102 in *Excavations at Jalame: Site of a Glass Factory in Late Roman Palestine*, ed. G. D. Weinberg. Columbia, MO.

Winter, T.

2006 "The Glass Vessels from 'Ein ez-Zeituna." *'Atiqot* (English Series) 51: 77–83.

2010 "The Glass Vessels." Pp. 155–68 in *Nahal Haggit: A Roman and Mamluk Farmstead in the Southern Carmel*, ed. J. Seligman. Israel Antiquities Authority Reports 43. Jerusalem.

Chapter 16

The Glassware:
Chemical Analysis

by Nadine Schibille and Patrick Degryse

The typology of the identifiable glass vessels from the 1937 excavations at Khirbet et-Tannur in the Glueck Archive in the Semitic Museum, Harvard University, and possible archaeological parallels have been discussed in detail by Margaret O'Hea in the preceding chapter. The objective of the present report is to discuss the results of the chemical analyses of the glass material, in light of our current understanding of the production of glass and its origins during the Late Roman period.

There is abundant evidence that during Roman and early mediaeval times raw glass was manufactured on a large scale in only a limited number of primary glassmaking sites located in Egypt (Nenna et al. 1997; Nenna et al. 2000) and on the Levantine coast (Gorin-Rosen 1995; 2000), although some suggestions have been made of early Roman primary glass making outside the eastern Mediterranean (Wedepohl and Baumann 2000; Jackson et al. 2003; Leslie et al. 2006; Silvestri et al. 2006; Degryse and Schneider 2008). A far-flung maritime trade network facilitated the supply of this primary glass to numerous secondary workshops throughout the Mediterranean region, including the Near East, as well as central and northern Europe, where the

glass was finally transformed into artefacts (Foy et al. 2000; Foy et al. 2003a; Foy et al. 2003b). Glass from consumer sites can be related back to primary glass production locations, and this provides insights into the economic and cultural connections linking specific archaeological sites to the wider ancient world.

As judged by the fabric, shape, and colour of the glass artefacts recovered from Khirbet et-Tannur, O'Hea concludes that the glasses were of a 3rd- or early to mid-4th century AD date (see Ch. 15). The AD 363 earthquake provides a *terminus ante quem*. Given this precise dating, it is likely that the raw glass was manufactured in the Roman tradition and corresponds to the Roman compositional type. Roman glasses have been shown to be relatively homogeneous until the 4th century AD, with minor variations only in terms of additives and trace elements (Sayre and Smith 1961; Sayre 1963; Fiori and Vandini 2004; Freestone 2005; 2006). To what extent the Khirbet et-Tannur glass may have been worked locally cannot be decided unequivocally based on its chemical composition. However, the current understanding of the primary production of Roman glass points to an origin of the raw glass from Khirbet et-Tannur either in Egypt or on the

Table 16.1   EPMA results and Corning ancient glass standard measurements.
Major and minor element composition of the 24 Tannur samples distinguished according to the identified groups (Tannur 1, Tannur 2, and three outliers). The mean of n ≥ 5 measurements are given (in weight% of the oxides). The precision and accuracy of the measurements was evaluated against Corning ancient glass standards A and B.

The complete dataset presented here is also available as a downloadable table in Open Context at: http://dx.doi.org/10.6078/M7D21VH7.

Tannur 1		SiO_2	Na_2O	CaO	K_2O	MgO	Al_2O_3	FeO	TiO_2	MnO	Sb_2O_5	P_2O_5	SO_3	Cl
Tannur002	greenish blue	64.99	16.66	9.92	0.88	0.66	2.72	0.63	0.09	0.97		0.22	0.17	0.86
Tannur003	greenish blue	65.67	16.37	9.71	0.94	0.68	2.82	0.51	0.11	0.90		0.20	0.13	0.84
Tannur004	colourless	68.51	15.18	8.04	0.87	0.62	2.75	0.37	0.08	0.88		0.10	0.24	0.86
Tannur005	greenish blue	65.70	15.77	9.80	0.96	0.63	2.99	0.51	0.10	0.99		0.16	0.12	0.82
Tannur008	greenish blue	67.43	15.45	9.24	0.88	0.89	2.88	0.62	0.11	1.19		0.16	0.18	0.82
Tannur009	greenish blue	67.25	15.42	9.11	0.83	0.88	2.84	0.58	0.12	1.21		0.17	0.16	0.85
Tannur018	greenish blue	68.22	15.47	7.60	0.99	0.62	2.70	0.39	0.10	1.23		0.10	0.28	0.82
Tannur019	pinkish	69.74	13.40	7.80	0.62	0.72	2.63	0.26	0.07	2.30		0.08	0.11	0.81
Tannur029	colourless	63.66	19.00	8.18	0.36	0.58	3.07	0.37	0.06	1.67		0.09	0.25	1.39
Tannur 2														
Tannur006	yellowish	68.06	18.74	6.77	0.68	0.58	2.14	0.48	0.09	0.17	0.66	0.11	0.35	1.20
Tannur007	greenish	67.71	17.77	8.20	0.73	0.64	2.11	0.46	0.12	0.15	0.46	0.11	0.32	0.96
Tannur010	greenish blue	65.79	16.62	9.03	1.04	0.67	2.41	0.52	0.10	0.56	0.32	0.25	0.17	0.78
Tannur011	greenish blue	66.52	16.67	9.25	1.05	0.65	2.42	0.59	0.08	0.57	0.36	0.22	0.17	0.83
Tannur013	greenish blue	68.05	17.42	7.95	1.02	0.64	2.24	0.45	0.11	0.35	0.49	0.22	0.22	0.97
Tannur014	bluish	67.17	16.01	9.53	1.01	0.62	2.56	0.51	0.09	0.72	0.27	0.20	0.13	0.73
Tannur015	colourless	69.03	17.07	7.35	0.77	0.58	2.34	0.38	0.10	0.64	0.40	0.15	0.23	1.15
Tannur016	greenish blue	67.40	17.31	8.40	1.00	0.62	2.08	0.44	0.09	0.32	0.38	0.25	0.24	0.99
Tannur017	greenish blue	67.33	16.55	8.48	1.07	0.72	2.33	0.48	0.09	0.53	0.43	0.22	0.21	0.94
Tannur020	greenish blue	68.18	17.40	7.57	0.87	0.59	2.27	0.47	0.10	0.51	0.49	0.16	0.26	1.07
Tannur025	aqua	68.27	17.21	7.30	0.80	0.57	2.35	0.44	0.09	0.70	0.39	0.15	0.18	1.10
Tannur028	colourless	67.79	17.09	7.13	0.82	0.54	2.31	0.35	0.08	0.57	0.38	0.13	0.23	1.09
Outliers														
Tannur001	greenish blue	72.85	12.55	8.17	0.90	0.67	2.78	0.40	0.08	0.11		0.12	0.04	0.88
Tannur012	greenish	69.10	18.58	6.01	0.60	0.46	2.02	0.40	0.08		0.72	0.08	0.27	1.35
Tannur022	greenish	67.12	19.73	5.66	0.43	0.78	2.70	0.75	0.23		0.58	0.05	0.33	1.48
Corning Standard A														
Average n=11		66.60	13.80	5.06	2.92	2.56	0.98	1.03	0.85	1.02	2.03	0.10	0.13	0.10
Standard deviation		0.25	0.18	0.09	0.04	0.05	0.03	0.04	0.03	0.06	0.13	0.01	0.04	0.01
Published values		66.56	14.30	5.03	2.87	2.66	1.00	1.09	0.79	1.00	1.75	0.13		
Absolute deviation		-0.04	0.50	-0.03	-0.05	0.10	0.02	0.06	-0.06	-0.02	-0.28	0.03	-0.13	-0.10
Relative deviation		-0.06	3.51	-0.51	-1.82	3.86	1.50	5.73	-7.46	-2.13	-16.28	21.73		
Corning Standard B														
Average n=15		61.65	16.62	8.69	1.07	0.99	4.40	0.32	0.12	0.23	0.43	0.83	0.51	0.19
Standard deviation		0.17	0.24	0.09	0.04	0.03	0.05	0.03	0.03	0.05	0.08	0.04	0.04	0.01
Published values		61.55	17.00	8.56	1.00	1.03	4.36	0.34	0.09	0.25	0.46	0.82	0.54	0.20
Absolute deviation		-0.10	0.38	-0.13	-0.07	0.04	-0.04	0.02	-0.03	0.02	0.03	-0.01	0.03	0.01
Relative deviation		-0.17	2.22	-1.49	-7.14	3.65	-0.85	4.88	-31.90	7.67	7.18	-0.97	5.21	6.87

Levantine coast (Foy et al. 2003b; Freestone 2005; Freestone et al. 2005; Schibille et al. 2008; Rehren et al. 2010). The practice of mixing and/or recycling different raw glasses could furthermore result in intermediate glass compositions and has to be taken into account (Freestone et al. 2002b). This chapter addresses these different options on the basis of chemical analyses and provides evidence for the origin of the Khirbet et-Tannur assemblage by comparison with established contemporary primary production groups. This in turn sheds light on how well Khirbet et-Tannur may have been integrated into the long distance trade network and to what extent it relied on regional or local supplies.

Materials and Methods

Twenty-four samples from Glueck's excavation that had previously been characterised typologically were subjected to electron microprobe analysis (EPMA), using a Jeol 8600 electron microprobe with four wavelength-dispersive spectrometers (WDS) (for details of the analytical parameters, see Schibille 2011). The reproducibility and accuracy of the EPMA measurements ($n \geq 5$ per sample) was generally within 5% relative standard deviation for all major and minor elements (SiO_2, Na_2O, CaO, MgO, K_2O, Al_2O_3, and FeO). A subset of fifteen fragments has additionally been analysed for trace elements by laser ablation-inductively coupled plasma-mass spectrometry (LA-ICP-MS) and published elsewhere (Schibille et al. 2012b). All sampled fragments stem exclusively from utilitarian vessels (beakers, bowls, flasks) and the majority of the glasses have a greenish blue or bluish green tinge, and occasionally include colourless, pinkish, yellowish, greenish, or bluish samples (Table 16.1). The sample numbers are the same as the catalogue numbers in Ch. 15, which gives their typological shapes. Despite their appearance, all the samples contain varying degrees of decolourants in the form of manganese, antimony, or a mixture of the two elements and can thus be classified as colourless glass (e.g., Foster and Jackson 2010), even though the decolourising effect is typically incomplete. At concentrations in excess of 0.2% both antimony and manganese

oxides have been proposed to indicate a deliberate addition in the attempt to counteract the colouring effect of iron present in the silica source (Sayre 1963). Silica sources, though, can contain variable amounts of manganese, and a more stringent threshold of ~ 0.4% MnO has thus been proposed for its intentional use (Brill 1988; Jackson 2005).

For isotopic analysis of six selected samples, about 100 mg of powdered material per sample was weighed into Savillex screw-top beakers and dissolved in a 3:1 mixture of 22 M HF and 14 M HNO_3 on a hot plate. Solutions were dried and the residues redissolved in aqua regia. After digestion was completed, the sample was evaporated to nearly dry, and the residue was taken up into 7 M HNO_3. The concentrations of Sr and Nd were checked semi-quantitatively using a quadrupole-based Perkin-Elmer SCIEX Elan 5000 ICP-MS instrument. Sr and Nd were isolated from the concomitant matrix using extraction chromatographic methods described by Ganio (Ganio et al. 2012). All Sr and Nd isotope ratio measurements were performed on a Thermo Scientific Neptune multi-collector inductively coupled plasma mass spectrometer (MC-ICP-MS), equipped with a micro-flow PFA-50 Teflon nebuliser, and running in static multi-collection mode. A concentration-matched solution of NIST SRM 987 $SrCO_3$ isotopic reference material was used as external standard ($^{86}Sr/^{88}Sr$ = 0.1194) to correct for instrumental mass discrimination. For the measurements of $^{143}Nd/^{144}Nd$, JNdi-1 reference material (Geological Survey of Japan) was used for the same purpose ($^{143}Nd/^{144}Nd$ = 0.51515, $^{146}Nd/^{144}Nd$ = 0.7219). On average, isotope ratios were measured with an internal precision (2s) better than 0.001 % for $^{86}Sr/^{88}Sr$ and 0.002 % for $^{143}Nd/^{144}Nd$.

The Compositional Characteristics

All the analysed samples are low-magnesia, low-potash soda-lime-silica glasses (Table 16.1) typical of Roman and post-Roman glass that has been produced from a mixture of natron and calcareous sand (Freestone et al. 2002a; Freestone et al. 2002b). The assemblage can be divided into two compositional groups and three outliers on

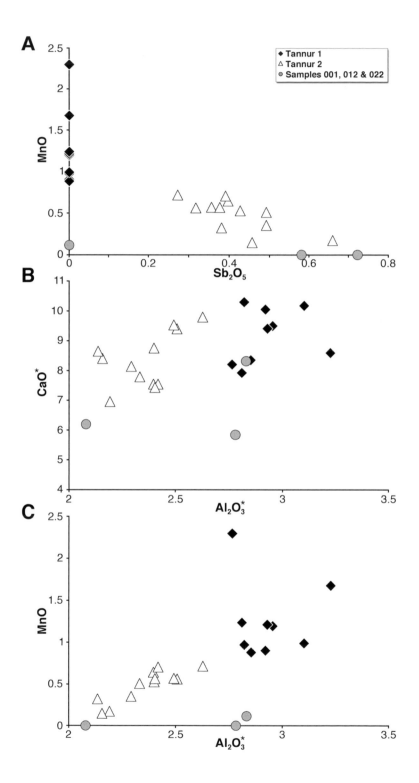

FIG. 16.1 *Base glass compositions and decolourants (EPMA): a. The comparison of antimony and manganese oxide concentrations (in weight %) identifies two main groups within the Tannur assemblage; b. The Tannur 1 samples have typically higher alumina concentrations than the Tannur 2 group; c. The positive correlation between manganese and aluminium oxide in the Tannur 2 glasses indicates that these glasses are the result of mixing. The asterisks indicate reduced and normalised data (to the seven base glass compounds SiO2, Na2O, CaO, MgO, K2O, Al2O3 and FeO).*

grounds of the use of manganese or a combination of manganese and antimony as decolourants (fig. 16.1a). Two fragments (samples 012 and 022) contain only antimony oxide at levels indicating its deliberate addition as a decolourant (~ 0.7% and 0.6%, respectively), and one sample (001) has neither antimony nor manganese at significant concentrations (Table 16.1). Sample 022 has furthermore an exceptional base glass composition with significant titanium oxide (0.23%), low lime (~ 5.7%), and slightly elevated iron oxide levels (~ 0.75%). The glasses from the Tannur 1 group (n=9) contain manganese oxide between 0.9% and 2.3%. The Tannur 2 samples (n=12) on the other hand are characterised by notable levels of antimony oxide (0.3%–0.7%) along with lower manganese oxide concentrations (~ 0.2% – 0.7%). Glasses belonging to the Tannur 1 group have on average higher alumina and lime concentrations than the Tannur 2 samples (fig. 16.1b, Table 16.1), indicating the use of different silica sources. Intriguingly, in the Tannur 2 glasses a strong positive correlation can be observed between manganese and aluminium (fig. 16.1c), whereas manganese is negatively correlated with antimony (fig. 16.1a). These effects are probably the result of the mixing of two types of raw glass that will be discussed below. Tannur 2 glasses have on average higher soda levels (~ 17.5%) than the Tannur 1 group (~ 15.5%), and while the soda levels of the Tannur 1 samples are negatively correlated with silica, no such trend is apparent in the Tannur 2 group. Except for sample 022, titanium and iron oxide contents are inconspicuous in both groups (< 0.1% and < 0.5%, respectively). The two groups are also very similar in terms of their trace element distribution, illustrating the use of mature sands that are depleted in heavy and clay minerals (fig. 16.2a). Barium contents show the greatest variations (~ 130–430 ppm) and are positively correlated with manganese (fig. 16.2b), suggesting that the majority of barium was introduced together with a manganese-bearing mineral such as psilomilan (Jackson 2005). Sample 022 is again exceptional as it contains elevated zirconium levels relative to the other samples (fig. 16.2a). In all samples that have been analysed by LA-ICP-MS, apart from specimens 019, 022,

and 029, copper and lead contents are somewhat elevated (fig. 16.2c), suggesting that the Khirbet et-Tannur vessels were produced at least partially from recycled material.

In summary, the glasses that were decolourised with manganese alone (Tannur 1) have higher alumina and lime and lower soda levels than the glasses decolourised by a mixture of manganese and antimony (Tannur 2). All other base glass components (alkali and rare earth elements) vary generally within narrow limits, although barium shows a relatively wide spread. It seems that barium in the glasses is derived only partially from the silica source (alkali feldspars) and to a large extent from the manganese-containing mineral. Manganese oxide is present at varying degrees, and it is consistently higher in the Tannur 1 group, where it can be assumed to be a deliberate addition to the glass. The lower concentrations of manganese oxide in the Tannur 2 group do not allow for the same conclusion. However, the antimony oxide contents in this group indicate its intentional use as a decolouring agent. Even though almost all samples contain notable levels of decolourants, most of the glasses are not truly colourless, possibly due to the contamination with transition metals that are usually responsible for the colouration of glass (i.e., copper).

All Tannur glass samples analyzed show a homogenous $^{87}Sr/^{86}Sr$ and $^{143}Nd/^{144}Nd$ composition, except for sample 022, which is slightly different (Table 16.2). All $^{87}Sr/^{86}Sr$ values are consistent with the Holocene seawater composition and point to the use of shell as a lime source in the primary raw material mixture of these glasses (Wedepohl and Baumann 2000). The Nd isotopic composition of all samples is between εNd -4 and -5, except for sample 022 showing an εNd of -5.77. The Nd isotopic composition of all glasses is consistent with the use of an eastern Mediterranean beach sand as a silica source (Degryse and Schneider 2008; Brems et al. 2012). In the present study, glass samples from Petra "Great Temple" also were analyzed for their Sr-Nd isotopic composition. All Petra samples, except one, have a $^{87}Sr/^{86}Sr$ composition consistent with the Holocene seawater composition. Sample P26 has a lower $^{87}Sr/^{86}Sr$ composition, consistent

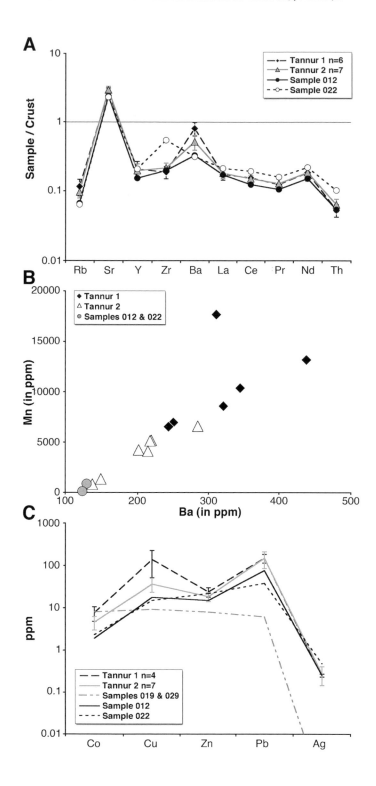

Fig. 16.2 *Trace elements (LA-ICP-MS): a. The mean trace element patterns of the two Tannur groups of those elements that were introduced with the silica source normalised to the mean continental crust (Kamber et al. 2005). Samples 012 and 022 are shown individually; b. Barium is positively correlated with manganese, indicating their concomitant introduction to the glass batch. Elemental concentrations are given in ppm; c. Comparison of the colourant-related transition metal concentrations (in ppm) of the two Tannur groups in addition to four exceptional samples (shown separately).*

Table 16.2   Elemental contents and Sr and Nd isotope ratio results.
The Nd isotope ratio results are also given as εNd (De Paolo and Wasserburg 1979).

Lab ID	Sample ID	$^{87}Sr/^{86}Sr$	Sr (ppm)	$^{143}Nd/^{144}Nd$	εNd	Nd (ppm)
T2	Tannur002	na	335	0.512380	-5.04	3.71
T3	Tannur003	0.70880	na	0.512396	-4.73	na
T4	Tannur004	0.70895	355	0.512414	-4.38	5.17
T5	Tannur005	0.70880	na	0.512425	-4.15	na
T22	Tannur022	0.70874	334	0.512342	-5.77	7.40
T25	Tannur025	0.70886	402	0.512389	-4.85	5.76
P12	PGT-012	0.70912	na	0.512427	-4.12	na
P13	PGT-013	0.70908	385	0.512361	-5.40	4.03
P16	PGT-016	0.70907	454	0.512378	-5.08	4.27
P21	PGT-021	0.70877	na	0.512410	-4.44	na
P26	PGT-026	0.70832	371	0.512363	-5.37	12.66
P31	PGT-031	0.70895	677	0.512367	-5.29	7.37

with HIMT glass (Table 16.2). The Nd isotopic composition of all Petra samples is between εNd -4.1 and -5.4, consistent with the use of an eastern Mediterranean beach sand as a silica source.

AFFILIATIONS: PROVENANCE AND RE-CYCLING

The compositional and isotopic characteristics of the Khirbet et-Tannur assemblage are broadly consistent with decolourised natron-type glasses typical of the Late Roman period from the eastern Mediterranean as well as Europe (e.g., Picon and Vichy 2003; Jackson 2005; Foster and Jackson 2010). A more refined picture emerges when the analytical data of the Tannur glass is evaluated against the major glass production groups that were prevalent during the 3rd and 4th centuries AD. In particular, the lime and alumina levels of soda-lime-silica glasses are considered diagnostic for the sand source and can give indications as to the type or the origin of the raw glass at consumer sites (Freestone et al. 2000). For comparison, a representative cross-section of 1st- to 4th-century Roman glasses, containing either antimony or manganese or a mixture of the two decolourants was selected from Romano-British (Baxter et al.

2005; Jackson 2005; Foster and Jackson 2010) and Italian assemblages (Mirti et al. 1993; Arletti et al. 2005; Silvestri et al. 2005; Silvestri 2008; Silvestri et al. 2008), in addition to 4th-century HIMT glass from Carthage, Billingsgate, and Augusta, and Levantine I samples that are associated with 4th- to 8th-century Palestinian glass working sites at Apollonia (Arsuf), Beth-Shean, and Dor, and with Late Roman glass from Jalame (courtesy of Ian Freestone). The comparison of the lime and alumina concentrations of the Tannur glasses with these reference groups allows for a tentative attribution of the Tannur glass groups (Fig. 16.3). The samples of the Tannur 1 group fall comfortably into the Levantine I cluster, supported by the Sr-Nd isotopic composition of the Tannur 1 samples that is also consistent with Levantine I glass (Degryse et al. 2006; Degryse and Schneider 2008). The Tannur 2 samples on the other hand overlap to a certain extent with Roman manganese-decolourised glass, yet the Tannur 2 samples tend to have higher lime concentrations (for further statistical analyses of these data, see Schibille et al. 2012b). The antimony-containing sample 022 with relatively high alumina (~ 2.8%) and low lime (~ 5.8%) is reminiscent of 4th-century HIMT

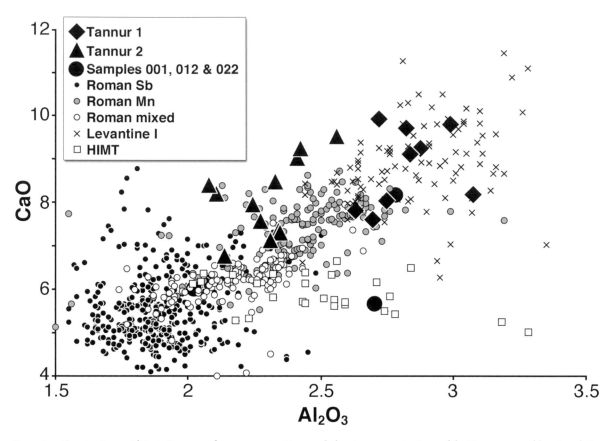

FIG. 16.3 *Comparison with Late Roman reference groups. Lime and alumina concentrations of the Tannur assemblage in relation to Roman glass from Britain (Baxter et al. 2005; Jackson 2005; Foster and Jackson 2010) and Italy (Mirti et al. 1993; Arletti et al. 2005; Silvestri 2008; Silvestri et al. 2005; Silvestri et al. 2008) as well as 4th-century HIMT glass and 4th- to 8th-century Levantine I glass (courtesy of I. Freestone). Note the overlap between Tannur 1 and Levantine I samples and the lack of correspondence between Tannur 2 and Roman mixed manganese/antimony glasses.*

glass (high iron, manganese, and titanium) in terms of its major and trace element composition (Freestone 1994) as well as its lower Sr and more negative Nd isotopic composition (Degryse et al. 2006; Degryse and Schneider 2008). However, manganese is missing entirely from this sample and iron is only slightly elevated (~ 0.8%); hence it cannot be unambiguously attributed to this primary production group.

The association between Tannur 1 and Levantine I glasses is somewhat unexpected, as the Levantine I primary production group supposedly post-dates the Tannur assemblage, which has a *terminus ante quem* of AD 363. To date, the Late Roman glass from Jalame (second half of the 4th century AD) is the earliest identified representative of the Levantine I glass group and was shown to have been made using coastal sand from the Syria-Palestinian coast (Brill 1988). It appears then that the Tannur 1 group is an exceptionally early example of Levantine I glasses, in agreement with the typological similarities between some of the Khirbet et-Tannur artefacts and vessels recovered from Jalame (notably samples 001, 005, and 018) (see Ch. 15).

Equally surprising is the lack of correspondence between the Tannur 2 samples and the contemporary Roman glasses with mixed antimony and manganese levels. Instead, Tannur 2 has higher lime and alumina concentrations and thus displays characteristics usually associated with Levantine I glass. The intermediate position of the Tannur 2 group between Roman and Levantine I strongly implies a component of mixing and/or recycling of these primary glass types. It has previously been

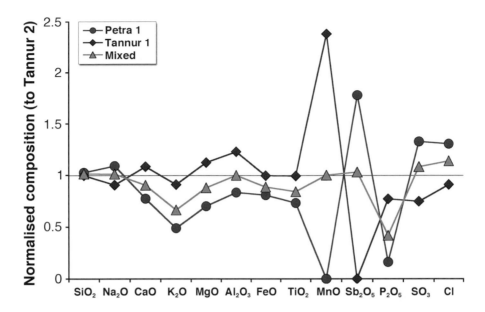

FIG. 16.4 *Computation of a mixed manganese/antimony glass composition. Averages of the Petra 1 and Tannur 1 glass compositions were normalised to the mean of the Tannur 2 group. A mixed Petra 1 + Tannur 1 composition (58% and 42%, respectively) was calculated.*

proposed that where both decolourising agents are present in Roman glasses, this was probably the result of mixing Roman antimony-decolourised with Roman manganese-containing (in some cases possibly HIMT) glasses (Foster and Jackson 2010). This trend is easily observed in the comparison of the lime and alumina concentrations of the different groups (fig. 16.3). The Roman mixed glasses fall on the mixing line between the Roman antimony and manganese groups. However, the mixing of the same primary glass groups for the production of Tannur 2 glasses is highly unlikely, due to their significantly higher lime contents relative to any of the Roman glass types. Rather, a combination of Roman antimony-decolourised glass with overall low levels of alumina and lime and Levantine I glasses that contain some manganese and considerably higher alumina and lime contents could explain the characteristics of the Tannur 2 samples.

That such mixing has most likely been carried out can be mathematically illustrated. For this analysis, the average concentrations of the Tannur 1 group and of antimony glasses from nearby Petra (group Petra 1 in Schibille et al. 2012b) were normalised to the average Tannur 2 data, showing the deviations

between these different glass groups (fig. 16.4). In addition, a mixed composition was calculated by adding Tannur 1 and Petra 1 glass in a ratio of 42% and 58%, respectively. Through this operation, the manganese concentration of the mixed glass is equivalent to that of Tannur 2 glass ($y = 1$, fig. 16.4). What is more, the calculated mixture matches the average Tannur 2 composition very closely (i.e., $y \approx 1$), with the exception of the potassium and phosphorous oxide contents that are significantly lower in the theoretical mixture. Contaminations from fuel ash and fumes during recycling and repeated heat treatment may explain this divergence (Schibille et al. 2012a). Indeed, elevated levels of phosphorous and alkali waste products have been observed in experimental glass that was exposed to the furnace atmosphere for a prolonged period of time (Paynter 2008). Recycling and mixing can also account for the strong positive correlation between manganese and aluminium (fig. 16.1c) and the negative correlation between manganese and antimony in the Tannur 2 group (fig. 16.1a). These observations clearly point to the mixing of two end members (Roman antimony and Levantine I manganese glass) rather than the addition of manganese to an antimony-decolourised glass. If manganese had been added on its own to antimony-containing glass, the alumina concentrations as well as the antimony levels would be expected to be unaltered from prototypical antimony-rich Roman glass compositions. Likewise, if antimony would have been added to glass decolourised by manganese oxide, the two oxides should not be negatively correlated.

Recycling of cullet and the accidental incorporation of some coloured glass may also explain the presence of elevated transition metals (including lead) in some of the glasses (fig. 16.2c). This pattern is not limited to the glass from the Tannur 2 group, but can be observed also with respect to most of the Tannur 1 samples. Only samples 019, 022, and 029 describe curves without an inflection and have transition metal contents typically below 10 ppm that are significantly lower than their relative abundance in the upper continental crust. It is thus unlikely that these glasses are the result of recycling. The remaining samples analysed by LA-ICP-MS, however, have copper and lead concentrations that are much higher than those of zinc and exceed in most cases their mean natural abundance. Hence, these glasses were most certainly contaminated with colourants (copper and lead), due to the addition of some coloured cullet during recycling (Freestone and Hughes 2006). Nonetheless, the degree of recycling must have been limited and exceedingly selective, as the level of the transition metals in all the samples is still relatively low.

It appears then that the majority of the glasses from Khirbet et-Tannur were produced using recycled material and are related to the Levantine I primary production group rather than Roman glasses. The only samples that can be considered pristine (i.e., non-recycled) glass are samples 019 and 029 belonging to the Tannur 1 group, and possibly sample 022 that may be related to HIMT glass. In this respect, the glass assemblage from Khirbet et-Tannur differs from the finds recovered from the "Great Temple" at Petra (Schibille et al. 2012b). At Petra, the proportion of non-recycled glass is larger than at Khirbet et-Tannur. Furthermore, no glasses have been identified in Petra that contain both antimony and manganese, and a significant part

of the assemblage corresponds to HIMT glass that is believed to originate from Egypt (Schibille et al. 2012b). Part of the underlying reason for the presence of different glass types at Khirbet et-Tannur and Petra might be the different socio-economic statuses of the two sites and their strategic positions along main trade arteries. In other words, the capital city had better access to imported high quality glass, whereas Khirbet et-Tannur relied more heavily on recycled materials. However, it is also noteworthy that although the glass finds from Khirbet et-Tannur and Petra represent overlapping chronological ranges, the chronological distribution of the Khirbet et-Tannur assemblage is confined to an exceptionally narrow time-span. The archaeological record of Khirbet et-Tannur glass reflects a very precise moment in time (3rd to early to mid-4th century AD) and purpose (i.e., use in the temple), and remained undisturbed after the earthquake in AD 363. Petra, on the other hand, was a city and an important trading centre with a much longer lifetime. Thus, while the glass vessels from Tannur may have in fact been produced or procured for a particular purpose (their use in the temple), the assemblage from Petra most certainly reflects multiple purposes and periods (Schibille et al. 2012b).

A further implication of the compositional differences between Khirbet et-Tannur and Petra is that they reflect chronological variations in both the base glass composition as well as in the use of antimony and manganese as decolouring agents. Given the attribution of the Khirbet et-Tannur finds to the 3rd, possibly the early 4th century AD and the dating of the Petra samples to either the 1st/2nd century or the 4th century, our data indicate that antimony and manganese oxides were simultaneously employed in Near Eastern glass production only in the 3rd and early 4th century AD. This is in agreement with the chronological pattern observed by Sayre (1963) as regards colourless glasses from European consumer sites. Sayre found that the majority of 2nd- and 3rd-century glass from Europe contained both antimony and manganese, whereas their combined use was remarkably rare in Late Roman glass from the eastern provinces (Sayre 1963). The Tannur 2 samples contradict this geographical distinction, and provide evidence for a greater incidence of mixed antimony/manganese glasses in the Near East than has previously been recognised. At the same time the chronological trends can be tentatively confirmed, with the simultaneous use of both decolourants being restricted to the 3rd and early 4th century AD.

CONCLUSIONS

In general terms, the major and minor elemental and Sr-Nd isotopic composition of the glasses from Khirbet et-Tannur is consistent with the characteristics of glass made using sands from the Levantine coast, inasmuch as both Roman and Levantine I glass groups ultimately derive from these coastal regions. Tannur 1 glasses have a chemical composition typical of Levantine I glass, even though they exhibit signs of limited recycling. Given the geographical proximity of Khirbet et-Tannur to the Syria-Palestinian coast and the origin of Levantine I glass, the prevalence of this primary glass production group might not be entirely unexpected. However, Levantine I glass is traditionally assigned to the 4th to 8th century AD, with the late 4th-century glass from Jalame being the earliest known example of this primary glass production group. Hence, the Khirbet et-Tannur assemblage seems to represent one of the earliest recognised instances of Levantine I raw glass and supports the model of centralised primary glass production during the later Roman period with the main location of glass making on the Levantine coast.

Our data furthermore suggest that a large proportion of glass dating to the later Roman period is the result of mixing and/or recycling even in the eastern provinces that are close to the primary production centres. The presence of both antimony and manganese oxides in the Tannur 2 group, for example, is most certainly the product of a combination of Roman antimony-decolourised glass with Levantine I manganese-decolourised glass. These results are consistent with other studies on Roman colourless glasses and the increased frequency of recycling during the 2nd and 3rd centuries AD. However, in the case of the Khirbet et-Tannur glasses, the recycling process must have been highly selective, contributing only minor contaminations in the form of transition metals to the batch. This is probably mainly a reflection of the availability of ample resources for recycling in the eastern provinces. Nonetheless, the glass assemblage from Khirbet et-Tannur proved compositionally quite distinct from that of nearby Petra, which may indicate different supply patterns, either due to chronological differences and/or different trade connections, wealth, and roles of the two Nabataean sites. As much of the material culture of Khirbet et-Tannur is closest to that of the nearby village of Khirbet edh-Dharih, it would not be surprising if it had to rely more on glass vessels produced from a locally available supply of recycled glass than the metropolis of Petra with its greater wealth and trade contacts.

ACKNOWLEDGEMENTS

This research was supported by a Marie Curie Intra-European Fellowship within the 7th European Community Framework Programme (to N. S.). We would also like to thank Norman Charnley (Department of Earth Sciences) and Chris Doherty (Research Laboratory for Archaeology and the History of Art) at the University of Oxford for technical help with the EPMA analyses, Tom Fenn of K. U. Leuven for analytical support with the isotope analyses, and Dr. Katherine Eremin of Harvard Art Museums for taking the samples.

References

Arletti, R.; Giordani, N.; Rarpini, R.;
and Vezzalini, G.
2005   "Archaeometrical Analysis of Glass of
       Western Emilia Romagna (Italy) from the
       Imperial Age." Pp. 80–84 in *Annales du
       16e congrès de l'association internationale
       pour l'histoire du verre, London*.

Baxter, M. J.; Cool, H. E. M.; and Jackson, C. M.
2005   "Further Studies in the Compositional
       Variability of Colourless Romano-British
       Vessel Glass." *Archaeometry* 47: 47–68.

Brems, D.; Ganio, M.; Walton, M.; and Degryse, P.
2012   "Mediterranean Sand Deposits as a Raw
       Material for Glass Production in Antiqui-
       ty." Pp. 120–27 In *Annales du 18e congrès
       de l'association internationale pour l'his-
       toire du verre, Thessaloniki*.

Brill, R. H.
1988   "Scientific Investigations of the Jalame
       Glass and Related Finds." Pp. 257–91
       in *Excavations at Jalame: Site of a Glass
       Factory in Late Roman Palestine*, ed. G. D.
       Weinberg. Columbia, MO.

De Paolo, D. J., and Wasserburg, G. J.
1976   "Nd Isotopic Variations and Petrogenic
       Models." *Geophysical Research Letters* 3:
       249–52.

Degryse, P., and Schneider, J.
2008   "Pliny the Elder and Sr-Nd Isotopes:
       Tracing the Provenance of Raw Materials
       for Roman Glass Production." *Journal of
       Archaeological Science* 35: 1993–2000.

Degryse, P.; Schneider, J.; Haack, U.; Lamers, V.;
Poblome, J.; Waelkens, A.; and Muchez, P.
2006   "Evidence for Glass 'Recycling' Using Pb
       and Sr Isotopic Ratios and Sr-Mixing Lines:
       The Case of Early Byzantine Sagalassos."
       Journal of Archaeological Science 33: 494–501.

Fiori, C., and Vandini, M.
2004   "Chemical Composition of Glass and its
       Raw Materials: Chronological and Geo-

graphical Development in the First Millennium AD." Pp. 151–94 in *When Glass
Matters: Studies in the History of Science
and Art from Graeco-Roman Antiquity to
Early Modern Era*, ed. M. Beretta. Florence.

Foster, H. E., and Jackson, C. M.
2010   "The Composition of Late Romano-
       British Colourless Vessel Glass: Glass
       Production and Consumption." *Journal of
       Archaeological Science* 37: 3068–3080.

Foy, D.; Picon, M.; and Vichy, M.
2003a "Verres omeyyades et abbasides d'origine
       égyptienne: les témoignages de l'archéo-
       logie et de l'archéométrie." Pp. 138–43
       in *Annales du 15e congrès de l'association
       internationale pour l'histoire du verre,
       Corning, New York*.

Foy, D.; Picon, M.; Vichy, M.; and Thirion-Merle, V.
2003b "Caractérisation des verres de la fin de
       l'antiquité en Méditerranée occiden-
       tale: l'émergence de nouveaux courants
       commerciaux." Pp. 41–85 in *Échanges et
       commerce du verre dans le monde antique:
       actes du colloque de l'Association française
       pour l'archéologie du verre, Aix-en-Pro-
       vence et Marseille, 7–9 juin 2001*, eds.
       D. Foy and M.-D. Nenna. Montagnac,
       France.

Foy, D.; Vichy, M.; and Picon, M.
2000   "Lingots de verre en Méditerranée occi-
       dentale." Pp. 51–57 in *Annales du 14e
       congrès de l'association internationale pour
       l'histoire du verre, Amsterdam*.

Freestone, I. C.
1994   "Appendix: Chemical Analysis of 'Raw'
       Glass Fragments." P. 290 in *Excavations at
       Carthage, Vol. II.1. The Circular Harbour,
       North Side. The Site and Finds Other than
       Pottery*, ed. H. R. Hurst. Oxford.
2005   "The Provenance of Ancient Glass
       Through Compositional Analysis." Pp.

195–208 in *Materials Issues in Art and Archaeology VII*, eds. P. B. Vandiver, J. L. Mass, and A. Murray. Warrendale, PA.

2006   "Glass Production in Late Antiquity and the Early Islamic Period: A Geochemical Perspective." Pp. 201–16 in *Geomaterials in Cultural Heritage*. eds. M. Maggetti and B. Messiga. Bath.

Freestone, I. C.; Gorin-Rosen, Y.;
and Hughes, M. J.
2000   "Primary Glass from Israel and the Production of Glass in Late Antiquity and the Early Islamic Period." Pp. 65–83 in *La Route du verre. Ateliers primaires et secondaires du second millénaire av. J.C. au Moyen Âge*, ed. M.-D. Nenna. Lyons.

Freestone, I. C.; Greenwood, R.;
and Gorin-Rosen, Y.
2002a   "Byzantine and Early Islamic Glassmaking in the Eastern Mediterranean: Production and Distribution of Primary Glass." Pp. 167–74 in *Hyalos-Vitrum-Glass: Proceedings of the First Hellenic Glass Conference*, ed. G. Kordas. Rhodes.

Freestone, I. C., and Hughes, M. J.
2006   "The Origins of the Jarrow Glass." Pp. 147–55 in *Wearmouth and Jarrow Monastic Sites*, ed. R. Cramp. Swindon.

Freestone, I. C.; Ponting, M.; and Hughes, M. J.
2002b   "The Origins of Byzantine Glass from Maroni Petrera, Cyprus." *Archaeometry* 44: 257–72.

Freestone, I. C.; Wolf, S.; and Thirlwall, M.
2005   "The Production of HIMT Glass: Elemental and Isotopic Evidence." Pp. 153–57 in *Annales du 16e congrès de l'association internationale pour l'histoire du verre, London*.

Ganio, M.; Latruwe, K.; Brems, D.; Muchez, P.;
Vanhaecke, F.; and Degryse, P.
2012   "Sr-Nd Isolation Procedure for Subsequent Isotopic Analysis Using Multicollector ICP – Mass Spectrometry in the Context of Provenance Studies on Archaeological Glass." *Journal of Analytical Atomic Spectrometry* 27: 1335–41.

Gorin-Rosen, Y.
1995   "Hadera, Bet Eliʿezer." *Excavations and Surveys in Israel* 13: 42–43.
2000   "The Ancient Glass Industry in Israel – Summary of the Finds and New Discoveries." Pp. 49–63 in *La Route du verre. Ateliers primaires et secondaires du second millénaire av. J.C. au Moyen Âge*, ed. M.-D. Nenna. Lyons.

Jackson, C. M.
2005   "Making Colourless Glass in the Roman Period." *Archaeometry* 47: 763–80.

Jackson, C. M.; Joyner, L.; Booth, C. A.; Day, P. M.;
Wager, E. C. W.; and Kilikoglou, V.
2003   "Roman Glass-Making at Coppergate, York? Analytical Evidence for the Nature of Production." *Archaeometry* 45: 435–56.

Kamber, B. S.; Greig, A.; and Collerson, K. D.
2005   "A New Estimate for the Composition of Weathered Young Upper Continental Crust from Alluvial Sediments, Queensland, Australia." *Geochimica et Cosmochimica Acta* 69: 1041–1058.

Leslie, K. A.; Freestone, I. C.; Lowry, D.;
and Thirlwall, M.
2006   "The Provenance and Technology of Near Eastern Glass: Oxygen Isotopes by Laser Fluorination as a Complement to Strontium." *Archaeometry* 48: 253–70.

Mirti, P.; Casoli, A.; and Appolonia, L.
1993   "Scientific Analysis of Roman Glass from Augusta-Praetoria." *Archaeometry* 35: 225–40.

Nenna, M.-D.; Picon, M.; and Vichy, M.
2000   "L'Atelier primaires et secondaires en Égypte a l'époque greco-romaine." Pp. 97–112 in *La Route du verre. Ateliers primaires et secondaires du second millénaire av. J.C. au Moyen Âge*, ed. M.-D. Nenna. Lyons.

Nenna, M.-D.; Vichy, M.; and Picon, M.
1997 "L'Atelier de verrier de Lyon, du 1er siècle après J.-C., et l'origine des verres 'Romains.'" *Revue d'archéométrie* 21: 81–87.

Paynter, S.
2008 "Experiments in the Reconstruction of Roman Wood-Fired Glassworking Furnaces: Waste Products and Their Formation Processes." *Journal of Glass Studies* 50: 271–90.

Picon, M., and Vichy, M.
2003 "D'Orient en occident: l'origine du verre à l'époque romaine et durant le haute Moyen Age." Pp. 17–31 in *Échanges et commerce du verre dans le monde antique: actes du colloque de l'association française pour l'archéologie du verre, Aix-en-Provence et Marseille, 7–9 juin 2001*, eds. D. Foy and M.-D. Nenna. Montagnac, France.

Rehren, T.; Marii, F.; Schibille, N.; Stanford, L.; and Swan, C.
2010 "Glass Supply and Circulation in Early Byzantine Southern Jordan." Pp. 65–81 in *Glass in Byzantium: Production, Usage, Analyses. RGZM - Tagungen 8*, eds. J. Drauschke and D. Keller. Mainz.

Sayre, E. V.
1963 "The Intentional Use of Antimony and Manganese in Ancient Glasses." Pp. 263–82 in *Advances in Glass Technology, Part 2*, eds. F. R. Matson and G. E. Rindone. New York, NY.

Sayre, E. V., and Smith, R. W.
1961 "Compositional Categories of Ancient Glass." *Science* 133: 1824–26.

Schibille, N.
2011 "Late Byzantine Mineral Soda High Alumina Glasses from Asia Minor: A New Primary Glass Production Group." *Plos One* 6(4): e18970. doi:10.1371/journal.pone.0018970

Schibille, N.; Degryse, P.; Corremans, M.; and Specht, C. G.
2012a "Chemical Characterisation of Glass Mosaic Tesserae from 6th-Century Sagalassos (South-West Turkey): Chronology and Production Techniques." *Journal of Archaeological Science* 39: 1480–92.

Schibille, N.; Degryse, P.; O'Hea, M.; Izmer, A.; Vanhaecke, F.; and McKenzie, J. S.
2012b "Late Roman Glass from the 'Great Temple' at Petra and Khirbet et-Tannur, Jordan –Technology and Provenance." *Archaeometry* 54.6: 997–1022.

Schibille, N.; Marii, F.; and Rehren, T.
2008 "Characterization and Provenance of Late Antique Window Glass from the Petra Church in Jordan." *Archaeometry* 50: 627–42.

Silvestri, A.
2008 "The Coloured Glass of Iulia Felix." *Journal of Archaeological Science* 35: 1489–1501.

Silvestri, A.; Molin, G.; and Salviulo, G.
2005 "Roman and Medieval Glass from the Italian Area: Bulk Characterization and Relationships with Production Technologies." *Archaeometry* 47: 797–816.
2008 "The Colourless Glass of Iulia Felix." *Journal of Archaeological Science* 35: 331–41.

Silvestri, A.; Molin, G.; Salviulo, G.; and Schievenin, R.
2006 "Sand for Roman Glass Production: An Experimental and Philological Study on Source of Supply." *Archaeometry* 48: 415–32.

Wedepohl, K. H., and Baumann, A.
2000 "The Use of Marine Molluskan Shells for Roman Glass and Local Raw Glass Production in the Eifel Area (Western Germany)." *Naturwissenschaften* 87: 129–32.

Chapter 17

The Lamps

by Deirdre G. Barrett

INTRODUCTION

During the seasons at Khirbet et-Tannur in 1937, Nelson Glueck recorded the discovery of many lamps and fragments in his excavation journal on 3, 4, 5 March and 7, 9, 15 April, and in his registration book on 1, 2, 3, 4 March and 2, 9 April. Although some of these entries are rather vague, e.g., "A number of complete lamps found inside" (GJ 5 March), ten lamps from the site were published in *Deities and Dolphins* (*DD* pl. 82a–b). Seven of these are in the Glueck Archive in the Semitic Museum. Harvard University, with thirty-two other lamp fragments from the site. An additional eight lamps, photographed by Glueck but not in the Glueck Archive, are included in the catalogue below. One lamp (no. 18) is in the Cincinnati Art Museum, but the current whereabouts of some other complete examples (nos. 29, 33, 37, and 42) and a polycandelon fragment (no. 3) are unknown. It is unclear if any of these were amongst the three lamps from Khirbet et-Tannur which Eleanor Vogel mentions were in the Cincinnati Hebrew Union College Museum in 1976,[1] but they could not be traced in 2011. The forty-eight lamps or fragments have been classified by type, period, or

region, where possible, and date from the beginning of the 2nd century AD to the 6th century AD.

This report was first completed in December 2003, and the material was included with the lamps from Petra in the PhD thesis of the author (Barrett 2005; 2008), the results of which were presented at a conference in Jordan in 2005 (Barrett 2011, with colour photographs). Since then, work has been done at a number of sites useful for comparanda and dating. These include in particular the excavations at the nearest site, Khirbet edh-Dharih, directed by François Villeneuve, for which he kindly sent us the report on the 1st- to 4th-century lamps by Caroline Durand (2011). Khirbet edh-Dharih not only has the closest parallels for the wheel-made round lamps and South Jordan "slipper" lamps but, most importantly, they are from dated archaeological contexts. Over 550 lamps from Pella, Deir 'Ain 'Abata, and Umm Qais (c. AD 300–700) were included in Kate da Costa's PhD thesis on Byzantine and early Umayyad ceramic lamps from Palaestina and Arabia (da Costa 2003), of which the Deir 'Ain 'Abata material has appeared (da Costa 2012). We are most grateful to these researchers for providing us with copies at the beginning of 2010, prior to their publications. Consequently, we re-examined the Khirbet et-Tannur lamps in January 2010 in the light of these reports, made some revisions to our classification, and also were able to suggest a more precise chronology for them, further assisted in some details by Kharieh 'Amr and Kate da Costa. We are also very grateful to the latter for additional references and comments. As a result of the more recent work, what is presented here updates, and sometimes consequently differs from, what was in the author's thesis (for which a Concordance is included, Table 17.2).

DISCUSSION

Although lamps were a necessary artifact to lighten darkness in both secular and sacred settings, the complex at Khirbet et-Tannur was built solely for religious purposes, thus obviating conjecture regarding the function of the site. The lack of an adjoining village or domestic quarters provides us with a relatively uncontaminated sample of lamps used for religious purposes. Of the lamps in the Glueck Archive, only one lamp is without signs of use, indicating that they were lit, rather than just being offerings as at some sites, such as Banias (Berlin 1999: 37). The evidence from nearby Khirbet edh-Dharih is the key to providing a more precise and accurate chronology for the lamps from Khirbet et-Tannur, which seems to have had similar periods of use in the Nabataean, Roman, and Byzantine periods. Pilgrims probably processed from Khirbet edh-Dharih, where there were more facilities, to the nearby hilltop sanctuary of Khirbet et-Tannur. Of the forty-eight lamps catalogued, only fragments of the earlier lamps have survived, while later ones, such as the South Jordan slipper lamps (mid-4th and 6th centuries AD) are often nearly complete.

This corpus of lamps, although small, is remarkable because of the association between lamp type and religious function it demonstrates as a result of the absence of two lamp types and also the presence of two others. Two ubiquitous Nabataean lamp types, "slash and rosette"/Negev Type 1 and "petal"/ Omega, are not attested at Khirbet et-Tannur. These two main volute Nabataean lamp types are the predominant types in the late Nabataean/early Roman

period at Petra (although the "petal"/Omega lamps are found in low numbers in the ez-Zantur housing area: Grawehr 2006: 307; Sarley 1988), and throughout the Nabataean kingdom (references in Grawehr 2006: 296–97, 307, for findspots in Sadagah, Khirbet edh-Dharih, Oboda, Mampsis, Timna, Humeyma, Khirbet el-Hassiya, Aila, Gaza, and Hegra, in addition to throughout Petra) and beyond (e.g., in Masada, Bailey 1994: 87, no. 177). Dating evidence remains poor. At ez-Zantur, the types seem to have been in use in the 1st century AD, with only residual fragments appearing in the early 2nd century (Grawehr 2006: 297–98). However, they are found at Khirbet edh-Dharih in early 2nd-century AD contexts (Durand 2011: nos. 3–12). Local mould-made round lamps are also associated with the construction date of the temple at Khirbet edh-Dharih, in the first half of the 2nd century AD (see below). Small fragments of the same types are found at Khirbet et-Tannur, and if the dates at Khirbet edh-Dharih for the "slash and rosette" and "petal"/ Omega lamps are indeed evidence of use, there should be examples at Khirbet et-Tannur, along with the local mould-made round lamps. In addition, the pottery indicates activity there in the 1st century AD, although the main phase commenced in the first half of the 2nd century. As there are no other lamp types at the site which must date to the 1st century, the reason for the absence of the early, "slash and rosette" and "petal" lamps is arguable, but on balance it appears that it is not an issue of chronology. It suggests that these types were only for everyday domestic use, and not religious functions.

Around AD 200 the sanctuary and facilities at Khirbet edh-Dharih were expanded and, possibly at this time or later in the 3rd century, the Altar Platform at Khirbet et-Tannur was enlarged and re-decorated and other Period 3 repairs were made. Lamps associated with use of the sanctuary there in the late 2nd and first half of the 3rd century include mould-made round lamps with large filling holes and unusual wheel-made round lamps. The examples of these both there and at Khirbet edh-Dharih are distinguished by the incorporation of the spout into the body of the lamp.

The use of purpose-made cultic lamps at Khirbet et-Tannur is seen in two lamp types which occur rarely elsewhere, and then only in religious contexts. Both of these types cast much light over a relatively short time, suggesting their use in night cults. The first type are multi-tiered polycandela, with tiers of rings with multiple spouts, which would have cast much light from their many wicks, like the examples from the 2nd–3rd century and c. AD 363–419 from the excavations in front of the Qasr el-Bint at Petra. The second type are "socket and saucer" lamps. These had a thick wick which was fed with oil from the surrounding saucer. The examples from Khirbet et-Tannur were fired with stands. The most intact one (no. 4) is dated from probably the late 1st century AD, although it could potentially be as late as the early 4th century AD. The attached stands suggest perhaps these were used in processions.

These lamps are very rare, but many examples (fired without stands) have been found at two sites in particular and dated from the 1st to 3rd centuries AD: Samaria in Palestine, associated with Kore (Crowfoot 1957: 373–74, Type 11) and Isthmia in Greece, associated with Palaimon (Broneer 1977: 35–52). The cult of Kore, celebrated in the Eleusinian mysteries, included a processional search for Kore with torches (Hornblower and Spawforth 1996: 1142). It should be noted that at the Sanctuary of Demeter and Kore in Corinth, only one fragment of a saucer and socket lamp was found; perhaps the special dining rituals at Corinth took precedence over night processions (Slane 1990: 11, cat. no. 10). Ritual at the sanctuary of Kore in Alexandria in the 4th century AD included a night-time procession with torch bearers (Bowersock 1990: 22).

Cult at the Palaimonion in Isthmia is more complex. Although there are no pre-Roman contexts which can securely be associated with the cult of Melikertes/Palaimon, it is likely that the legend of the death, burial, and divinization of Melikertes was associated with the beginning of the Isthmian Games, thus reaching far back into pre-Roman history (Gebhard and Dickie 1999). Plutarch discusses a night-time contest, and Melikertes/Palaimon was of course linked with Poseidon, who himself is associated with Demeter and Kore at Isthmia (Gebhard 1993: 136–37). The socket and saucer lamps (in association with locally made

plain wheelmade lamps, Type XVI) were found in some quantity in the sacrificial pits associated with ritual at the Palaimonion (Broneer 1977: 92).

The clay used for both of these ritual types at Khirbet et-Tannur (the socket and saucer lamps and the polycandela) was not well-levigated, often a factor in locally-made ceramics. Donald Bailey (pers. comm.) has confirmed that unique lamps were often produced specifically for sanctuaries. The nearest place where these lamps might have been made is Khirbet edh-Dharih, as we know other lamps were made there because a mould has been found (Durand 2011: no. 52). However, it is notable that no polycandela or saucer and socket lamps have been found at Khirbet edh-Dharih, suggesting that they were not used in its sanctuary, but were locally specific to the different ritual at Khirbet et-Tannur.

The discovery of South Jordan slipper lamps around the repaired Altar Platform (fig. 17.49) and in some of the dining rooms off the temple Forecourt suggests that Khirbet et-Tannur was used for pagan worship as late as the mid-4th century AD, based on the dated evidence of similar lamps at Khirbet edh-Dharih. The survival of two from the same mould (nos. 33 and 34) in Room 14 and in the Inner Temenos Enclosure suggests that these areas were both still in use at the same time. The fact that many of the slipper lamps were largely intact accords with their being abandoned at the time of the main cessation of worship at Khirbet et-Tannur with the AD 363 earthquake, which also led to Khirbet edh-Dharih being abandoned for over a century. That an example (no. 37) comes from the same mould as a lamp found in Petra raises the possibility that perhaps this example was brought from there.

The latest lamps at Khirbet et-Tannur were probably brought there by early 6th-century visitors after Khirbet edh-Dharih was re-occupied (and its temple shell re-fitted as a church). These include a Small Candlestick lamp with a cross, probably brought from north of the Wādī al-Mujib, and one (probably two) large South Jordan slipper lamp(s) of grey ware with a high tongue handle.

The socket and saucer lamps clearly had a ritual use and, because of their association elsewhere directly and indirectly with the cult of Kore, raise the question: was Kore worshipped at Khirbet et-Tannur? The identity of the Vegetation Goddess on the tympanum above the doorway of the Inner Temenos Enclosure (Period 2) (Vol. 1, figs. 92, 160) is not certain, although Wenning (2009: 582–83) has recently suggested that she represents the goddess of the spring of La'abān (near Khirbet edh-Dharih) which is mentioned in an inscription from Khirbet et-Tannur (Ch. 9, inscription no. 1). Glueck believed she represented the Syrian goddess Atargatis in the role of "the mother of nature," seeing the goddess as "the source of fertility," surrounded as she was by symbols of fecundity, e.g., vines, figs, and pomegranates. He compared her with, amongst others, Persephone/Kore pressing a pomegranate between her breasts – another representation of fruitfulness (*DD* 290). Cumont suggested that Kore was assimilated to the Great Syrian goddess, citing an inscription found in Britain which assimilated the Syrian goddess to Peace, Virtue, Ceres, Cybele, and even to the sign of the Virgin (Cumont 1911: 132, citing *CIL* VII.759).

The Vegetation Goddess was not the only sculptural deity at Khirbet et-Tannur connected with a bounteous harvest, for a "Grain Goddess" was discovered on one of the panels of the Period 3 Altar Platform. Glueck (1965: 316) identified her as another manifestation of Atargatis, naming her alter egos Hera, Fortuna, Tyche, and Demeter, the mother of Persephone/Kore, who often shared in cult worship of her daughter. However, the iconography and context of the Grain Goddess has since been re-evaluated, and it is now believed that she represents the zodiacal Virgo (see Vol. 1, p. 221; McKenzie et al. 2002: 77). Scholars have re-evaluated the role of Atargatis as one of the main Nabataean deities, suggesting that she was of interest to only a small minority of Nabataeans (Zayadine 1979: 194–97), with uncertain evidence for her presence at Khirbet et-Tannur, despite the apparent use of her form for the female cult statue (Healey 2001: 141) (but see Vol. 1, pp. 196–201).

The socket and saucer lamps at Khirbet et-Tannur therefore invite us to consider further the identity of the deity or deities worshipped within the temple, the types of night cultic activity there, and the possible worship of a goddess whose attributes might include aspects of Kore.

CATALOGUE

For abbreviations see pp. xvii–xviii.

The information is given in the following order:

- Catalogue number of this publication (assigned January 2010);
- Fig. number(s) in the current work.
- *DD* reference, if illustrated;
- GA photograph, if there is one;
- Locus, if known (marked on fig. 6.2);
- GA Unit, as explained above, pp. 7–9. (The lamps and fragments are now stored together, not in the bags of pottery.)
- GP reference, if in it;
- GR number, if in it;
- GJ reference, if lamp apparently mentioned;
- GA lamp number, if in GA. (These are the same as their catalogue numbers.)
- Munsell description;
- Dimensions;
- Description;
- Glueck label, if present.

Wheel-Made Polycandela

Polycandela have a number of spouts attached to a circular tube which is filled with oil. It was assumed that those with a single row of spouts were used for lighting larger rooms and thought to be hung by metal hooks from the ceiling or placed on stands (Slane 1990: 10–11 "corona lamps;" Barag and Hershkovitz 1994: 58).

However, da Costa (2012: "Polilychnos Wheel-made") reports that polycandela are very rare in Jordan and all examples found there in archaeological contexts are associated with religious buildings (although at Masada two ring lamps come from the Western Palace, suggesting night lighting in a secular context, Barag and Hershkovitz 1994: 58). Da Costa (pers. comm.) also notes that they provide a great deal of light for a relatively short period.

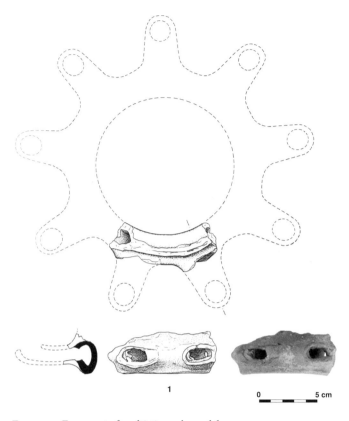

FIG. 17.1 *Fragment of multi-tier polycandelon.*

Comparanda for single-ring polycandela: Ayalon 1996 (attached to bowl); Barag and Hershkovitz 1994: 42, 58, nos. 99–101 (c. 37 BC–AD 115); da Costa 2012: nos. 80–84; Parker 2006: 350, fig. 16.75 = sherd 376, pl. 16.1 (late Byzantine, AD 502–551, with superstructure) = Parker 1987: 545–46, fig. 124, pl. 94.
Comparanda for complex Nabataean multi-tier polycandela: Renel (in press).

1.
Fig. 17.1. *DD* pl. 82a top row centre (= GA photo. I-36c-2).
Locus 20: Room 13; GA Unit 47-01K. GP no. 25; GJ April 14. GA lamp 1.
Munsell: clay 2.5YR 5/6 red; core 7.6YR 6/3 light brown. Coarse ware.
l. 9.0 cm; w. 3.6 cm; estimated diam. 10.9 cm; inner w. of apertures 1.5 cm, 1.4 cm.
Partial tubular polycandelon with two broken spouts. The tube is broken off along the top.

2.
Fig. 17.2.
Locus: "debris"; GA Unit 47-01J. GA lamp 2.
Munsell: clay and core 5YR 5/8 yellowish red.
l. 5.7 cm; w. 3.8 cm; th. 0.5 cm; inner w. of aperture: 1.5 cm.
Partial tubular polycandelon with one broken spout, and flat vertical ring above, broken off. Smaller diameter ring, and lamp, than no. 1 above.

3.
Fig. 17.3. (= GA photo. I-36c-6; drawing in GA). *DD* pl. 82a third row, far right (= GA photo. I-36c-6)
Locus: provenience unknown; GP no. 23. Whereabouts unknown May 2010.
Traces of grey slip, according to GP.
Estimated measurements: l. 6.5 cm; w. 5.5 cm; h. 1.8 cm; inner w. of spout 1.5 cm.
Partial tubular polycandelon with one spout. Apparently traces of sooting on edge of spout.

The only example at Khirbet et-Tannur for which a find place was recorded (no. 1) was from Room 13, opposite the Inner Temenos Enclosure. Close examination of nos. 1 and 2 reveals that the tubular ring was not a single ring, but part of a tiered lamp with more than one such ring. Similar fragments from a large number of complex examples with more than one tier have been found at Petra in the excavations in front of the Qasr el-Bint in Byzantine layers dated c. AD 363–419 (fig. 17.50) (Renel, in press) . There were also examples from the 2nd or possibly 3rd century AD (fig. 17.51) with nozzles like fragment no. 48. The fragments from Khirbet et-Tannur probably pre-date the AD 363 destruction and could date from the 2nd to 3rd century. No fragments of polycandela were found at Khirbet edh-Dharih, or in the Petra "Great Temple" excavations, further confirming their narrow religious use, specific to only some sanctuaries.

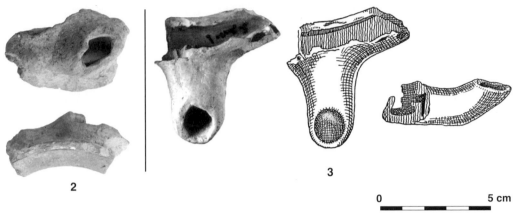

Figs. 17.2–3 *Polycandela fragments.*

Wheel-Made Socket and Saucer Lamps

So-called socket and saucer lamps are designed to provide intense light for a short period, and thus are associated with night cults. They take a very thick wick which receives the oil through slits in the surrounding saucer. The most intact example at Khirbet et-Tannur (no. 4) is attached to a nearly complete stand. Although broken, the other examples also had attached stands (visible on nos. 5–8, 10). They are the "number of peculiar lamps" Glueck (GJ 15 April) mentions finding in Room 14, with nos. 4 and 5 visible in the foreground of the photograph of the west end of it (Vol. 1, fig. 226) and no. 6 also found in Room 14.

The most complete example (no. 4) is of particular interest because of its "buff" ware and incised decoration, which are identical to those of "Nabataean cream ware" strainer jug necks. The other socket and saucer lamps at Khirbet et-Tannur are generally of "light red" pottery (nos. 5–11), sometimes with a thick cream coating (no. 6). The ware of nos. 5–7 is less well levigated (i.e., is coarser) than that of nos. 8–9. They have soot on the wick hole, indicating that they were used.

No unbroken example has been found, and the saucer fragments at Khirbet et-Tannur are all broken around the rim. The fragments from the lamp stand upper rim still attached to the saucer indicate that the potter must have formed the saucer and socket lamp on the wheel, inserted it into the top of a leather-hard ceramic lamp stand, using slip for adhesive, and then fired the completed vessel in the kiln. This combination of saucer, socket, and stand would have provided more stability for the lamp, especially if it were placed on an uneven surface.

The proportion of seven examples out of a total of forty-eight lamps from Khirbet et-Tannur is significant, especially as socket and saucer lamps are generally very rare. No examples were found at Khirbet edh-Dharih (François Villeneuve, pers. comm., January 2011), and Barrett recorded none at Petra. Elsewhere, they have been found in sanctuaries associated with the cult of Kore or night cults (see *Discussion* above).

Comparanda

A large cache of ninety-six socket and saucer lamps, without stands, was found at Samaria connected with the worship of Kore (Crowfoot 1957: 373–74, fig. 88.11; Broneer 1977: 83). These lamps were found in several sections of the site, but fifty of them were found in the Sanctuary of Kore, whose identification is based on an inscription found in the temple (Sukenik 1942), and another twenty in the stadium, which also had several graffiti and dipinti mentioning Kore (Crowfoot 1942). Many of these lamps were discovered with Roman pottery (Crowfoot 1957: 374). Unlike the Khirbet et-Tannur examples they lack an attached stand (fig. 17.52).

Over a thousand socket and saucer lamps, without stands, were discovered in the Sanctuary of

Palaimon at Isthmia and catalogued by Broneer (1977: 3, 35–52). Although the panhellenic sanctuary was primarily sacred to Poseidon, it also included the hero cult of Melikertes/Palaimon, a Theban youth who had drowned along with his mother. Broneer describes the lamp type:

"It is in a true sense of the word a cult vessel, designed exclusively for the Sanctuary of Palaimon. The lamps are wheel-made, consisting of a large bowl that contained the oil and in the centre a tubular wick-holder with one or more openings to permit the oil to reach the wick. Nearly all the lamps show blackening at the top of their sockets. The wick would have been large and was probably rolled into a tube, as on large modern kerosene lamps. A solid wick large enough to fill the socket would have used up oil too fast and would probably have produced an undue amount of smoke. The base is slightly raised and in most cases it is rough underneath, showing the marks of the string used for removing the lamp from the wheel. On several of the lamps, however, the base has been trimmed after removal from the wheel.

The Palaimonion lamps have no handle; consequently they were intended to be set on the ground or on some lamp stand" (Broneer 1977: 35).

The Isthmian lamps were divided into two main groups. Group A lamps, the most frequently found, have a socket lower than the saucer rim. The fabric varies from a brick red to a pale yellow without glaze or wash, but with "traces of a white chalky surfacing applied both on the inside and the outside, and even on the base and inside the socket. This crumbly substance, which seems to be pure lime, can hardly have been made for decoration. I would venture a guess that it is mere white wash applied at times for purification of the whole area. This would seem to follow from the fact that in some cases, it has been splashed over fragmentary and probably discarded lamps" (Broneer 1977: 37). Group B lamps, less common and apparently later in date, were made of dark brown gritty clay, were smaller than the Group A lamps, but had

sockets higher than the bowl rim, which was normally simple and incurving (Broneer 1977: 48–52). More socket and saucer lamps were discovered in the pits of the Palaimonion and surrounding areas during the excavations of the University of Chicago team (Gebhard et al. 1998: 436, 443). These excavations have revised Broneer's chronology and show the lamps were introduced by AD 80, and used until the cult ceased around AD 220–240 (Gebhard et al. 1998: 445–46).

In her catalogue of over 550 lamps, especially from Deir 'Ain 'Abata, Pella, and Umm Qais, and largely dated to c. AD 300–700, da Costa reports only one, probably re-used, example from Deir 'Ain 'Abata (da Costa 2012: no. 79, fig. 541). Similar saucer lamps, without socket, were used in this period in Christian contexts in Egypt, at Kellia (Egloff 1977: 161–63, pl. 85.5–14).

4.
Fig. 17.4 (= GA photo. III-6-9; drawing in GA).
Locus 21: apparently west end of Room 14 (visible in foreground of Vol. 1, Fig. 226); GP no. 12. Department of Antiquities main store, Amman, Jordan. inv. 40.782 – J3293. *Non vidi.*
"Buff" coloured ware (Department of Antiquities record card; GP).
h. 10.8 cm (ditto).

Wheel-made lamp and stand with handle. The stand is in the form of a hollow cylinder with a handle placed beneath the flaring rim, with broken edge. The lower exterior body of the vessel is decorated with an incised zigzagging line above two incised straight bands. The lamp saucer is nestled inside the stand rim. This is the only example with a surviving stand, but other examples (nos. 5–8, 10) have traces of stands on the undersides of their saucers.

Kharieh 'Amr observes (pers. comm., February 2010) that this lamp is otherwise identical to a "Nabataean cream ware" strainer jug neck. She dates it from probably the late 1st to early 2nd century AD, although there are later prototypes going into the 3rd century, and probably even the early 4th century. Room 14 was still in use in the 4th century, and to narrow the date of this lamp would require examining the fabric firsthand (our attempts to do

4

0 _____ 5 cm

FIG. 17.4 *Socket and saucer lamp, with attached stand.*

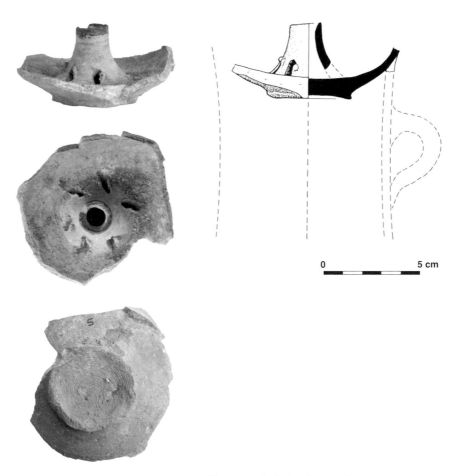

0 _____ 5 cm

5   FIG. 17.5 *Socket and saucer lamp.*

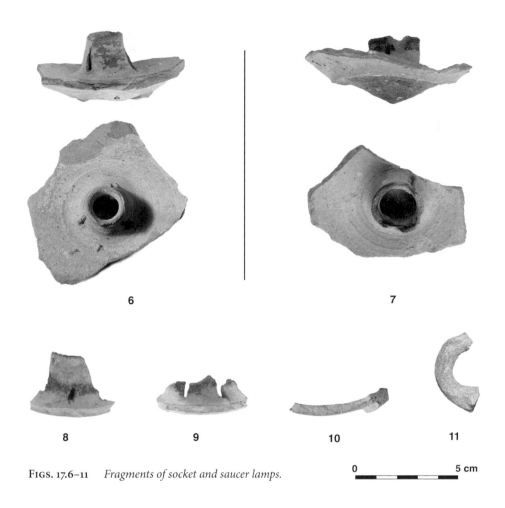

6   7

8   9   10   11

FIGS. 17.6–11   *Fragments of socket and saucer lamps.*

0   5 cm

so in 2010 and 2011 were unsuccessful). "Nabataean cream ware" ('Amr 1992; Schneider 1996: 138–39, 142, figs. 579–91, nos. 124–36 "Green Ware") should not be confused with Islamic Mahesh ware (Whitcomb 1989).

5.
Fig. 17.5; Vol. 1, fig. 367b. *DD* pl. 82a top left (= GA photo. I-36c-1).
Locus 21: apparently west part of Room 14 (visible in foreground of Vol. 1, fig. 226); GA Unit 20-B04. GA lamp 5.
Munsell: clay and core 2.5YR 6/8 light red.
h. 3.9 cm; surviving diam. of saucer 8.4 cm; th. at centre point of base 1.2 cm; th. of socket 0.4 cm; inner diam. of socket (wick hole) 1.0 cm; average slit length 0.4 cm.

Wheel-made socket and saucer lamp with six perpendicular slits around the base of socket. The

small socket, with a sooted rim, is set within a saucer with a string-cut base. The saucer rim is broken (original diameter unknown), with a fragment from the stand adhering to one edge.

6.
Fig. 17.6.
Locus 21: Room 14; GA Unit 20-B05; GJ 15 April. GA lamp 6.
Munsell: clay and core 2.5YR 6/6 light red; coating: 2.5Y 8/3 pale yellow.
h. 3.3 cm; diam. of saucer 7.9 cm; th. at centre point of base 1.5 cm; th. of socket 0.6 cm; inner diam. of socket (wick hole) 1.1 cm; average slit length: 1.3 cm.

Wheel-made socket and saucer lamp with three perpendicular slits around the base of the socket, which has faint traces of soot. The saucer has a broken rim. The base is damaged revealing the socket base, and that the socket and saucer were made on the wheel in a single process. The lamp has a thick creamy yellow coating inside and out (see description of comparanda from Isthmia, above).

7.
Fig. 17.7.
Locus: provenience unknown; GA Unit 20-B01. GA lamp 7.
Munsell: clay 2.5YR 6/6 light red; core 2.5YR 5/1 reddish grey; underside of saucer 7.5YR 4/1 dark grey.
h. 3.2 cm; diam. of saucer 8.0 cm; th. of socket 0.3 cm; inner diam. of socket 1.8 cm; average slit length 1.3 cm; thickness at centre point of base of socket 1.7 cm.

Wheel-made socket and saucer lamp with two perpendicular slits around the base of the socket, which has a sooted rim. The saucer has a broken rim. The base (which has a nearly black surface) of the socket projects in a cone-shape beneath the saucer.

8.
Fig. 17.8.
Locus: "debris"; GA Unit 47-19. GA lamp 8.
Munsell: clay 5YR 6/6 reddish yellow; core 2.5YR 7/6 light red.
h. 3.0 cm; th. of socket base 0.3 cm; slit length 0.7 cm.

Wheel-made socket fragment with one surviving slit and two broken slits at the base of the socket, which is heavily sooted.

9.
Fig. 17.9.
Locus: "debris"; GA Unit 47-19. GA lamp 9.
Munsell: clay and core 2.5YR 5/6 red; splashes 10YR 7/2 light grey on exterior and inside edges (could be lime encrustation).
h. 1.9 cm; th. of socket base 0.3 cm.

Wheel-made socket fragment with part of two slits, and a sooted rim, set within a broken saucer fragment.

10.
Fig. 17.10.
Locus: "debris"; GA Unit 48-04. GA lamp 10.

Munsell: clay 2.5YR 6/8 light red; exterior wash 10YR 7/2 light grey.
l. 4.9 cm; w. 1.8 cm; h. 0.9 cm; th. of base 0.5 cm.

Wheel-made saucer fragment with small clay lip where the lamp stand was sealed to the saucer.

11.
Fig. 17.11.
Locus: provenience unknown; GA Unit A-17. GA lamp 11.
Munsell: clay and core 10YR 8/3 very pale brown.
h. 3.8 cm; maximum w. 2.0 cm; th. at centre 1.0 cm.

Vertical handle, apparently from socket and saucer lamp.

Wheel-Made Round Lamps

Comparanda

The wheel-made round lamps from Khirbet et-Tannur are unusual as they differ from other, earlier, wheel-made examples, such as "Herodian lamps" (Barag and Hershkovitz 1994: 24–58, Type C), because the spout is nearly contained within the line of the circular body, and they have small pinched handles. However, very close parallels have been excavated at nearby Khirbet edh-Dharih in dated contexts (Durand 2011: nos. 26–28). They appear there in the second half of the 2nd century or beginning of the 3rd century. They were found in the "Rectangular Building" and "Caravanserai" which continued in use in the first half of the 3rd century. Examples were found at Petra, but not in dated contexts ('Amr 1987: 34, 279, 329, pl. 18, nos. PL42 and PL43 = Type 11). None are known from ez-Zantur.

A striking parallel should be noted: the second most common lamp type at the Palaimonion in Isthmia, after the saucer and socket lamps, was a plain wheelmade lamp (Type XVI), rarely found outside Corinth and Isthmia and therefore certainly locally made (Broneer 1977: 26–35).

12.
Fig. 17.12 (incl. GA photos. I-36a-5, I-36b-5). *DD* pl. 82a second row, far right (= GA photo. I-36c-3).
Locus 16: SW corner of Room 9; GA Unit 20-B01;

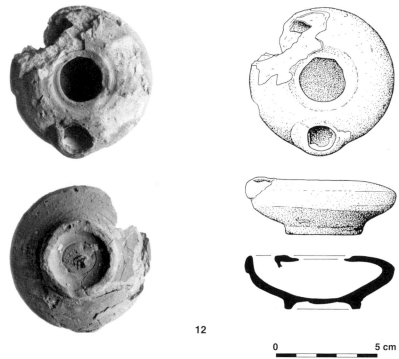

12

0 _____ 5 cm

FIG. 17.12 *Wheel-made round lamp.*

GP no. 17; GR no. 81; GJ 9 April. GA lamp 12.
Munsell: clay and core 10YR 8/3 very pale brown;
slip 2.5YR 5/6 red. Coarser ware than nos. 13–14
below.
diam. 7.0 cm; h. 2.7 cm; filling hole diam. 2.2 cm;
inner w. of spout 1.3 cm.

An almost complete wheel-made, red-slipped
round lamp with the spout incorporated within
its circumference. The oil reservoir is flattened and
level with the large central filling hole which has a
faint ridge around it. The base ring is footed. It is
unclear if there was a handle due to damage at rear
of the shoulder. There is some lime encrustation on
the shoulder and sooting around the spout.

Apparently found with no. 18 below.

13.
Fig. 17.13.
Locus: "debris"; GA Unit 47-19. GA lamp 13.
Munsell: clay and core 2.5YR 7/8 red. Some limey
inclusions. Finer ware than no. 12 above.
l. 8.1 cm; h. 1.9 cm; th. 0.4 cm; filling hole diam. 1.8 cm.

Partial wheel-made round lamp, including edge
of spout, with sooting in that area. Complete large

filling hole with two slight ridges around it. At the
rear shoulder of the lamp there is a vestigial handle,
added by hand. It is mounted flat and unclear if it
had a vertical component. The oil reservoir is flattened and level with the large central filling hole.
Some lime encrustation.

14.
Fig. 17.14.
Locus: "debris"; GA Unit 47-19. GA lamp 14.
Munsell: clay and core 5YR 6/6 reddish yellow;
slip traces 2.5YR 5/6 red. Some limey inclusions.
Levigation of ware close to no. 13 above.
l. 7.5 cm; estimated diam. 7.9 cm; h. 3.5 cm; filling
hole diam. 2.3 cm.
Fragment of upper shoulder and partial base
of wheel-made round lamp, with edge of spout,
sooted in that area. Partial large filling hole with
two slight ridges round it.

15.
Fig. 17.15.
Locus 14A: ditch to n. of Inner Temenos Enclosure;
GA Unit 4A-19. GA lamp 15.

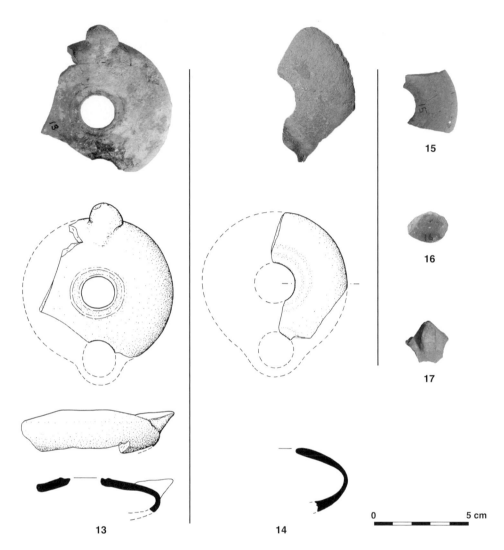

FIGS. 17.13–17 *Fragments of wheel-made round lamps.*

Munsell: clay 2.5YR 6/6 light red; core 2.5Y 5/1 grey. l. 3.3 cm; estimated diam. 6.5 cm; th. 0.3 cm; filling hole diam. 2.2 cm.

Upper shoulder fragment from a wheel-made round lamp, with a partial large filling hole, with some sooting.

In bag labelled "91 fine sherds from a ditch on north side of north court, also 2 pieces of glass, green; (bottle mouth)."

16.
Fig. 17.16.
Locus: provenience unknown; GA Unit A-13. GA lamp 16.
Munsell: clay 2.5YR 5/8 red; core 2.5Y 5/1 grey.

w. 1.5 cm; h. 2.1 cm.

Very worn unperforated handle, with slight upward curve, from local wheel-made round lamp to which it was apparently attached horizontally.

17.
Fig. 17.17.
Locus: provenience unknown; GA Unit A-13. GA lamp 17.
Munsell: clay 10R 6/6 light red; core 2.5Y 6/1 grey.
Ware like no. 14 above.
w. 2.3 cm; h. 1.8 cm.

Unperforated vertical handle from local wheel-made round lamp.

Levantine Copies of Discus Lamps

Comparanda for no. 18: Eagles on Broneer (1930) Type XXIII lamps (same motif, different from no. 18): Bailey 1965: 33, nos. 44–46; Bailey 1988: nos. Q2414, Q2415, Q2416, Q2417, Q2443 and Q2518; Rosenthal-Heginbottom 1981: 115, no. F-13 "Adler." General type: Grawehr 2006: 309–21, Type I Rundlampen mit kleinem Fülloch, although at ez-Zantur lamps with decorated discuses tend to also have decorated shoulders, and no lamps, local or imported, were found at ez-Zantur with an eagle on the discus. Dates from the references above range from late 1st century AD to the 4th century.

Comparanda for no. 19: General: Horsfield and Horsfield 1942: no. 435, pl. 46. Dated to 1st century AD based on shoulder form: Loeschcke form IIb; Broneer (1930) Type XXII/XXIII.

18.
Fig. 17.18 (= GA photos. I-36a-2, I-36b-2).
Locus 16: in south-west corner of Room 9; GR no. 80; GJ 9 April. Cincinnati Art Museum no. 1939.243.
l. 9.5 cm; w. 7.0 cm; h. 2.5 cm; filling hole diam. 0.8 cm; inner w. of spout 1.0 cm. (Dimensions provided by the late Glenn Markoe.)

Mould-made ovoid lamp with plain rim and decorated discus surrounded by two slight ridges. The discus motif appears to be a simplified eagle, facing right. The spout is rounded, and the handle is pinched and unperforated, emanating from the raised base ring. Apparently found with no. 12 above.

19.
Fig. 17.19.
Locus: provenience unknown; GA Unit A-13. GA lamp 19.
Munsell: clay and core 5YR 6/6 reddish yellow. Limey inclusions.
l. 4.4 cm; h. 1.6 cm; th. 0.3 cm.

Very worn shoulder rim fragment from discus lamp.

Nabataean Mould-Made Lamps

Comparanda for no. 20: Generally: Broneer XXV/Loeschcke VIII; Khairy 1990: 12, no. 19 (1st century AD), different shoulder motif. Ware like Nabataean and quite fine. No exact parallels for shoulder rim decoration. No parallels known from Petra. Syro-Palestinian version: Israeli and Avida 1988: 32, no. 43. Egyptian version: Selesnow 1988: 154, no. 217.

Comparanda for no. 21: Possibly Grawehr 2006: 309–21, Type I Rundlampen mit kleinem Fülloch, e.g., no. 243. However, large handles joined to the base ring are more common in northern Jordan on lamps with larger filling holes (see next type) (Lankester Harding 1950: 84–85, pl. 25 "Jabal Jofeh lamps"). Large handles like this, joined to base rings, are also known in Egypt, but those handles have a notch at the top (Mlynarczyk 1995).

20.
Fig. 17.20.
Locus: "debris"; GA Unit 47-19. GA lamp 20.
Munsell: clay 5YR 6/6 reddish yellow; core 10YR 5/1 grey. Ware like Nabataean and quite fine.
l. 3.9 cm; w. 2.5 cm; th. 0.3 cm.

Small fragment from a mould-made lamp, with a rosette on a slightly depressed discus, with only four partial petals present. There is a triangular ridged design and circle with raised dot on shoulder rim.

21.
Fig. 17.21.
Locus 21: Room 14; GA Unit 47-01F. GA lamp 21.
Munsell: clay and core 5YR 7/6 reddish yellow; slip 2.5YR 5/8 red;
l. 4.5 cm; w. 3.9 cm; h. 2.3 cm.

Ridged handle attached to a small base fragment. The ridge on the handle extends down to the base ring. Well-levigated ware, but clumsy manufacture.

Label: "8 – room II 13 April". [Apparently S room II, i.e., Room 14].

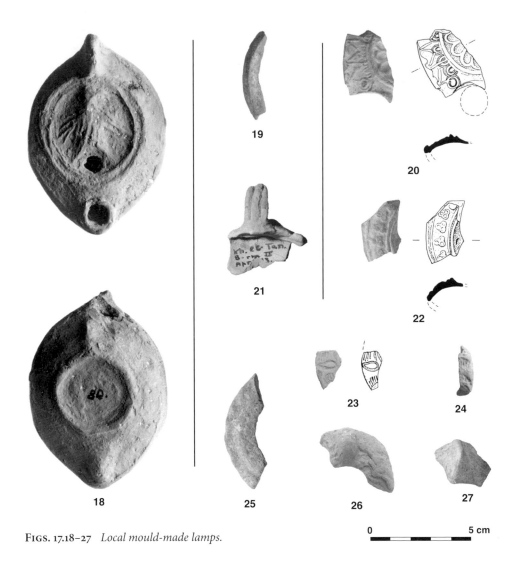

FIGS. 17.18–27 *Local mould-made lamps.*

0   5 cm

Levantine Copies of Mould-Made Round Lamps

Nos. 25–28 are all the same poorly levigated (coarse) ware.

Comparanda for shape (Nos. 22–26): Broneer Type XXV/Loeschcke VIII, late 1st to 3rd centuries AD = Bailey Type O (1979: 239–44) and Q (1979: 336); Grawehr 2006: 309–20, Type I Round lamps with small filling holes.

Comparanda for decoration:
For no. 22: No lamps found with similar three-dot decoration.
For nos. 23–24 impressed teardrop (or egg) and lines shoulder decoration: No exact parallels found, but

examples with a related teardrop patterns were excavated at Khirbet edh-Dharih. They include the lamp mould from the foundations of the sanctuary dated to the beginning of the 2nd century AD (Durand 2011: no. 52), and a lamp with simpler teardrops from the olive oil press V10 which was destroyed at the beginning of the 2nd century AD (Durand 2011: no. 14). Teardrop pattern on Grawehr 2006: 361, no. 601, Type C2 Jerash Round Lamps (imported to Petra).

22.
Fig. 17.22.
Locus: provenience unknown; GA Unit A-12. GA lamp 22.

Munsell: clay and core 2.5YR 7/6 light red. Some limey inclusions.

l. 3.5 cm, w. 2.1 cm, th. 0.3 cm.

Small shoulder fragment. The rim, bordered with ridging, is decorated with four groups of three raised dots, each with raised outline and raised centre.

23.
Fig. 17.23.
Locus: "debris"; GA Unit 47-19. GA lamp 23.
Munsell: clay and core 5YR 7/6 reddish yellow; slip 2.5YR 3/6 dark red. Fine ware.
l. 1.9 cm; w.1.3 cm; th. 0.2 cm.

Very small shoulder fragment, decorated with an impressed outlined teardrop, flanked by impressed lines. Possibly part of the same lamp as no. 24 below.

24.
Fig. 17.24.
Locus: provenience unknown; GA Unit A-13. GA lamp 24.
Munsell: clay and core 5YR 7/6 reddish yellow; slip traces 2.5YR 3/6 dark red.
l. 2.4 cm; w. 0.8 cm; h. 1.2 cm; th. 0.4 cm.

Very small shoulder fragment, decorated with an impressed outlined teardrop, flanked by impressed lines. Possibly part of the same lamp as no. 23 above.

25.
Fig. 17.25.
Locus: provenience unknown; GA Unit A-13. GA lamp 25.
Munsell: clay 2.5YR 6/8 light red; core 10YR 7/3 very pale brown.
l. 5.6 cm; w. 1.8 cm; th. 0.4 cm.

Worn mould-made shoulder rim with partial large filling hole with raised ridge. Some moulded decoration discernible on the rim, possibly ovolos.

26.
Fig. 17.26.
Locus: provenience unknown; GA Unit A-12. GA lamp 26.
Munsell: clay and core 2.5YR 6/8 light red. Some limey inclusions.
l. 4.5 cm; w. 2.1 cm; th. 0.4 cm; h. of handle 1.7 cm.

Worn mould-made shoulder rim with unperforated raised handle. Partial large central filling hole, possibly surrounded by two ridges. Any decoration on the rim is not discernible.

27.
Fig. 17.27.
Locus: provenience unknown; GA Unit A-17. GA lamp 27.
Munsell: clay 2.5YR 5/8 red; core 10YR 7/3 light grey.
w. 2.9 cm; h. 2.2 cm.

Unperforated handle from mould-made round lamp, with thin shoulder.

28.
Locus: "debris"; GA Unit 48-05. GA lamp 28.
Munsell: clay 2.5YR 6/8 light red; core 10YR 7/3 light grey. Core has chalky texture.
l. 3.1 cm; w. 2.2 cm; th. 0.3 cm.

Small base fragment of mould-made round lamp with partial raised base ring.

Mould-Made Round Lamps with Large Filling Holes

Mould-made round lamps with large filling holes appear at nearby Khirbet edh-Dharih in the late 2nd century or beginning of the 3rd century AD (Durand 2011: nos. 32–34), with two of them in an area (S7) which was destroyed in the second half of the 3rd century AD (Durand 2011: nos. 32–33). They do not have identical shoulder decoration to those at Khirbet et-Tannur. Similar lamps appear at ez-Zantur in Petra, although dated there on parallels to northern finds (Grawehr 2006: 321–32, Type J Round lamps with large filling holes, 2nd to end of 3rd century). Northern versions are well-known at Jerash (Kehrberg 2007: fig. 8, no. 125) from the late 2nd to early 3rd centuries (JUTZ lamps). The type continues at Pella until the 4th century (da Costa et al. 2002: 517–18, fig. 12: RN192002 and RN192003 from a destruction of the very late 4th century).

Comparanda for no. 29: Very close: Grawehr 2006: 322, no. 327, Type J1 variant c, and p. 331, no. 416, Type J3 variant c. Similar: da Costa 2012:

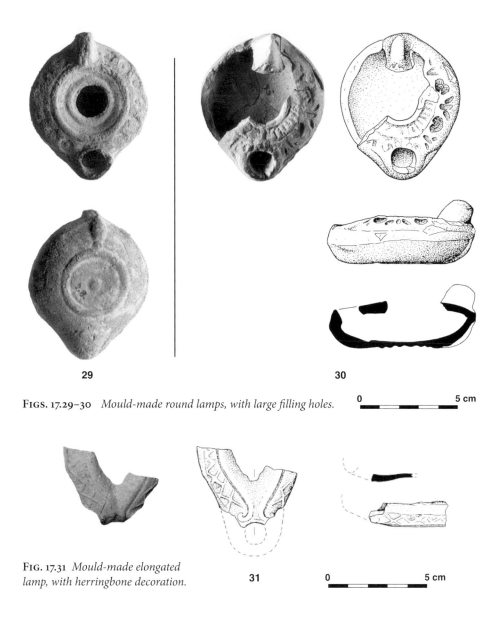

FIGS. 17.29–30 *Mould-made round lamps, with large filling holes.*

0   5 cm

FIG. 17.31 *Mould-made elongated lamp, with herringbone decoration.*

31   0   5 cm

no. 4; Rosenthal and Sivan 1978: 127, no. 522, "Late Roman" (3rd–4th century).

Comparanda for no. 30: Zayadine 1986: 15–16, nos. 13–19, especially no. 16; Lapp 1997: 49–52, 323, fig. 29: "Gerasan type" (2nd–4th century AD); Harding 1950: pl. 25, no. 25.

29.
Fig. 17.29 (= GA photos. I-36a-3, I-36b-3).
Locus 2: north-west corner of Inner Temenos Enclosure; GR no. 28. Whereabouts unknown May 2010.

Estimated measurements: l. 7.6 cm; w. 6.5 cm; filling hole diam. 1.5 cm; inner w. of spout 1.0 cm.

Mould-made round lamp. Large central filling hole decorated with two wide ridges. Spout is sooted. On shoulder impressed design of circles with centred dots. Raised base ring with raised centre dot. Unperforated raised handle.

30.
Fig. 17.30 (incl. GA photo. I-36c-9). *DD* pl. 82a bottom row, far right (= GA photo. I-36c-9).
Locus: provenience unknown; GA Unit 20-B07; GP no. 21. GA lamp 30.

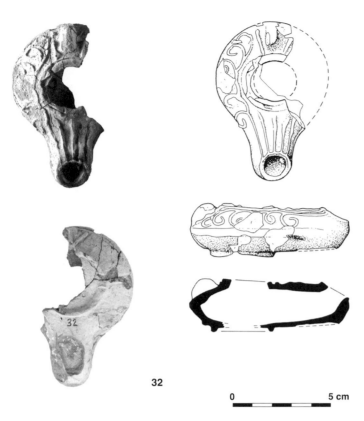

32

0   5 cm

Fɪɢ. 17.32 *South Jordan slipper lamp, with volutes on shoulder.*

Munsell: clay and core 2.5YR 5/8 red. Some limey inclusions.
l. 7.5 cm; w. 6.2 cm; h. 2.5 cm; th. 0.5 cm; h. incl. handle 3.1 cm; filling hole diam. 2.0 cm; inner w. of spout 1.1 cm.

Two-thirds of mould-made round lamp. Large central filling hole encircled by wide ridge and impressed radiating lines. Spout is sooted. There is an impressed design on the shoulder that may represent fruit and leaves. About half of the upper section of the lamp is missing. Small knob handle at the rear of lamp. Base has three raised concentric circles.

Mould-Made Elongated Lamp with Raised Herringbone Decoration

Comparanda: Rosenthal and Sivan 1978: 98, no. 400, without discussion but acquired in Petra in 1934 and grouped with Nabataean lamps; Sussman 1989: no. 49, Type 6E northern stamped, with im-

pressed decoration, but similar form; possibly North African/Egyptian, although the closest known parallel seems too late: Bailey 1988: 232, Q2266, Alexandrian copying Levantine Late Roman/early Islamic 7th-century.

31.
Fig. 17.31.
Locus: provenience unknown; GA Unit A-13. GA lamp 31.
Munsell: clay 5YR 6/6 reddish yellow; core 2.5YR 5/4 reddish brown.
l. 4.7 cm; w. 5.3 cm; h. 1.1 cm; th. 0.4 cm.

Partial upper shoulder fragment from an elongated lamp with a tongued discus; with edge of spout, which has some sooting. Shoulder rim is decorated with a raised relief of an open herringbone design with a trace of a volute on either side of the spout. The filling hole is missing.

South Jordan Slipper Lamps

Nos. 32–38 are all related by ware. No. 39 is coarser, less red, with a darker core. No. 40 is more like nos. 32–38, but they are redder and slipped. Nos. 33 and 34 come from the same mould, while no. 37 comes from the same mould as a lamp found in Petra.

These mould-made lamps are characterized by a variety of relief decoration on the shoulder and lines on the spout, a large central filling hole, a vestigial knob handle and a raised base ring. They are commonly called "slipper lamps" because of their shape, although they are named "Peträisch-Frühbyzantinische Lampen" at ez-Zantur (Grawehr 2006: 340–49). All Byzantine lamps are sometimes called slipper lamps, indiscriminately. Da Costa (2012: nos. 33–69) has suggested that the term "South Jordan lamps" is more specific. In order to avoid confusion they are referred to here as "South Jordan slipper lamps." Glueck called them Nabataean lamps in his excavation records because he had apparently already made the association between where they are found and Nabataean territory, also noted by Khairy (1990: 19–20). Most examples have ridged radiating lines on the shoulder, suggesting that they were descended from the earlier (late 1st century BC to 2nd cent AD) Nabataean "slash and rosette" lamp types (so too Zanoni 1996: 324; Durand 2011; da Costa 2012), although the issue of the chronological gap has not been solved.

Over 693 fragments of this type have been found at ez-Zantur, firmly establishing the introduction of the type by AD 363 (Grawehr 2006: 340–42). They were also found in AD 363 contexts at 'En Hazeva in the eastern Negev (Erickson-Gini 2010: 146, figs. 61–62, 155, nos. 61–62, 156). Da Costa notes that the absence of the slipper lamps at Lejjun before AD 300 suggests that they were not introduced before then, and the evidence from Deir 'Ain 'Abata indicates that late forms were in use throughout the Umayyad period (da Costa 2012).

Very close parallels for the types at Khirbet et-Tannur (nos. 32–34, 37–38, 41) have been excavated at nearby Khirbet edh-Dharih (Durand 2011: nos. 39, 40, 42, 46) in a drain which was destroyed in an earthquake in the mid-4th century AD. In this drain of the north temenos of the sanctuary, these complete lamps were found with twelve bronze coins, mostly of the first half of the 4th century (none later than AD 363). After the AD 363 earthquake Khirbet edh-Dharih was deserted until the beginning of the 6th century, and there seems to have been a similar pattern of human presence at Khirbet et-Tannur. Thus, the South Jordan slipper lamps at Khirbet et-Tannur, nos. 32–41, are probably dated to the first half of the 4th century, before AD 363.

Comparanda for no. 32, with volutes on shoulder: Very close, Khirbet edh-Dharih: Durand 2011: no. 40. Earliest version ez-Zantur: Grawehr 2006: 342, no. 481. Similar: Deir 'Ain 'Abata: da Costa 2012: no. 51, fig. 514. Ez-Zantur: Grawehr 2006: 344, no. 498.

Comparanda for nos. 33–34, with dots and lines: Similar Khirbet edh-Dharih: Durand 2011: no. 39. Ez-Zantur: Grawehr 2006: 347, no. 513 (grey ware). It is possible that the groups of dots represent grapes, as they have a line leading to each group.

Comparanda for no. 37: No. 37 has mould match with ez-Zantur: Grawehr 2006: 346, no. 509. See single short line in centre of left shoulder, shape of curves on lines on spout, and imperfections in base rings (K. da Costa, pers. comm., 2011).

Comparanda for 41: Ez-Zantur: Grawehr 2006: 345, no. 504. Khirbet edh-Dharih: Durand 2011: no. 45 (single ring around filling hole).

Comparanda for 42: No exact parallels at ez-Zantur or Khirbet edh-Dharih, as generally these lamps do not have such large handles, but a similar lamp at Deir 'Ain 'Abata: da Costa 2012: no. 67, fig. 530.

32.
Fig. 17.32 (incl. GA photo. I-36c-7).
Locus: provenience unknown; GA Unit 20-B01 and 20-B06; GP no. 24; GR no. 23. GA lamp 32.
Munsell: clay and core 2.5YR 5/6 red; slip 10YR 8/2 very pale brown.
l. 8.2 cm; w. 4.2 cm; h. 2.7 cm; th. 0.1 cm; w. of spout 2.1 cm; inner w. of spout 1.1 cm.

Two-thirds of mould-made slipper lamp with five raised lines running down the nozzle, the outer two ending in a volute. The nozzle is sooted. There is a vestigial knob handle at the rear of the shoulder, flanked by three dots trailed together. On the base there is a partial raised ring, with two or three joining lines under the handle. There is some curved ridging of repeated volutes on the shoulder.

33.
Fig. 17.33; Vol. 1, fig. 368a (= GA photos. I-36a-6, I-36b-6).
Locus 1: south-west corner of Altar Platform; GP no. 18; GR no. 27; GJ 3 March. Whereabouts unknown in 2010.
Estimated measurements: l. 8.5 cm; w. 5.8 cm; filling hole diam. 2.3 cm; inner w. of spout 1.0 cm.

Mould-made complete slipper lamp. Vestigial knob handle at the rear of the shoulder. Shoulder rim is decorated with raised dots and herringbone ridging with two large dots on either side of the handle. Sooted spout is decorated with three lines emanating from dots beside the filling hole, which is surrounded by a ridge. Raised base ring with a

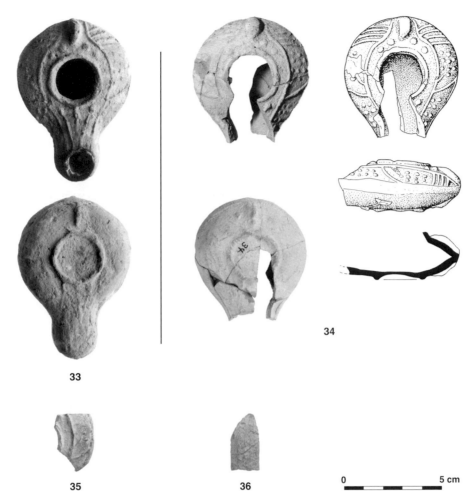

33

34

35   **36**

0   5 cm

FIGS. 17.33–36   *South Jordan slipper lamps.*

ridge that runs from the ring towards the handle on the upper section of the lamp. Same mould as no. 34 below.

34.
Fig. 17.34; Vol. 1, fig. 368b. *DD* pl. 82a centre of bottom row (= GA photo. I-36c-8).
Locus 21: Room 14; GA Unit 20-B06; GP no. 20. GA lamp 34.
Munsell: clay 2.5YR 5/6 red; core 7.5YR 5/2 brown; slip 10YR 8/3 very pale brown. Slip and ware similar to no. 32 above.
l. 6.4 cm; w. 5.8 cm; h. 2.6 cm; th. of base 0.2 cm; filling hole diam. 2.3 cm.

Most of mould-made lamp, except nozzle. Vestigial knob handle at the rear of the shoulder. The large filling hole is surrounded by a ridge, with

two raised dots on either side of the handle. A raised line runs from either side of the handle along the rim to the spout. Shoulder rim has four lines on either side running towards the handle. The rest of the rim on either side is decorated with two groups of small raised dots separated by a raised line, with a single line running into the back set of dots. Raised base ring with a ridge that runs from the ring towards the handle. Same mould as no. 33 above.

35.
Fig. 17.35.
Locus: provenience unknown; GA Unit A-13. GA lamp 35.
Munsell: clay 2.5YR 5/6 red; slip 10YR 8/2 very pale brown.
l. 2.9 cm; w. 1.8 cm; th. 0.3 cm.

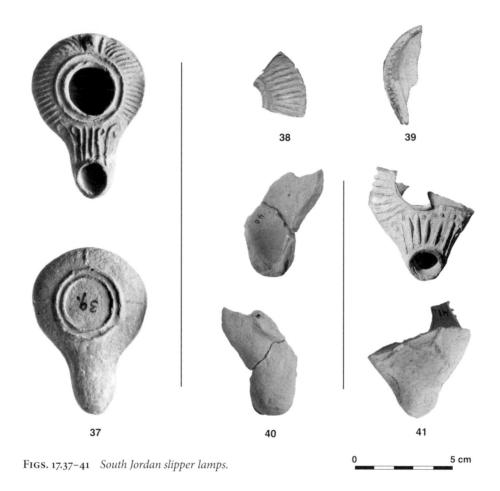

FIGS. 17.37–41 *South Jordan slipper lamps.*

0   5 cm

Shoulder fragment of mould-made slipper lamp with edge of filling hole and ridged border enclosing line and raised dots. From lamp similar to no. 34 above.

36.
Fig. 17.36.
Locus: provenience unknown; GA Unit A-13. GA lamp 36.
Munsell: clay 2.5YR 5/6 red; core: 2.5YR 4/2 weak red; slip 10YR 8/3 very pale brown.
l. 2.9 cm; w. 1.4 cm; th. 0.3 cm.
Rim fragment of mould-made slipper lamp with ridged decoration.

37.
Fig. 17.37 (= GA photos. I-36a-1, I-36b-1).
Locus 6: east part of Inner Temenos Enclosure; GR no. 39; GJ 4 March. Whereabouts unknown May 2010.

Estimated measurements: l. 8.5 cm; w. 6.1 cm; filling hole diam. 2.3 cm; inner w. of spout 1.3 cm.

Mould-made complete slipper lamp. Radial ridging on shoulder rim and a vestigial knob handle at the rear of the shoulder. The large filling hole is surrounded by two ridges. On the nozzle are two pairs of volutes encasing two straight ridges which follow the filling hole to the spout. There are two ridges delineating the base ring with a short ridge running from the rear to the upper shoulder.

38.
Fig. 17.38.
Locus 13: inside north wall of Forecourt; GA Unit 47-7D. GA lamp 38.
Munsell: clay and core 2.5YR 6/8 light red. Some limey inclusions. Ware related to 32 and 34 above.
l. 3.6 cm; w. 2.2 cm; th. 0.3 cm.
Small shoulder fragment from mould-made

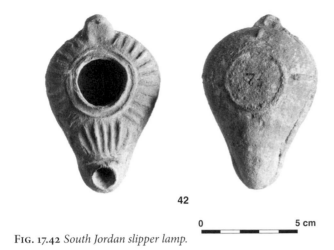

42

0   5 cm

FIG. 17.42 *South Jordan slipper lamp.*

slipper lamp. Radial ridging encircles a large filling hole.

Label: "found inside north wall of main court."

39.
Fig. 17.39.
Locus: Room 14. GA lamp 39.
Munsell: clay 2.5YR 5/6 red; core 7.5YR 4/1 dark
grey.
l. 5.2 cm; h. 1.7 cm; th. 0.3 cm.

Small base fragment with a fraction of a raised
base ring and upper shoulder rim from a slipper
lamp, which is decorated with raised radial lines.
Label: "room 14" on base.

40.
Fig. 17.40.
Locus 6: in front of Altar Platform, Inner Temenos
Enclosure; GA Unit 4A-25. GA lamp 40.
Munsell: clay and core 5YR 6/6 reddish yellow.
Some limey inclusions.
l. 6.2 cm; h. 1.8 cm; inner w. of spout 1.1 cm.

A quarter of the lower part of a mould-made
slipper lamp with spout, sooted on its upper rim,
and a small section of a raised base ring.
Label: "In front of main shrine."

41.
Fig. 17.41. *DD* pl. 82a second row, far left (= GA
photo. I-36c-4).

Locus: provenience unknown; GA
Unit 20-B02; GP no. 22; GR no. 17.
GA lamp 41.
Munsell: clay 2.5YR 5/8 red; slip
10YR 8/4 very pale brown; interior
10YR 6/2 light brownish grey.
l. 6.0 cm; w. 5.1 cm; h. 2.6 cm; th. 0.3
cm; inner w. of spout 1.1 cm.

Mould-made slipper lamp fragment of nozzle and part of filling
hole. Two single volutes bordering
five high ridges run down the nozzle,
which is sooted. There is a raised dot
in both volutes and a dot at the end
of, or beside, each of the five ridges
beside the raised edge of the filling
hole. There are raised radial lines on
the shoulder. There is a partial base ring with ridges
flanking the nozzle base.

42.
Fig. 17.42 (= GA photos. I-36a-4, I-36b-4).
Locus 15: Room 8; GP no. 33; GR no. 72. Glueck
records as "Missing." Whereabouts unknown May
2010.
Estimated measurements: l. 8.5 cm; w. 6.3 cm;
filling hole diam. 2.5 cm; inner w. of spout 1.3 cm.

Mould-made complete slipper lamp with radial
ridging on shoulder rim and seven ridges running
down nozzle. Large filling hole surrounded by two
ridges, and a tongue-like handle at the rear of the
shoulder. Single base ring with three straight ridges
extending up from the base ring to the upper shoulder, below the handle and half way along each side.

Small Candlestick Lamp

Small Candlestick lamps are very rare in south
Jordan, south of the Wādī al-Mujib, but com-
mon across the Dead Sea (da Costa 2001: 245;
Rosenthal and Sivan 1978: 112–16). The conven-
tional date range is 4th to 5th century, although
Magness suggests they may have been in use into
the 6th century (Magness 1993: 250–52, Oil lamps
Form 2 "Small Candlestick Lamps"). They are no
later than the early 6th century. As Khirbet edh-
Dharih was deserted after the AD 363 earthquake

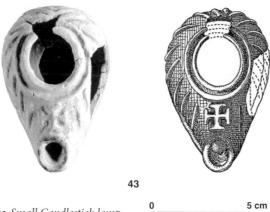

43

FIG. 17.43 *Small Candlestick lamp.*

0   5 cm

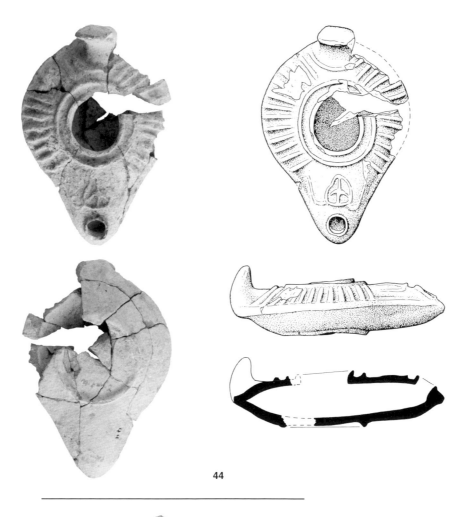

44

45

FIGS. 17.44–45 *Large grey South Jordan slipper lamps.*

0   5 cm

for over a century, it is most likely that it was brought to Khirbet et-Tannur by a visitor to the site after Khirbet edh-Dharih was re-occupied at the beginning of the 6th century. However, Khirbet et-Tannur also could have been visited in the late 4th or 5th century.

Comparanda: Deir ʿAin ʿAbata: da Costa 2012: no. 22, fig. 485 (5th to early 6th century AD); Kennedy 1963: Type 17b, no. 640.

43.
Fig. 17.43 (= GA photo. I-35c; drawing in GA). *DD* pl. 82b (= GA photo. I-35c).
Locus: in "debris" of east part of Room 14 (*DD* 183); GP no. 16. Rockefeller Museum card inv. 40.781. Whereabouts unknown in 2010.
"Red ware."
l. 8.6 cm; w. 5.7 cm.

Almost complete mould-made slipper lamp with a raised, widely spaced, radial pattern on the rim and a "Maltese" cross on the nozzle. Sooted spout. The large filling hole has two ridges around it. It was made without a handle. Rear rim and right-hand shoulder are damaged.

Large Grey South Jordan Slipper Lamps

Lamp no. 44 is distinguished from the South Jordan slipper lamps above by its distinctive high handle, size, and ware which is grey all the way through (with a thin cream slip). It is also distinguished by its coarse, widely spaced, radiating shoulder decoration. No exact parallels could be found, especially with a handle like this, although a Byzantine lamp from Masada is close (Barag and Hershkovitz 1994: 99, no. 202). No. 44 is probably dated to the 6th century AD and presumably left by 6th-century visitors (or worshippers) after Khirbet edh-Dharih was re-occupied in the early 6th century. (A 6th-century date for no. 44 is the consensus after pers. comm. 2010 from Elias Khamis, Kate da Costa, Kharieh ʿAmr, Donald Whitcomb, and François Villeneuve.)

44.
Fig. 17.44; Vol. 1, fig. 369. *DD* pl. 82a second row, centre (= GA photo. I-36c-5); GA photo. III-6-7.

Locus 16: Room 9; GA Unit 20-B02; GP no. 19; GA lamp 44.
Munsell: clay 10YR 8/3 very pale brown; core 10YR 5/1 grey.
l. 11.2 cm; w. 7.8 cm; h. 3.6 cm; th. 0.7 cm; filling hole diam. 2.3 cm; inner w. of spout 0.9 cm.

Mould-made lamp. The body is a pointed oval shape and biconical in profile, with a raised base ring. There is a large central filling-hole surrounded by two high ridges. Sooted spout. High radial ridging on the shoulder. High projecting tongue handle at the rear, springing from the back of the shoulder. A raised 'drooping' cross or arrowhead, with a raised line around it, is placed on the nozzle which has a raised edge.
Label on base: "n. room 2" [Room 9].

45.
Fig. 17.45.
Locus: provenience unknown; GA Unit A-13. GA lamp 45.
Munsell: clay and core 2.5Y 5/2 greyish brown.
l. 3.6 cm; w. 2.2 cm; th. 0.3 cm.

Small shoulder fragment from mould-made lamp with high radial ridges and part of raised line around filling hole. Grey ware colour and line thickness of decoration almost identical to no. 44 above.

Non-Diagnostic Nozzle Fragments

46.
Fig. 17.46.
Locus: "debris"; GA Unit 47-19; GA lamp 46.
Munsell: clay and core 5YR 6/6 reddish yellow; slip 10YR 8/3 very pale brown. Some limey inclusions.
l. 3.5 cm; w. 3.4 cm; h. 2.8 cm, th. 0.3 cm; inner w. of spout 1.4 cm.

Elongated undecorated rounded spout. No sooting. The hand-made spout was added to the lamp after it had dried to a leather-hard stage. Possibly from a polycandelon.

47.
Fig. 17.47.
Locus 16: Room 9; GA Unit 47-13I; GA lamp 47.
Munsell: clay and core 2.5YR 6/6 light red.

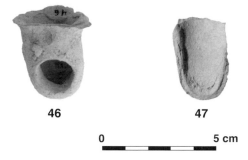

FIGS. 17.46–47 *Nozzles.*

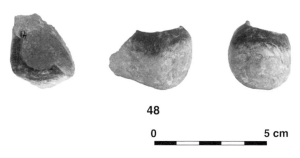

FIG. 17.48 *Nozzle fragment, probably from a multi-tier polycandelon, as in fig. 17.51.*

l. 3.5 cm; w. 2.2 cm; th. 0.3 cm; inner w. of spout 1.7 cm.
Base of an elongated mould-made spout.
Label "n. room II" [Room 9].

48.
Fig. 17.48.
Locus: "debris"; GA Unit 47-19. GA lamp 48.
Munsell: clay and core 5YR 5/6 yellowish red.
Coarse ware.
l. 3.6 cm; h. 2.9 cm; th. 0.3 cm; inner w. of spout 1.5 cm.

Large partial spout of unusual shape, with flattened end, sooted around rim. Probably oval-shaped wick hole, incomplete. Probably from a polycandelon, like the 2nd- or 3rd-century example from the excavations in front of the Qasr el-Bint at Petra (fig. 17.51; colour: Vol. 1, fig. 366).

NOTE

1   E. Vogel letter to Dr C. Gavin of the Semitic Museum, Harvard University, 3 November 1976. We are grateful to Jean Eglinton of the Skirball Museum of the Hebrew Union College in Cincinnati and Catherine Aurora of the Skirball Cultural Centre in Los Angeles for checking their collections.

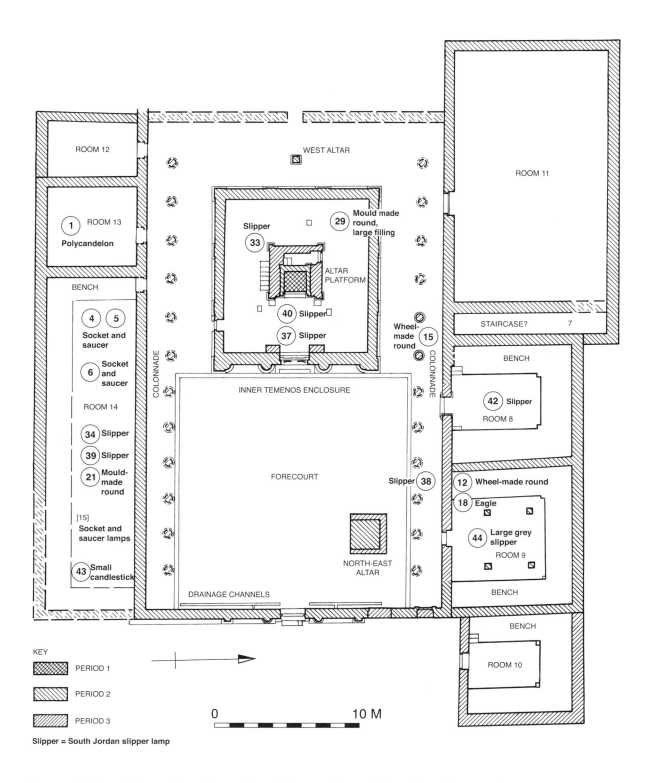

FIG. 17.49 *Khirbet et-Tannur, plan with approximate find-spots of lamps, indicated by catalogue number.*

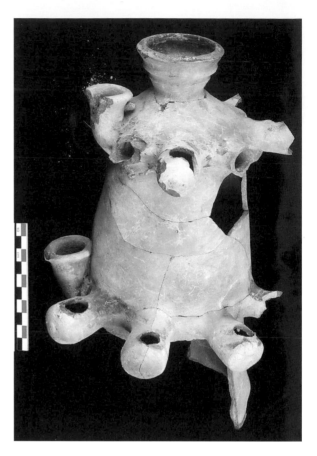

FIG. 17.50 *Petra, area beside exedra in front of the Qasr el-Bint: fragment of tubular ring, from a multi-tier polycandelon, c. AD 363–419.*

FIG. 17.51 *Petra, area beside exedra in front of the Qasr el-Bint: two-tier polycandelon of 2nd or possibly 3rd century AD.*

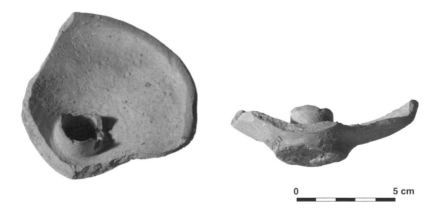

FIG. 17.52 *Samaria, socket and saucer lamp (Semitic Museum, Harvard University, inv. 1934.9.636).*

Table 17.1   Lamps at Khirbet et-Tannur (by context).

Locus	Location	Lamp Catalogue Number	Date in excavation journal, 1937	Glueck Archive Unit or whereabouts
1	SW corner of Altar Platform	33 (South Jordan slipper, lines and dots)	3 March	Whereabouts unknown in 2010
2	NW corner of Inner Temenos Enclosure	29 (mould-made round, large filling hole)	GR no. 28, 4 March	Whereabouts unknown in 2010
6	E part of Inner Temenos Enclosure	37 (South Jordan slipper, radial lines)	4 March	Whereabouts unknown in 2010
	In front of Altar Platform	40 (South Jordan slipper)	-	4A-25
13	Inside N wall of Forecourt	38 (South Jordan slipper, radial lines)	-	47-07D
14A	Ditch N of N wall of Inner Temenos Enclosure	15 (wheel-made round)	This area 7, 11 March, 4 May, 6 December	4A-19
15	Room 8	42 (South Jordan slipper, radial lines, late)	GR no. 72, 2 April	Missing
16	SW corner of Room 9	12 (wheel-made round)	9 April	20-B01
		18 (discus with eagle)	9 April	Cincinnati Art Museum 1939.243
	Room 9	44 (large grey South Jordan slipper)	-	20-B02
		47 (unidentified)	-	47-13I
20	Room 13	1 (polycandelon)	14 April	47-01K
21	Room 14	4, 5 (socket and saucer)	-	Jordan Department of Antiquities 40.782 – J3293; 20-B04
		6 (socket and saucer)	15 April	20-B05
		21 (Nabataean)	Label: 13 April	47-01F
		34 (South Jordan slipper, lines and dots)	-	20-B06
		39 (South Jordan slipper, radial lines)	-	none
		43 (Small Candlestick with cross)	DD 183	Rockefeller 40.481; whereabouts unknown 2010

Table 17.1 (cont.)   Lamps at Khirbet et-Tannur (by context).

LOCUS	LOCATION	LAMP CATALOGUE NUMBER	DATE IN EXCAVATION JOURNAL, 1937	GLUECK ARCHIVE UNIT OR WHEREABOUTS
-	"Debris"	2 (polycandelon)	-	47-01J
		8, 9 (socket and saucer)	-	47-19
		13, 14 (wheel-made round)	-	47-19
		20 (Nabataean)	-	47-19
		23 (mould-made round, teardrops and lines)	-	47-19
		46, 48 (unidentified)	-	47-19
-	"Debris" on bag	10 (socket and saucer)	-	48-04
		28 (mould-made round)	-	48-05
-	Provenience unknown	3 (polycandelon)	-	Whereabouts unknown 2010
		7, 11 (socket and saucer)	-	20-B01; A-17
		16, 17 (wheel-made round)	-	A-13
		19 (discus)	-	A-13
		22 (mould-made round, three dots)	-	A-12
		24 (mould-made round, teardrops and lines)	-	A-13
		25, 26, 27 (mould-made round)	-	A-13; A-12; A-17
		30 (mould-made round, large filling hole)	-	20-B07
		31 (mould-made elongated, herringbone)	-	A-13
		32 (South Jordan slipper, volutes)	GR no. 23, 2 March	20-B01 and 20-B06
		35 (South Jordan slipper, lines and dots)	-	A-13
		36 (South Jordan slipper)	-	A-13
		41 (South Jordan slipper, radial lines)	GR no. 17, 1 March	20-B02
		45 (large grey South Jordan slipper)	-	A-13

Table 17.2   Concordance of Khirbet et-Tannur lamp catalogue numbers.

Present catalogue in order	Barrett 2005 and 2008	Barrett 2005 and 2008, in order	Present catalogue
1	Kh.et-L-34	Kh.et-L-1	20
2	Kh.et-L-35	Kh.et-L-2	19
3	Kh.et-L-36	Kh.et-L-3	26
4	Kh.et-L-11	Kh.et-L-4	25
5	Kh.et-L-5	Kh.et-L-5	5
6	Kh.et-L-6	Kh.et-L-6	6
7	Kh.et-L-7	Kh.et-L-7	7
8	Kh.et-L-8	Kh.et-L-8	8
9	Kh.et-L-9	Kh.et-L-9	9
10	Kh.et-L-10	Kh.et-L-10	10
11	Kh.et-T-48	Kh.et-L-11	4
12	Kh.et-L-30	Kh.et-L-12	30
13	Kh.et-L-31	Kh.et-L-13	29
14	Kh.et-L-32	Kh.et-L-14	18
15	Kh.et-L-33	Kh.et-L-15	31
16	Kh.et-L-44	Kh.et-L-16	34
17	Kh.et-L-43	Kh.et-L-17	35
18	Kh.et-L-14	–	36
19	Kh.et-L-2	Kh.et-L-18	33
20	Kh.et-L-1	Kh.et-L-19	37
21	Kh.et-L-40	Kh.et-L-20	41
22	Kh.et-L-47	Kh.et-L-21	42
23	Kh.et-L-45	Kh.et-L-22	32
24	Kh.et-L-46	Kh.et-L-23	–
25	Kh.et-L-4	Kh.et-L-24	38
26	Kh.et-L-3	Kh.et-L-25	45
27	Kh.et-L-42	Kh.et-L-26	39
28	Kh.et-L-41	Kh.et-L-27	40
29	Kh.et-L-13	Kh.et-L-28	43
30	Kh.et-L-12	Kh.et-L-29	44
31	Kh.et-L-15	Kh.et-L-30	12
32	Kh.et-L-22	Kh.et-L-31	13
33	Kh.et-L-18	Kh.et-L-32	14
34	Kh.et-L-16	Kh.et-L-33	15
35	Kh.et-L-17	Kh.et-L-34	1
36	–	Kh.et-L-35	2
37	Kh.et-L-19	Kh.et-L-36	3
38	Kh.et-L-24	Kh.et-L-37	46
39	Kh.et-L-26	Kh.et-L-38	47
40	Kh.et-L-27	Kh.et-L-39	48
41	Kh.et-L-20	Kh.et-L-40	21
42	Kh.et-L-21	Kh.et-L-41	28
43	Kh.et-L-28	Kh.et-L-42	27
44	Kh.et-L-29	Kh.et-L-43	17
45	Kh.et-L-25	Kh.et-L-44	16
46	Kh.et-L-37	Kh.et-L-45	23
47	Kh.et-L-38	Kh.et-L-46	24
48	Kh.et-L-39	Kh.et-L 47	22
–	Kh.et-L-23	Kh.et-T-48	11

References

'Amr, K.
1987   *The Pottery from Petra: A Neutron Activation Analysis Study*. British Archaeological Reports, International Series 324. Oxford.
1992   "Islamic or Nabataean? The Case of a First to Early Second Century AD Cream Ware." *Studies in the History and Archaeology of Jordan* 4: 221–25.

Ayalon, E.
1996   "A Rare Multinozzled Byzantine Lamp from Kiludiya." *'Atiqot* 29: 61–67.

Bailey, D. M.
1965   "Lamps in the Victoria and Albert Museum." *Opuscula Atheniensia* 4: 1–83.
1979   *A Catalogue of the Lamps in the British Museum 2: Roman Lamps Made in Italy*. London.
1988   *A Catalogue of the Lamps in the British Museum 3: Roman Provincial Lamps*. London.
1994   "Imported Lamps and Local Copies." Pp. 79–99 in *Masada IV: The Yigael Yadin Excavations 1963–1965, Final Reports: Lamps from Masada*, eds. D. Barag and M. Hershkovitz. Jerusalem.

Barag, D., and Hershkovitz, M. (eds.)
1994   *Masada IV: The Yigael Yadin Excavations 1963–1965, Final Reports: Lamps from Masada*. Jerusalem.

Barrett, D. G.
2005   The Ceramic Oil Lamp as an Indicator of Cultural Change within Nabataean Society in Petra and its Environs circa CE 106. PhD thesis, Brown University (UMI). (with printed tables)
2008   *The Ceramic Oil Lamp as an Indicator of Cultural Change within Nabataean Society in Petra and its Environs circa CE 106*. Piscataway, NJ. (with tables on a CD)
2011   "The Lamps at Khirbet et-Tannur." Pp. 75–102 in *Lampes antiques du Bilad es Sham: Jordanie, Syrie, Liban, Palestine – Ancient Lamps of Bilad es Sham. Actes du colloque de Pétra–Amman (6–13 novembre 2005)*, eds. D. Frangié and J.-F. Salles. Paris. (with colour photographs)

Berlin, A.
1999   "The Archaeology of Ritual: The Sanctuary of Pan at Banias / Caesarea Philippi." *Bulletin of the American Schools of Oriental Research* 315: 27–45.

Bowersock, G. W.
1990   *Hellenism in Late Antiquity*. Ann Arbor, MI.

Broneer, O.
1930   *Corinth Vol. IV: Terracotta Lamps*. Cambridge, MA.
1977   *Isthmia Vol. III: Terracotta Lamps*. Princeton, NJ.

Crowfoot, G. M.
1957   "Lamps and an Early Stone Lamp Holder." Pp. 365–78 in *The Objects from Samaria*, eds. J. M. Crowfoot, G. M. Crowfoot, and K. Kenyon. London.

Crowfoot, J. M.; Kenyon, K. M.; and Sukenik, E. L.
1942   *The Buildings at Samaria*. London.

Cumont, F. V. M.
1911   *Oriental Religions in Roman Paganism*. Chicago, IL.

da Costa, K.
2001   "Byzantine and Early Islamic Lamps: Typology and Distribution." Pp. 241–57 in *La Céramique byzantine et proto-islamique en Syrie-Jordanie (IVe-VIIIe siècles apr. J.-C.). Actes du colloque tenu à Amman, 3–5 décembre. 1994*, eds. P. Watson and E. Villeneuve. Beirut.
2003   Byzantine and Early Umayyad Ceramic Lamps from Palaestina and Arabia (ca 300-700 A.D.). Unpublished PhD thesis, University of Sydney.
2012   "V.5 The Ceramic Lamps." Pp. 223–91 in K. D. Politis, *Sanctuary of Lot at Deir 'Ain 'Abata in Jordan, Excavations 1988–2003*. Amman.

da Costa, K., et al.
2002 "New Light on Late Antique Pella: Sydney University Excavations in Area XXXV, 1997." *Annual of the Department of Antiquities of Jordan* 46: 503–33.

Durand, C.
2011 "Lampes nabatéennes et romaines de Khirbet edh-Dharih (Jordanie) Ier – IVème siècles après J.-C." Pp. 43–73 in *Lampes antiques du Bilad es Sham: Jordanie, Syrie, Liban, Palestine – Ancient Lamps of Bilad es Sham. Actes du colloque de Pétra–Amman (6–13 novembre 2005)*, eds. D. Frangié and J.-F. Salles. Paris.

Egloff, M.
1977 *Kellia: la poterie copte. Quatre siècles d'artisanat et d'échanges en Basse-Égypt, Tomes 1 et 2*. Geneva.

Erickson-Gini, T.
2010 *Nabataean Settlement and Self-Organized Economy in the Central Negev, Crisis and Renewal*. British Archaeological Reports, International Series 2054. Oxford.

Gebhard, E. R.
1993 "The Evolution of a Pan-Hellenic Sanctuary: From Archaeology Towards History at Isthmia." Pp. 123–41 in *Greek Sanctuaries: New Approaches*, eds. N. Marinatos and R. Hägg. London.

Gebhard, E. R., and Dickie, M. W.
1999 "Melikertes-Palaimon, Hero of the Isthmian Games." Pp. 159–65 in *Proceedings of the Fifth International Seminar on Ancient Greek Cult, Organized by the Department of Classical Archaeology and Ancient History, Göteborg University, 21–23 April, 1995*, ed. R. Hägg. Stockholm.

Gebhard, E. R.; Hemans, F. P.; and Hayes, J. W.
1998 "University of Chicago Excavations at Isthmia, 1989: III." *Hesperia* 67: 405–56.

Glueck, N.
1965 *Deities and Dolphins*. New York, NY.

Grawehr, M.
2006 *Die Lampen der Grabungen auf ez-Zantur in Petra. Petra – Ez Zantur III.2: Ergebnisse der Schweizerisch-Liechtensteinischen Ausgrabungen*. Terra Archaeologica 5. Monographien der Schweizerisch-Liechtensteinischen Stiftung für archäologische Forschungen im Ausland [SLSA / FSLA]. Mainz.

Harding, L.
1950 "A Roman Family Vault on Jebel Jofeh, Amman." *Quarterly of the Department of Antiquities of Palestine* 14: 81–94.

Healey, J. F.
2001 *The Religion of the Nabataeans: A Conspectus*. Religions in the Graeco-Roman World 136. Leiden.

Hornblower, S., and Spawforth, A. (eds.)
1996 *Oxford Classical Dictionary*. 3rd edition. Oxford.

Horsfield, G., and Horsfield, A.
1942 "Sela-Petra, the Rock of Edom and Nabatene, Ch. 4, The Finds." *Quarterly of the Department of Antiquities in Palestine* 9: 105–204.

Israeli, Y., and Avida, U.
1988 *Oil-lamps from Eretz Israel: The Louis and Carmen Warschaw Collection at the Israel Museum*. Jerusalem.

Kehrberg, I.
2007 "Gerasa as Provider for Roman Frontier Stations: A View Seen from Late Roman Potters' Waste at the Hippodrome and the Upper Zeus Temple." *Studies in the History and Archaeology of Jordan* 9: 31–48.

Kennedy, C.
1963 "The Development of the Lamp in Palestine." *Berytus* 14: 67–115.

Khairy, N. I.
1990 *The 1981 Petra Excavations*. Wiesbaden.

Lapp, E. C.
1997   The Archaeology of Light: The Cultural Significance of the Oil Lamp from Roman Palestine. Unpublished PhD thesis, Duke University.

Loeschcke, S.
1919   *Lampen aus Vindonissa*. Zürich.

Magness, J.
1993   *Jerusalem Ceramic Chronology ca. 200–800 CE*. Sheffield.

McKenzie, J. S.; Gibson, S.; and Reyes, A. T.
2002   "Reconstruction of the Nabataean Temple Complex at Khirbet et-Tannur." *Palestine Exploration Quarterly* 134: 44–83.

Mlynarczyk, J.
1995   "New Data on the Chronology of Late Roman Lamps in Alexandria." *Études et travaux* 17: 137–79.

Parker, S. T.
1987   *The Roman Frontier in Central Jordan: Interim Report on the Limes Arabicus Project, 1980–1985*, Vols. 1 and 2. British Archaeological Reports, International Series 340, Oxford.
2006   *The Roman Frontier in Central Jordan: Final Report on the Limes Arabicus Project 1980–1989*. Washington, DC.

Renel, F.
in press   "L'Abandon du secteur du Qasr al-Bint à Pétra: nouveaux éléments archéologiques." *Studies in the History and Archaeology in Jordan* 11.

Rosenthal, R., and Sivan, R.
1978   *Ancient Lamps in the Schloessinger Collection*. Jerusalem.

Rosenthal-Heginbottom, R.
1981   *Römische Bildlampen aus östlichen Werkstätten*. Wiesbaden.

Sarley, M.
1988   A Typological Study of Lamps from the Petra Excavations 1958–64. Unpublished BA thesis, University College, London.

Schneider, C.
1996   "Die Importkeramik." Pp. 129–42 in *Petra – Ez Zantur I: Ergebnisse der Schweizerisch-Liechtensteinischen Ausgrabungen 1988–1992*, eds. A. Bignasca et al. Terra archaeologica 2. Monographien der Schweizerisch-Liechtensteinischen Stiftung für archäologische Forschungen im Ausland [SLSA / FSLA]). Mainz.

Selesnow, W.
1988   *Bildwerke der Sammlung Kaufmann II: Lampen aus Ton und Bronze*. Melsungen.

Slane, K. W.
1990   *Corinth XVIII.II: The Sanctuary of Demeter and Kore. The Roman Pottery and Lamps*. Princeton, NJ.

Sukenik, E. L.
1942   "G. The Temple of the Kore." Pp. 62–67 in *The Buildings at Samaria*, eds. J. M. Crowfoot, Kenyon, K. M., and Sukenik, E. L. London.

Sussman, V.
1989   "Northern Stamped Oil-lamps and their Typology." *Michmanim* 4: 22–58.

Wenning, R.
2009   "The Message of the Sculpture from Khirbat at-Tannur." *Studies in the History and Archaeology of Jordan* 10: 577–84.

Whitcomb, D.
1989   "Mahesh Ware: Evidence of Early Abbasid Occupation from Southern Jordan." *Annual of the Department of Antiquities of Jordan* 33: 269–85.

Zanoni, I.
1996   "Tonlampen." Pp. 311–36 in *Petra – Ez Zantur I: Ergebnisse der Schweizerisch-Liechtensteinischen Ausgrabungen 1988–1992*, eds. A. Bignasca *et al*. Terra archaeologica 2. Monographien der Schweizerisch-Liechtensteinischen Stiftung für archäologische Forschungen im Ausland [SLSA / FSLA]. Mainz.

Zayadine, F.
1979   "Excavations at Petra (1976–1978)." *Annual of the Department of Antiquities of Jordan* 23: 185–97.
1986   "The Jerash Project for Excavation and Restoration: A Synopsis with Special Reference to the Work of the Department of Antiquities." Pp. 7–20 in *Jerash Archaeological Project 1981–1983*, ed. F. Zayadine. Amman.

Chapter 18

The Pottery

by Stephan G. Schmid, Catherine S. Alexander, and Judith S. McKenzie

INTRODUCTION

This chapter deals with the pottery from the 1937 Khirbet et-Tannur excavations stored in the Glueck Archive in the Semitic Museum, Harvard University. Thanks to the meticulous efforts of Judith McKenzie, many boxes and bags of pottery, labelled in the present work as Glueck Archive Units (as explained below, pp. 7–11) and simply referred to in this chapter as Units, could be ascribed to specific locations within the sanctuary: the Inner Temenos Enclosure, the Forecourt, and the colonnades and rooms on either side of the Court (fig. 6.3). An attempt has been made to identify each of the over 5,600 sherds in the Semitic Museum in terms of provenience and chronology. The few more complete vessels (not stored there) and the lamps have also been included.

The pottery with "Loci" numbers established by McKenzie (Nos. 1 to 21 marked on fig. 6.2) is presented in the catalogue first and (within each Locus) is listed by Glueck Archive Unit. After this, the unprovenienced Glueck Archive Units are presented (i.e., those that so far could not be ascribed to a specific location). The main results are presented in the *Discussion* preceding the Catalogue. More details about some units are given in the *Catalogue*. These have not been selected out and presented separately, as might normally be expected. This is to avoid giving a misleading impression that they are the most reliably dated units. We do not know if they are, because we are lacking adequate information about the stratigraphic origin of the units.

Although for much of the pottery the Loci we have are locations on a plan, it is a position in two dimensions, because we lack precise information for the third dimension, i.e., the stratigraphy, other than the fact that the pottery is largely from above the paving of Period 2 of the temple complex, which was repaired in Period 3. This has some influence on the validity of the results obtained from the study of the pottery.

Another point that affects these results is the uncertainty regarding the selection criteria for the pottery collected on site, and also of that transported to Harvard. Was virtually all the pottery brought to the United States, and did that which was brought all reach the Semitic Museum? Some units suggest all the pottery collected is there, because they almost exclusively contain undecorated coarse ware body sherds, something that otherwise would not be selected compared to, for instance,

207

Table 18.1   Chronology of Schmid's Dekorphases of painted Nabataean fine ware.

DEKORPHASE	CHRONOLOGICAL RANGE
1	end of the 2nd and the first half of the 1st century BC (but see *Discussion* below for possibly an earlier beginning)
2a	third quarter of the 1st century BC
2b	last quarter of the 1st century BC
2c	first quarter of the 1st century AD
3a	second and third quarters of the 1st century AD
3b	last quarter of the 1st century AD with decreasing continuation
3c	starts c. AD 100 and continues into the 4th century AD
4	present in contexts dated to AD 363

painted Nabataean pottery. However, since we are not sure about this, the results obtained cannot be considered as absolute.

This said, the pottery can be looked at from two main points of interest: chronology and typological composition. The interest of the first issue is evident; the second one will be of interest for the role of the different structures and rooms of the sanctuary. This is possible because the site had a sole (religious) function, as it did not have an adjoining village and was not later converted into a church, and as it is at the top of a hill, it was not affected by wash from higher up the site, unlike, for example, the "Great Temple" at Petra.

DISCUSSION

Three main conclusions have been established from the pottery analysis:

- By far the majority of the pottery belongs to the 2nd to 4th centuries AD, with the 2nd century AD being the most prominently represented.
- There clearly is, although in small amounts, earlier pottery, covering the whole range of Nabataean painted fine ware from the late 2nd/early 1st century BC onwards, with a few coarser examples possibly of the late 2nd century BC.
- According to the shapes and types of the pottery, drinking and eating were clearly the main activities at the sanctuary, especially in the rooms identified as triclinia.

The prominent place occupied by pottery from the 2nd century AD is surely not a surprise, since it corresponds with the major building phase (Period 2) of the surviving complex (cf. Vol. 1, Ch. 2). Most of the identifiable Nabataean painted pottery in terms of chronology belongs to Schmid's Dekorphase 3c and even 4 (after Schmid 2000), starting around AD 100 and covering a good part of the 2nd and 3rd centuries AD that would seem to be the, or at least one, main period of use of the sanctuary (figs. 18.3–7, nos. **15–26**) (see Table 18.1). How long this lasted is difficult to determine from the pottery alone, but there are some distinctive pottery types that indicate regular use of the site at least until the 4th century AD (e.g., African Red Slip, fig. 18.16, no. **68**: of Hayes 1972: Form 50; red ware plate, fig. 18.16, no. **70**, and Vol. 1, fig. 25b; possibly casserole, fig. 18.17, no. **73**). Cooking pots from Nabataean sites are still difficult to date because those from stratified contexts at Petra, such as ez-Zantur, have not yet been fully published (bibliography in Gerber 2013: 111). However, there are some cooking pots at Khirbet et-Tannur which date to the 3rd–4th centuries (e.g., fig. 18.29, nos. **119–120**; fig. 18.32, no. **128**) or could (fig. 18.27, nos. **109**, **112**; fig. 18.29, no. **121**; fig. 18.32, no. **129**). There is also pottery that seems much later, such as two vertical handles from Unit 47-01G in Locus 21. The continuation of cultic use into the 4th century is suggested by the evidence of the lamps (Ch. 17), while some glass could also date to this period (Ch. 15). The few examples of later pottery would seem to reflect occasional visits to the site in the 5th or 6th century, as also suggested by some of the lamps (figs. 17.43–44, lamp nos. 43–44).

The pottery from the 1st centuries BC and AD is equally interesting, since it indicates that the site was regularly visited, although we do not know much about its character then. In terms of statistics, pottery belonging to Schmid's Dekorphase 3b (last quarter of the 1st century AD) is more prominent (c. 287 sherds) than previous phases (fig. 18.3, nos. **11–14**). This could indicate the beginning of a more intense use of the site. Pottery dated before that occurs in equal proportions in the different sub-phases. This is somewhat surprising since, for instance, Dekorphase 2c (corresponding to the middle of the reign of Aretas IV, 9 BC–AD 40) at other sites produced huge amounts of pottery compared to earlier periods and, therefore, one would expect more pottery belonging to this phase. The increase at Khirbet et-Tannur does not begin until the next phase 3a (c. 88 sherds), with by far the predominant number in phase 3c (c. 1072 sherds, figs. 18.3–6, nos. **15–24**). The evidence for phase 3c, in contrast to 3b, includes substantial remains of at least four bowls (figs. 18.3, no. **16**; 18.5, no. **21**; 18.6, nos. **23–24**), mostly with just palmettes. By contrast, there are just a few (c. 17) sherds from Dekorphases 3c/4 and 4 (fig. 18.7, nos. **25–26**).

While some of the earliest sherds with painted wavy lines (fig. 18.2, nos. **5–6**) can belong to Schmid's Dekorphase 1 (late 2nd to mid-1st century BC), at least three of the sherds from Unit 48-10 certainly belong to it and indicate, together with corresponding plain sherds, an early use of the site. The same can be said about two painted

sherds from Unit 48-17 of unknown provenience. In total we have five sherds clearly belonging to Schmid's phase 1 and thirty-one belonging to his phase 1 or 2a. Given the topographical situation of Khirbet et-Tannur, it is very unlikely that this earlier pottery is unrelated to whatever activity was taking place on the site under the open sky, with some built installations such as an altar. This was apparently by the late 2nd or early 1st century BC, judging by the base of a bowl with a cross painted inside it, from Locus 3, Unit 4A-24 (fig. 18.1, no. **1**) found inside Altar 1 under the packed lime layer (Vol. 1, figs. 33a, 34) with burnt bones. The base of a huge storage vessel with a pattern painted around the exterior of the base (fig. 18.33, no. **131**), which was also found in this locus, is related to examples in the late Hellenistic levels beside the Qasr el-Bint at Petra (F. Renel, pers. comm., 2010).

The bowl mentioned with the cross painted inside it (fig. 18.1, no. **1**) is possibly the earliest sherd from the site. P. Bienkowski (pers. comm.) could not find an exact parallel for it but considered the shape, base, and ware very much like those of Iron II, whilst not having an exact parallel for the painted cross. However, early Nabataean pottery (Schmid's phase 1) does have painted crosses inside it, even if on smaller vessels (Schmid 2000: 27–28, figs. 73–76). This combination, i.e., a shape at least reminiscent of Iron II forms and a painted décor related to the earliest known painted decorations securely attributable to Nabataean pottery, could be one of the missing links looked for in recent research in order to bridge the gap between the end of the Edomite and the beginning of Nabataean material culture. On the one hand, Bienkowski could clearly show that at Busayra occupation continued until the 4th, and possibly even the 3rd, century BC (Bienkowski 2002: 344–48, 350–51, 477; 2013: 29–30). On the other hand, the recent French investigations in the area underneath and around the altar of the Qasr el-Bint indicate, in all likelihood, an early occupation going back to the 4th and 3rd centuries BC (Renel et al. 2012; Mouton 2012; Graf 2013: 45).

Finally, one has to bear in mind that in suggesting a date for the beginning of phase 1 on ez-Zantur in the later 2nd century BC, Schmid (2000) was dependent on the earliest layers from ez-Zantur yielding phase 1 pottery combined with Eastern Terra Sigillata A (ESA) fragments. Since the excavation there stopped without exploring deeper layers, one cannot exclude an earlier beginning for phase 1 on ez-Zantur also (cf. Schmid 2000: 10–25 and especially 24 with note 117; Hoffmann 2013: 100 n. 12, 103). That at least some forms of early Nabataean pottery seem to be based on prototypes found at Edomite sites can be shown from a specific form of carinated bowl, sometimes with painting of Dekorphase 1 (Schmid 2000: 55–56, figs. 189–91), that has very good parallels in Edomite fine ware bowls found, for example, at Busayra (Bienkowski 2002: 282–83, bowls type J). Recent excavations in the city centre of Petra, namely around the Qasr el-Bint and along the (later) Colonnaded Street, which are yielding pottery from the 4th to 2nd centuries BC, are likely to shed more light on these questions (Graf et al. 2005; 2007; Graf 2012; Mouton 2012; Renel et al. 2012; Renel and Mouton 2013).

The other point which needs to be made is the overlap between Dekorphases and regional variations in how long particular Dekorphases continued in particular areas, as well as what they might reflect about the dates of occupation of those areas; for example, the preponderance of phase 3c compared with 3b at Khirbet et-Tannur contrasts with the situation in the Negev, where phase 3b (i.e., palmettes and other images with a background of fine lines; as in fig. 18.3, nos. **11–12**) is the most ubiquitous Nabataean painted fine ware bowl type (T. Erickson-Gini, pers. comm.), and extending through the 2nd century AD, with Dekorphases 3c and 3b found together at Mezad Hazeva in the early 3rd century (Erickson-Gini 2010: 107 and 117, nos. 1–2, with triangles and large blobs, not just palmettes). In general terms, one has to bear in mind that new elements in material culture usually do not abruptly replace older elements, and that it is good archaeological practice to use the *youngest* elements in order to date archaeological contexts. In relevant contexts containing enough Nabataean pottery in order to be able to draw statistical and chronological conclusions, the overlapping of, for example, phases 3b and 3c is quite obvious. This is the case, for instance, with several units from ez-

Zantur in Petra, dated around AD 100 or slightly later, according to coins and Eastern Sigillata A (ESA): in all cases pottery belonging to Schmid's phase 3c was predominantly present, together with substantial amounts of pottery from Schmid's phase 3b (Schmid 2000: 35–36, 38, with Beil. 58–66 for detailed statistics and graphs).

It would also be very interesting if we could obtain information about the earlier building phases of the sanctuary, for instance regarding the first shrine and its first enclosure (but the pottery that might be associated with these is either not in the Glueck Archive or no longer labelled). However, all the other units that could be interesting in this respect are heterogeneous in terms of pottery. The most eloquent example may be the small Unit 4A-11 from Locus 3, the north-east offertory box (Vol. 1, figs. 398–99) within the Inner Temenos Enclosure (location marked on fig. 6.3). In his excavation journal, Glueck wrote, "In n.e. side of temple court is a fairly square break in the stone-black pavement (which encircles the central altar). In it Hassan is finding bits of fine (bird?) egg-shell, fragments of Nabataean pottery, charcoal and grains" (GJ 6 March). This unit (4A-11) contains sherds belonging to Schmid's Dekorphases 1 or 2a (fig. 18.2, nos. **4, 6**) and phases 2b or 2c, but it also contained pottery clearly belonging to his phase 3c (following Schmid 2000). The same is true for other units (e.g., Unit 4A-26 of uncertain provenience), which have a similar composition.

Glueck realised that most of the pottery found immediately beneath the level of the pavement was mixed. This becomes clear, for instance from his comments on the finds from the "ditch" in the *balatah* floor beside the paving on the north side of the colonnade (Loci 14A and 14B, marked on fig. 6.2):

"Digging the ditch on the north side of the court outside the north inner court of the shrine, revealed that it is full of rubbish, containing fine painted sherds, and that apparently this rubbish goes under the pavement of the court and under the temple proper. The conclusion would be that the entire temple is a secondary construction built over earlier Nabataean debris. It is a fact that the only sherds and vessels found in the temple proper and above the *balatah* of the courtyard are of the coarser, black, and to an extent ribbed type. Most of the painted sherds found seem to be on the outside of the main building complex." (GJ 7 March)

From his subsequent entries it becomes clear that Glueck had realised that there were different building phases and, in general terms, the relative sequence of the phases at Khirbet et-Tannur was well established. He had noticed that each new building period followed earthquake damage to the preceding structures (Vol. 1, Ch. 2). Consequently, the most intact vessels and lamps date to the last phase of worship, before the AD 363 earthquake, with a few left by later visitors. It is also possible that some of the mixed layers, such as in the "ditch," relate to clearance after earthquakes, before re-building.

In order to establish a more precise relative and absolute sequence, Glueck decided to lift a few slabs of the pavement near the "ditch" mentioned (north of the Inner Temenos Enclosure), discovering that there was a floor of stamped lime on which a burnt layer and mixed Nabataean pottery were resting (GJ 11 March). Further information on the different phases can be gained from his comment: "We also lifted 4 stones in the back of the west wall of the inner shrine, finding a burned level beneath the stones, which were joined together with plaster. Beneath this burned level, resting apparently on a rubble foundation of an earlier floor, and beneath this earlier floor level, we are finding Nab. pottery, mostly fine, and bones" (GJ 11 April). It is a pity that Glueck did not specify what kind of Nabataean pottery they found, and so we are not sure whether this is one of the units we have but which has lost its label, or that it is not amongst them. Furthermore, we can be more or less confident that in the 1930s only Nabataean pottery from Schmid's phases 2a onwards (following Schmid 2000) was recognised as such, as is confirmed when looking through Glueck's *Deities and Dolphins*, as well as his *Explorations in Eastern Palestine*.

Since we cannot be sure which types of fine Nabataean pottery the excavators found in the different relevant units, the pottery, as it is preserved today, does not give a definitive answer for the chronology of the building phases, even though it provides some indication of the periods of use of the site. Together with the comments above and the analysis of the different architectural and sculptural elements, it probably becomes possible to narrow the picture somewhat. At least the question about the *terminus post quem* for the final paving of the Inner Temenos Enclosure, as for all other "final" paving, could probably be resolved by lifting a few slabs and trying to collect some (pottery) evidence from beneath it. With luck, this would also allow one to verify and date the earlier phases of *balatah* floors and burnt levels. The only unit that seems to contain no later pottery than Schmid's phase 3b (last quarter of the 1st century AD) is Unit 48-10, but as it is labelled "debris" it is possible that this consistency might have resulted from Glueck sorting it.

What is astonishing at Khirbet et-Tannur is the small quantity of Nabataean plain ware forms, such as plates and bowls. It has been shown that the painted bowls and the plain bowls and plates usually form a kind of dinner service, with the painted bowls used for drinking and the plain ones for eating (Schmid 2000: 91–92). The material at Harvard shows a striking dominance of painted sherds throughout all phases. At first sight this could lead to the conclusion that people only (or mostly) drank in the sanctuary and did not to eat so much. However, this conclusion is probably erroneous as is indicated by the respectable number of cooking pots, jugs, flasks, and other coarse ware shapes. Maybe the painted sherds were more intensively collected? This would seem logical, because more or less the same picture is obtained from Glueck's survey publications as well as from *Deities and Dolphins*. However, as so many cooking pot body sherds were collected, it makes it unlikely that disproportionately few Nabataean plain ware sherds were collected. Another possible explanation would be that at sanctuaries such as Khirbet et-Tannur mostly grilled and roasted dishes were consumed and fewer boiled ones. But again, the considerable number of cooking pots would not favour this hypothesis. This raises the question of whether the painted bowls were also used (in addition to the plain Nabataean fine ware ones) for eating associated with religious celebrations in a sanctuary context, but their lack of bases makes them impractical for this.

The variety of types of pottery is notably much narrower than that found at the nearby settlement of Khirbet edh-Dharih, reflecting Khirbet et-Tannur's single (religious) function. For example, the pottery from a 3rd-century AD context at Khirbet edh-Dharih (S7 OW/04: stratigraphic units 10, 11, and mostly 21; S7 OR/03: stratigraphic unit 04; S7 E: SU 24, 17, 16; S7 C: SU 05; provided by François Villeneuve) includes not only types found at Khirbet et-Tannur, but also additional forms not found there. Bowls of identical types to those found at Khirbet et-Tannur include Dekorphase 3c bowls with palmettes, those related to African Red Slip (ARS) Hayes form 50, red ware ones with a ledge (like fig. 18.16, nos. **69–70**) related to ARS forms, one with an outward-splaying straight side (an E8a-derivation like no. **50**, but without rouletted decoration), and E8a-derivations with an incised line around the top and a pair of incised lines midway down the straight side (like fig. 18.14, nos. **57–59**). Both sites have cooking pots, but Khirbet edh-Dharih has more wide-necked jugs/storage vessels and jugs. However, this 3rd-century AD context at Khirbet edh-Dharih includes notable types absent at Khirbet et-Tannur – especially ornate kraters and some tiny oil or perfume containers.

This contrasts with the lamps (Ch. 17). Some forms which occur at Khirbet et-Tannur are absent at Khirbet edh-Dharih. These are polycandela (with many wicks) and socket and saucer lamps (with thick wicks) used in some (not all) sanctuaries when much light was required for night-time activities, which are also evidenced by fragments of lanterns (fig. 18.39, nos. **146–47**). Finally, the handle of the cover of an incense burner (fig. 18.40, no. **148**) confirms the burning of incense which is also indicated by the incense altars (Ch. 10).

Beside the Nabataean and Nabataean-style pottery mentioned so far, the picture of eating and especially drinking being the main activities at Khirbet et-Tannur can be supported by other categories as well. Notably, most of the Eastern Terra Sigillata (ESA) fragments found belong to closed shapes such as jugs (fig. 18.18, nos. **74–75**) and/or bottles. As they are quite rare in ESA compared to bowls and plates, these ESA jugs and/or bottles were most probably carried up the hill because of their contents. Other obviously imported wares include two Parthian green glazed vessels, attested by two small sherds (fig. 18.38, no. **145**).

Like the ESA jugs, the jugs of "green ware" with an interior strainer were probably also brought to the site because of their contents. This specific category of pottery (also called "cream ware") occurs only in a very restricted number of shapes, the most prominent being the shape, always with a strainer, which is attested at Khirbet et-Tannur (fig. 18.24, no. **97**). Interestingly, one socket and saucer lamp (fig. 17.4) appears to be of this ware with incised decoration like that used on necks of jugs of it. Although the exact provenience(s) of "green ware" pottery is still debated, the function of these vessels clearly was to contain a liquid that needed to be purified before drinking (such as beer or wine), and it is very likely that they were imported to Nabataea because of their contents. This pottery is found at Petra and other Nabataean sites from the second quarter of the 1st century AD onwards. However, its exact place of manufacture remains largely unknown (Murray and Ellis 1940: pl. 25.15; Negev 1986: 71; 'Amr 1992: *passim*; Schneider 1996: 138–39). Recently, a study dealing with pottery from Aqaba proposed a subdivision into several groups, some of them being produced at Aqaba, but the group to which no. **97** belongs still remains enigmatic (Dolinka 2003: 63–64). Some years ago a Parthian provenience for this kind of pottery was proposed, based on analogies of shape and clay (Schmid 2000: 136–37, fig. 424). The abundant finds from Kallirhoé (Clamer 1997: 73–79), on the shores of the Dead Sea, suggest it could be another candidate.

The presence at Khirbet et-Tannur of these vessels, together with the great number of drinking cups, cooking pots, storage devices, etc., shows that banquets were regularly held there. The many cooking pots (figs. 18.26–32, nos. **104–29**) indicate the preparation of food on the top of the hill. That this was planned for some time ahead is suggested by the very large storage vessels (figs. 18.33–36, nos. **131–38**).

Compared with Nabataean pottery in most other contexts, one observes the absence or comparably small number of some of the most characteristic forms. This is the case, for example, with the small cups (type E3a2 in Schmid 2000: 9, figs. 57–59) which are very common in Nabataean houses and also occur in funerary contexts (Bikai and Perry 2001: fig. 8.3, 6–7). A very large number of these small cups was discovered in a basement below the Temple of the Winged Lions at Petra (Hammond 1987), so that at first sight the small number of these cups at Khirbet et-Tannur would seem surprising. However, these cups were not inside the temple of the Winged Lions, but were concentrated in an adjoining area that was apparently a painters' workshop, next to the "marble workshop." Therefore, as they cannot be explained there as being normally present in a sanctuary, there is no reason that they would necessarily be expected at Khirbet et-Tannur.

Thus, the types of pottery vessels present (or absent) and their relative numbers in the temple complex on Jabal et-Tannur, like the lamps, are clearly specific to their functions and the rituals for which they were used there, in a sanctuary whose design is unique (Vol. 1, pp. 247, 253).

ARRANGEMENT OF THE CATALOGUE

"Locus" refers to the loci re-established by J. McKenzie (as explained above, p. 11, and marked on figs. 6.2–3). "Unit" refers to the Glueck Archive Unit (GA Unit) which is based on number for the bag and box in which the sherds were stored in 2001 (as explained on pp. 7–11).

Entries are presented in the following order: those with a Locus number, followed by "Debris," "Provenience Unclear," and "Provenience Unknown." Within each Locus, they are arranged by Glueck Archive Unit number. Within each Unit, the sherds are listed in the order outlined below. The lamps have also been included, with their numbers from the lamp catalogue (Ch. 17).

Abbreviations

The following abbreviations are used for the descriptions of pottery:

CW — coarse ware
FW — fine ware
semi-FW — usually sherds belonging to vessels with fine forms (thin walls) but with ware showing inclusions similar to CW

ARS — African Red Slip Ware
ESA — Eastern Terra Sigillata A
GW — green ware; also known as cream ware
RW — red ware, referring to a mat or shiny red surface, but not actual ARS or ESA

RS — rim sherd
BS — body sherd
base — base

OF — open form
CF — closed form
E — open forms in Schmid's classification (Schmid 2000)
F — cups or goblets, about as wide as they are high, in Schmid's classification (Schmid 2000)
G — closed forms, such as jugs, in Schmid's classification (Schmid 2000)

"Phase" refers to the "Dekorphases" of painting on Nabataean fine ware following Schmid's classification (Schmid 2000). For its chronology, see Table 18.1.

The following abbreviations are used for provenience:
CAM — Cincinnati Art Museum
GA — ASOR Nelson Glueck Archive in the Semitic Museum, Harvard University
GJ — Nelson Glueck's excavation journal, in GA (reproduced here in Ch. 7)
GP — Glueck's List of Pottery, in GA
GR — Glueck's Registration Book, in GA (reproduced here in Ch. 8)
JAM — Jordan Archaeological Museum
(For other abbreviations, see pp. xvii–xviii)

Typology and Order in which the
Sherds are Presented within a Unit

The different components of each Unit are described with the abbreviations above. The first distinction is made according to ware, within each Unit. If there is any, fine ware (FW) pottery is put first, since it usually allows a more precise dating, followed by coarse ware (CW) pottery. Within each category, the different remains of vessels are given from top to bottom, i.e., the rim sherds (RS) first, followed by handles, body sherds (BS), and bases. This is except for painted sherds within the fine ware pottery which, because they allow a more precise dating, are put first, no matter whether rim or body sherds, etc.

If rim sherds, especially of Nabataean fine ware pottery, are identifiable, their type is given according to the classification in Schmid 2000. This gives indications such as E1b10 (a very typical flat painted Nabataean drinking bowl, cf. Schmid 2000: 28–29, figs. 90–92, 378–79, pls. 5, 7–10). The classification according to Schmid 2000 contains a letter (E for open forms, F for deep cups, G for closed forms), a number followed by a letter (for example 1b, according to the evolution of forms within each category), and a final number (for example 10, identifying each individual type). This typology was developed based mainly on the huge quantity of Nabataean fine ware pottery from the 1st centuries BC and AD. So far, no specific study has been made on Nabataean or Nabataean-style pottery from the 2nd to 4th centuries AD in Petra, in contrast to the Negev (Erickson-Gini 2010). Yet we know that this characteristic pottery continued to be produced at least until the late 4th and possibly even until the 6th century AD ('Amr 1991; 'Amr and al-Momani 1991). Many forms from these centuries seem to be based on typical forms of the Nabataean fine ware repertoire established during the later 1st century AD. Thus, they are called "derivations" of such and such types. In addition, in some cases it is clear that a form is close to a well-known type of earlier times without exactly corresponding to it. In this case, only the first part of the type identification is given (for example E1b and not E1b10), indicating that the general form is the same but

that there is no exact match. The phases of painted Nabataean fine ware pottery are given, according to Schmid 2000, in brackets at the end of the entry (for dates, see Table 18.1).

Thus, an entry may look like this:
10 FW RS OF E1b10 (3b) = ten fine ware rim sherds from open forms belonging to type E1b10 and decorated with painting of phase 3b,
or:
20 CW BS CF (cooking pots) = twenty coarse ware body sherds of closed forms belonging to cooking pots

Arrangement of the Pottery Figures

The sherds, for which numbers are given, are illustrated in figs. 18.1–18.40. They are presented typologically grouped, in the following sequence, with open forms before closed forms:

18.1	Painted and plain coarse ware bowls
18.2–7	Painted Nabataean fine ware bowls
18.8	Nabataean fine ware goblets, etc.
18.9	Beakers and cups
18.10	Plain Nabataean bowls
18.11	Fine ware bowls
18.12–13	Bowls, with rouletted decoration
18.14	Fine and semi-fine ware bowls, related to type E8a
18.15	Miscellaneous open forms
18.16	Open forms of African Red Slip, its imitations, and red ware
18.17	Casseroles
18.18–21	Jugs and juglets, including Eastern Sigillata A
18.22–23	Jugs or bottles/jars
18.24	Green (cream) ware closed forms
18.25	Miscellaneous closed forms
18.26–32	Cooking pots
18.33	Painted coarse ware closed forms
18.34–36	Huge storage vessels and closed forms
18.37–38	Miscellaneous, including Parthian green/brown glazed
18.39	Lanterns
18.40	Incense burner cover

Because all of the types in Schmid's typology identified at Khirbet et-Tannur are not illustrated here, or only with an incomplete indication of a vessel shape from a rim sherd or occasionally a base, Table 18.2 (on pp. 314–16) provides references to illustrations of those types in Schmid 2000. The pots drawn by Schmid were Munselled by him, and those later drawn by Catherine Alexander (largely coarse wares and unpainted bowls) were Munselled by Semitic Museum intern Meseret Oldjira. Although lighting conditions lead to inevitable variations, they at least provide some indications of the colours of the fabrics and paint.

Catalogue

Inner Temenos Enclosure

Locus 1, Inner Temenos Enclosure

GR 27
Lamp no. 33 (South Jordan slipper; fig. 17.33)

*Locus 2, North-West Corner
of Inner Temenos Enclosure*

GR 28
Lamp no. 29 (mould-made round, large filling hole; fig. 17.29)

Unit 4A-23 (fig. 18.24, no. 98)
12 CW BS CF (cooking pots)
2 CW handles CF (cooking pots)
1 CW RS CF with handle (cooking pot)
4 GW BS CF
1 GW base CF (No. **98**)

Unit 47-01C
1 CW BS CF (Nabataean cooking pot)
1 CW base CF (Nabataean cooking pot)

Unit 47-13G
1 CW base CF (Nabataean cooking pot)

Locus 3, North-East Offertory Box

Unit 4A-11 (fig. 18.2 nos. 4, 6)
1 FW RS OF E4b83 (1/2a) (No. **4**)
2 FW RS OF E1b10 (3c)

1 FW BS OF (1/2a) (No. **6**)
2 FW BS OF (2b/2c)
2 FW BS OF (3c)
10 FW BS OF (Nabataean)
4 CW BS CF (Nabataean)

Both nos. **4** and **6** show a characteristic painted décor, typical of late phase 1 and early phase 2, i.e., second and third quarters of the 1st century BC (cf. Schmid 2000: 27–42). However, other painted fragments from this unit belong to phase 3c, including a rim sherd of one of the main painted types of that phase, i.e., the early 2nd century AD. As in most units, the pottery in this one is quite heterogeneous.

Locus 4, West Offertory Box

Unit 4A-10
3 CW BS CF (from a single pot, jug, or bottle, dark ware with intrusions)

*Locus 5, South Wall East of Squatters' House
in Inner Temenos Enclosure*

Unit 4A-06
1 FW BS OF
1 CW RS with vertical handle CF
2 CW horizontal handles
1 CW base CF (cooking pot)
19 CW BS CF (cooking pot)

Unit 47-01D
1 CW base CF

Unit 47-13D "inside wall east of squatters' house"
1 FW vertical handle CF
1 FW BS CF with rouletted decoration

Locus 6, In Front of Altar Platform

GR 39
Lamp no. 37 (South Jordan slipper; fig. 17.37)

Unit 4A-25
Lamp no. 40 (South Jordan slipper; fig. 17.40)
1 FW base CF (small juglet)
10 CW BS CF (cooking pots)

Unit 47-07E
　　1 CW BS CF (cooking pot)

Altar Platform

Locus 7, Inside Altar Platform (Altar 1)

Unit 4A-24 (figs. 18.1, no. 1; 18.33, no. 131; 18.35, no. 134)
　　1 FW RS CF
　　1 CW RS CF, 2 joining fragments join fragment from Unit 47-05I, provenience unknown (No. **134**)
　　6 CW BS CF
　　1 CW base CF (painted) 4 joining fragments join base fragment from Unit 47-01K, provenience unknown (No. **131**)
　　1 CW base OF (painted) (No. **1**; Vol. 1, fig. 34)
This unit has 17 sherds from "the bottom of the east shrine [Altar 1] where the burnt bones were found," from below the packed lime layer. According to shape and ware, no. **1** could belong to the Hellenistic period (see *Discussion* above). The fragment has some features reminiscent of Iron II Edomite examples (P. Bienkowski, pers. comm., 2006 and 2012), while examples related to no. **131** were found in the late Hellenistic levels beside the Qasr el-Bint (F. Renel, pers. comm., 2010).

Forecourt

Locus 8, Forecourt

Unit 4A-21 (figs. 18.8, no. 30; 18.9, nos. 32–33; 18.22, no. 93; 18.26, nos. 106, 108)
　　1 FW RS OF E1b10 (3c)
　　1 FW BS OF (3c)
　　2 FW RS OF E18a187 or E18a 379
　　3 FW RS CF F5a (Nos. **32–33**)
　　4 FW BS OF (Nabataean)
　　1 FW RS lid (Nabataean) (No. **30**)
　　3 CW RS CF (Nabataean-style cooking pots) (Nos. **106, 108**)
　　5 CW RS CF (jugs, ? amphorae, etc.) (No. **93**)
　　1 CW RS OF
　　5 CW handle CF
　　2 CW BS CF (incised decoration)

　　69 CW BS CF (mostly Nabataean style cooking pots)
　　2 CW base CF (cooking pots)
　　1 BS CF (amphora)
　　1 GW base CF
The pottery in this unit seems rather homogeneous and would belong to the early 2nd century AD. No. **32** belongs to a beaker typical of phases 3b and 3c, i.e., the end of the 1st and the 2nd century AD. The same is true for the small cooking pots nos. **106** and **108**. In general terms, in the second half of the 1st century AD, Nabataean pottery produces a great variety of small closed shapes such as small pots, jugs, etc. Similar forms to nos. **106** and **108** can even be found in Nabataean fine ware of that period (Schmid 2000: figs. 249–57). In total, this unit contains 110 sherds from the Forecourt. Most of them are from cooking pots and other coarse ware shapes. Most of the material seems more or less homogeneous for the period from the end of the 1st to the 2nd century AD.

Locus 9, South-West End of Forecourt

Unit 4A-12
　　1 FW RS CF (bottle, typical "fine" ware of the 2nd century AD)
　　1 CW vertical handle CF
　　23 CW BS CF (mostly belonging to a few specimens of cooking pots)
Despite the small statistical basis, the pottery in this unit seems to belong to the 2nd century AD.

Unit 4A-14 (figs. 18.19, no. 83; 18.21, no. 88; 18.22, no. 91)
　　3 FW RS CF (jug or bottle, typical "fine" ware of the 2nd century AD), close to G21a/b (No. **91**)
　　1 FW BS CF (typical "fine" ware of the 2nd century AD)
　　7 FW fragments, including 1 RS, from same jug (No. **83**), resembling a degenerated version of G25
　　40 CW BS CF (they seem to belong to only a few specimens of cooking pots and jugs) (No. **88**)
Much of the pottery in this unit is characteristic of the 2nd century AD.

Locus 10, Inside South Wall of Forecourt

Unit 4A-13
   1 FW RS OF E3a2
   2 FW BS OF (Nabataean)
   1 CW base CF (cooking pot)
   1 CW handle CF (cooking pot)
   32 CW BS CF (cooking pots)
As far as one can tell, the pottery in this unit belongs to the 2nd century AD.

No Box/Bag no. "inside S wall of main outer court"
   13 CW BS CF + 1 CW base CF (all from same cooking pot, greyish surface, possibly burnt)

Locus 11, East Side of Forecourt

Unit 4A-15
   1 FW RS OF E1b10 (3c)
   1 FW RS OF E1c8 (very coarse and degenerated variant, i.e., 2nd/3rd century AD)
   2 FW BS OF (3c)
   1 FW BS OF
   1 CW RS OF
   2 CW RS CF (cooking pots)
   1 CW vertical handle
   19 CW BS CF (cooking pots)
   1 CW base CF
The pottery in this unit clearly belongs in the 2nd century AD.

Unit 4A-16
   2 FW BS OF
   1 CW RS CF (cooking pot)
   13 CW BS CF (cooking pots, several sherds belonging to the same specimen)

Locus 12, Outside South Wall of Room 9

Unit 4A-02
   3 CW BS CF (probably belonging to the same cooking pot)
   1 CW vertical handle CF (cooking pot)

Unit 4A-28
   1 FW BS OF (3b)
   2 FW RS OF E1b10 (3c)

   6 FW BS OF (3c)
   6 FW BS OF
   1 FW RW RS OF + 5 FW RW BS OF + 1 FW RW base OF, belonging to the same plate, very similar to RW plate (no. **70**) from Unit A-01 below
   1 FW RW BS CF
   1 semi-FW
   3 CW RS CF (cooking pots)
   1 CW vertical handle CF (cooking pot)
   45 CW BS CF (cooking pots)
   6 CW BS OF
   2 CW base CF (cooking pots)
This unit clearly belongs to the early 2nd century AD. An early date within the 2nd century AD is suggested by the presence of one painted sherd belonging to phase 3b (last quarter 1st century AD).

Unit A-01 (fig. 18.16, no. 70)
   3 FW RW RS OF + 1 FW RW BS OF belonging to the same plate (No. **70**; Vol. 1, fig. 25b)
   2 semi-FW BS CF
Sherd no. **70** illustrates quite well the problems with identifying and dating pottery from scanty contexts or without reliable contexts at all. On the one hand, the smoothly rounded shape as well as the red surface would point to Hellenistic traditions and the comparisons quoted support a rather early date, i.e., in the 1st century BC. On the other hand, equally similar forms and wares, including the smooth red slip, can be paralleled by typical examples of Late Roman pottery, for example "Late Roman C" ware or ARS (Hayes 1972: 96–100, ARS form 59; 327–29, Late Roman C form 2). Meanwhile, "Late Roman C" has also become known as Phocean Red Slip Ware (Hayes 2008: 237–38, figs. 237–47, form 2 and variants) and the specific forms last well into the 5th century AD. The small ledge on the inner lip, as well as parallels from a 3rd-century AD deposit at Khirbet edh-Dharih (see *Discussion* above), would indicate a rather late date for the sherd from Khirbet et-Tannur.

Locus 13, Inside North Wall of Forecourt

Unit 4A-08
    2 semi-FW BS OF
    1 CW RS with handle CF (cooking pot)
    1 CW RS CF (cooking pot)
    2 CW vertical handle CF (cooking pots)
    20 CW BS CF (cooking pots)

Unit 47-01B
    1 CW vertical handle CF

Unit 47-05C
    1 CW BS CF

Unit 47-07D
    Lamp no. 38 (South Jordan slipper; fig. 17.38)
    1 FW BS CF

Unit 47-13C (figs. 18.13, no. 56; 18.37, no. 143)
    1 FW RS OF with rouletted decoration (No. **56**)
    1 CW BS CF with comb-incised decoration
      (No. **143**)
    1 CW BS CF (cooking pot)
    1 CW base CF

The rouletted fine ware rim sherd (no. **56**) is reminiscent of one of the earlier (pre-AD 106) Nabataean types such as E8a, of which it could be a later variant. The kind of incised decoration as on no. **143** on coarse ware does not occur before the late 1st century AD and then lasts quite long. Therefore, the pottery in this unit probably belongs to the 2nd century AD, with possibly some later elements.

"Ditch"

Locus 14A, "Ditch," North of North Wall of Inner Temenos Enclosure

Unit 4A-03
    10 CW BS CF (all belonging to the same jug or
      bottle)

Unit 4A-17 (figs. 18.3, nos. 11–12, 15; 18.10, no. 40; 18.25, no. 102; 18.38 no. 145)
    2 FW RS OF E1b10 (3b) (No. **12**)

3 FW BS OF (3b) (No. **11**)
1 FW RS OF E1b10 (3c) (No. **15**)
5 FW BS OF (3c)
1 FW RS OF E4a4
1 FW RS OF E1c7
1 FW RS OF E1c8 (No. **40**)
1 FW BS OF with rouletted decoration
3 FW RW base OF
2 FW RW BS CF
1 FW Parthian green / brown glazed BS (No. **145**)
17 CW BS CF (cooking pots)
6 CW BS CF (amphora)
2 CW vertical handles CF (cooking pots)
3 CW base CF (No. **102**)

The pottery illustrated from this unit belongs to the last quarter of the 1st and the beginning of the 2nd century AD. This is confirmed by several more painted fragments, not illustrated here, also belonging to phases 3b and 3c and, therefore, covering the same chronological range. Furthermore, this unit includes 21 rim sherds and two base sherds of cooking pots, underlining the regular use of this kind of pottery within the sanctuary. The question is whether or not the two chronological groups (it and Unit 4A-19 below) belong together.

Unit 4A-19 (figs. 18.2, no. 5; 18.3, no. 16; 18.4, no. 19; 18.10, no. 39; 18.16, no. 68; 18.27, no. 111)
    Lamp no. 15 (wheel-made round; fig. 17.15)
    1 FW BS OF (1/2a) (No. **5**)
    1 FW BS OF (3a)
    2 FW RS OF E1b10 (3a/3b)
    2 FW BS OF (3b)
    11 FW RS OF E1b10 (3c) (Nos. **16, 19**)
    38 FW BS OF (3c)
    2 FW BS CF (3c)
    1 FW RS OF E1c7 (No. **39**)
    1 FW RS OF E3a2
    1 FW ARS base / BS OF (No. **68**)
    6 FW BS OF
    4 FW BS CF
    1 FW base CF
    1 CW RS CF (cooking pot) (No. **111**)
    1 CW vertical handle CF (cooking pot)
    13 CW BS CF (cooking pots)
    3 CW base CF (cooking pots)

Although the vast majority of pottery in this unit clearly belongs to the (early) 2nd century AD, there are some interesting earlier fragments that can be explained by the corresponding entries in Glueck's excavation journal (e.g., GJ 7 March).

Body sherd no. **5** has painted decoration typical for the late phase 1 and early phase 2, i.e., the second to third quarter of the 1st century BC. It belongs, therefore, to the earliest examples of pottery from Khirbet et-Tannur. The painted rim sherd No. **16** belongs to a typical Nabataean bowl, with the somewhat clumsy rim as well as the absence of the background lines that are characteristic for the later 1st century AD, clearly showing that this specimen belongs to the 2nd century AD, i.e., phase 3c. No. **39** is one of the most frequent plain bowl types in Nabataean fine ware pottery from AD 20 to the end of the 1st century AD. In total there are 11 rim and 37 body sherds with painting of phase 3c from this unit, clearly forming the main part of the unit.

The general form of rim no. **111** occurs in the Nabataean coarse ware corpus from the later 1st century AD onwards and still exists in Late Roman times (Gerber 2001: fig. 2; Fellmann Brogli 1996: figs. 738–41). The fragment of African Red Slip Ware (ARS) no. **68**, related to Hayes Form 50 (Hayes 1972: 68–73), confirms that this unit contains some material from the Late Roman period.

Unit 20-B11, North-east end of north ditch
   1 FW ESA BS OF

Unit 47-05E, North-east end of north ditch
   1 FW ESA BS CF

Locus 14B, South of "Ditch"

Unit 47-13B
   1 CW BS CF (same cooking pot as the sherd in Unit 47-20B below)

Unit 47-20B
   1 CW BS CF (same cooking pot as the sherd in Unit 47-13B above)

Room 8

Locus 15, Room 8

GR 72
   Lamp no. 42 (South Jordan slipper; fig. 17.42)

Unit 47-07F
   1 FW BS OF (plate)

Unit 47-07I
   1 CW BS CF (probably cooking pot, burnt)

Unit 47-13H
   1 CW base CF (cooking pot, two joining fragments, burnt)

Unit A-05
Unit misplaced 2004–2011, so pottery not identified by S. Schmid: 9 rims, 5 handles, 3 bases, 17 body sherds, 1 painted body sherd

Unit A-14 (figs. 18.15, nos. 65, 67; 18.30, no. 122; 18.35, no. 135)
   1 FW BS OF (3c)
   1 FW RS OF E4a4
   1 FW RS OF E1c7
   1 FW RS OF E13b-derivation, 2nd century AD (No. **65**)
   1 FW RS CF F3a
   1 FW RW BS CF
   1 FW base CF
   4 CW RS CF (cooking pots) (No. **122**)
   1 CW RS OF (plate with out-turning rim) (No. **67**)
   1 CW RS CF (jug)
   4 CW vertical handles CF (cooking pots)
   1 CW horizontal handle (large storage vessel) (No. **135**)
   15 CW BS CF (mostly cooking pots)
   3 CW base CF (cooking pots)

Room 9

Locus 16, Room 9

20-B01
    Lamp no. 12 (wheel-made round; fig. 17.12)

20-B02
    Lamp no. 44 (large grey South Jordan slipper; fig. 17.44)

GR 80 (CAM 1939.243)
    Lamp no. 18 (discus with eagle; fig. 17.18)

Unit 47-11B
    1 CW BS CF two joining fragments (amphora or a huge cooking pot)

Unit 47-13I
    Lamp no. 47 (unidentified; fig. 17.47)
    1 CW RS OF (with joining BS)
    1 CW base CF
General impression: 2nd–4th century AD.

Unit A-03
    2 CW RS CF (large jug or cooking pot)
    45 CW BS CF (large jug or cooking pot)
Probably all from the same vessel of greyish brown ware with a relatively fine greyish surface.

Unit A-10 (fig. 18.28, no. 115)
    3 FW BS OF (3c/4, very thick)
    1 FW RW RS OF
    7 FW BS CF
    4 CW RS CF (cooking pots) (No. **115**)
    1 CW RS CF (jug)
    1 CW RS CF (amphora?)
    15 CW BS CF (mostly cooking pots)
    1 CW GW base CF (two joining fragments)
The general impression, as well as the very thick painted sherds, indicate a date for this unit in the 2nd–4th centuries AD.

Unit A-11, South-west end of Room 9 (fig. 18.7, no. 25)
    3 FW RS OF E1b176 (3c/4) (No. **25**)
    5 FW BS OF (3c), from the same bowl

    3 FW BS OF (3c), from a different bowl
    1 FW base OF
    1 CW base CF
The shape and decoration of the painted sherds clearly indicate a date within the 2nd–3rd centuries AD.

Room 10

Locus 17, Room 10

Unit 47-07F
    1 FW ESA BS CF

Unit 47-07G
    1 CW BS CF with rouletted decoration

Unit 47-13F
    1 FW ESA BS CF

Unit A-02 (figs. 18.9, no. 36; 18.14, no. 61; 18.26, no. 105)
    3 FW BS OF (3c/4)
    3 FW RS OF E1c8, late derivation
    3 FW RS OF E8a, late derivation (No. **61**)
    2 FW RS OF E13b, late derivation
    1 FW RS CF F5, late derivation (No. **36**)
    4 CW RS CF (cooking pots) (No. **105**)
    4 CW RS CF (jugs, bottles)
    9 CW vertical handles CF (mostly cooking pots)
    2 CW BS CF
    3 CW bases OF
    3 CW bases CF
This unit clearly belongs in the 2nd–3rd centuries AD, as is indicated by the painted sherds as well as the numerous rim sherds of bowls which are late versions of "classical" Nabataean shapes of the 1st century AD.

Unit A-09 (fig. 18.10, no. 41)
    4 FW RS OF E1c8, late derivation (No. **41**)
    1 CW BS CF
No. **41** is one of the characteristic plates used for eating during most of the 1st century AD, more precisely AD 20–100. The basic form continues to be used into the 2nd century AD, but it gets thicker and rounder.

GP 06 (JAM J3292, missing February 2010; GA photo. III-6-1) (fig. 18.19, no. 84)
ESA or imitation, jug, nearly complete (No. **84**)

South-East Corner of Room 10

No number (Whereabouts unknown May 2010; GA photo. I-35b-middle) (fig. 18.10, no. 42)
1 FW RS OF E1c8, late derivation, 3 joining fragments (No. **42**)

In Front of Room 10

Locus 18, Outside South Wall of Room 10

Unit 47-01I (fig. 18.16, no. 71)
1 RS RW OF, two joining fragments of a deep bowl with steep body and flat base, reminiscent of ARS shapes (No. **71**)

Locus 19, Outside Northmost Door to Forecourt

Unit 4A-09 (figs. 18.3, no. 10; 18.15, no. 66; 18.18, no. 75)
1 FW RS OF E1b10 (3a/3b) (No. **10**)
1 FW RS OF E1b10 (3c/4)
1 FW BS OF (3c/4)
1 FW RS OF E1c8, burnt
2 FW RS OF (2nd–3rd century AD) (No. **66**)
1 FW BS OF
2 FW BS CF
1 FW ESA RS CF (jug) (No. **75**)
1 FW ESA BS CF (jug)
1 CW vertical handle CF
5 CW BS CF

No. **10** is a rim sherd of one of the characteristic Nabataean painted drinking bowls; in this case, form and decoration are typical for phase 3a, 3b at the latest, ranging from c. AD 20–70/80 (AD 100 at the latest). This small unit further contains two fragments of an Eastern Sigillata A (ESA) closed shape such as a jug or a flask. As in the case of a similar shape from Locus 21, Unit 47-01G (no. **74**), it belongs to a general Hellenistic form (see Unit 47-01G for further information).

Unit 47-05B
1 semi-FW vertical handle CF (jug)

Unit 47-15 (fig. 18.20, no. 86)
1 CW base CF (green surface on the outside, small flat base) (No. **86**)

No number (JAM J1472; GA photo. I-35b-lower) (fig. 18.7, no. 26)
1 FW RS OF E1b175-177 (4) about 6 joining fragments of a Nabataean painted bowl (No. **26**)

GP 08 (CAM 1939.245; GA photo. I-35a; *DD* pl. 75a) (fig. 18.6, no. 24)
1 FW RS OF E1b170 (3c) about 5 joining fragments of a Nabataean painted bowl (No. **24**)

GR 32 (JAM J3298; GA photo. III-6-3; GP 03) (fig. 18.31, no. 125)
CW CF cooking pot, nearly complete (No. **125**)

GR 33 (Whereabouts unknown May 2010; GA photo. III-6-4; GP 04) (fig. 18.30, no. 124)
CW CF cooking pot, base missing (No. **124**)

Room 13

Locus 20, Room 13

Unit 47-01E (fig. 18.27, no. 110)
3 CW RS CF (cooking pots) (No. **110**)
1 CW BS CF (cooking pot)
1 CW BS CF (cooking pot) with impressed decoration
1 CW base CF

Unit 47-01K
Lamp no.1 (polycandelon; fig. 17.1)

Unit 47-05F (figs. 18.18, no. 81; 18.27, no. 113; 18.36, no. 137)
1 FW RS CF F5a
1 FW RS CF G15b (No. **81**)
1 CW RS CF (cooking pot) (No. **113**)
1 CW BS CF with impressed decoration (No. **137**)

Despite the small number of sherds, a date for this unit within the late 1st or early 2nd century AD seems likely.

Unit 47-09A
  1 CW base CF

Unit 47-10A
  1 CW BS CF (cooking pot)

Unit 47-13E
  1 FW ESA BS CF (3 joining fragments of a jug or a bottle)

Unit 47-14A (fig. 18.39, no. 146)
  4 CW BS lantern fragments, with holes, 3 fragments join a fragment from Unit 47-14B, provenience unknown (No. **146**)

Room 14

Locus 21, Room 14

No Unit number
  Lamp no. 39 (South Jordan slipper; fig. 17.39)

20-B04
  Lamp no. 5 (socket and saucer; fig. 17.5)

20-B05
  Lamp no. 6 (socket and saucer; fig. 17.6)

20-B06
  Lamp no. 34 (South Jordan slipper; fig. 17.34)

GP 12 Department of Antiquities, Amman, Jordan, inv. 40.782 – J3293
  Lamp no. 4 (socket and saucer; fig. 17.4)

GP 16
  Lamp no. 43 (Small Candlestick, with cross; fig. 17.43)

47-01F
  Lamp no. 21 (Nabataean; fig. 17.21)

Unit 47-01G (figs. 18.8, nos. 29, 31; 18.18, nos. 74, 77–80; 18.20, no. 85; 18.22, no. 92; 18.27, nos. 109, 112; 18.29, no. 121; 18.32, no. 129; 18.38, no. 144; 18.40, no. 148)
  1 FW ESA RS CF (jug) (No. **74**)
  1 FW vertical handle CF (jug) (No. **78**)
  1 FW BS CF (unguentarium) (No. **31**)
  2 FW BS CF, one with rouletted decoration (No. **77**)
  2 FW base CF (No. **29**)
  6 CW RS CF (mostly cooking pots, stretching from the later 1st century AD until 3rd century AD) (Nos. **109, 112, 129**) (No. **121**, joins fragments from Locus 21, Unit 47-05A)
  1 FW RS CF (jug, typical 2nd/3rd century AD (No. **80**)
  1 semi-FW RS CF (jug, typical 2nd/3rd century AD) (No. **79**)
  1 CW RS CF (jug or bottle, typical 2nd/3rd century AD) (No. **92**)
  1 CW RS CF (jug or juglet, typical 2nd/3rd century AD) (No. **85**)
  5 CW vertical handles CF (cooking pots)
  1 CW vertical handle CF (huge storage vessel)
  1 CW horizontal handle CF
  2 CW vertical handles CF (typical Late Antique to Middle Ages)
  2 CW BS CF (cooking pot)
  1 CW BS CF (amphora)
  4 CW base CF
  1 CW huge handle CF (? aquamanile antler) with impressed decoration (No. **144**)
  1 CW circular handle, from incense burner cover (No. **148**)

Whilst there is a nice assemblage from the late 1st–2nd century AD, some sherds clearly belong to later centuries, as is best illustrated by two very coarse handles.

The Eastern Sigillata A (ESA) jug or flask no. **74** has no exact parallel in Hayes (1985), but this is not really surprising as closed forms are very rare in ESA; open forms such as plates, dishes, and bowls are far more frequent. However, the general shape of no. **74** here stands in a clearly Hellenistic tradition, and a date somewhere in the 1st century BC seems reasonable. The big variety of small and fine closed shapes, such as nos. **31, 78–80** is characteristic for the second half of the 1st century AD and the early 2nd century AD. This is also true for the thin-walled body sherd with rouletted decoration no. **77**. Beside the pottery illustrated above, a considerable number of sherds belonging to cooking pots and other coarse ware forms comes from this unit. In general terms, most of that pottery seems to date from the late 1st and the 2nd–3rd centuries AD.

Unit 47-03 (fig. 18.23, nos. 95–96)
  2 CW RS CF (jugs) with incised decoration (Nos. **95–96**)
The two rims, nos. **95** and **96**, from coarse ware closed shapes show incised decoration, a common feature of some coarse ware forms from the late 1st century AD onwards well into the Byzantine period (cf., for instance, Fellmann Brogli 1996: figs. 728, 729, 768, 790; Watson 2001: fig. 13.7, 1).

Unit 47-05A (fig. 18.29, no. 121)
  2 CW RS CF (cooking pots) (No. **121**, joins fragments from Locus 21, Unit 47-01G)
  1 CW vertical handle (jug)
  1 CW BS CF (cooking pot)
  1 CW base CF

Unit 47-06A (figs. 18.29, no. 119; 18.32, no. 128)
  2 CW RS CF (cooking pot) join fragments from Unit 47-06C, provenience unknown (No. **119**)
  1 CW RS + 2 CW BS CF (belonging to same cooking pot) (No. **128**)
Both forms nos. **119** and **128** would seem to be later developments of initially Nabataean cooking pots, covering a chronological range from the 2nd century AD up to the Late Roman period.

Unit 47-07A (figs. 18.28, no. 118; 18.36, no. 138)
  1 FW base OF
  1 CW RS CF (cooking pot) (No. **118**)
  1 CW RS CF (jug)
  2 CW vertical handles CF (huge pot)
  2 CW BS CF (huge storage vessel) with impressed decoration (No. **138**)

Unit 47-09B
  1 CW base CF (cooking pot)

Unit 47-11A (figs. 18.9, no. 34; 18.24, no. 97)
  1 FW RS CF F5a (No. **34**)
  1 CW GW BS CF (jug with sieve) (No. **97**)
Both shapes in this Unit are typical of the 2nd–3rd centuries AD. No. **34** is a beaker or small pot from the increasingly rich spectrum of this form within the late 1st and the early 2nd centuries AD (cf., for some similar forms, Schmid 2000: figs. 224–29). No. **97** belongs to a jug or amphora with high neck and integrated strainer. Its form, ware, and surface are very characteristic of a category of pottery, commonly called "green ware" or "cream ware." However, its exact place of origin remains largely unknown (see *Discussion* above). Whatever the case, the strainer shows that these jugs or amphorae did contain a specific kind of liquid, and it is very likely that they were imported to Nabataea because of their contents.

Unit 47-12A (figs. 18.8, no. 27; 18.18, no. 76)
  1 FW RS CF F2c64, 247, 248 (3c) (No. **27**)
  1 FW BS CF with rouletted decoration (No. **76**)
Both shapes (Nos. **27, 76**) from this unit are typical of the 2nd–3rd centuries AD. They are characteristic of the increasing diversity in Nabataean fine ware forms at the end of the 1st/beginning of the 2nd century AD, especially a great variety of small beakers, cups, and the like.

Unit 47-13D (figs. 18.1, nos. 2–3; 18.13, no. 54; 18.15, no. 62; 18.28, no. 117; 18.32, no. 127; 18.33, no. 130; 18.37, no. 141)
  1 FW RS OF E10a136 (No. **62**)
  1 FW RW RS OF E4a4
  1 FW BS CF
  4 FW BS CF with rouletted decoration (No. **54**)
  1 FW ESA BS CF (jug or bottle)
  1 FW base OF
  3 FW base CF
  6 CW RS CF (cooking pots) (Nos. **117, 127**)
  1 CW RS CF (jug, with incised decoration) related to No. **96**
  3 CW RS OF (plates, bowls) (Nos. **2–3**)
  4 CW vertical handles CF (cooking pots)
  1 CW BS CF
  8 CW base CF

1 CW base CF with paint or slip, joins base fragment from Unit 47-16B, provenience unknown (No. **130**)

1 CW BS with thumb-impressed decoration (No. **141**)

Beside the specimens illustrated, in this unit there is an Eastern Sigillata A (ESA) fragment from a closed shape, similar to the one from Locus 21, Unit 47-01G (no. **74**). This ESA jug or flask has no exact parallel in Hayes (1985), but this is not really surprising, as closed forms are very rare in ESA; open forms such as plates, dishes and bowls being far more frequent. However, the general shape here stands in a clearly Hellenistic tradition, and a date somewhere in the 1st century BC seems reasonable. There is also a rim sherd from a cooking pot with applied impressed decoration (no. **127**), usually not in use before the end of the 1st century AD. Like most other units, this one is rather heterogeneous.

Unit 47-13J
2 semi-FW RS OF
1 CW RS CF (jug or cooking pot)
1 CW vertical handle CF (cooking pot)

Unit 47-16A
1 semi-FW base CF (big bottle)

Unit 47-20C (fig. 18.14, no. 60)
3 semi-FW RS OF E8a-derivation with horizontal handle, 2nd – 3rd centuries AD (No. **60**)

Unit 48-15
1 CW BS + base CF several joining fragments of a huge cooking pot, maybe the same as in Unit 48-16 below, No. **120**)

Unit 48-16 (fig. 18.29, no. 120)
1 FW BS OF (3c)
1 CW RS CF several joining fragments of a huge cooking pot, perhaps same pot as in Unit 48-15 above (No. **120**)

Cooking pot no. **120** would seem to be a developed version of a Nabataean form. The rounded rim, compared to the more sharply formed rims of cooking pots from the late 1st to early 2nd cen-

tury AD, indicates a date from the 2nd to the 4th century AD.

Unit A-16
1 FW RS OF E1b10 (3c)
1 FW RS OF E3a2
2 FW BS OF
2 FW BS CF
1 CW RS CF (cooking pot)
2 CW RS CF (jug)
38 CW BS CF (mostly cooking pot)
1 CW BS CF (jug)
2 CW BS CF (amphora)
2 CW base CF

20-B03 (fig. 18.20, no. 87)
1 CW base CF (No. **87**)

Unit 47-01H, East part of Room 14 ("Room 15")
1 CW vertical handle CF (cooking pot)

GR 94, East part of Room 14 ("Room 15") (CAM 1939.244; GP 10; GA photo. III-6-5) (fig. 18.11, no. 47)
Complete Nabataean bowl E3b188 (No. **47**)

"Debris"

"Debris" Written on Individual Sherds by Glueck, i.e., no Provenience

20-B08
1 CW small base CF

Unit 47-01J (figs. 18.14, no. 58; 18.21, no. 89; 18.25, no. 99)
Lamp no. 2 (polycandelon; fig. 17.2)
1 FW RS OF E8a-derivation (No. **58**)
1 FW RS OF (bowl, typical 2nd–3rd centuries AD)
1 FW BS CF
1 CW RS CF (krater, with thumb impressed decoration) (No. **99**)
1 CW vertical handle (cooking pot)
1 CW vertical handle (jug)
1 CW vertical handle (huge storage/transport vessel)

1 CW base CF (jug) (No. **89**)
1 CW base CF

Unit 47-05H (figs. 18.18, no. 82; 18.25, no. 103; 18.30, no. 123)
  1 FW BS OF (3c)
  1 FW RS CF G15b (No. **82**)
  1 FW base CF
  2 CW RS CF (cooking pots) (No. **123**)
  1 CW base CF
  1 CW neck CF (No. **103**)

Unit 47-07J (fig. 18.28, no. 116)
  1 FW BS OF (3c)
  2 CW RS CF (cooking pot) (No. **116**)
  1 CW vertical handle CF (cooking pot)

Unit 47-13L (figs. 18.12, no. 48; 18.37, no. 142)
  1 FW BS OF (2b/2c)
  1 FW BS OF (3c)
  1 FW RS OF E1a12
  1 FW RS OF E4a4
  1 FW RS OF E1c7
  1 FW RS OF E8a-derivation with rouletted decoration (No. **48**)
  1 FW RS CF (juglet)
  2 FW BS OF
  1 FW base OF
  1 CW RS CF (cooking pot)
  1 CW vertical handle CF (huge storage/transport vessel)
  7 CW BS CF with incised and thumb impressed decoration (No. **142**)
  1 CW base CF

Unit 47-19
  Lamps nos.:
  8 and 9 (socket and saucer; figs. 17.8–9)
  13 and 14 (wheel-made round; figs. 17.13–14)
  20 (Nabataean; fig. 17.20)
  23 (mould-made round; fig. 17.23)
  46 and 48 (unidentified; figs. 17.46, 17.48)

In Bags Labelled "Debris"

Unit 48-01 (fig. 18.4, no. 20)
  2 FW BS OF (1/2a)

  6 FW BS OF (3b)
  14 FW RS OF E1b170 (3c) (No. **20**)
  31 FW BS OF (3c)
  1 FW RS OF E1c7-derivation
  5 FW BS OF
  1 FW base OF
  2 FW bases CF

The clear majority of the pottery in this unit belongs to the 2nd–3rd centuries AD, and there seems to be no later material. There is, however, a small selection of earlier pottery, going back to the 1st century BC. Due to the small size of the two painted body sherds preserved, it is not possible to decide whether they belong to phase 1 (late 2nd/first half 1st century BC) or to phase 2a (third quarter of the 1st century BC).

Unit 48-02
  1 FW BS OF (3b)
  2 FW RS CF (jug or bottle)
  2 FW BS OF
  2 FW base OF
  1 FW base CF
  1 FW ARS-imitation RS OF
  1 semi-FW RS CF (jug)
  2 semi-FW vertical handles CF (jug)
  1 CW RS OF
  1 CW RS CF (huge storage vessel)
  2 CW vertical handle CF (cooking pots)
  1 CW vertical handle CF (huge storage vessel)
  14 CW BS CF (mostly cooking pots)
  1 CW BS CF with a hole
  2 CW bases CF (cooking pots)
  2 CW bases CF (jug or bottle)

Unit 48-03
  1 FW BS OF (2c)
  5 FW BS OF (3a)
  7 FW RS OF E1b10 (3b)
  33 FW BS OF (3b)
  24 FW RS OF E1b10 (3c)
  104 FW BS OF (3c)
  3 FW RS OF E2e/f
  6 FW RS OF E1c7
  9 FW RS OF E1c8
  1 FW RS OF E1c8-derivation
  4 FW RS OF E3a2

2 FW RS CF F2a
70 FW BS OF
10 FW BS CF
2 FW bases OF
2 FW bases CF
56 CW BS CF (mostly cooking pots)
1 CW BS strainer (with triangular holes)

Unit 48-04
Lamp no. 10 (socket and saucer; fig. 17.10)
3 FW BS OF (1/2a)
1 FW RS OF E1b10 (3a)
5 FW BS OF (3a)
3 FW BS OF (3a/3b)
6 FW BS OF (3b)
8 FW RS OF E1b10 + derivations (3c)
22 FW BS OF (3c)
2 FW RS OF E2e/f
2 FW RS OF E4a4
4 FW RS OF E1c8
1 FW RS OF E3a2
1 FW RS OF E8a-derivation
2 FW RS OF
2 FW RS CF F2a
1 FW vertical handle CF
20 FW BS OF
4 FW BS CF
3 FW bases OF
2 FW bases CF
3 CW RS CF (cooking pots)
1 CW RS OF (huge mortar)
3 CW vertical handles CF (cooking pots)
181 CW BS CF (mostly cooking pots)
10 CW BS CF (transport/storage-vessels)
2 CW bases CF
2 CW GW BS CF

The clear majority of this unit belongs to the 2nd–3rd centuries AD, and there seems to be no later material. There is, however, a small selection of earlier pottery, going back to the late 2nd century or first to third quarters of the 1st century BC, painted (phase 1/2) and unpainted (E2e/f).

Unit 48-05
Lamp no. 28 (mould-made round)
1 FW vertical handle CF (3c)
2 FW BS OF (3c)

1 FW BS CF (3c)
1 FW RS CF F2a
4 FW BS CF
4 CW RS CF (cooking pots)
6 CW vertical handles CF (cooking pots)
55 CW BS CF (mostly cooking pots)
1 CW base CF (cooking pot)
1 CW base CF (jug or bottle)

Unit 48-06
1 FW RS OF E1b10 (3c)
1 FW BS OF (3c)
2 FW RS OF (small bowl, typical for 2nd–3rd centuries AD)
5 FW BS CF
2 FW bases CF
1 FW ARS BS OF
8 CW BS CF
1 CW RS CF
1 CW vertical handle CF

Unit 48-07 (fig. 18.4, no. 17)
1 FW RS OF (1/2a)
1 FW BS OF (2b/2c)
3 FW RS OF E1b10 (3a)
6 FW BS OF (3a)
1 FW RS OF E1b10 (3b)
18 FW BS OF (3b)
12 FW RS OF E1b10 (3c) (No. **17**)
31 FW BS OF (3c)
1 FW vertical handle CF (3c)
3 FW RS OF E1c7
2 FW RS OF E1c8
3 FW RS OF
18 FW BS OF
5 FW BS CF
5 FW bases OF
2 FW bases CF
1 FW ARS-imitation(?) BS OF
1 CW RS CF
44 CW BS CF (mostly cooking pots)
5 CW bases CF

The clear majority of the unit belongs to the 2nd–3rd centuries AD, and there seems to be no later material. There is, however, a small selection of earlier pottery, going back to the 1st century BC. Due to the small size of the painted rim sherd preserved, it is not possible to decide whether it belongs to phase 1 (late 2nd/first half of the 1st century BC) or to phase 2a (third quarter of the 1st century BC).

Unit 48-08 (fig. 18.11, nos. 44–45)
  1 FW BS OF (2a)
  3 FW BS OF (3a)
  1 FW RS OF E1b10 (3b)
  10 FW BS OF (3b)
  3 FW RS OF E1b10 (3c)
  17 FW BS OF (3c)
  2 FW RS OF E2e/f (Nos. **44–45**)
  1 FW RS OF E1c8
  2 FW RS OF E1c7
  2 FW RS OF E9a
  10 FW BS OF
  3 FW bases OF
  1 FW base CF
  1 FW ARS BS+base OF
  4 CW RS CF (cooking pots)
  1 CW RS CF (jug)
  1 CW RS OF
  15 CW BS CF (mostly cooking pots)

The clear majority of this unit belongs to the 2nd–3rd centuries AD, and there seems to be no later material. There is, however, a small selection of earlier pottery, going back to the second and third quarters of the 1st century BC, painted (phase 2a, third quarter of the 1st century BC) and unpainted (E2e/f, late 2nd century/first to third quarter of the 1st century BC) (nos. **44–45**).

Unit 48-09 (figs. 18.10, no. 38; 18.26, no. 107)
  5 FW RS OF E4b83 (1/2a)
  3 FW BS OF (1/2a)
  1 FW RS OF E2a356 (2c)
  1 FW RS OF E1b10 (3a)
  1 FW BS OF (3a)
  2 FW RS OF E1b10 (3b)
  16 FW BS OF (3b)
  2 FW RS OF E1b10 (3c)
  3 FW BS OF (3c)
  5 FW RS OF E1a12 (No. **38**)
  5 FW RS OF E4a4
  5 FW RS OF E24b
  1 FW RS OF E3a2

  9 FW RS OF E1c8
  5 FW RS OF E1c7
  4 FW RS CF G3a
  4 FW vertical handle CF (jug)
  107 FW BS OF
  29 FW BS CF
  1 FW BS CF with rouletted decoration
  8 FW bases OF
  6 FW bases CF
  4 semi-FW RS CF (juglets)
  5 CW RS CF (cooking pots) (No. **107**)
  1 CW RS CF (amphora)
  1 CW RS OF
  7 CW vertical handles CF (cooking pots)
  1 CW vertical handle CF (jug)
  346 CW BS CF (mostly cooking pots)
  10 CW BS CF (huge storage / transport vessels)
  8 CW bases CF
  4 CW bases OF
  5 CW GW BS CF
  1 CW GW base CF

The unit is surprising because of the huge number of coarse ware body sherds compared to the small number of corresponding coarse ware rim sherds. In addition, the emphasis of the unit seems to be within phase 3b (last quarter of the 1st century AD), despite some earlier (up to late 2nd/first to third quarter 1st century BC) and a few later sherds (phase 3c, early 2nd century AD).

Unit 48-10
  2 FW BS OF (1)
  1 FW RS OF E4b83 (1)
  1 FW BS OF (2a)
  1 FW BS OF (2b/2c)
  1 FW BS OF (3a)
  17 FW BS (3b)
  3 FW RS OF E24b
  3 FW RS OF E1c7
  2 FW RS OF E1c8
  2 FW RS OF E3a2
  2 FW RS OF
  1 FW RS CF
  1 FW vertical handle CF
  103 FW BS OF
  29 FW BS CF
  1 FW base OF

1 FW ESA BS OF
319 CW BS CF (mostly cooking pots)
6 CW BS CF (storage/transport vessel)
2 CW vertical handle CF
1 CW base CF
5 CW GW BS CF

This would seem to be the only unit that contains no material later than the late 1st century AD (phase 3b). This impression is confirmed by unpainted fine ware and coarse ware that do not seem to contain any later elements. If this is not a coincidence, it would be interesting to know where the unit comes from. There is also, as is frequently the case with units (i.e., bags) from Box 48, earlier material, including sherds from the late 2nd/early 1st century BC.

Unit 48-11
1 FW BS OF (3a)
1 FW BS OF (3b)
2 FW RS OF E1b10 (3c)
5 FW BS OF (3c)
2 FW BS OF
2 CW BS CF

Unit 48-12
1 FW BS OF (3c)
1 FW RS CF F3a (characteristic for the 2nd–3rd centuries AD)
3 CW RS CF (cooking pots)
2 CW RS CF (very coarse, Late Antique–Mediaeval)
1 CW vertical handle CF
40 CW BS CF (some of the very coarse, Late Antique–Mediaeval)
1 CW base CF

Unit 48-13 (fig. 18.22, no. 94)
2 FW BS OF (1/2a)
17 FW BS OF (3a)
2 FW RS OF E1b10 (3b)
20 FW BS OF (3b)
2 FW RS OF E1b10 (3c)
11 FW BS OF (3c)
1 FW RS OF E1c7
1 FW RS OF E1c8
1 FW vertical handle CF

4 FW BS OF
2 FW BS CF
3 FW bases OF
3 FW bases CF
1 FW ESA BS OF
1 FW Parthian green glazed BS CF
1 CW RS CF (cooking pot)
1 CW RS CF (jar, with pie-crust edge) (No. **94**)
1 CW vertical handle CF (cooking pot)
4 CW BS CF

Unit 48-14 (fig. 18.8, no. 28)
1 FW RS OF E4b83 (1/2a)
1 FW BS OF (1/2a)
1 FW RS OF E2a16b (2b/2c)
1 FW RS OF E1b10 (3a)
5 FW BS OF (3a)
2 FW RS OF E1b10 (3b)
12 FW BS OF (3b)
31 FW RS OF E1b10 (3c)
1 FW RS F2c248 (3c) (No. **28**)
133 FW BS OF (3c)
2 FW BS CF (3c)
3 FW RS OF E1c7
3 FW RS OF E1c8
34 FW BS OF
2 FW bases OF
1 CW RS CF (cooking pot)
1 CW RS CF (jug)
1 CW RS lid
2 CW BS CF

Provenience Unclear
(i.e., with incomplete labels, so that the find-locations are ambiguous)

Unit 47-07B, "Room II"
1 CW BS CF

Unit 47-05G, "Room 3" [= Room 10 or east part of Room 14] (fig. 18.13, no. 53)
1 CW RS OF with rouletted decoration, similar to E22e238 (No. **53**)

Unit 47-07C, "Room 3" [= Room 10 or east part of Room 14]
1 CW BS CF

Unit 47-13K, "Room 3" [= Room 10 or east part of Room 14] (fig. 18.12, no. 49)
  1 FW RS OF E8a (No. **49**)
  1 FW ESA BS CF
  1 CW RS CF
  1 CW BS sieve

Unit A-15, "room III or VII" (fig. 18.12, no. 51)
  2 FW RS OF E1b10 (3b)
  2 FW BS OF (3b)
  3 FW RS OF E1b10 (3c)
  8 FW BS OF (3c)
  1 FW RS OF E1c7-derivation
  3 FW RS OF E8a-derivation, one with rouletted decoration (No. **51**)
  2 FW RS OF (bowls, typical 2nd–3rd centuries AD)
  6 FW BS OF
  1 FW base OF
  3 CW RS CF (cooking pots)
  2 CW RS CF (jugs, bottles)
  1 CW RS OF
  38 CW BS CF (mostly cooking pots)
  1 CW base CF
This unit belongs to the 2nd–3rd centuries AD, with a few sherds of the late 1st century AD.

Unit 47-01F "8-room II or N. room II"
  3 CW RS CF (cooking pot)
  1 CW RS CF (jug)
  4 CW vertical handle CF (cooking pot)
  1 CW vertical handle CF (jug)
  1 CW vertical handle CF (huge storage vessel)
  1 CW BS CF
  2 CW bases CF

Unit 47-05D "room 6" (fig. 18.13, no. 55)
  1 CW base OF with rouletted decoration (No. **55**)

Unit 4A-26 "Room 6"
  1 FW RS OF E18a (3a)
  3 FW BS OF (3a)
  1 FW RS OF E1b10 (3b)
  6 FW BS OF (3b)
  7 FW RS OF E1b10 (3c)

  13 FW BS OF (3c)
  1 FW BS CF (3c)
  2 FW RS OF E1c7
  2 FW RS OF E1c8
  1 FW RS OF E8a
  4 FW RS OF E3a2
  28 FW BS OF
  16 FW BS CF
  2 FW bases OF
  2 FW bases CF
  2 CW bases CF
This unit contains surprisingly little coarse ware compared to fine ware. The Nabataean pottery covers most of the 1st century AD (phases 3a and 3b) and stretches into the 2nd century AD (phase 3c), where the main quantity (20 painted sherds) is to be situated. Chronologically speaking, the composition of the unit seems like Locus 3 (northeast offertory box) Unit 4A-11, i.e., some earlier Nabataean sherds mixed with 2nd century AD sherds, and it could, therefore, come from a similar context.

Unit 47-01A "E. court and outside to north"
  1 CW RS CF (jug)
  2 CW bases CF

Unit 47-06B "NE end of portico outside ne. corner of temple courtyard" (fig. 18.17, no. 73)
  1 semi-FW RS OF casserole (characteristic 2nd – 4th centuries AD) (No. **73**)

Unit 47-20A "N. east end of portico outside ne. corner of temple courtyard"
  1 CW RS OF (characteristic 2nd–4th centuries AD)

Provenience Unknown
(i.e., where there is no longer any record of the find-location)

20-B01
  Lamp no. 7 (socket and saucer; fig. 17.7)

20-B01 and 20-B06
  Lamp no. 32 (South Jordan slipper; fig. 17.32)

20-B02
Lamp no. 41 (South Jordan slipper; fig. 17.41)

20-B07
Lamp no. 30 (mould-made round, large filling hole; fig. 17.30)

GP 23
Lamp no. 3 (polycandelon; fig. 17.3)

Unit 47-01K (figs. 18.25, no. 101; 18.33, no. 131)
1 FW RS CF G3a
1 FW RS CF G26c, similar (No. **101**)
1 CW vertical handle CF (cooking pot)
1 CW vertical handle CF (huge storage/transport vessel)
2 CW BS CF
1 CW BS CF (huge storage/transport vessel)
2 CW bases CF, one joins 4 fragments from Locus 7, Unit 4A-24 (No. **131**)
1 CW GW BS CF

Unit 47-05I (figs. 18.26, no. 104; 18.35, no. 134)
1 FW ARS (or imitation) RS OF
2 CW RS CF (cooking pot) (No. **104**)
1 CW RS CF (huge storage vessel) (No. **134**)
2 CW BS CF
1 CW BS CF
1 CW GW BS CF

Unit 47-06C (fig. 18.29, no. 119)
2 CW RS CF (cooking pot) join fragments from Locus 21, Unit 47-06A (No. **119**)
1 CW RS CF (amphora?)
2 CW BS CF (cooking pot, probably from same pot as the RS)
1 CW BS CF with imprinted decoration

Unit 47-07H
1 CW RS CF (cooking pot)
1 CW RS CF (jug)
4 CW BS CF
1 CW base CF
1 CW GW RS CF

Unit 47-08
1 CW BS CF (huge amphora)

Unit 47-10B
1 FW RS OF E1c8-derivation

Unit 47-12C
1 FW RS OF E2a16b (2b/2c)
3 FW BS OF (3a)
7 FW BS OF (3b)
1 FW BS OF (3c)
2 FW BS OF
1 FW BS CF with rouletted decoration
11 CW BS CF

Unit 47-13M (figs. 18.21, no. 90; 18.28, no. 114)
5 FW BS OF (3c)
1 FW RS OF E1c8
4 FW BS OF
1 FW BS CF
1 FW BS CF with rouletted decoration
1 FW base OF
2 CW RS CF (cooking pot) (No. **114**)
1 CW vertical handle CF (cooking pot)
1 CW vertical twist handle CF (No. **90**)
22 CW BS CF (mostly cooking pots)
3 CW GW BS CF

Unit 47-14B (figs. 18.39, nos. 146–47)
1 CW BS lantern (No. **147**)
1 CW BS lantern, joins 3 fragments from Locus 20, Unit 47-14A (No. **146**)

Unit 47-16B (fig. 18.33, no. 130)
1 FW BS CF
2 FW bases CF, one joins base fragment from Locus 21, Unit 47-13D (No. **130**)

Unit 47-17 (fig. 18.34, no. 132)
1 CW BS + vertical handle CF (storage / transport vessel) (No. **132**)

Unit 47-18 (fig. 18.36, no. 136)
1 CW BS CF (huge amphora) with thumb impressed decoration (No. **136**)

Unit 47-20D
1 CW RS CF (jug or amphora)

Unit 48-17
    1 FW RS OF E4b83 (1)
    1 FW BS OF (1)
    1 FW RS OF E2a356 (2c)
    6 FW BS OF (3a)
    7 FW RS OF E1b10 (3b)
    18 FW BS OF (3b)
    6 FW RS OF E1b10 (3c)
    1 FW RS CF (3c)
    4 FW BS OF (3c)
    1 FW RS OF E2e/f
    2 FW RS OF E1a12
    2 FW RS OF E4a35
    1 FW RS OF E16a
    4 FW RS OF E1c7
    13 FW RS OF E1c8
    1 FW RS OF E3a2
    2 FW BS OF
    3 FW BS CF
    10 FW base OF
    3 FW base CF
    4 semi-FW RS CF (juglets)
    9 CW RS CF
    1 CW RS OF
    4 CW vertical handle CF
    6 CW bases CF
    2 CW GW bases CF

This is the only unit that has an undeniable and clearly identified sherd (fine ware rim sherd E4b83) from phase 1, i.e., the late 2nd/first half of the 1st century BC. This situation is confirmed by another painted sherd of either phase 1 or phase 2a, as well as plain fine ware such as E2e/f and E1a12. Therefore, we have definite evidence that the summit of the hill was occupied or visited in one form or another before the middle of the 1st century BC, as also suggested by some sherds from Locus 7 (inside Altar 1) 4A-24, possibly going back to the 2nd century BC (see *Discussion* above). Otherwise, this unit has a cluster of pottery belonging to the late 1st century AD.

Unit A-12 (fig. 18.37, nos. 139–40)
    Lamps nos. 22 and 26 (mould-made round; figs. 17.22, 17.26)
    2 FW BS OF (3a)
    5 FW BS OF (3b)

20 FW BS OF (3c)
1 FW RS OF E3a2
1 FW RS OF E8a-derivation
1 FW RS CF G14d
1 FW BS CF (unguentarium)
49 FW BS OF
16 FW BS CF
1 CW RS CF (cooking pot)
1 CW RS CF with impressed decoration (No. **140**)
1 CW BS CF with impressed decoration (No. **139**)
181 CW BS CF (mostly cooking pots)
17 CW BS CF (storage and transport vessels)
25 CW BS OF
2 CW BS CF (very coarse, Mediaeval?)
1 CW base CF
3 CW GW BS CF

Unit A-13 (figs. 18.2, no. 7; 18.5, no. 22; 18.9, no. 35; 18.10, no. 37; 18.11, no. 43; 18.12, nos. 50, 52; 18.15, no. 63)
    Lamps nos.:
    16 and 17 (wheel-made round; figs. 17.16–17)
    19 (discus; fig. 17.19)
    24 and 25 (mould-made round; figs. 17.24–25)
    31 (mould-made elongated; fig. 17.31)
    35 and 36 (South Jordan slipper; figs. 17.35–36)
    45 (large grey South Jordan slipper; fig. 17.45).
    6 FW BS OF (1/2a)
    1 FW BS OF (2a)
    1 FW RS OF E2a16b (2b) (No. 7)
    3 FW BS OF (2b/2c)
    1 FW RS OF E18a (3a)
    20 FW BS OF (3a)
    15 FW RS OF E1b10 (3b)
    51 FW BS OF (3b)
    84 FW RS OF E1b10 (3c)
    1 FW RS OF E1b170 (3c) (No. **22**)
    242 FW BS OF (3c)
    5 FW BS CF (3c)
    1 FW base OF (3c)
    4 FW RS OF E2e/f (phase 1/2a) (No. **43**)
    1 FW RS OF E1a12 (phase 2a) (No. **37**)
    1 FW RW RS OF E4a4
    1 FW RS OF E4a5
    20 FW RS OF E1c8 ("real" ones and derivations, typical for late 1st–2nd century AD)

21 FW RS OF E1c7 ("real" ones and derivations, typical for late 1st–2nd century AD)

8 FW RS OF E8a (derivations of an earlier type, typical for the 2nd century AD) (Nos. **50**, **52**)

7 FW RS OF E11a (? derivations of an earlier type, typical for the 2nd century AD) (No. **63**)

11 FW RS CF F5a (typical for late 1st–2nd century AD) (No. **35**)

2 FW BS CF with rouletted decoration

34 FW BS OF

12 FW BS CF

11 FW bases OF

5 FW bases CF

26 CW RS CF (cooking pots)

1 CW RS lid

12 CW RS CF (jugs)

6 CW RS OF

20 CW vertical handles CF (cooking pots)

5 CW vertical handles CF (jugs)

257 CW BS CF (mostly cooking pots)

37 CW bases CF (mostly cooking pots)

1 CW GW BS CF

1 FW ESA BS OF

3 FW ESA BS CF

The unit shows a clear focal point in the 2nd century AD (phase 3c) with some earlier specimens, and later lamps (Lamps nos. 35–36, 45). In terms of statistics, this seems to give a rather valuable overview for the pottery to be found on top of Khirbet et-Tannur.

Unit A-17 (figs. 18.11, no. 46; 18.14, nos. 57, 59; 18.15, no. 64; 18.16, no. 69; 18.25, no. 100; 18.34, no. 133)

    Lamps nos. 11 (socket and saucer) and 27 (mould-made round) (figs. 17.11, 17.27)

    3 FW RS OF E1b10 (3b)

    14 FW RS OF E1b10 (3c)

    3 FW RS OF E2e/f (No. **46**)

    2 FW RS OF E1a12

    1 FW RS OF E4a5

    13 FW RS OF E1c8 ("real" and derivations)

    8 FW RS OF E1c7 ("real" and derivations)

    7 FW RS OF E8a-derivations (Nos. **57**, **59**)

    5 FW RS OF E13b-derivations (No. **64**)

    6 FW RS CF F9a/b

    1 FW RS CF G13a/b (No. **100**)

    3 FW RS CF G14d

4 FW RS CF (juglets, bottles)

4 FW vertical handles CF

13 FW bases OF

7 FW bases CF

1 FW ARS-imitation RS OF, similar to Hayes 1972: form 45 (No. **69**)

1 FW ESA or imitation, vertical handle CF

25 CW RS CF (cooking pots)

6 CW RS CF (jugs, bottles)

3 CW RS CF (huge transport/storage vessel)

11 CW RS OF

24 CW vertical handles CF (mostly cooking pots)

9 CW vertical handles CF (huge transport/storage vessels) (No. **133**)

16 CW bases CF (mostly cooking pots)

5 CW bases CF

1 CW base CF (huge transport/storage vessel)

1 CW GW RS CF (jug or amphora)

Despite a few earlier sherds going back to the 1st century BC (E2e/f, E1a12), the vast majority of this unit belongs to the 2nd–3rd centuries AD.

Unit A-18 (figs. 18.2, nos. 8–9; 18.3, nos. 13–14; 18.4, no. 18)

    1 FW BS OF (1/2a)

    1 FW BS OF E2a16b (2b) (No. **8**)

    1 FW BS OF (2b) (No. **9**)

    1 FW BS OF (3a)

    2 FW RS OF E1b10 (3a/3b) (Nos. **13–14**)

    4 FW BS OF (3a/3b)

    1 FW RS OF E1b10 (3b)

    6 FW BS OF (3b)

    20 FW RS OF E1b10 (3c) (No. **18**)

    73 FW BS OF (3c), including one thick base (?3c/4)

    1 FW BS CF (3c)

    4 FW BS OF

This unit shows the entire spectrum of Nabataean painted pottery from the mid-1st century BC to the 2nd century AD with a clear emphasis in the 2nd century AD (94 out of 111 painted sherds).

Although very fragmentary, nos. **8** and **9** are of the greatest interest because they belong within the earliest surely datable pottery remains so far recorded from Khirbet et-Tannur. No. **9**, with concentrically applied small branches, belongs to the lower part of a Nabataean drinking bowl; such a combination is only possible within phase 2b and, therefore, the last quarter of the 1st century BC (cf. Schmid 2000: 27–42 for detailed argument). The same is true for no. **8**. Although the painted decoration is absent from the fragment actually preserved, the shape with the fine step in the wall is a characteristic detail only observed on a few forms, all belonging to the last quarter of the 1st century BC.

Nos. **13** and **14** are typical representatives of Nabataean drinking bowls from the second and third quarters of the 1st century AD.

In terms of painted pottery Unit A-18 contains 2 body sherds of phase 2b (25–1 BC), 6 body sherds of phase 3a (AD 20–70/80), 2 rim and 5 body sherds of phase 3b (AD 70/80–106), and 21 rim and 78 body sherds of phase 3c (AD 100 to 3rd century). These turn out to be quite representative statistics for the entire pottery from Khirbet et-Tannur, i.e., a few early remains covering the later 1st century BC and the 1st century AD and a considerable amount of pottery from the 2nd–3rd centuries AD.

GP 02 (JAM J3291, missing February 2010; GA photos. III-7a, III-7b, III-7c) (fig. 18.17, no. 72)

   CW OF casserole, nearly complete, with two thumb impressed ledge handles (No. **72**)

GP 05 (Whereabouts unknown May 2010; GA photo. III-6-2) (fig. 18.31, no. 126)

   CW CF cooking pot, nearly complete (No. **126**)

GP 34 (JAM J1471; GA photo. I-35d; *DD* pls. 73a, 74) (fig. 18.5, no. 21)

   1 FW RS OF E1b170 (3c) about 24 joining fragments of about half of a Nabataean bowl with painted palmettes and pomegrantes (No. **21**)

No number (Whereabouts unknown May 2010; GA photo. I-35e; *DD* pl. 75b) (fig. 18.6, no. 23)

   1 FW RS OF E1b170 (3c) about 8 joining fragments of about a quarter of a Nabataean bowl (No. **23**)

FIG. 18.1　Coarse ware bowls.

Painted coarse ware bowl

1.　Locus 7, inside Altar Platform, Unit 4A-24 (Vol. 1, fig. 34)
　　Base sherd, painted coarse ware, open form
　　ware: 10YR 6/2.5 light brownish grey–pale brown, with mica
　　inner and outer surfaces: 2.5Y 4.5/1 dark grey
　　paint: 5YR 4/3 reddish brown.

Plain coarse ware bowls

2.　Locus 21, Room 14, Unit 47-13D
　　Rim and body sherd, coarse ware
　　ware: 10YR 4/1 very dark grey
　　inner and outer surfaces: 5YR 5/5 reddish brown–yellowish red.

3.　Locus 21, Room 14, Unit 47-13D
　　Rim and body sherd, coarse ware
　　ware: 7.5YR 6.5/4 pink-light brown, with big inclusions
　　inner and outer surfaces: 2.5Y 7.5/3 pale yellow.

COARSE WARE BOWLS Fig. 18.1

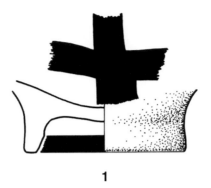

1

Painted coarse ware bowl

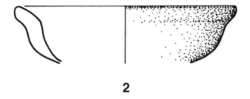

2

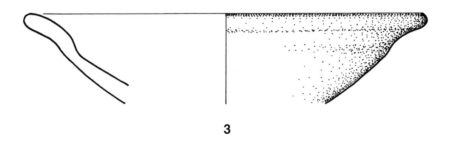

3

Plain coarse ware bowls

0   5 cm

Fig. 18.2   Painted Nabataean fine ware bowls.

Phase 1/2

4.   Locus 3, north-east offertory box, Unit 4A-11
     Rim sherd, Nabataean painted, type E4b83 (phase 1 or 2a)
     ware: 5YR 6/8 reddish yellow
     inner surface: 5YR 6/8 reddish yellow
     outer surface: 5YR 5/6 yellowish red
     paint: 2.5YR 4/8 dark red.

5.   Locus 14A, "ditch", Unit 4A-19
     Body sherd, Nabataean painted (phase 1/2a)
     ware: 5YR 6.5/6 reddish yellow
     inner and outer surfaces: 5YR 6/6 reddish yellow
     paint: 2.5YR 4.5/6 dark red.

6.   Locus 3, north-east offertory box, Unit 4A-11
     Body sherd, Nabataean painted (phase 1 or 2a)
     ware: 5YR 6/8 reddish yellow
     inner surface: 5YR 6/8 reddish yellow
     outer surface: 5YR 5/6 yellowish red
     paint: 2.5YR 4/8 dark red.

Type E2a16b (phase 2b)

7.   Provenience unknown, Unit A-13
     Rim sherd, Nabataean painted, type E2a16b (phase 2b)
     ware: 2.5YR 5.5/6 red
     inner surface: 2.5YR 5.5/8 red
     outer surface: 2.5YR 6/6 light red.

8.   Provenience unknown, Unit A-18
     Body sherd, Nabataean painted, type E2a16b (phase 2b)
     ware: 2.5YR 5/7 red
     inner surface: 2.5YR 4/6 dark red
     outer surface: 7.5YR 4/2.5 brown
     parallels: Schmid 2000: figs. 83–85.

Phase 2b

9.   Provenience unknown, Unit A-18
     Body sherd, Nabataean painted (phase 2b)
     ware: 7.5YR 7/6 reddish yellow
     inner and outer surfaces: 5YR 6.5/6 reddish yellow
     paint: 10R 4/6 red
     parallels: Schmid 2000: figs. 84–85.

PAINTED NABATAEAN FINE WARE BOWLS

FIG. 18.2

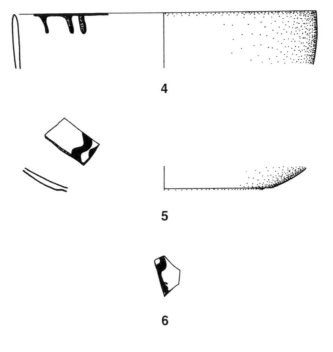

4

5

6

Phase 1/2

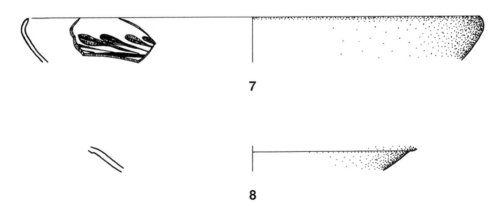

7

8

Type E2a16b (phase 2b)

9

Phase 2b

0   5 cm

FIG. 18.3   Painted Nabataean fine ware bowls.

Type E1b10 (phase 3a/3b)

10.   Locus 19, outside northmost door to Forecourt,
       Unit 4A-09
       Rim sherd, Nabataean painted, type E1b10
       (phase 3a/3b)
       ware: 5YR 6.5/6 reddish yellow
       inner and outer surfaces: 5YR 6.5/6 reddish
       yellow
       paint: 2.5YR 4/6 dark red
       parallels: Schmid 2000: figs. 89–90.

Phase 3b

11.   Locus 14A, "ditch", Unit 4A-17
       Body sherd, Nabataean painted (phase 3b)
       ware: 7.5YR 3.5/1 very dark grey
       inner surface: 5YR 6/7 reddish yellow
       outer surface: 5YR 6.5/8 reddish yellow
       paint: 5YR 3/3 dark reddish brown.

Type E1b10 (phase 3b)

12.   Locus 14A, "ditch", Unit 4A-17
       Rim sherd, Nabataean painted, type E1b10
       (phase 3b)
       ware: 5YR 5.5/6 reddish yellow–yellowish red
       inner and outer surfaces: 5YR 5.5/6 reddish
       yellow–yellowish red
       paint: 7.5YR 2.75/2 very dark brown
       parallels: Schmid 2000: figs. 90–91.

13.   Provenience unknown, Unit A-18
       Rim sherd, Nabataean painted, type E1b10
       (phase 3b)
       ware: 5YR 7/6 reddish yellow
       inner surface: 5YR 6/6 reddish yellow
       outer surface: 5YR 6.5/7 reddish yellow
       paint: 5YR dark reddish brown
       parallels: Schmid 2000: fig. 91.

14.   Provenience unknown, Unit A-18
       Rim sherd, Nabataean painted, type E1b10
       (phase 3b)
       ware: 5YR 7/6 reddish yellow
       inner and outer surfaces: 5YR 6/6 reddish
       yellow
       paint: 5YR 3/1 very dark grey
       parallels: Schmid 2000: fig. 91.

Type E1b10 (phase 3c)

15.   Locus 14A, "ditch", Unit 4A-17
       Rim sherd, Nabataean painted, type E1b10
       (phase 3c)
       ware: 7.5YR 6.5/6 reddish yellow
       inner and outer surfaces: 5YR/7.5YR 6/6 red-
       dish yellow
       paint: 2.5YR 3/4 dusky red
       parallels: Schmid 2000: figs. 92–93.

16.   Locus 14A, "ditch", Unit 4A-19 (Vol. 1, fig. 404a
       right)
       Rim sherds, Nabataean painted, type E1b10
       (phase 3c)
       ware: 10YR 5/2 greyish brown
       inner and outer surfaces: 5YR 5/6 yellowish red
       paint: 7.5YR 3/1 very dark grey
       parallels: Schmid 2000: fig. 93.

PAINTED NABATAEAN FINE WARE BOWLS

Fig. 18.3

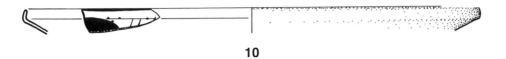

10

Type E1b10 (phase 3a/3b)

11

Phase 3b

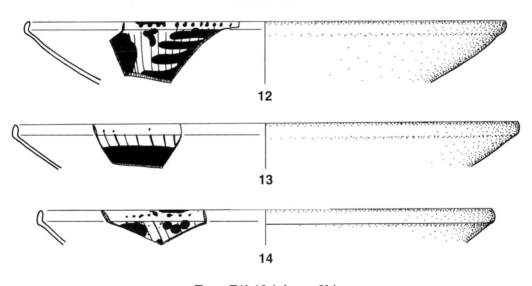

12

13

14

Type E1b10 (phase 3b)

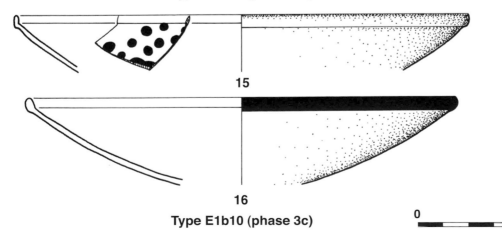

15

16

Type E1b10 (phase 3c)

0   5 cm

Fig. 18.4   Painted Nabataean fine ware bowls.

Type E1b10 (phase 3c)

17.   Debris, Unit 48-07
   Rim sherd, Nabataean painted, type E1b10 (phase 3c)
   ware: 2.5YR 5/6 red
   inner surface: 2.5YR 6/6–6/8 light red
   outer surface: 2.5YR 6/8 light red
   paint: 2.5YR 3.5/4 dark reddish brown.

18.   Provenience unknown, Unit A-18
   Base fragment, Nabataean painted, type E1b10 (phase 3c)
   ware: 2.5YR 4/0 dark grey
   inner surface: 2.5YR 6/6 light red
   outer surface: 2.5YR 6/6–6/8 reddish brown
   paint: 2.5YR 3/4 dark reddish brown.

19.   Locus 14A, "ditch", Unit 4A-19 (Vol. 1, fig. 404a middle)
   Rim sherd, Nabataean painted, type E1b10 (phase 3c)
   ware: 2.5YR 5.5/6 red
   inner surface: 2.5YR 6/8 light red
   outer surface: 2.5YR 5.6/8 red
   paint: 2.5YR 3.5/4 dark reddish brown.

Type E1b170 (phase 3c)

20.   Debris, Unit 48-01
   Rim sherd, Nabataean painted, type E1b170 (phase 3c)
   ware: 2.5YR 5/6 red
   inner surface: 2.5YR 6/6 light red
   outer surface: 5YR 7/6 reddish yellow
   paint: 2.5YR 3.5/4 dark reddish brown.

PAINTED NABATAEAN FINE WARE BOWLS

Fig. 18.4

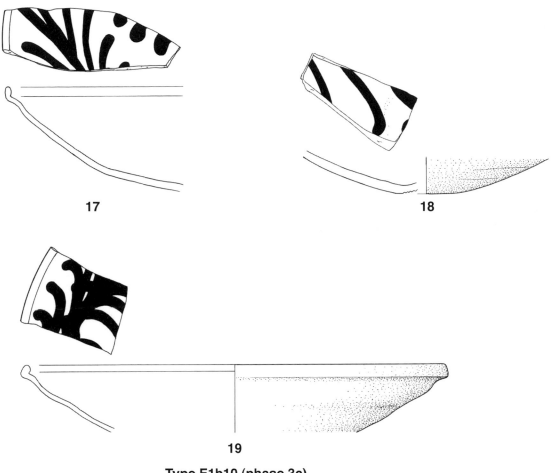

17

18

19

Type E1b10 (phase 3c)

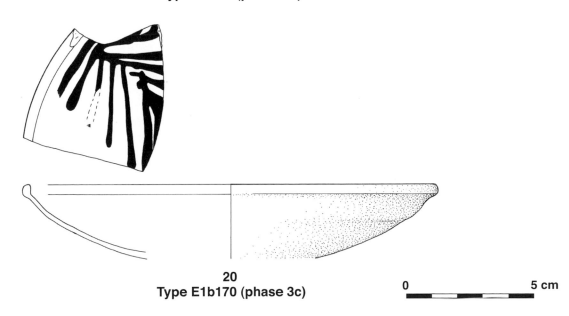

20
Type E1b170 (phase 3c)

0   5 cm

FIG. 18.5   Painted Nabataean fine ware bowls.

Type E1b170 (phase 3c)

21.   Provenience unknown, GP 34, GA drawing; JAM J1471
       More than half of a Nabataean painted bowl, type E1b170 (phase 3c).

22.   Provenience unknown, Unit A-13
       Rim sherd, Nabataean painted, type E1b170 (phase 3c)
       ware: 2.5YR 6/6 light red
       inner surface: 2.5YR 6/6–5/6 light red
       outer surface: 2.5YR 6/6 light red.

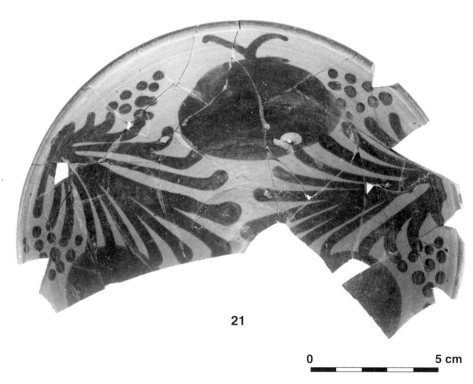

21

0   5 cm

FIG. 18.5*

PAINTED NABATAEAN FINE WARE BOWLS

Fig. 18.5

21

22

Type E1b170 (phase 3c)

0   5 cm

Fig. 18.6   Painted Nabataean fine ware bowls.

Type E1b170 (phase 3c)

23.   Provenience unknown, no number; whereabouts unknown May 2010
      Rim and body sherds, Nabataean painted, type E1b170 (phase 3c).

24.   Locus 19, outside northmost door to Forecourt, GP 08; CAM 1939.245
      (exact dimensions unknown)
      Rim and body sherds, Nabataean painted, type E1b170 (phase 3c).

PAINTED NABATAEAN FINE WARE BOWLS   Fig. 18.6

0 ▬▬▬▬▬▬ 5 cm

23

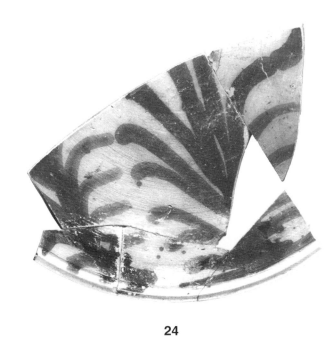

24

Type E1b170 (phase 3c)

Fig. 18.7   Painted Nabataean fine ware bowls.

Type E1b176 (phase 3c/4)

25.   Locus 16, Room 9, Unit A-11
       Rim sherd, Nabataean painted, type E1b176 (phase 3c/4)
       ware: 2.5YR 5/6 red
       inner surface: 2.5YR 6/6–6/8 light red
       outer surface: 2.5YR 6/6 light red
       paint: 2.5YR 4/4 reddish brown.

Type E1b175–177 (phase 4)

26.   Locus 19, outside northmost door to Forecourt, no number, GA drawing; JAM J1472
       Rim and body sherds, Nabataean painted, type E1b175–177 (phase 4).

PAINTED NABATAEAN FINE WARE BOWLS

FIG. 18.7

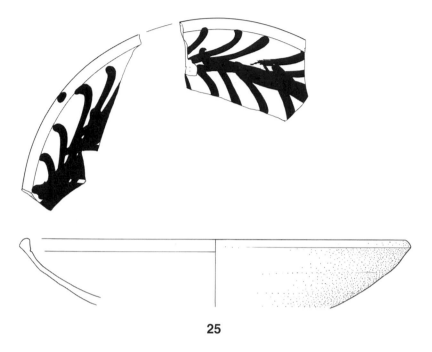

25

Type Eb176 (phase 3c/4)

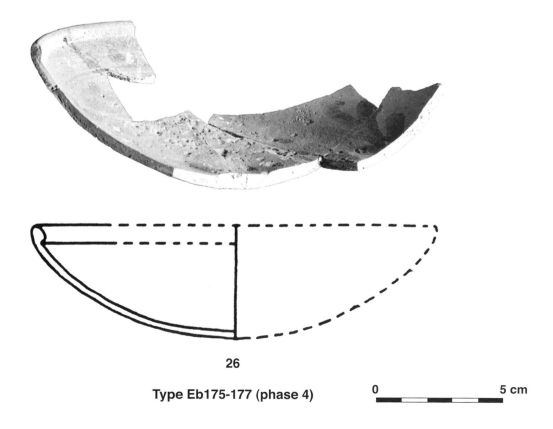

26

Type Eb175-177 (phase 4)

0 _____ 5 cm

Fig. 18.8   Nabataean fine ware.

Painted goblets, versions of type F2c (phase 3c)

27.   Locus 21, Room 14, Unit 47-12A
      Rim sherd with handle, Nabataean painted, type F2c64, F2c247, F2c248 (phase 3c)
      ware: 2.5YR 6/8 red
      inner and outer surfaces: 2.5YR 5/7 red
      paint: 7.5YR 3/1 very dark grey
      parallels: Schmid 2000: figs. 212–14.

28.   Debris, Unit 48-14
      Rim sherd, Nabataean painted, type F2c248 (phase 3c)
      ware: 2.5YR 4/0 dark grey
      inner surface: 2.5YR 6/6–6/8 light red
      outer surface: 2.5YR 5/6 red
      paint: 2.5YR 3.5/4 dark reddish brown.

Goblet

29.   Locus 21, Room 14, Unit 47-01G
      Base fragment, Nabataean fine ware
      ware: 5Y 4.5/1 dark grey
      inner surface: 5YR 6/6 reddish yellow
      outer surface: 7.5YR 5/2.5 brown.

Lid

30.   Locus 8, Forecourt, Unit 4A-21
      Rim sherd, Nabataean fine ware, lid
      ware: 10R 6/8 red
      inner surface: 10R 5/6 red
      outer surface: 2.5YR 6/6 light red.

Unguentarium

31.   Locus 21, Room 14, Unit 47-01G
      Body sherd, Nabataean fine ware, unguentarium
      ware: 5YR 6/7 reddish yellow
      inner and outer surfaces: 5YR 6/7 reddish yellow
      parallels: Schmid 2000: figs. 317–19.

NABATAEAN FINE WARE

Fig. 18.8

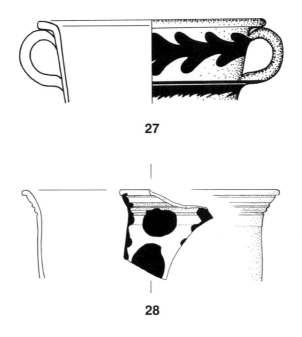

27

28

Painted goblets, versions of type F2c (phase 3c)

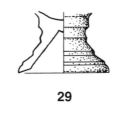

29

Goblet

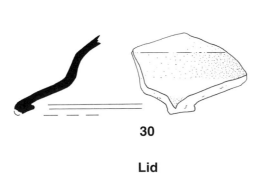

30

Lid

31

Unguentarium

0   5 cm

Fig. 18.9   Beakers and cups.

Type F5a

32. Locus 8, Forecourt, Unit 4A-21
     Rim sherd, Nabataean fine ware, type F5a
     ware: 10YR 5/2 greyish brown
     inner and outer surfaces: 5YR 6/6 reddish yellow
     parallels: Schmid 2000: figs. 224–25.

33. Locus 8, Forecourt, Unit 4A-21
     Rim sherd, fine ware, closed form, type F5a
     ware: 5YR 7/6 reddish yellow
     inner surface: 5YR 7/6 reddish yellow
     outer surface: 5YR 7/4 pink.

34. Locus 21, Room 14, Unit 47-11A
     Rim and body sherd, Nabataean plain ware, type F5a
     ware: 5YR 5/6 yellowish red
     inner surface: 10YR 6.5/3 very pale brown
     outer surface: 10YR–2.5Y 8/2 very pale brown–pale yellow.

35. Provenience unknown, Unit A-13
     Rim sherd, red ware, cup, type F5a
     ware: 5YR 6/4 light reddish brown
     inner surface: 2.5 6/6 light red
     dark rim: 2.5YR 2.5/0 black
     outer surface: 5YR 7/6 reddish yellow
     dark rim: 5YR 4/1 dark grey.

Type F5, late derivation

36. Locus 17, Room 10, Unit A-02
     Rim sherd, fine ware, open form, similar to type F5, late derivation
     ware: 2.5YR 5.5/8 light red
     inner surface: 10R 5/6 red
     outer surface: 2.5YR 5.5/6 light red.

BEAKERS AND CUPS Fig. 18.9

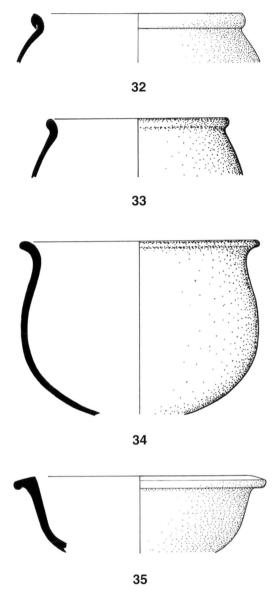

32

33

34

35

Type F5a

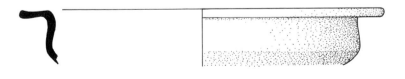

36

Type F5, late derivation

0   5 cm

FIG. 18.10   Plain Nabataean bowls.

Type E1a12

37. Provenience unknown, Unit A-13
     Rim sherd, fine ware, type E1a12
     ware: 5YR 7/6 reddish yellow
     inner surface: 5YR 7/4–7/6 pink / reddish yellow
     outer surface: 10YR 8/4 very pale brown.

38. Debris, Unit 48-09
     Rim sherd, fine ware, type E1a12
     ware: 2.5YR 5/2 weak red
     inner surface: 10YR 6/3 pale brown
     outer surface: 7.5YR 6/4 light brown
     slip below rim: 5YR 5.5/2 reddish grey.

Type E1c7

39. Locus 14A, "ditch", Unit 4A-19
     Rim sherd, Nabataean plain, type E1c7 (phase 3)
     ware: 2.5YR 5.5/6 red
     inner and outer surfaces: 5YR 5/6 yellowish red
     parallels: Schmid 2000: figs. 54–56.

Type E1c8 and derivations

40. Locus 14A, "ditch", Unit 4A-17
     Rim sherd, Nabataean plain, type E1c8 (phase 3)
     ware: 7.5YR 6/5 light brown-reddish yellow
     inner and outer surfaces: 7.5YR 6/5 light brown-reddish yellow
     parallels: Schmid 2000: figs. 52–53.

41. Locus 17, Room 10, Unit A-09
     Rim and body sherd, Nabataean plain, type E1c8 (phase 3)
     ware: 7.5YR 4.5/1 dark grey
     inner and outer surfaces: 7.5YR 5.5/4 light brown
     parallels: Schmid 2000: figs. 52–53.

42. Locus 17, Room 10, no number; whereabouts unknown 2010
     Rim sherd, fine ware, type E1c8, late derivation.

PLAIN NABATAEAN BOWLS

FIG. 18.10

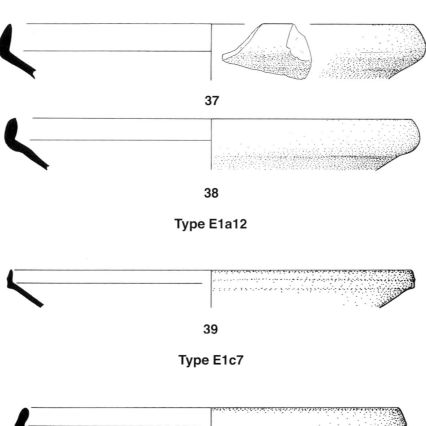

37

38

Type E1a12

39

Type E1c7

40

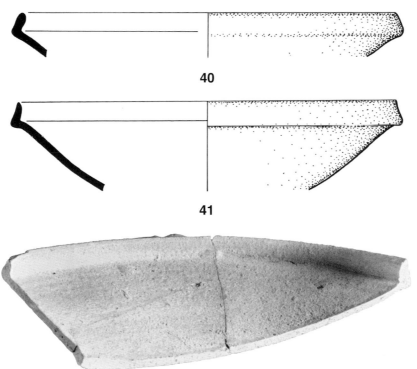

41

42

Type E1c8 and derivations

0   5 cm

FIG. 18.11   Fine ware bowls.

Type E2e/f

43. Provenience unknown, Unit A-13
     Rim sherd, fine ware, open form, type E2e/f (phase 1/2a)
     ware: 2.5YR 6/8 light red
     inner and outer surfaces: 5YR 7/6 reddish yellow.

44. Debris, Unit 48-08
     Rim sherd, fine ware, open form, type E2e/f
     ware: 7.5YR 7/4 pink
     inner and outer surfaces: 5YR 7/6–7/8 reddish yellow.

45. Debris, Unit 48-08
     Rim sherd, fine ware, open form, type E2e/f
     ware: 2.5YR 6/6 light red
     inner surface: 2.5YR 6/8 light red
     outer surface: 2.5YR 5/6 red.

46. Provenience unknown, Unit A-17
     Rim sherd, fine ware, open form, type E2e/f
     ware: 2.5YR 5/6 red
     inner surface: 2.5YR 6/6 light red
     outer surface: 7.5YR 7/4 pink.

Type E3b188

47. Locus 21, Room 14, GR 94; CAM 1939.244
     Complete Nabataean bowl, type E3b188.

FINE WARE BOWLS   FIG. 18.11

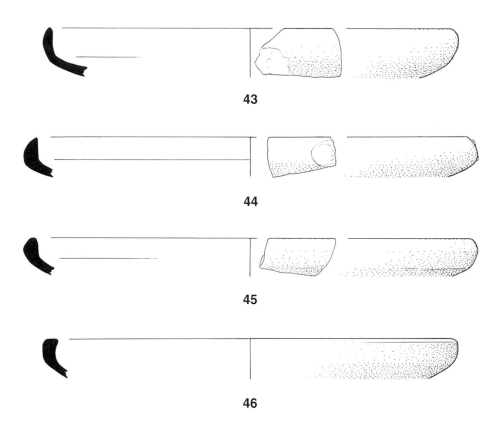

43

44

45

46

Type E2e/f

47

Type E3b188

0   5 cm

FIG. 18.12   **Fine ware bowls, with rouletted decoration.**

Type E8a and derivations

48.   Debris, Unit 47-13L
Rim sherd, fine ware, open form, with rouletted decoration, type E8a-derivation
ware: 2.5YR 6/6 light red
inner surface: 2.5YR 6/8 light red
outer surface: 2.5YR 5/6 light red.

49.   Provenience unclear, Unit 47-13K
Rim sherd, fine ware, open form, with rouletted decoration, type E8a
ware: 2.5YR 6/6 light red
inner surface: 2.5YR 5/4 reddish brown
outer surface: 2.5YR 6/4 light reddish brown.

50.   Provenience unknown, Unit A-13
Rim sherd, fine ware, open form, with rouletted decoration, type E8a-derivation
ware: 2.5YR 6/8 light red
inner surface: 5YR 7/4 pink
outer surface: 2.5YR 5/6 red.

51.   Provenience unclear, Unit A-15
Rim sherd, fine ware, open form, with rouletted decoration, type E8a-derivation
ware: 2.5YR 6/4 light red
inner surface: 2.5YR 6/8 light red
outer surface: 2.5YR 6/6 light red.

52.   Provenience unknown, Unit A-13
Rim sherd, fine ware, open form, with rouletted decoration, type E8a-derivation
ware: 2.5YR 6/6 light red
inner surface: 2.5YR 6.6 light red
outer surface: 5YR 7/4 pink.

FINE WARE BOWLS, WITH ROULETTED DECORATION Fig. 18.12

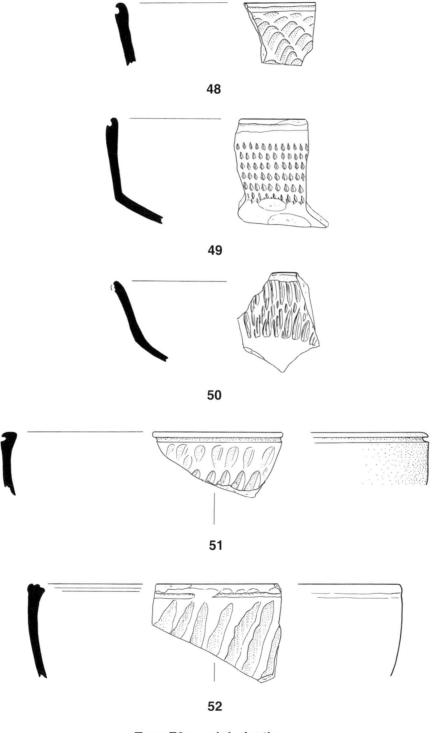

48

49

50

51

52

Type E8a and derivations

0   5 cm

Fig. 18.13 Bowls, with rouletted decoration.

53. Provenience unclear, Unit 47-05G
    Rim sherd, coarse ware, open form, with rouletted decoration, similar to type E22e238
    ware: 2.5YR 5/8 red
    inner surface: 10R 4/8 red
    outer surface: 2.5YR 5/6 red.

54. Locus 21, Room 14, Unit 47-13D
    Body sherd, Nabataean, open form, with rouletted decoration
    ware: 2.5YR 6/8 light red
    inner surface: 2.5YR 5/6 red
    outer surface: 2.5YR 5/8 red.

55. Provenience unclear, Unit 47-05D
    Base sherd, coarse ware, open form, with rouletted decoration
    ware: 2.5YR 6/6 light red
    inner and outer surfaces: 2.5YR 6/6 light red.

56. Locus 13, inside north wall of Forecourt, Unit 47-13C
    Rim sherd, Nabataean fine ware, with rouletted decoration
    ware: 10R 6/6 light red
    inner surface: 10R 5/6 red
    outer surface: 10R 6/6 light red.

BOWLS, WITH ROULETTED DECORATION

Fig. 18.13

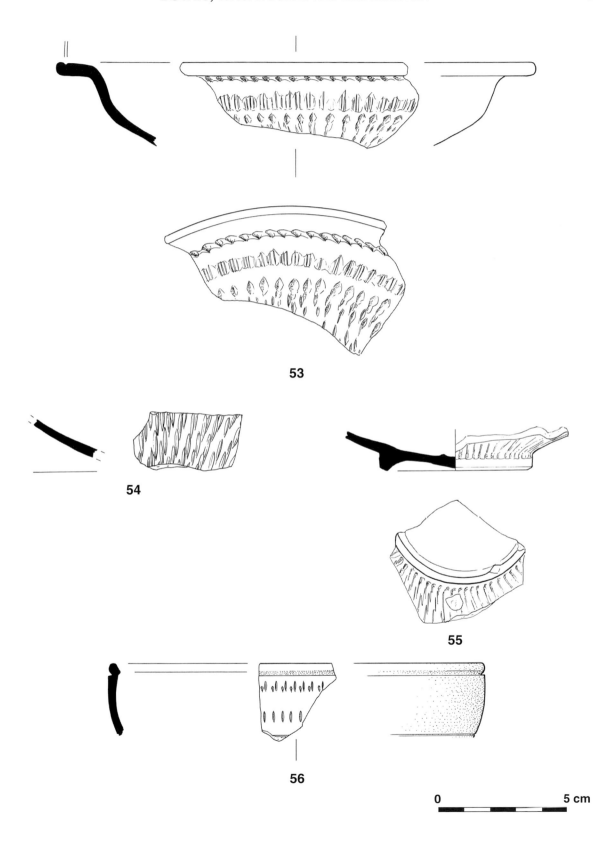

53

54

55

56

0   5 cm

Fig. 18.14   Fine and semi-fine ware bowls.

Type E8a and derivations

57. Provenience unknown, Unit A-17
     Rim sherd, fine ware, open form, type E8a-derivation
     ware: 2.5YR 6/8 light red
     inner surface: 2.5YR 6/8 light red
     outer surface: 10R 5/6 red.

58. Debris, Unit 47-01J
     Rim sherd, fine ware, open form, type E8a-derivation
     ware: 2.5YR 5/6 red (dark core)
     inner surface: 2.5YR 6/8 light red
     outer surface: 2.5YR 5/6 red.

59. Provenience unknown, Unit A-17
     Rim sherd, fine ware, open form, type E8a-derivation
     ware: 10R 5/6 red
     inner surface: 2.5YR 6/8 light red
     outer surface: 10R 5/4 weak red.

60. Locus 21, Room 14, Unit 47-20C
     Rim sherd, semi-fine ware, open form, type E8a-derivation
     ware: 5YR 7/4 pink
     inner surface: 5YR 7/6 reddish yellow
     outer surface: 5YR 8/4 pink.

61. Locus 17, Room 10, Unit A-02
     Rim sherd, fine ware, open form, similar to type E8a, degenerated
     ware: 2.5YR 6/8 light red
     inner surface: 2.5YR 6/6 light red
     outer surface: 2.5YR 6/4 light red.

FINE AND SEMI-FINE WARE BOWLS

Fig. 18.14

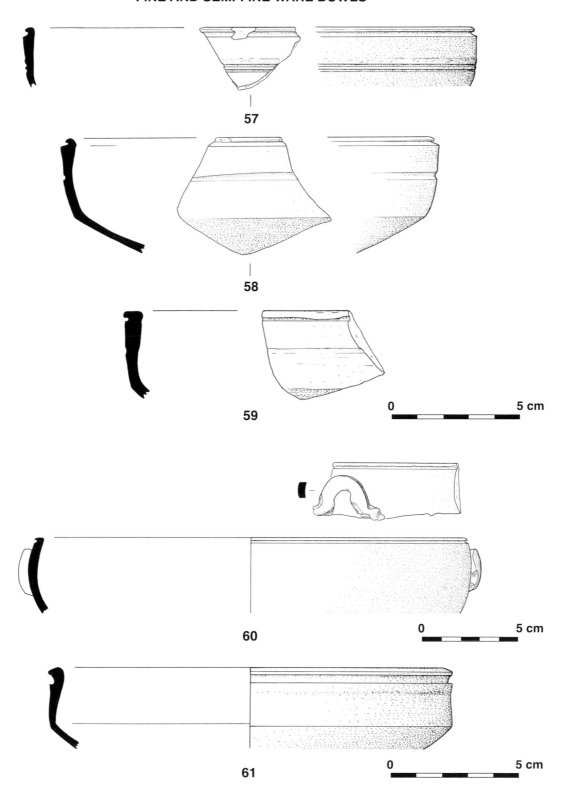

Type E8a and derivations

Fig. 18.15   **Miscellaneous open forms.**

Type E10a136

62.   Locus 21, Room 14, Unit 47-13D
      Rim sherd, fine ware, open form, type E10a136
      ware: 5YR 5/4 reddish brown
      inner surface: 5YR 6/6 yellowish red
      outer surface: 5YR 6/4–6/6 light reddish brown.

Type E11a-derivation

63.   Provenience unknown, Unit A-13
      Rim sherd, fine ware, open form, type E11a-derivation
      ware: 2.5YR 5.5/8 red
      inner surface: 2.5YR 6/8 light red
      outer surface: 2.5YR 6/6 light red.

Type E13b-derivations

64.   Provenience unknown, Unit A-17
      Rim sherd, fine ware, open form, type E13b-derivation
      ware: 2.5YR 6/8 light red
      inner surface: 2.5YR 5.5/6 light red
      outer surface: 5Y 8/3 pale yellow.

65.   Locus 15, Room 8, Unit A-14
      Rim sherd, Nabataean fine ware, open plate or bowl, type E13b-derivation
      ware: 2.5YR 6/6–6/8 light red
      inner surface: 2.5YR 6/6 light red
      outer surface: 5YR 7/13 pink.

Other

66.   Locus 19, outside northmost door to Forecourt, Unit 4A-09
      Rim sherd, fine ware, open form
      ware: 2.5YR 5/6 red
      original ware: 2.5YR 3/6 dark red
      inner surface: 2.5YR 5/6 red
      outer surface: 2.5YR 6/6 light red.

67.   Locus 15, Room 8, Unit A-14
      Rim sherd, coarse ware, open form
      ware: 2.5YR 5/6 red (thin dark core)
      inner surface: 2.5YR 6/6 light red
      outer surface: 5YR 7/4 pink
      outer rim: 2.5YR 6/8 light red.

MISCELLANEOUS OPEN FORMS

FIG. 18.15

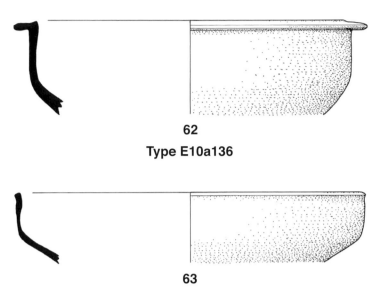

62

Type E10a136

63

Type E11a-derivation

64

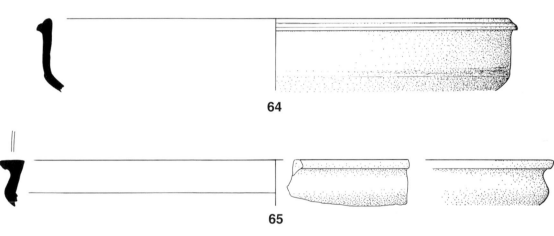

65

Type E13b-derivation

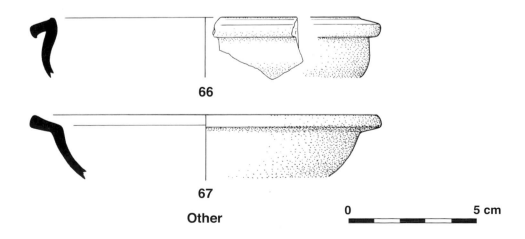

66

67

Other

0   5 cm

Fig. 18.16   African Red Slip (ARS), imitations, and red ware open forms.

African Red Slip and imitations

68. Locus 14A, "ditch", Unit 4A-19
     Body sherd, African Red Slip ware
     ware: 5YR 6/8 reddish yellow
     inner and outer surfaces: 2.5YR/5YR 6/8 reddish yellow
     parallels: related to Hayes 1972: form 50.

69. Provenience unknown, Unit A-17
     Rim sherd, fine ware, open form, African Red Slip imitation
     ware: 2.5YR 5/6 red
     inner surface: 2.5YR 5.5/8 red / light red
     outer surface: 2.5YR 6/8 light red
     parallels: similar to Hayes 1972: form 45.

Red ware

70. Locus 12, outside south wall of Room 9, Unit A-01 (Vol. 1, fig. 25b)
     Rim and body sherds, red ware, open form
     ware: 5YR 6/7 reddish yellow
     inner surface: 2.5YR 4/7 dark red
     outer surface: 5YR 6/6 reddish yellow
     parallels: Schmid 2000: figs. 22–24, 164; related to Hayes 1972: African Red Slip form 59.

71. Locus 18, outside south wall of Room 10, Unit 47-01I
     Rim sherd, red ware, open form, reminiscent of African Red Slip shapes
     ware: 2.5YR 6/8 light red
     inner surface: 2.5YR 5.6 red
     outer surface: 2.5YR 6.8 light red.

AFRICAN RED SLIP (ARS), IMITATIONS, AND RED WARE OPEN FORMS   Fig. 18.16

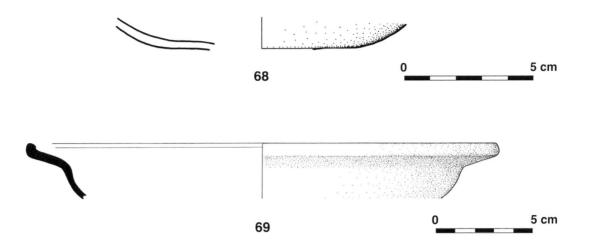

68

0   5 cm

69

0   5 cm

African Red Slip and imitations

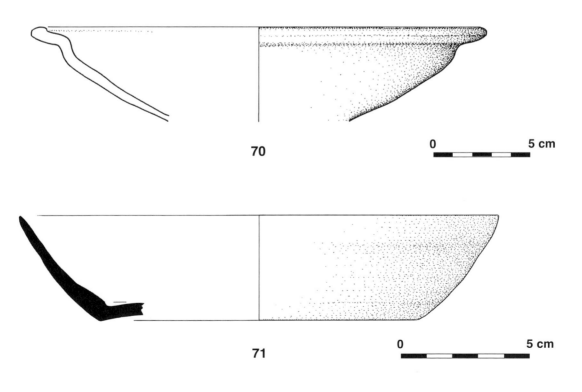

70

0   5 cm

71

0   5 cm

Red ware

FIG. 18.17   Casseroles.

72.   Provenience unknown, GP 02; JAM J3291
      Nearly complete, coarse ware, casserole, with thumb impressed ledge handles.

73.   Provenience unclear, Unit 47-06B
      Rim sherd with handle, semi-fine ware, casserole
      ware: 2.5YR 6/8 light red
      inner surface: 2.5YR 6/6 light red
      outer surface: 2.5Y 7/4 pale yellow.

72   0   5 cm

FIG. 18.17*

CASSEROLES   Fig. 18.17

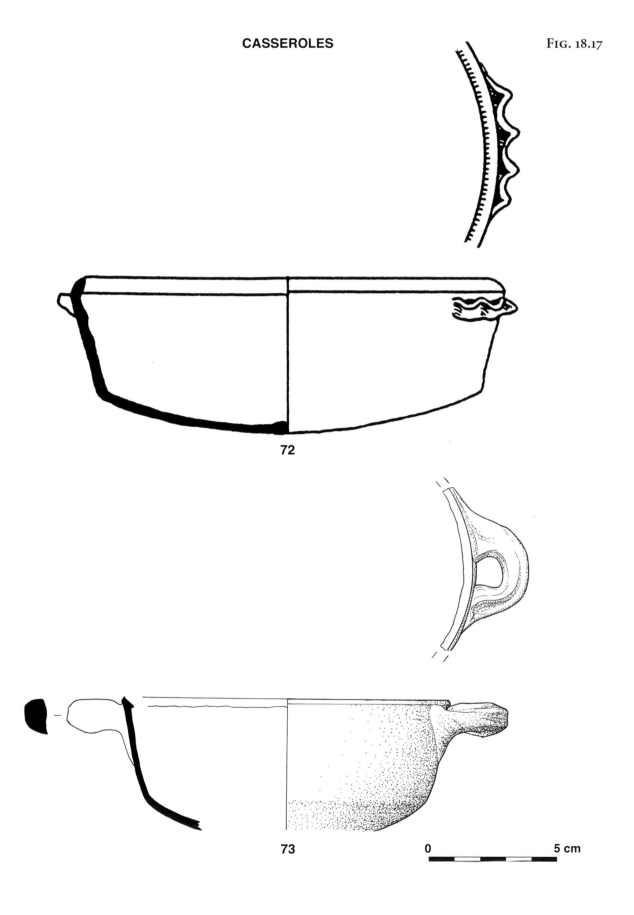

72

73   0   5 cm

FIG. 18.18   Fine ware jugs.

Eastern Sigillata A (ESA)

74.   Locus 21, Room 14, Unit 47-01G
Rim and body fragment, jug, ESA
ware: 7.5YR 7.5/4 pink
inner and outer surfaces: 2.5YR 4.8 dark red.

75.   Locus 19, outside northmost door to
Forecourt, Unit 4A-09
Rim sherd, fine ware, jug, ESA
ware: 5YR 8/4 pink
rim: 2.5YR 4/8 red
inner surface: 5YR 8/4 pink
outer surface: 2.5YR 4/8 red.

Nabataean

76.   Locus 21, Room 14, Unit 47-12A
Body sherd, Nabataean fine ware, closed
form, with rouletted decoration
ware: 5Y 4.5/1 dark grey
inner surface: 7.5YR 5.5/4 light brown
outer surface: 2.5/5YR 6/8 reddish yellow
parallels: Schmid 2000: fig. 371.

77.   Locus 21, Room 14, Unit 47-01G
Body fragment, Nabataean fine ware,
closed form, with rouletted decoration
ware: 5Y 4.5/1 dark grey
inner surface: 7.5YR 5.5/4 light brown
outer surface: 2.5/5YR 6/8 reddish yellow
parallels: Schmid 2000: fig. 371.

78.   Locus 21, Room 14, Unit 47-01G
Large handle, Nabataean fine ware, jug
ware: 2.5Y 6/1.5 light brownish grey
inner and outer surfaces: 5YR 6/8
reddish yellow.

79.   Locus 21, Room 14, Unit 47-01G
Rim sherd with part of handle, Nabataean
semi-fine ware, jug
ware: 2.5Y 6/1.5 light brownish grey
inner and outer surfaces: 5YR 5/7 yellowish red.

80.   Locus 21, Room 14, Unit 47-01G
Rim fragment, Nabataean fine ware, jug
ware: 5YR 7/7 reddish yellow
inner surface: 5YR 5/7 yellowish red
outer surface: 5YR 5/7 yellowish red, traces of
whitish slip
parallels: Schmid 2000: figs. 330, 351.

Type G15b

81.   Locus 20, Room 13, Unit 47-05F
Rim sherd with handle, fine ware, juglet, type
G15b
ware: 10R 5/6 red
inner surface: 2.5YR 5/4 reddish brown
outer surface: 2.5YR 5/6 red.

82.   Debris, Unit 47-05H
Near rim sherd, fine ware, closed form, type
G15b
ware: 2.5YR 6/6 light red
inner surface: 2.5YR 6/8 light red
outer surface: 5YR 4.5/2 dark reddish grey.

FINE WARE JUGS

Fig. 18.18

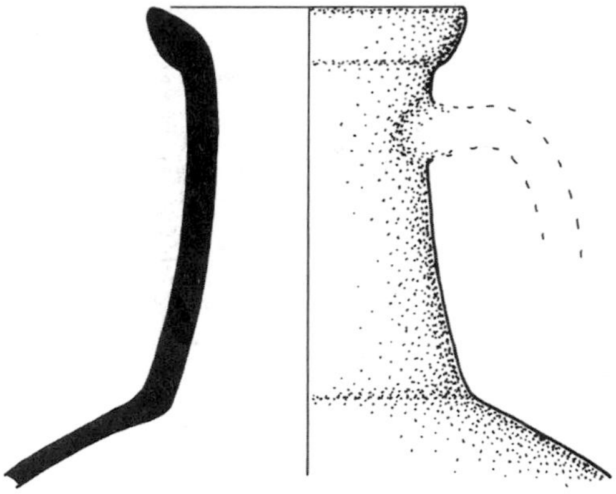

74

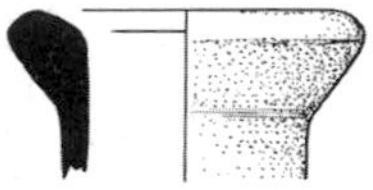

75

Eastern Sigillata A (ESA)

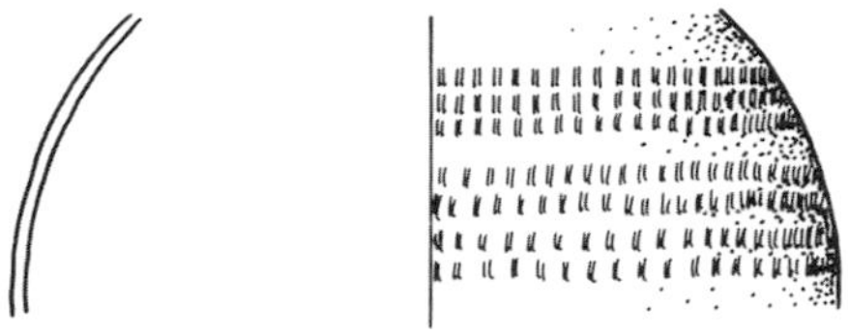

76

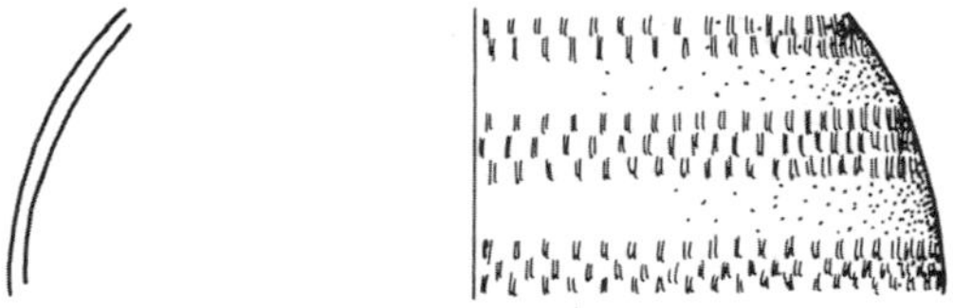

77

78

79

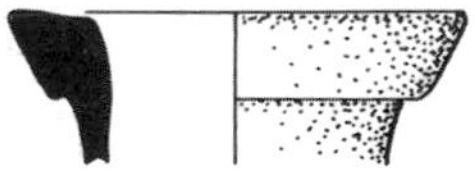

80

Nabataean

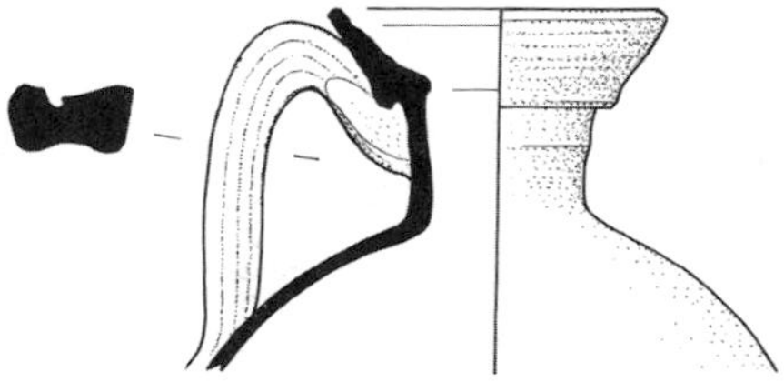

81

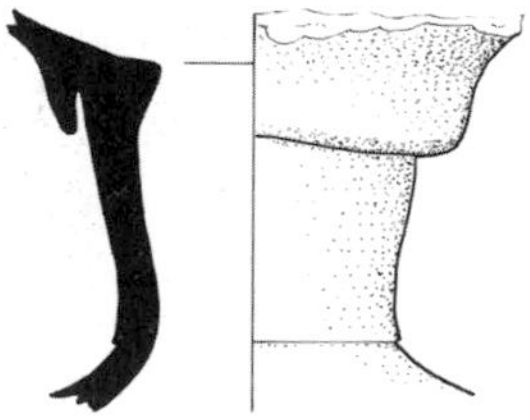

82

Type G15b

0   5 cm

FIG. 18.19   Fine ware jugs.

Type G25

83. Locus 9, south-west end of Forecourt, Unit 4A-14
Rim sherd, fine ware, jug, type G25, ? degenerate version
ware: 5YR 7/6–7/8 reddish yellow
inner surface: 5YR 7/6 reddish yellow
outer surface: 5YR 6/4–6/6 light reddish brown.

Eastern Sigillata A (ESA) or imitation

84. Locus 17, Room 10, GP 06, GA drawing; JAM J3292
Almost complete, fine ware, jug, Eastern Sigillata A (ESA) or imitation.

84   0   5 cm

FIG. 18.19*

FINE WARE JUGS

FIG. 18.19

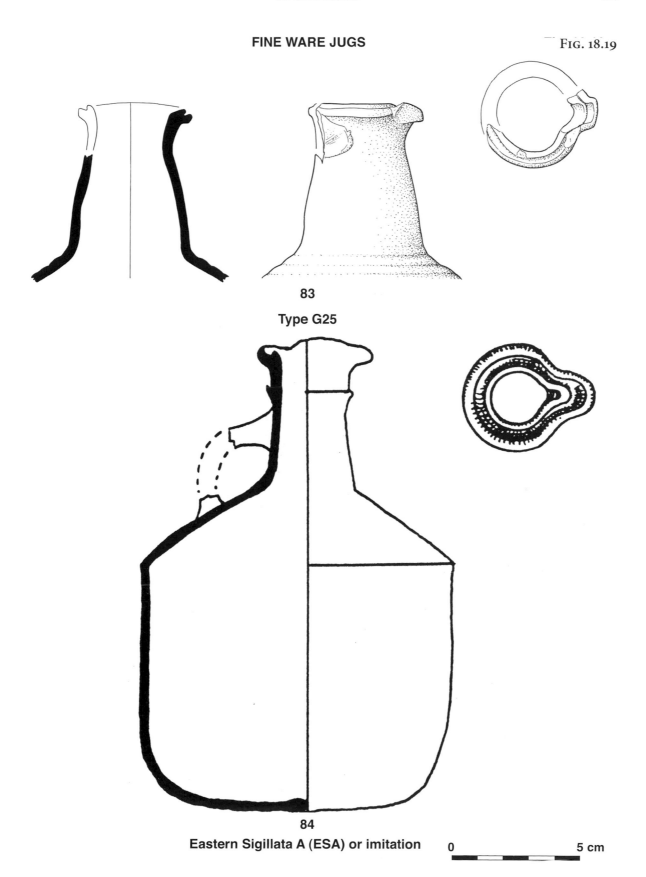

83

Type G25

84

Eastern Sigillata A (ESA) or imitation

0   5 cm

FIG. 18.20   Coarse ware juglets.

85.   Locus 21, Room 14, Unit 47-01G
    Rim sherd with part of handle, coarse ware, jug or juglet
    ware: 5YR 6.5/6 reddish yellow
    inner and outer surfaces: 10YR 8/3.5 very pale brown.

86.   Locus 19, outside northmost door to Forecourt, Unit 47-15
    Base and body fragment, coarse ware, closed form
    ware: 5YR 7/4 pink
    inner surface: 2.5YR 8/4 pale yellow
    outer surface: 5Y 8/3 pale yellow.

87.   Locus 21, Room 14, Unit 20-B03
    Base and body fragment, coarse ware, closed form
    ware: 5Y 8/2 white
    inner surface: 5Y 7/3 pale yellow
    outer surface: 5Y 8/3 pale yellow.

COARSE WARE JUGLETS

Fig. 18.20

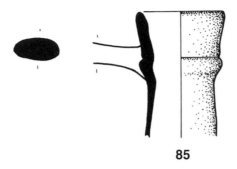

85

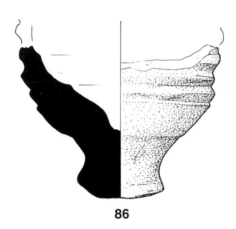

86

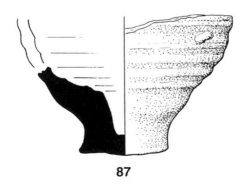

87

0   5 cm

FIG. 18.21   Coarse ware jugs.

88.   Locus 9, south-west end of Forecourt, Unit 4A-14
       Body and base sherd, coarse ware, jug
       ware: 2.5YR 5/6–5/8 red
       inner surface: 2.5YR 5/6 red
       outer surface: 10YR 8/4 very pale brown.

89.   Debris, Unit 47-01J
       Base sherd, coarse ware, jug
       ware: 2.5YR 5/6 red (thin dark core)
       inner surface: 2.5YR 5/2 weak red
       outer surface: 2.5YR 5/6 red.

Twisted handle

90.   Provenience unknown, Unit 47-13M
       Vertical handle, twisted, coarse ware, closed form
       ware: 2.5YR 5.5/6 red
       outer surface: 2.5YR 5/6 red.

COARSE WARE JUGS   FIG. 18.21

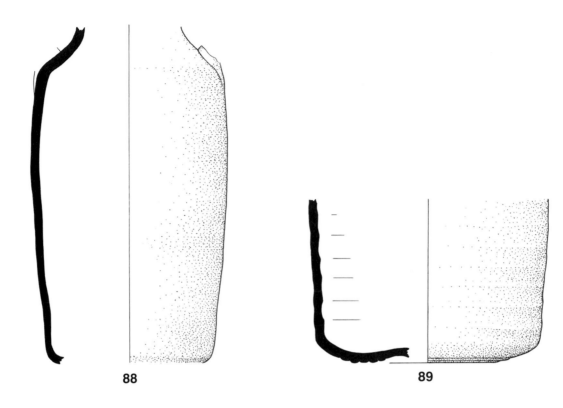

88   89

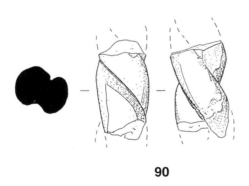

90

Twisted handle

0   5 cm

Fig. 18.22   Jugs or bottles/jars.

Type G21a/b

91. Locus 9, south-west end of Forecourt, Unit 4A-14
     Rim sherd, fine ware, jug or bottle, close to type G21a/b
     ware: 5YR 7/6 reddish yellow
     inner surface: 10YR 8/4 very pale yellow
     outer surface: 10YR 8/4–7/4 very pale yellow.

Other

92. Locus 21, Room 14, Unit 47-01G
     Rim sherd, coarse ware, jug or bottle
     ware: 5YR 7/8 reddish yellow
     inner surface: 7.5YR 8/3.5 pink
     outer surface: 7.5YR 8/3.5 pink, grey sinter, possibly from ash.

93. Locus 8, Forecourt, Unit 4A-21
     Rim sherd, coarse ware, jug or amphora
     ware: 10YR 5/1.5 greyish brown, with small mica
     inner and outer surfaces: 7.5YR/10YR 7/4 pink-very pale brown.

94. Debris, Unit 48-13
     Rim sherd, coarse ware, jar, with pie-crust edge
     ware: 2.5YR 5/6 red
     inner surface: 2.5YR 7/4 pale yellow
     outer surface: 7.5YR 7/4 pink
     on rim: 5YR 3/1 very dark grey.

JUGS OR BOTTLES / JARS

Fig. 18.22

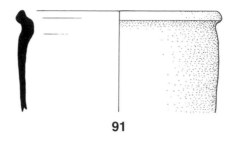

91

Type G21a/b

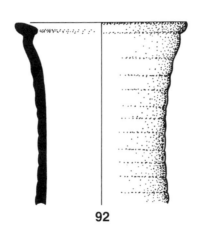

92

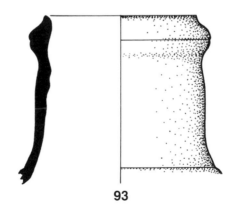

93

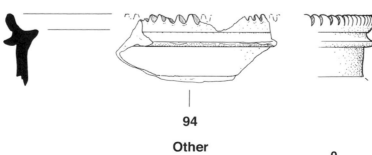

94

Other

0   5 cm

Fig. 18.23   Coarse ware jugs or jars, with incised decoration.

95.   Locus 21, Room 14, Unit 47-03
      Rim sherd, coarse ware, closed form, with incised decoration
      ware: 7.5YR 6/7 reddish yellow
      inner and outer surfaces: 7.5YR 6.5/4 pink–light brown.

96.   Locus 21, Room 14, Unit 47-03
      Rim sherd, coarse ware, closed form, with incised decoration
      ware: 5YR 5.5/6 reddish yellow–yellowish red
      inner and outer surfaces: 10YR 5/1.5 greyish brown.

COARSE WARE JUGS OR JARS, WITH INCISED DECORATION

FIG. 18.23

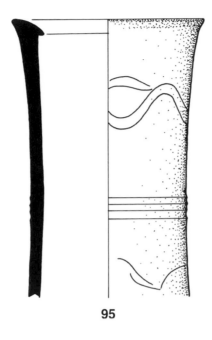

95

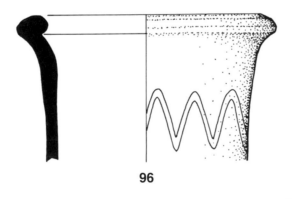

96

0   5 cm

FIG. 18.24   Green (cream) ware closed forms.

97.   Locus 21, Room 14, Unit 47-11A
      Body sherd, green ware, jug with sieving device
      ware: 2.5Y 8/3 pale yellow
      inner and outer surfaces: 2.5Y 7.5/3 pale yellow
      parallels: Schneider 1996: figs. 579–90, especially fig. 588.

98.   Locus 2, north-west corner of Inner Temenos Enclosure, Unit 4A-23
      Base sherd, green ware, closed form
      ware: 10YR 8/4 very pale yellow
      inner surface: 2.5Y 8/2 white
      outer surface: 2.5Y 8/4 pale yellow.

GREEN (CREAM) WARE CLOSED FORMS   Fig. 18.24

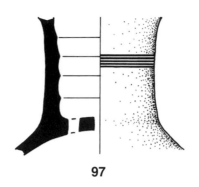

97

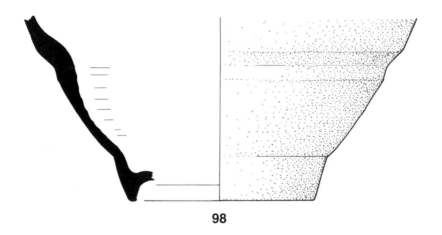

98

0 ▮▮▮▮▮ 5 cm

FIG. 18.25   Miscellaneous closed forms.

Krater

99.   Debris, Unit 47-01J
       Rim sherd, coarse ware, closed form, krater, with thumb impressed decoration
       ware: 2.5YR 6/8 light red
       inner surface: 2.5YR 6/8 light red
       outer surface: 2.5YR 6/6 light red.

Type G13a/b

100.   Provenience unknown, Unit A-17
       Rim sherd, closed form, type G13a/b
       ware: 2.5YR 6/6 light red
       inner and outer surfaces: 10R 5/6 red.

Type G26c

101.   Provenience unknown, Unit 47-01K
       Rim sherd, fine ware, small jar, type G26c, similar
       ware: 2.5YR 5.5/6 light red / red
       inner surface: 2.5YR 5/6 red
       outer surface: 2.5YR 5.5/8 red.

Nabataean plain ware

102.   Locus 14A, "ditch", Unit 4A-17
       Base sherd, Nabataean plain, closed form
       ware: 5YR 6.5/6 reddish yellow
       inner and outer surfaces: 5YR 6.5/6 reddish yellow.

? Neck

103.   Debris, Unit 47-05H
       ? neck, ?closed form
       ware: 2.5YR 6/8 light red
       inner and outer surfaces: 2.5YR 6/8 light red.

MISCELLANEOUS CLOSED FORMS

Fig. 18.25

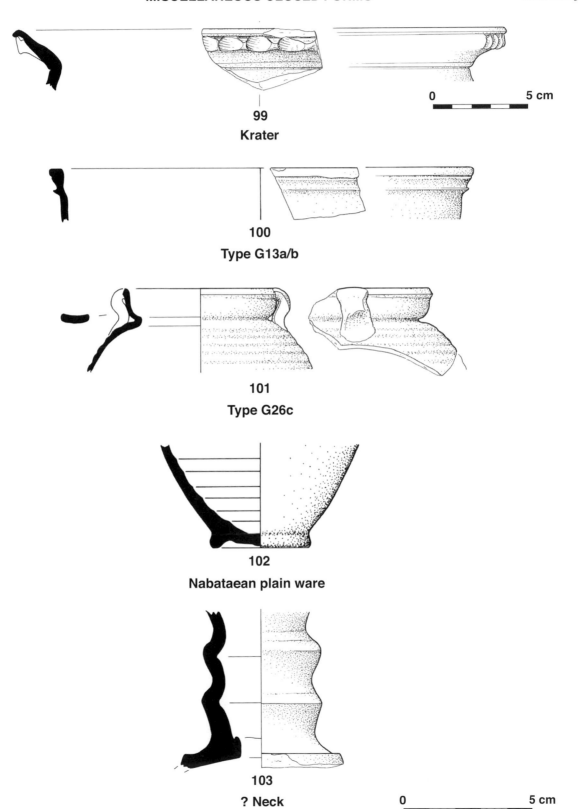

99
Krater

0   5 cm

100
Type G13a/b

101
Type G26c

102
Nabataean plain ware

103
? Neck

0   5 cm

FIG. 18.26   Cooking pots.

104. Provenience unknown, Unit 47-05I
      Rim sherd with handle, coarse ware, cooking pot
      ware: 2.5YR 5/0 grey
      inner surface: 2.5YR 5/0 grey
      outer surface: 2.5YR 4/0 dark grey.

105. Locus 17, Room 10, Unit A-02
      Rim sherd with handle, coarse ware, cooking pot
      ware: 5YR 7/6 reddish yellow
      inner surface: 5YR 6/6 reddish yellow
      outer surface: 2.5Y 6/6 light brownish grey.

106. Locus 8, Forecourt, Unit 4A-21
      Rim sherd with handle, Nabataean coarse ware, cooking pot
      ware: 7.5YR 6/6 reddish yellow, with small mica
      inner and outer surfaces: 5YR 5.5/6 reddish yellow–yellowish red.

107. Debris, Unit 48-09
      Rim sherd with handle, coarse ware, cooking pot
      ware: 2.5YR 6/6 light red
      inner surface: 5YR 7/4–7/6 pink / reddish yellow
      outer surface: 2.5YR 5/6 red.

108. Locus 8, Forecourt, Unit 4A-21
      Rim sherd, Nabataean coarse ware, cooking pot, but quite fine
      ware: 10YR 7/4 very pale brown, with small mica
      inner surface: 5YR 6/6 reddish yellow
      outer surface: 7.5YR 4/1.5 dark grey / brown.

COOKING POTS   Fig. 18.26

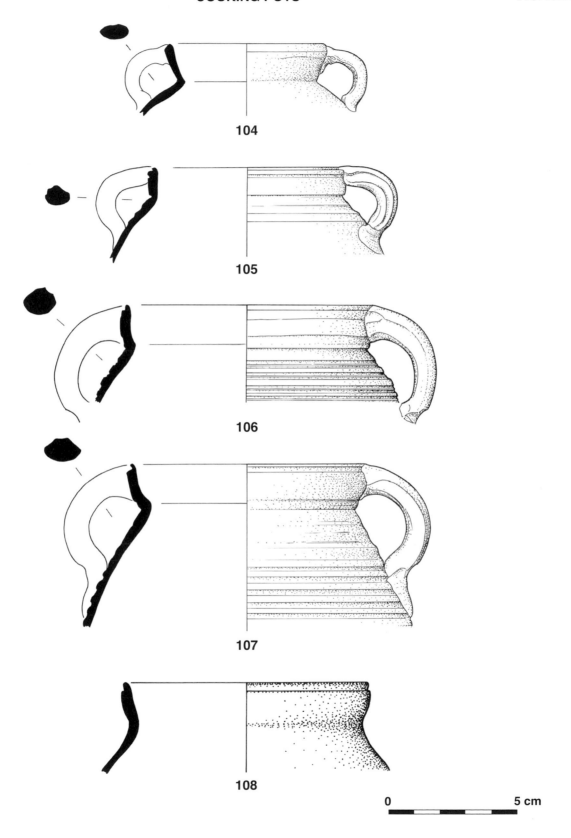

Fig. 18.27   Cooking pots.

109. Locus 21, Room 14, Unit 47-01G
     Rim sherd with part of handle, Nabataean coarse ware, cooking pot
     ware: 10YR 8/3 very pale brown
     inner surface: 10YR 7.5/3 very pale brown
     outer surface: 7.5YR 5/4 brown, grey sinter, maybe from ash.

110. Locus 20, Room 13, Unit 47-01E
     Rim sherd with handle, coarse ware, cooking pot
     ware: 2.5YR 5/8 red
     inner surface: 2.5YR 5/4 reddish brown
     outer surface: 2.5YR 5/8 red.

111. Locus 14A, "ditch", Unit 4A-19
     Rim sherd, coarse ware, cooking pot
     ware: 5YR 5.5/6 reddish yellow-yellowish red
     inner surface: 5YR 5.5/6 reddish yellow-yellowish red
     outer surface: 5YR 5.5/6 reddish yellow–yellowish red, remains of whitish slip
     parallels: Gerber 1996: fig. 32E.

112. Locus 21, Room 14, Unit 47-01G
     Rim sherd with handle, Nabataean coarse ware, cooking pot
     ware: 5YR 7/7 reddish yellow
     inner surface: 5YR 6/8 reddish yellow
     outer surface: 10YR 8/3 very pale brown, slip.

113. Locus 20, Room 13, Unit 47-05F
     Rim sherd with handle, coarse ware, cooking pot
     ware: 2.5YR 5/6 red
     inner surface: 2.5YR 8/4 pale yellow
     outer surface: 2.5YR 5.5/8 red.

COOKING POTS

FIG. 18.27

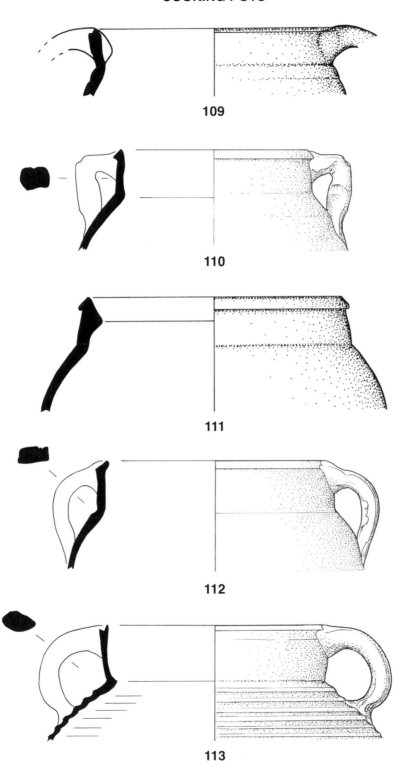

109

110

111

112

113

0   5 cm

Fig. 18.28   Cooking pots.

114.   Provenience unknown, Unit 47-13M
       Rim sherd with handle, coarse ware, cooking pot
       ware: 2.5YR 5.5/6 red
       inner surface: 2.5YR 5/8 red
       outer surface: 2.5YR 5/6 red.

115.   Locus 16, Room 9, Unit A-10
       Rim sherd with handle, coarse ware, cooking pot
       ware: 2.5YR 6/6 red
       inner surface: 5YR 7/6 reddish yellow
       outer surface: 2.5YR 5.5/6 red.

116.   Debris, Unit 47-07J
       Rim sherd with handle, coarse ware, cooking pot
       ware: 2.5YR 6/6 light red
       inner surface: 2.5YR 5.5/8 red
       outer surface: 2.5YR 5/6 red.

117.   Locus 21, Room 14, Unit 47-13D
       Rim sherd with handle, coarse ware, cooking pot
       ware: 2.5YR 6/6–6/8 light red
       inner surface: 2.5YR 5.5/6 red
       outer surface: 2.5YR 5/6 red.

118.   Locus 21, Room 14, Unit 47-07A
       Rim sherd with handle, coarse ware, cooking pot
       ware: 2.5YR 5.5/6 red
       inner surface: 2.5YR 5/6 red
       outer surface: 2.5YR 5/6–5/8 red.

COOKING POTS

Fig. 18.28

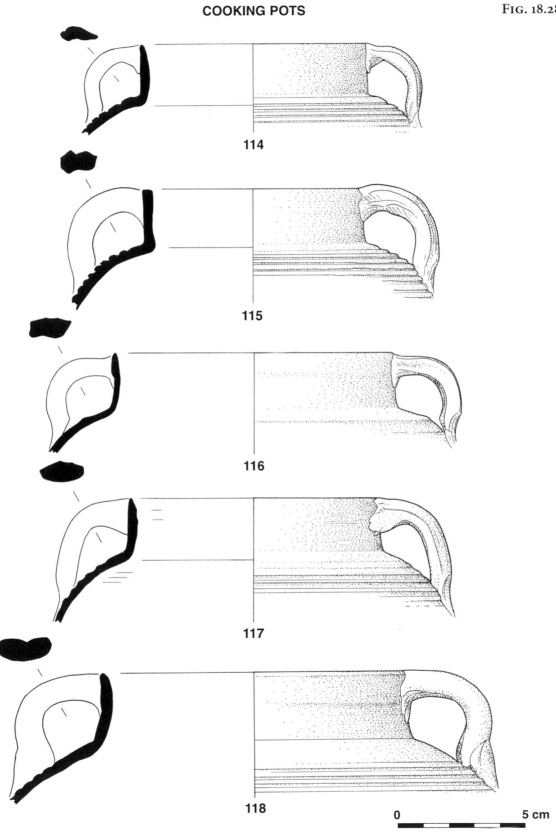

114

115

116

117

118

0   5 cm

FIG. 18.29   Cooking pots.

119. Locus 21, Room 14, Unit 47-06A (and Unit 47-06C, provenience unknown)
     Rim and body sherd with handle, coarse ware, cooking pot
     ware: 5YR 4.5/6 yellowish red
     inner surface: 5YR 5/6 yellowish red
     outer surface: 5YR 5/6 yellowish red, traces of whitish slip
     parallels: Gerber 2001: fig. 3B.

120. Locus 21, Room 14, Unit 48-16
     Rim and body sherds with handle, Nabataean coarse ware, cooking pot
     ware: 5YR 5.5/6 reddish yellow-yellowish red, with whitish mica
     inner surface: 5YR 6/6 reddish yellow
     outer surface: 5YR 6/4 reddish yellow, traces of whitish mica
     parallels: Fellmann Brogli 1996: figs. 728–30; Gerber 2001: figs. 3D–3E.

121. Locus 21, Room 14, Units 47-05A and 47-01G
     Rim and body sherd with handle, Nabataean coarse ware, cooking pot
     ware: 10YR 5/1.5 greyish brown
     inner and outer surfaces: 10YR 5/1.5 greyish brown
     parallels: Gerber 2001: fig. 2B.

COOKING POTS

FIG. 18.29

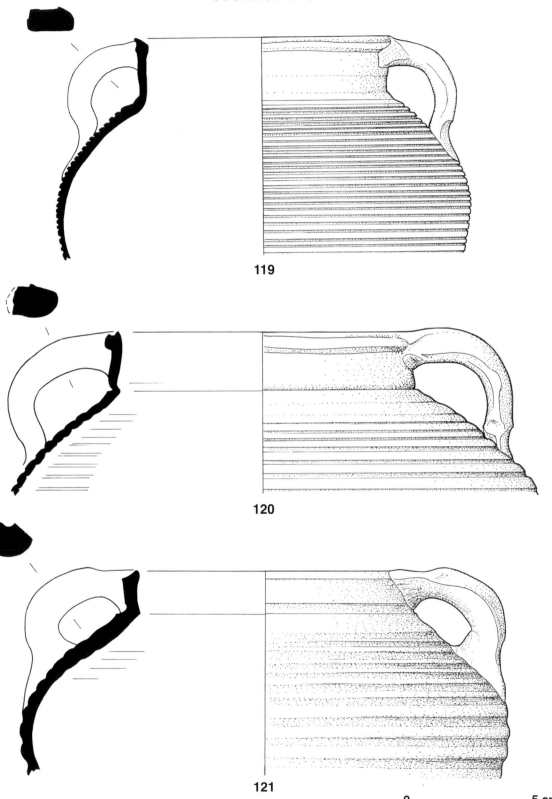

119

120

121

0   5 cm

Fig. 18.30   Cooking pots.

122. Locus 15, Room 8, Unit A-14
      Rim sherd with handle, coarse ware, cooking pot
      ware: 2.5YR 5/8 red
      inner surface: 2.5YR 6/8 light red
      outer surface: 10YR 8/4 very pale brown.

123. Debris, Unit 47-05H
      Rim sherd with handle, coarse ware, cooking pot
      ware: 2.5YR 6/8 light red
      inner surface: 2.5YR 5/6 red
      outer surface: 2.5YR 4.5/6 red.

124. Locus 19, outside northmost door to Forecourt, GR 33, GA drawing;
      whereabouts unknown 2010
      Nearly complete (base missing), coarse ware, cooking pot.

124

Fig. 18.30*

COOKING POTS Fig. 18.30

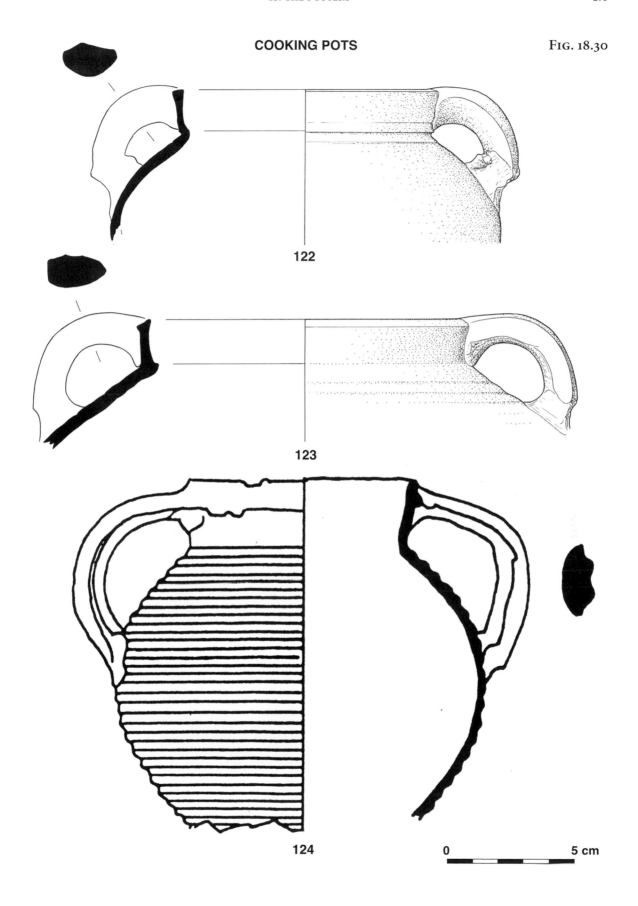

122

123

124

0   5 cm

FIG. 18.31   Cooking pots.

125. Locus 19, outside northmost door to Forecourt, GR 32, GA drawing; JAM J3298
Nearly complete, coarse ware, cooking pot.

126. Provenience unknown, GP 05, GA drawing; whereabouts unknown 2010
Nearly complete, coarse ware, cooking pot.

125

126

FIG. 18.31*

COOKING POTS

Fig. 18.31

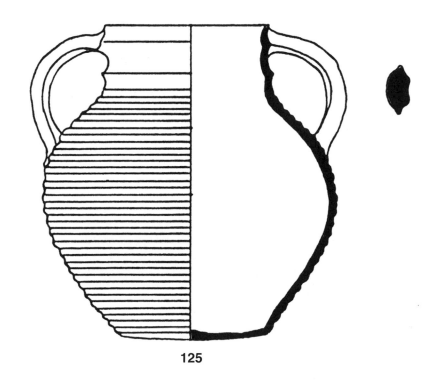

125

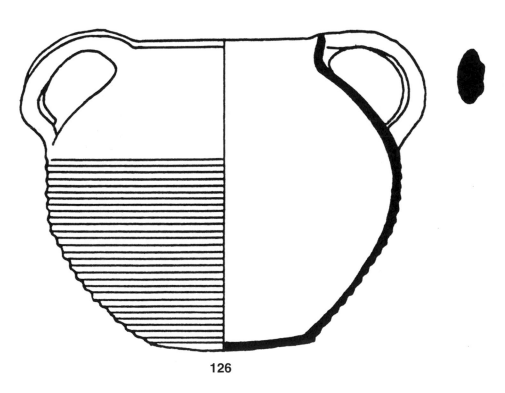

126

0   5 cm

Fig. 18.32   Cooking pots.

127.   Locus 21, Room 14, Unit 47-13D
Rim sherd, coarse ware, cooking pot, with thumb impressed decoration
ware: 10R 6/6 light red
core: 10R 5/1 reddish grey
inner surface: 2.5YR 6/2 pale red
outer surface: 10YR 6/2 weak red.

128.   Locus 21, Room 14, Unit 47-06A
Rim and body sherd, coarse ware, cooking pot
ware: 5YR 5/6 yellowish red
inner and outer surfaces: 10YR 4/1.5 dark greyish brown
parallels: Fellmann Brogli 1996: fig. 763; Gerber 2001: fig. 20.

129.   Locus 21, Room 14, Unit 47-01G
Rim sherd, coarse ware, cooking pot
ware: 5YR 6/7 reddish yellow
inner surface: 5YR 6/7 reddish yellow
outer surface: 5YR 6/7 reddish yellow, trace of whitish slip
parallels: Gerber 1996: pl. 32A.

COOKING POTS

Fig. 18.32

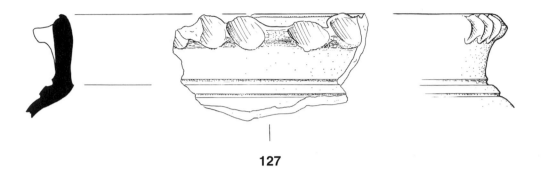

127

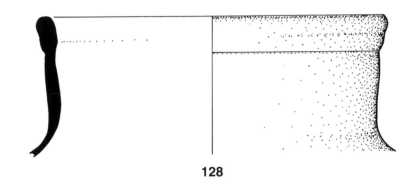

128

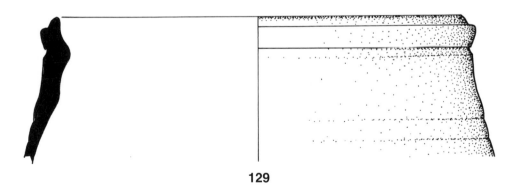

129

0   5 cm

Fig. 18.33   Painted coarse ware closed forms.

130. Locus 21, Room 14, Unit 47-13D (and Unit 47-16B, no provenience)
      Base sherds, coarse ware, closed form, with reddish paint (? or slip)
      ware: 2.5YR 5/8 red
      inner surface: 10R 5/6 red
      outer surface: 2.5YR 6/8 light red
      paint (fine hatching): 10R 4/6 red
      paint (coarse hatching): 2.5YR 6/6 light red.

131. Locus 7, inside Altar Platform, Unit 4A-24 (and Unit 47-01K, provenience unknown)
      Base sherds, coarse ware, closed form, storage / transport vessel
      ware: 2.5YR 6/6–6/8 light red
      core: 7.5YR 4.5/2 brown
      inner surface: 2.5YR 6/6–6/8 light red
      outer surface: 2.5YR 6/6 light red
      paint or slip (hatched): 2.5YR 4.5/8 red.

PAINTED COARSE WARE CLOSED FORMS Fig. 18.33

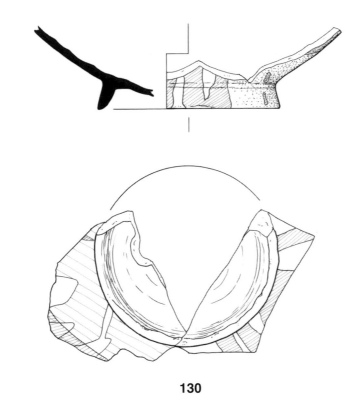

130

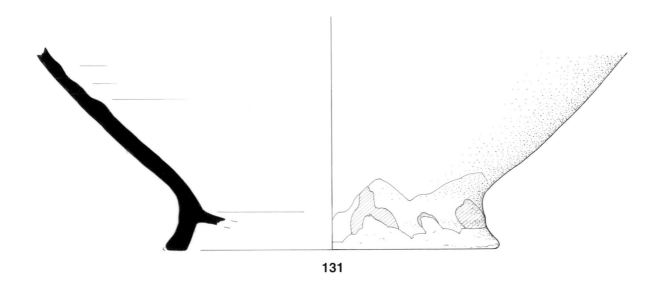

131

0   5 cm

Fig. 18.34   Huge storage vessels.

132. Provenience unknown, Unit 47-17
      Body sherd and part of handle, coarse ware, closed form, huge storage vessel
      ware: 2.5Y 8/4 pale yellow
      inner and outer surfaces: 2.5Y 8/4 pale yellow.

133. Provenience unknown, Unit A-17
      Rim sherd with part of handle, coarse ware, closed form, huge storage vessel
      ware: 2.5YR 6/8 light red
      core: 10YR 5/2 greyish brown
      inner surface: 2.5YR 6/8 light red
      outer surface: 2.5Y 8/2 white.

HUGE STORAGE VESSELS

Fig. 18.34

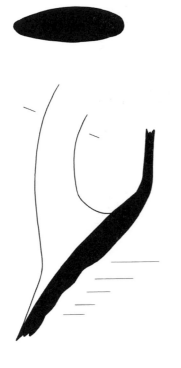

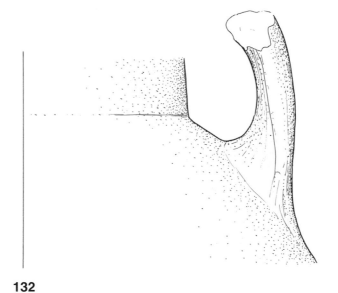

132

133

0   5 cm

FIG. 18.35   Huge storage vessels, with ribbed bodies.

134. Locus 7, inside Altar Platform, Unit 4A-24 (and Unit 47-05I, provenience unknown)
Rim sherd, coarse ware, closed form, huge storage vessel
ware: 2.5YR 6/4 reddish brown
inner surface: 2.5YR 6/4 light reddish brown
outer surface: 2.5YR 5/2 weak red.

135. Locus 15, Room 8, Unit A-14
Body sherd with horizontal handle, coarse ware, closed form, huge storage vessel
ware: 2.5YR 6/8 light red
inner surface: 2.5YR 6/8 light red
outer surface: 2.5Y 8/2 white.

HUGE STORAGE VESSELS, WITH RIBBED BODIES

Fig. 18.35

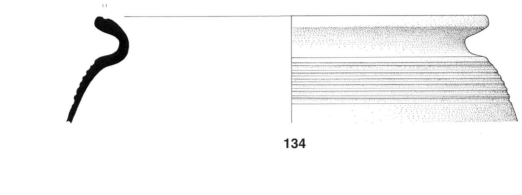

134

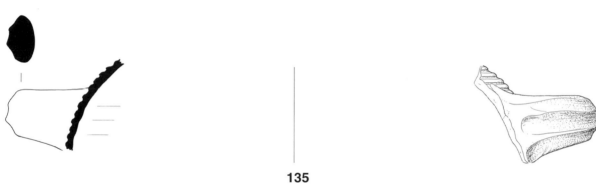

135

0   5 cm

Fig. 18.36   **Huge closed vessels, with impressed decoration.**

136. Provenience unknown, Unit 47-18
Body fragment, painted coarse ware, amphora, with thumb impressed decoration
ware: 5YR 6/6 reddish yellow
core: 10YR 4/2 dark greyish brown
inner surface: 5YR 5/3 reddish brown
outer surface: 5YR 4/1 dark grey
paint (hatched): 2.5YR 3/4 dark red.

137. Locus 20, Room 13, Unit 47-05F
Body sherd, coarse ware, closed form, with thumb impressed decoration
ware: 2.5YR 6/8 light red
inner surface: 2.5YR 6/6 light red
outer surface: 2.5YR 5/8 red.

138. Locus 21, Room 14, Unit 47-07A
Body sherd, coarse ware, closed form, huge storage vessel, with impressed decoration
ware: 7.5YR 6/2 pinkish grey
inner surface: 10YR 7/3 very pale yellow
outer surface: 10YR 7/4 very pale yellow
paint (hatched): 2.5 YR 4/8 reddish brown.

HUGE CLOSED VESSELS, WITH IMPRESSED DECORATION

FIG. 18.36

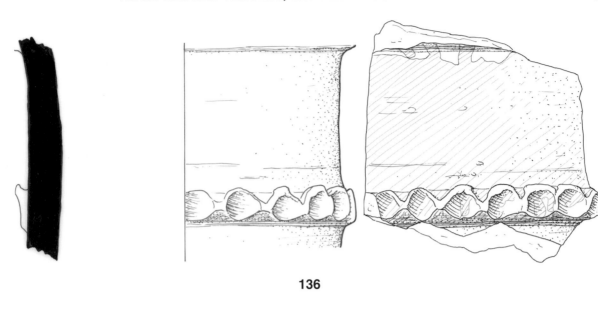

136

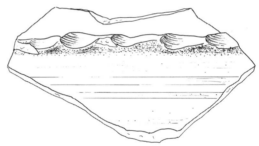

137

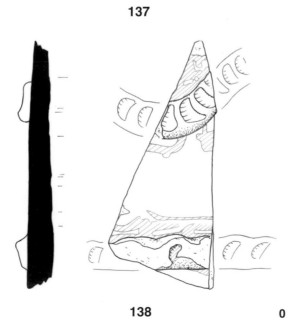

138

0   5 cm

Fig. 18.37   **Miscellaneous, with impressed and/or incised decoration.**

139. Provenience unknown, Unit A-12
      Body sherd, coarse ware, closed form, with trail and thumb impressed decoration
      ware: 2.5YR 6/8 light red
      inner surface: 5YR 8/4 pink
      outer surface: 10R 3/6 dark red.

140. Provenience unknown, Unit A-12
      Body sherd, coarse ware, closed form, with thumb impressed decoration
      ware: 2.5YR 6/8 light red
      inner surface: 2.5YR 6/8 light red
      outer surface: 2.5YR 6/6 light red.

141. Locus 21, Room 14, Unit 47-13D
      Body sherd, coarse ware, unidentified form, with thumb impressed decoration
      ware: 10R 6/6 light red
      core: 2.5YR 5/0 grey
      inner surface: 2.5YR 4/0 dark grey
      outer surface: 2.5YR 5/2 weak red.

142. Debris, Unit 47-13L
      Body sherd, coarse ware, closed form, with incised and thumb impressed decoration
      ware: 5YR 6/6 reddish yellow
      inner surface: 5YR 6/6 reddish yellow
      outer surface: 5YR 5/6 yellowish red.

143. Locus 13, inside north wall of Forecourt, Unit 47-13C
      Body sherd, coarse ware, closed form, with comb-incised decoration and indentations
      ware: 10YR 6/4 light yellowish brown
      inner surface: 10YR 6/6 brownish yellow
      outer surface: 10YR 5/8 yellow brown to 10YR 4/6 dark yellowish brown.

MISCELLANEOUS, WITH IMPRESSED AND / OR INCISED DECORATION   FIG. 18.37

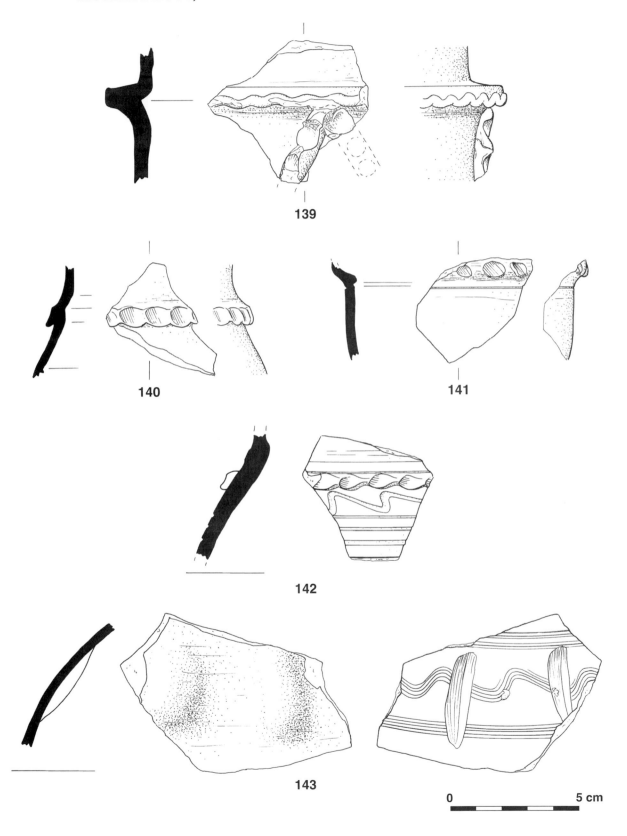

139

140

141

142

143

0   5 cm

FIG. 18.38   Miscellaneous.

Handle of coarse ware closed form, ? aquamanile antler

144. Locus 21, Room 14, Unit 47-01G
      Large handle, coarse ware, closed form, ? aquamanile antler, with impressed decoration
      ware: 2.5YR 6/8 light red
      core: 10YR 4/2 dark greyish brown
      inner surface: 10R 4/6 red
      outer surface: 2.5YR 6/6 light red
      paint (hatched): 2.5YR 4.2 weak red.

Parthian green/brown glazed

145. Locus 14A, "ditch", Unit 4A-17
      Body sherd, Parthian green / brown glazed
      ware: 10YR 8/2.5 very pale brown
      inner surface: 2.5Y 4.5/4 light olive brown
      outer surface: 5G 5/2 greyish green
      parallels: for finds from Petra: Schneider 1996: 138 with further references.

MISCELLANEOUS Fig. 18.38

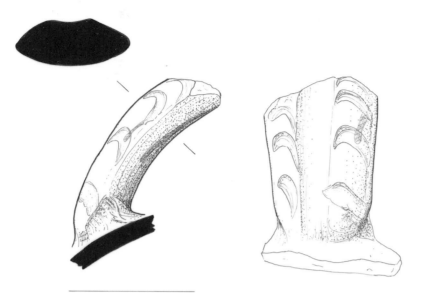

144

Handle of coarse ware closed form, ? aquamanile antler

145

Parthian green / brown glazed

0   5 cm

Fig. 18.39 Lanterns.

146. Locus 20, Room 13, Unit 47-14A (and Unit 47-14B, provenience unknown)
Body and shoulder fragments, coarse ware, lantern
ware: 2.5YR 6/6–6/8 light red
inner and outer surfaces: 2.5YR 6/8 light red.

147. Provenience unknown, Unit 47-14B
Body fragment, coarse ware, lantern
ware: 2.5YR 6/6 light red
inner surface: 2.5YR 6/8 light red
outer surface: 2.5YR 6/6 light red.

LANTERNS

FIG. 18.39

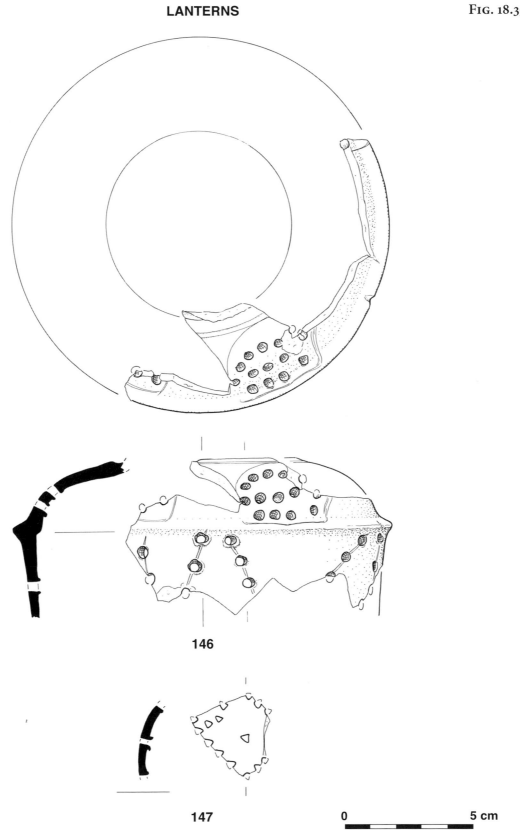

146

147

0   5 cm

FIG. 18.40   Incense burner cover.

148. Locus 21, Room 14, Unit 47-01G
     Circular handle, coarse ware, incense burner cover
     ware: 2.5YR 6/8 light red
     outer surface: 2.5YR 6/6 light red.

INCENSE BURNER COVER   FIG. 18.40

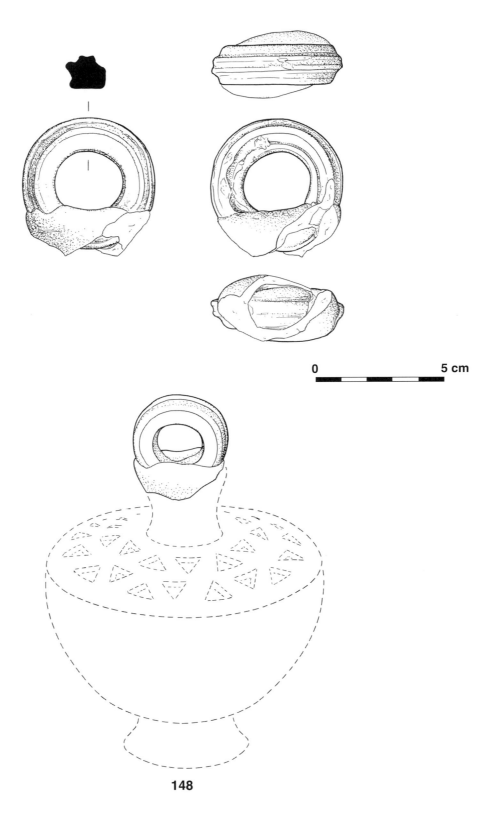

0   5 cm

148

Table 18.2   Schmid's Nabataean pottery forms (types) at Khirbet et-Tannur.

SCHMID 2000 TYPE/FORM (PHASE)	NO. OF SHERDS	NO. IN PRESENT VOL. (Figs. 18.1–25)	SHAPE (E = open; F = cups/goblets; G = closed)	SCHMID 2000 REFERENCE
E1a12	11	37–38	Bowl	181, nos. 46–47, figs 46–47
E1b10 (3a)	3	–	Bowl	184, no. 90, fig. 90
E1b10 (3a/b)	5	10	Bowl	184, nos. 90 (3a), 91 (3b), figs. 90–91
E1b10 (3b)	43	12–14	Bowl	184, no. 91, fig. 91
E1b10 (3c)	228	15-19	Bowl	184, no. 92, fig. 92
E1b10 (3c/4)	1	–	Bowl	184, no. 92 (3c), fig. 92
E1b170 (3c)	18	20–24	Bowl	184, no. 93, fig. 93
E1b176 (3c/4)	3	25	Bowl	184, no. 95, fig. 95
E1b175–177 (4)	1	26	Bowl	184, nos. 94 (E1b175), 95 (E1b176), 96 (E1b177), figs. 94–96
E1c7	33	39	Bowl	182, nos. 54–56, figs. 54–56
E1c7 and derivations	31	–	Bowl	
E1c8	49	–	Bowl	182, nos. 52–53, figs. 52–53
E1c8 and derivations	35	40–42	Bowl	
E1c8 late derivations	9	–	Bowl	
E2a16b (2b)	2	7–8	Carinated bowl	183, nos. 84–85, figs. 84–85
E2a16b (2b/c)	2	–	Carinated bowl	183–84, nos. 84–85, 88, figs. 84–85, 88
E2a356 (2c)	1	–	Bowl	184, no. 88, fig. 88
F.2e/f	15	43–44	Bowl	179, nos. 10–14, figs. 10–14
E3a2	16	–	Shallow cup	182, nos. 57–59, figs. 57–59
E3b188	1	47	Cup	182, no. 60, fig. 60
E4a4	12	–	Cup	181, nos. 38–39, figs 38–39
E4a5	2	–	Cup	181, nos. 42–43, figs 42–43
E4a35	2	–	Shallow cup	181, nos. 40–41, figs. 40–41
E4b83 (1/2a)	9	4	Cup	183, nos. 73–74, figs. 73–74

Table 18.2 (cont.)   Schmid's Nabataean pottery forms (types) at Khirbet et-Tannur.

SCHMID 2000 TYPE /FORM (PHASE)	NO. OF SHERDS	NO. IN PRESENT VOL. (Figs. 18.1–25)	SHAPE (E = open; F = cups/ goblets; G = closed)	SCHMID 2000 REFERENCE
E8a	2	–	Bowl	182, nos. 61–65, figs. 61–65
E8a and derivations	28	48–52, 57–61	Bowl	
E9a	2	–	Bowl	187–88, nos. 161–63, figs. 161–63
E10a136	1	62	Bowl	186, no. 127, fig. 127
E11a	–	–	Bowl	186, nos. 128–32, figs. 128–32
E11a? derivations	7	63	Bowl	
E13b	–	–	Bowl	183, nos. 70–72, figs. 70–72
E13b derivations	6	64–65	Bowl	
E13b late derivations	2	–	Bowl	
E16a	1	–	Bowl	180, nos. 22–29, figs. 22–29
E18a187 or 379	3	–	Bowl	199, nos. 199 (E18a187), 200 (E18a379), figs. 199–200
E18a (3a)	2		Bowl	199, nos. 199–200, figs. 199–200
E22e238, similar	1	53	Bowl with distinct lip	188, no. 169, fig. 169
E24b	8	–	Bowl/cup with straight sides	189, no. 183, fig. 183
F2a	5	–	Cup with lip	190, nos. 206–208, figs. 206–208
F2c (3c)	1	–	Cup with lip and handle	190, nos. 212–14, figs. 212–14
F2c64,247,248 (3c)	1	27	Cup with lip and handle	190, nos. 212 (F2c64), 213 (F2c247), 214 (F2c248), figs. 212–14
F2c248 (3c)	1	28	Cup with lip and handle	190, no. 214, fig. 214
F3a	2	–	Cup (rouletted)	191, no. 219, fig. 219
F5a	17	32–35	Inward turning beaker	191, nos. 224–25, figs. 224–25

Table 18.2 (cont.)   Schmid's Nabataean pottery forms (types) at Khirbet et-Tannur.

SCHMID 2000 TYPE /FORM (PHASE)	NO. OF SHERDS	NO. IN PRESENT VOL. (Figs. 18.1–25)	SHAPE (E = open; F = cups/ goblets; G = closed)	SCHMID 2000 REFERENCE
F5a70 or 252	1	–	Inward turning beaker	191, nos. 224 (F5a70), 25 (F5a252), figs. 224–25
F5, late derivation	1	36	Inward turning beaker	
F9a/b	6	–	Beaker with lip	192, nos. 241–42, figs. 241–42
G3a	5	–	Convex flask	193, nos. 265–67, figs. 265–67
G13a/b	1	100	Jug or amphora, with distinct lip	195, nos. 306–14, figs. 306–14
G14d	4	–	Juglet	196, nos. 321–25, figs. 321–25
G15b	2	81–82	Flask	196, nos. 331–32, figs. 331–32
G21a/b, close to	1	91	Jug or bottle	197, nos. 342–44, figs. 342–44
G25, degenerated	1	83	Jug	197, nos. 350–51, figs. 350–51
G26c, similar	1	101	Small jar	192, no. 255, fig. 255

REFERENCES

'Amr, K.
1991   "Preliminary Report on the 1991 Season at Zurrabah." *Annual of the Department of Antiquities of Jordan* 35: 313–23.
1992   "Islamic or Nabataean? The Case of a First to Early Second Century AD Cream Ware." *Studies in the History and Archaeology of Jordan* 4: 221–25.

'Amr, K., and al-Momani, A.
1999   "The Discovery of Two Additional Pottery Kilns at az-Zurraba, Wadi Musa." *Annual of the Department of Antiquities of Jordan* 43: 175–94.

Bienkowski, P.
2002   *Busayra. Excavations by Crystal-M. Bennett 1971–1980*. Oxford.

2013   "The Iron Age in Petra and the Issue of Continuity with Nabataean Occupation." Pp. 23–34 in *Men on the Rocks, The Formation of Nabataean Petra*, eds. M. Mouton and S. G. Schmid. Berlin.

Bikai, P., and Perry, M.
2001   "Petra North Ridge Tombs 1 and 2: Preliminary Report." *Bulletin of the American Schools of Oriental Research* 324: 59–78.

Clamer, C.
1997   *Fouilles archéologiques de 'Aïn ez-Zâra / Callirhoé, villégiature hérodienne*. Beirut.

Dolinka, B. J.
2003   *Nabataean Aila (Aqaba, Jordan) from a Ceramic Perspective*. British Archaeological Reports, International Series 1116. Oxford.

Erickson-Gini, T.
2010 *Nabataean Settlement and Self-Organized Economy in the Central Negev, Crisis and Renewal*, British Archaeological Reports, International Series 2054. Oxford.

Fellmann Brogli, R.
1996 "Die Keramik aus den spätrömischen Bauten." Pp. 219–81 in *Petra – Ez Zantur I. Ergebnisse der Schweizerisch-Liechtensteinischen Ausgrabungen 1988–1992*, eds. A. Bignasca et al. Terra Archaeologica 2. Monographien der Schweizerisch-Liechtensteinischen Stiftung für Archäologische Forschungen im Ausland [SLSA/FSLA]. Mainz.

Gerber, Y.
1996 "Die Entwicklung der lokalen nabatäischen Grosskeramik aus Petra / Jordanien." Pp. 147–51 in *Hellenistische und kaiserzeitliche Keramik des östlichen Mittelmeergebietes*, eds. M. Herfort-Koch, U. Mandel, and U. Schädler. Frankfurt.
1997 "The Nabataean Coarse Ware Pottery: A Sequence from the End of the Second Century BC to the Beginning of the Second Century AD." *Studies in the History and Archaeology of Jordan* 6: 407–11.
2001 "A Glimpse of the Recent Excavations on ez-Zantur / Petra: The Late Roman Pottery and its Prototypes in the 2nd and 3rd Centuries AD." Pp. 7–12 in *La Céramique byzantine et proto-islamique en Syrie-Jordanie (IVe – VIIIe siècles apr. J.-C.)*, eds. E. Villeneuve and P. M. Watson. Beirut.
2013 "Archaeometric Investigations on Nabataean Common Ware Pottery." Pp. 107–111 in *Men on the Rocks, The Formation of Nabataean Petra*, eds. M. Mouton and S. G. Schmid. Berlin.

Graf, D. F.
2012 "Das hellenistiche Petra." Pp. 131–33 in *Begleitbuch zur Ausstellung "Petra – Wunder in der Wüste. Auf den Spuren von J. L. Burckhardt alias Scheich Ibrahim,"* eds. E. van der Meijden and S. G. Schmid. Basel.

2013 "Petra and the Nabataeans in the Early Hellenistic Period: The Literary and Archaeological Evidence." Pp. 35–56 in *Men on the Rocks, The Formation of Nabataean Petra*, eds. M. Mouton and S. G. Schmid. Berlin.

Graf, D. F.; Bedal, L. A.; Schmid, S. G.; and Sidebotham, S. E.
2005 "The Hellenistic Petra Project. Excavations in the Civic Center, Preliminary Report of the First Season, 2004." *Annual of the Department of Antiquities of Jordan* 49: 417–41.

Graf, D. F.; Schmid, S. G.; Ronza, E.; and Sidebotham, S. E.
2007 "The Hellenistic Petra Project: Excavations in the Qasr al-Bint Temenos Area. Preliminary Report of the Second Season, 2005." *Annual of the Department of Antiquities of Jordan* 51: 223–38.

Hammond, P. C.
1987 "Three Workshops at Petra (Jordan)." *Palestine Exploration Quarterly* 119: 129–41.

Hayes, J. W.
1972 *Late Roman Pottery*. London.
1980 *A Supplement to Late Roman Pottery*. London.
1985 "Sigillate Orientali." Pp. 1–96 in *Enciclopedia dell'arte antica, classica e orientale. Atlante delle forme ceramiche, II. Ceramica fine romana nel bacino mediterraneo*. Rome.
2008 *Roman Pottery. Fine Ware Imports, The Athenian Agora*, 32. Princeton, NJ.

Hoffmann, S.
2013 "Indications for 'Early Petra' based on Pottery Finds in the City Centre: El-Habis as a Case Study." Pp. 93–105 in *Men on the Rocks, The Formation of Nabataean Petra*, eds. M. Mouton and S. G. Schmid. Berlin.

McKenzie, J. S.; Gibson, S.; and Reyes, A. T.
2002 "Reconstruction of the Nabataean Temple Complex at Khirbet et-Tannur." *Palestine Exploration Quarterly* 134: 44–83.

Mouton, M.
2012   "Die frühe nabatäische Besiedlung Petras."
     Pp. 127–30 in *Begleitbuch zur Ausstellung*
     "Petra – Wunder in der Wüste. Auf den
     Spuren von J. L. Burckhardt alias *Scheich*
     Ibrahim," eds. E. van der Meijden and S.
     G. Schmid. Basel.

Murray, M. A., and Ellis, J. C.
1940   *A Street in Petra.* London.

Negev, A.
1986   *The Late Hellenistic and Early Roman*
     Pottery of Nabatean Oboda: Final Report.
     Qedem 22. Jerusalem.

Negev, A., and Sivan, R.
1977   "The Pottery of the Nabatean Necropolis
     at Mampsis." Pp. 109–131 in *Rei Cretariae*
     Romanae Fautorum, Acta XVII/XVIII.
     Zurich.

Renel, F., and Mouton, M.
2013   "The Architectural Remains and Pottery
     Assemblage from the Early Phases at the
     Qasr al-Bint." Pp. 57–77 in *Men on the*
     Rocks, The Formation of Nabataean Petra,
     eds. M. Mouton and S. G. Schmid. Berlin.

Renel, F.; Mouton, M.; Augé, C.; Gauthier, C.;
Hatté, C.; Saliège, J.-F.; and Zazzo, A.
2012   "Dating the Early Phases under the
     Temenos of the Qasr al-Bint at Petra."

Pp. 39–54 in *The Nabataeans in Focus.*
Current Archaeological Research at Petra,
eds. L. Nehmé and L. Wadeson. Supplement to Proceedings for the Seminar for
Arabian Studies 42. Oxford.

Schmid, S. G.
2000   *Die Feinkeramik der Nabatäer. Typologie,*
     Chronologie und kulturhistorische Hinter-
     gründe. Petra – Ez Zantur II 1. Ergebnisse
     der Schweizerisch-Liechtensteinischen
     Ausgrabungen. Terra archaeologica 4. Monographien der Schweizerisch-Liechtensteinischen Stiftung für Archäologische
     Forschungen im Ausland [SLSA/FSLA].
     Mainz.

Schneider, C.
1996   "Die Importkeramik." Pp. 129–49 in *Petra*
     – Ez Zantur I. Ergebnisse der Schweize-
     risch-Liechtensteinischen Ausgrabungen
     1988-1992, eds. A. Bignasca et al. Terra archaeologica 2. Monographien der Schweizerisch-Liechtensteinischen Stiftung für
     Archäologische Forschungen im Ausland
     [SLSA/FSLA]. Mainz.

Watson, P.
2001   "The Byzantine Period." Pp. 461–502 in
     The Archaeology of Jordan, eds. B. MacDonald, R. Adams, and P. Bienkowski.
     Sheffield.

Illustration Credits

Photographs with a prefix 18, 20, etc. (i.e., of the form 18.123, etc.) were taken by S. J. Schweig of the Palestine Archaeological Museum. Images with GA prefix are in the ASOR Nelson Glueck Archive in the Semitic Museum, Harvard University. Those with three or four digit numbers (329, etc.) were taken by Nelson Glueck, except where indicated by Peake Pasha. GA images with no number given here lack Glueck numbers. The images in the GA also include some photographs from the Cincinnati Art Museum (CAM) and the Department of Antiquities of Jordan.

Numbers of the form II-2a, etc., refer to the volume, page number, and print in Glueck's three albums of prints of the above images, e.g., II-2a-1 is volume II, page 2, print a, object 1. Those numbers are also the numbers under which prints were filed and labelled by Eleanor Vogel. Consequently, occasionally two different images of the same object have the same number, sometimes indicated here by "bis."

For other images, the name of the photographer (and sometimes negative number), artist, or source is given. Bibliographic references can be found in the bibliography on pp. 303–17. Where the images are also reproduced in *Deities and Dolphins* (*DD*), even if cropped, the references are included in the figure list for convenient identification. Where the *DD* image of a fragment is not used "same block as *DD* pl. ..." is indicated for convenience.

CAM numbers refer to the Cincinnati Art Museum inventory numbers which all have the prefix "1939."

For other abbreviations, see pp. xvii–xviii.

Copyright for drawings and photographs by Sheila Gibson and Judith S. McKenzie rests with the latter, and they may be reproduced in academic printed publications, with full acknowledgement, without the need to contact her. Images from Manar al-Athar contributors may be downloaded from the Manar al-Athar website for use in academic publications, with acknowledgement.

13.8   No. 8. Sealing from sealing ring, with head facing right (A. T. Reyes).

13.9a   No. 9. Spatula, actual size (18.578; GA I-38d).

13.9b   No. 9. Spatula, with detail of decoration and base of spoon (C. Alexander).

13.10a–b No. 10. Seleucid coin of Antiochus III.
    a   Obverse (GA I-38a; *DD* pl. 57e).
    b   Reverse (GA I-38b; *DD* pl. 57f).

13.11a–b No. 12. Nabataean coin of Aretas IV.
    a   Obverse (GA I-37a; *DD* pl. 57a).
    b   Reverse (GA I-37b; *DD* pl. 57b).

13.12   No. 17. Possible metal mould (GA I-20b; *DD* pl. 191d).

14.1   The main surviving part of the totally corroded and heavily fissured lower hinge block, with tongue, top view (B. Gilmour).

14.2   Side view of the main hinge block in fig. 14.1, without tongue (B. Gilmour).

14.3a–b   X-ray image (original and inverted) showing the remains of the swivel pin projecting downwards from the end of the tongue into the lower locating steel block of the hinge (B. Gilmour).

14.4   Polished section of a fragment from the lower hinge block showing traces of black voids left by the secondary corrosion of grain boundary and needles (plates) of iron carbide (cementite) within an amorphous ground-mass of greyish ferrous corrosion products from the primary corrosion of the matrix (in this case steel): thus a surviving relic ultra-high carbon steel structure. Field of view 0.9 mm wide (B. Gilmour).

15.1   Profiles of glass, with catalogue and Type Series (TS) numbers (M. O'Hea).

15.2   Glass, with catalogue and Type Series (TS) numbers, actual size (S. Vanderhooft).

16.1   Base glass compositions and decolourants (EPMA) (N. Schibille).

16.2   Trace elements (LA-ICP-MS) (N. Schibille).

16.3   Comparison with Late Roman reference groups (N. Schibille).

16.4   Computation of a mixed manganese/antimony glass composition. (N. Schibille).

17.1   Fragment of multi-tier polycandelon (S. Vanderhooft; drawing: C. Alexander).

17.2–3   Polycandela fragments.
    17.2 (S. Vanderhooft).
    17.3 (GA I-36c-6; *DD* pl. 82a; drawing: GA).

17.4   Socket and saucer lamp, with attached stand (GA III-6-9; drawing: GA).

17.5   Socket and saucer lamp (S. Vanderhooft; drawing: C. Alexander).

17.6–11   Fragments of socket and saucer lamps.

17.6   (S. Vanderhooft; D. G. Barrett).

17.7   (S. Vanderhooft).

17.8   (S. Vanderhooft).

17.9   (S. Vanderhooft).

17.10   (S. Vanderhooft).

17.11   (D. G. Barrett).

17.12   Wheel-made round lamp (GA I-36a-5; GA I-36b-5; drawing: C. Alexander).

17.13–17 Fragments of wheel-made round lamps.
    17.13 (S. Vanderhooft; drawing: C. Alexander).
    17.14 (D. G. Barrett; drawing: C. Alexander).
    17.15 (S. Vanderhooft).
    17.16 (S. Vanderhooft).
    17.17 (D. G. Barrett).

17.18–27 Local mould-made lamps.
    17.18 (GA I-36a-2; GA I-36b-2).
    17.19 (S. Vanderhooft).
    17.20 (S. Vanderhooft; drawing: C. Alexander).
    17.21 (D. G. Barrett).
    17.22 (S. Vanderhooft; drawing: C. Alexander).
    17.23 (D. G. Barrett; drawing: C. Alexander).
    17.24 (S. Vanderhooft).
    17.25 (S. Vanderhooft).
    17.26 (S. Vanderhooft).
    17.27 (S. Vanderhooft).

17.29–30 Mould-made round lamps, with large filling holes.
    17.29 (GA I-36a-3: GA I-36b-3).
    17.30 (GA I-36c-9; *DD* pl. 82a; drawing: C. Alexander).

17.31   Mould-made elongated lamp, with herringbone decoration (D. G. Barrett; drawing: C. Alexander).

17.32   South Jordan slipper lamp, with volutes on shoulder (GA I-36c-7; *DD* pl. 82a; S. Vanderhooft; drawing: C. Alexander).

17.33–36 South Jordan slipper lamps.
    17.33 (GA I-36a-6; GA I-36b-6).
    17.34 (D. G. Barrett; S. Vanderhooft; drawing: C. Alexander).
    17.35 (S. Vanderhooft).
    17.36 (S. Vanderhooft).

17.37–41 South Jordan slipper lamps.
    17.37 (GA I-36a-1; GA I-36b-1).
    17.38 (D. G. Barrett).
    17.39 (D. G. Barrett).
    17.40 (S. Vanderhooft).
    17.41 (D. G. Barrett; S. Vanderhooft).

17.42   South Jordan slipper lamp (GA I-36a-4; GA I-36b-4).

17.43   Small Candlestick lamp (GA I-35c; *DD* pl. 82b; drawing: GA).

17.44–45 Large grey South Jordan slipper lamps.
    17.44 (S. Vanderhooft; drawing: C. Alexander).
    17.45 (S. Vanderhooft).

17.46–47 Nozzles.
    17.46 (S. Vanderhooft).
    17.47 (D. G. Barrett).

17.48   Nozzle fragment, probably from multi-tier polycandelon, as in fig. 17.51 (S. Vanderhooft).

17.49   Khirbet et-Tannur, plan with approximate find-spots of lamps, indicated by catalogue number (J. S. McKenzie).

17.50   Petra, area beside exedra in front of the Qasr el-Bint: fragment of tubular ring, from a multi-tier polycandelon, ca. AD 363–419 (A. Pelle, CNRS / MFQB).

17.51   Petra, area beside exedra in front of the Qasr el-Bint: two-tier polycandelon of 2nd or possibly 3rd century AD (A. Pelle, CNRS/MFQB).

17.52   Samaria, socket and saucer lamp (Semitic Museum, Harvard University inv. 1934.9.636) (D. G. Barrett).

18.1–18.40   Pottery drawings (S. G. Schmid and C. Alexander, except those indicated below).

18.5*	no. 21	(15.449; GA I-35d).
18.5	no. 21	(GA).
18.6	no. 23	(GA I-35e).
	no. 24	(19.930; GA I-35a).
18.7	no. 26	(GA I-35b lower; GA drawing).
18.10	no. 42	(GA I-35b-middle).
18.11	no. 47	(GA III-6-5).
18.17*	no. 72	(GA III-7c).
18.17	no. 72	(GA drawing).
18.19*	no. 84	(GA III-6-1).
18.19	no. 84	(GA drawing).
18.30*	no. 124	(GA III-6-4).
18.30	no. 124	(GA drawing).
18.31*	nos. 125–26	(GA III-6-3; GA III-6-2).
18.31	no. 125	(GA drawing).
	no. 126	(GA drawing).

Index

Note: For references in Glueck's excavation journal (GJ) and registration book (GR) to the contexts of specific types of finds, see Table 6.1 on pp. 12–18; with more detail: for bones Table 11.4 on p. 77; for plant remains Tables 12.1–2 on pp. 118–19; for glass Table 15.1 on p. 146; for lamps Table 17.1 on pp. 199–200.

Useful references to parts of the building (Altar Platform, Inner Temenos Enclosure, etc.) mentioned in GJ can be found in the discussion in Ch. 2, and through the index for them in Vol. 1.

Wadi al-Mujib, lamps 175, 193
Wadi Musa 50
Wadi Ramm (Iram) 50
Wadi Sabra 125
Wadi Sirhan 33
Waechter, J. d'A. 27
weed seeds 122
wheat 117–23, figs. 12.1–3
Willoughby, Harold R. 25
willow 125, 126

wine 152, 212
wood 3, 117, 123–25, 129, 131, 139, figs. 12.6–7
Wood, Lynn H. 20, 24

Z
Zayd'el 48, 49, 50
Zeus 57
zinc 132
Zodiac Tyche 42
Zosimos of Panopolis 142